Advance Praise for David Ray Griffin's
The New Pearl Harbor Revisited

"President Bush and Vice President Cheney have many questions to answer in light of this book. This time they should have to testify separately and under oath. Unlike their testimony at the 9/11 Commission, behind closed doors, this should be open testimony."
—*Jesse Ventura, Governor of Minnesota, 1999–2003*

"Citizens in many countries are waging a war on the cover-up of the basis for the so-called war on terror—this basis being the official interpretation of the 9/11 attacks. Along with the Internet, which has equipped both public figures and ordinary citizens to wage this war on the cover-up, David Ray Griffin has revealed dozens of omissions, distortions, and contradictions in the official story in a way that provides undeniable evidence of its falsity. *The New Pearl Harbor Revisited* presents a powerful exposé of the false narrative that has been driving the mainstream political agenda since 9/11. It is now up to politicians and journalists around the world to expose this truth to our peoples."
—*Yukihisa Fujita, member of the House of Councilors, the Diet of Japan*

"Circuses use people to clean up their elephants—a dirty job, but someone has to do it. The 9/11 Commissioners evidently likened themselves to circus workers, cleaning up after the (Republican) elephant. They did a very sloppy job, making it easy to see that 9/11 was an inside job. The contrary view—that the 9/11 attacks were perpetrated by Arab Muslims—has been the source of innumerable evils, which threaten to destroy our country and the world itself. David Griffin's *New Pearl Harbor Revisited* contains everything needed by Congress and the press to see through the most massive crime and cover-up in our history."
—*Edward Asner, actor and citizen*

"With this work, Dr. Griffin cements his place as the preeminent spokesperson for the growing number of people who demand answers to an expanding list of questions about 9/11. . . . Even those members of the 9/11 Truth Movement who have immersed themselves thoroughly in the subject will find new information here, presented in the precise and very readable style Dr. Griffin has brought to each of his books. . . . Absent a revival of investigative journalism—a dim prospect at best, in view of the media ownership concentration—books like this one, arming the informed citizen with solid information and providing a basis for demanding direct action, appear to be our best hope."

—*Shelton F. Lankford, Lt. Col. US Marine Corps (Ret.)*

"You and I, along with all citizens of the world, are victims of a heinous crime. The conspiracy that generated the Twin Tower photo-op, blamed the 9/11 attacks on Arab Muslims, and misdirected truth-seekers by destruction of evidence and willful misrepresentation is masterfully exposed in this book. Who had the motive, means and opportunity to demolish three skyscrapers, including Building 7, which was not even attacked by a mere airplane? Who could penetrate the Earth's most heavily defended air space and fortress—the Pentagon? What was their motive? Greed to concentrate power, to control access to the last drop of Gaia's reserve hydrocarbon energy? But, alas, who thinks of our children? David Ray Griffin, apolitical scholar and theologian, was transformed by the coup d'etat into a superb scientist-journalist. By documenting the tragic 9/11 crime, this consummate educator has done us victims a profound service."

—*Lynn Margulis, Distinguished University Professor, Department of Geosciences, University of Massachusetts-Amherst, and National Medal of Science recipient*

"Mr. Griffin has again painstakingly laid bare the many lingering questions and inconsistencies of the official story regarding the horrific attacks of September 11, 2001. Sadly, millions of taxpayer dollars have been squandered on investigations that yielded no accountability, few answers, and fewer reforms. Yet, the attacks of September 11, 2001 have been wantonly used as political and policy fodder. Without truth, there can be no accountability. Without accountability, there can be no real change. Without change, we remain at risk."

—*Monica Gabrielle, widow of Richard Gabrielle, who was killed at WTC2 on 9/11/01, member of the Family Steering Committee for the 9/11 Commission*

THE NEW PEARL HARBOR REVISITED

9/11, THE COVER-UP, AND THE EXPOSÉ

DAVID RAY GRIFFIN

ARRIS BOOKS
An imprint of Arris Publishing Ltd
Gloucestershire

First published in Great Britain in 2008 by

ARRIS BOOKS
An imprint of Arris Publishing Ltd
PO Box 75
Moreton-in-Marsh
GL56 0WA
www.arrisbooks.com

ISBN 978-1-84437-076-4

Printed and bound in the United States of America

Telephone: 01608 659328
Visit our website at www.arrisbooks.com or email us at info@arrisbooks.com

CONTENTS

ACKNOWLEDGMENTS

I n acknowledging the tremendous amount of help and support I received in writing this book, I wish to begin by mentioning *the* indispensable source for 9/11-related stories published in the mainstream press: *The Complete 9/11 Timeline* at History Commons (formerly known as Cooperative Research). Started in 2002 by Paul Thompson, it has surely become, through the continuing work of Thompson and his colleagues, the greatest feat of annotated, investigative journal indexing ever achieved on a volunteer basis. Having served as the source of about half of my references in *The New Pearl Harbor*, this timeline has been equally indispensable for *The New Pearl Harbor Revisited*.

Whereas most of the people on whose work I drew for this book are named in the notes, I received additional assistance from Dylan Avery, Rob Balsamo, Elias Davidsson, Kee Dewdney, Eric Douglas, Mark Gaffney, Allan Giles, Ed Haas, Barbara Honegger, Jim Hoffman, Robin Hordon, Jay Kolar, Stephen Jones, Alan Miller, Rowland Morgan, Ted Muga, Ralph Omholt, Kevin Ryan, and Russ Wittenberg.

I owe special gratitude to three individuals who provided extraordinary assistance in the actual writing of the book: Matthew Everett, Tod Fletcher, and Elizabeth Woodworth. Besides being three of the best proofreaders in the world, they helped in many other ways. Matthew, who through his work on *The Complete 9/11 Timeline* has become a gold mine of information, brought to my attention many of the sources I employed. Tod, who seems to know a lot about everything, provided valuable help with every chapter. Elizabeth, who has served as my virtual assistant, employed her gifts as acute critic and research librarian extraordinaire throughout the process, helping in countless ways, including creating the index.

I also wish to express my continuing gratitude to my editor, Pam Thompson, and publisher, Michel Moushabeck, who took the risk to publish *The New Pearl Harbor* when the 9/11 truth movement had little intellectual or professional support.

As always, my main source of daily support is my wife, Ann Jaqua.

M y first book about 9/11, *The New Pearl Harbor: Disturbing Questions about the Bush Administration and 9/11* (henceforth NPH), was published early in 2004, with a second, updated edition appearing a few months later. The present volume was prompted by two facts about the discussion of 9/11 in the intervening years. On the one hand, although 9/11 was indisputably the most fateful event of our time, from which enormous consequences—almost entirely negative—have flowed, neither Congress nor the mainstream media have investigated the reasons provided by independent researchers from many professions for considering the official account false. On the other hand, five major developments have occurred that have changed the discussion since the appearance of NPH.

One major development was the publication of *The 9/11 Commission Report* in July 2004. Prior to its publication, a portion of the community of researchers seeking the truth about 9/11 still hoped that the 9/11 Commission would prove to be a truth-seeking body. Some of these optimistic researchers, hoping to assist the Commission, even sent it copies of *The New Pearl Harbor*, which was widely regarded as the best summary of the main discoveries made by this community of independent researchers, generally called "the 9/11 truth movement." But when the Commission's report appeared, it confirmed the expectations of the movement's most pessimistic members. Rather than confronting the evidence summarized in NPH and elsewhere that suggested official complicity, the Commission simply presupposed the truth of the government's theory, according to which the 9/11 attacks resulted from a conspiracy involving only Osama bin Laden and other Arab Muslims. All the contrary information provided in NPH and elsewhere was either distorted or simply omitted in the Commission's final report. One of the most remarkable omissions was its failure even to mention that Building 7 of the World Trade Center had collapsed—perhaps because FEMA, which had put out a preliminary report on the World Trade Center in 2002, admitted that its best explanation for this collapse had "only a low probability of occurrence."

A second major development was the publication in 2005 of the official report on the destruction of the Twin Towers by the National Institute of Standards and Technology (NIST). Although this report has been accepted by the mainstream press as an authoritative explanation, many scientists have argued that NIST could appear to explain the collapses of these buildings only by ignoring several types of evidence and even violating various laws of physics. Further criticisms of NIST's report have been evoked by the fact that, although it was supposed to deal not only with the Twin Towers but also with WTC 7, NIST has repeatedly delayed its explanation for this third building's collapse.

A third major development was the publication in 2006 of two polls indicating that a significant percentage of the American people rejected, or at least doubted, the official account of 9/11. A Zogby poll indicated that 42 percent of the population believed "the US government and its 9/11 Commission concealed. . . critical evidence that contradicts their official explanation of the September 11th attacks." Even more significant was a Scripps Howard/Ohio University poll, which found 36 percent of the public believing that "federal officials either participated in the attacks on the World Trade Center and the Pentagon or took no action to stop them 'because they wanted the United States to go to war in the Middle East.'" This latter poll led *Time* magazine to comment: "Thirty-six percent adds up to a lot of people. This is not a fringe phenomenon. It is a mainstream political reality."

These polls suggested that the 9/11 truth movement, in spite of the hostility of the mainstream press, had been increasingly successful. That success—which, to anyone paying attention, had been apparent long before those polls publicized the fact—perhaps lay behind a new approach to the 9/11 truth movement adopted by defenders of the official account. Prior to the summer of 2006, the official reports had dealt with the movement by ignoring it;

the reports by NIST and the 9/11 Commission did not even acknowledge the existence of an alternative account of 9/11, according to which it was an inside job—whether fully or at least in part. But in August 2006, four official and semi-official publications appeared that explicitly sought to debunk this alternative account. One of the semi-official publications was a book by *Popular Mechanics* entitled *Debunking 9/11 Myths*. This new strategy constituted a fourth major development.

A fifth major development was a large influx of intellectuals and professionals into the 9/11 truth community. This community now includes various organizations of intellectuals—such as Scholars for 9/11 Truth, Scholars for 9/11 Truth and Justice, and S.P.I.N.E.: The Scientific Panel Investigating Nine-Eleven. Partly to emphasize this development, Peter Dale Scott and I edited a 2006 book entitled *9/11 and American Empire: Intellectuals Speak Out*. The movement also now includes a growing number of professionals, many of whom belong to some specialized organization, such as Veterans for 9/11 Truth, Pilots for 9/11 Truth, and Architects and Engineers for 9/11 Truth. This influx of intellectuals and professionals also led to the creation of a scholarly journal, *The Journal of 9/11 Studies*. Statements by hundreds of intellectuals and professionals who believe that a new investigation is needed can now conveniently be read online at Patriots Question 9/11.

Thanks to the growing number of intellectuals and professionals—including physicists, chemists, architects, engineers, pilots, military officers, intelligence officers, and political leaders—who have publicly rejected the official story, the case against that story is now much stronger than in 2004 (as I showed in a 2007 book, *Debunking 9/11 Debunking*, in which I responded to the four documents of August 2006 that tried to refute the claims of the 9/11 truth movement).

This strengthening of the 9/11 truth movement's composition and its case against the official story may help explain the fact that a Scripps Howard/Ohio University poll taken in late 2007 showed a dramatic decrease in the number of Americans who are confident about the truth of the official account: Only 30 percent of the respondents considered "not likely" the idea that federal officials had received specific warnings about the 9/11 attacks but decided to ignore them. This finding suggests that a clear majority of the American people would be ready for a true investigation into 9/11.

Even after all of these developments, however, both Congress and the mainstream press have continued to refuse to investigate the dozens of reasons the 9/11 truth community has provided for considering the official account false.

These reasons include the fact that the 9/11 Commission's report contains dozens of falsehoods, whether explicit or merely implicit (as I showed in my 2005 critique, *The 9/11 Commission Report: Omissions and Distortions*). These reasons also include the existence of massive contradictions between the official theory and some basic laws of physics (as I documented in *Debunking 9/11 Debunking*, citing the analyses of Steven Jones, Kevin Ryan, and other scientists). These reasons include, moreover, many internal contradictions within the official story (as I demonstrated in my first 2008 book, *9/11 Contradictions: An Open Letter to Congress and the Press*). Nevertheless, while acknowledging that the Bush administration's response to 9/11, based on its public account of it, has been overwhelmingly destructive for both America and the rest of the world, both our elected representatives and our "fourth estate" have thus far ignored the massive amount of evidence pointing to the falsity of that account.

The idea of writing *The New Pearl Harbor Revisited* arose because of a two-fold fact about NPH. On the one hand, besides containing some errors, it had become increasingly out of date. On the other hand, it continued to be, in spite of these flaws, widely regarded as the best and most readable introduction to the issues. During the past few years, therefore, many people had urged me to write an updated edition.

Although they knew that I had responded to some of the new developments in the aforementioned books, they pointed out that it would be important to have all of the information most essential for evaluating the official story in an easily accessible form. Besides being helpful for ordinary citizens who have come to suspect the falsity of the official story, this would be vital if Congress and the press were finally to decide to investigate the problems in that story. Busy senators, representatives, and journalists could not be expected to search through several books to find the relevant information about a given issue. The question was how to update NPH without losing two of its oft-remarked virtues, its brevity and readability.

The publisher and I arrived at the following solution: NPH is reprinted as the first volume of a two-volume set. The second volume, *The New Pearl Harbor Revisited* (NPHR), is a chapter-by-chapter commentary on the first volume, in which its discussion is brought up to date and, where necessary, corrected. The updating consists partly of information contained here and there in my intervening books, and partly of information I had not previously discussed. In some cases, this new information involves developments that occurred shortly before the book went to press.

The fact that NPH and NPHR have been published as companion volumes in a two-book set does not mean that they must be purchased together; readers who already have NPH may simply purchase NPHR by itself. What it does mean is that neither book is intended to be used as a stand-alone volume. NPH is no longer self-sufficient for the reasons already mentioned: Besides containing some errors, it is several years out of date, having appeared prior to the publication of *The 9/11 Commission Report*, NIST's report on the Twin Towers, and many other developments. Likewise, NPHR is not intended to be read by itself: As a commentary on NPH, it presupposes that its readers have already studied that earlier volume. Indeed, it consists of chapters paralleling those in NPH, so that readers can turn immediately from a chapter in that book to the updating of its information in the present book.

The full title of the present book is *The New Pearl Harbor Revisited: 9/11, the Cover-Up, and the Exposé*. NPH dealt with the official account of 9/11, on the one hand, and the 9/11 truth community's exposé of that account as a cover-up of what really happened, on the other hand, as they both existed in early 2004. The present volume deals with the official account in the form in which it has existed since the appearance of *The 9/11 Commission Report* (July 2004), which offered a radically new explanation of why the hijacked airliners were not intercepted, and the appearance of NIST's report on the Twin Towers (2005), which provided a new and supposedly definitive account of why they came down. Besides explaining these revisions of the official story, this book also summarizes the 9/11 truth movement's ongoing exposé of these revisions as further attempts to cover up the truth about what really occurred on 9/11—an exposé that, thanks to the influx of large numbers of intellectuals and professionals into the movement, is now so compelling as to be virtually undeniable by anyone who will take the time to study it.

A s I pointed out in the preface, much has changed since *The New Pearl Harbor* (NPH) was published. Those changes led me over the years to express growing certainty about the falsity of the official account of 9/11. In NPH, I described the evidence for official complicity as merely *prima facie*, but I dropped this qualification after writing *The 9/11 Commission Report: Omissions and Distortions* (henceforth 9/11CROD),[1] saying in that book's final paragraph:

> [F]ar from lessening my suspicions about official complicity, [the 9/11 Commission's report] has served to confirm them. Why would the minds in charge of this final report engage in such deception if they were not trying to cover up very high crimes?[2]

The deception to which I referred was considerable. In a brief essay summarizing 9/11CROD, I listed 115 lies of omission and distortion in the Commission's report that my book had identified.[3]

In my next book, *Christian Faith and the Truth behind 9/11*, I explained the significance of the 9/11 Commission's report in the following way:

> In a criminal trial, once the prosecution has presented its initial case, the defense asks the judge for a dismissal on the grounds that a *prima facie* case for guilt has not been presented. However, if the judge declares that such a case *has* been made, then the defense must rebut the various elements in the prosecution's case. . . . If the defense fails to offer a convincing rebuttal, the *prima facie* case is presumed to be conclusive. . . . The 9/11 Commission, under the direction of Bush administration insider Philip Zelikow, had the opportunity to rebut the [9/11 truth movement's] *prima facie* case against the Bush administration. But as [its] . . . omissions and distortions show, it completely

failed to do so. As a result, the *prima facie* case that the Bush administration orchestrated the attacks of 9/11 remained unrefuted. The publication of *The 9/11 Commission Report* should, accordingly, be recognized as a decisive event: the moment at which the *prima facie* case against the Bush administration became a *conclusive* case.[4]

The experience of writing my next book, *Debunking 9/11 Debunking* (henceforth D9D)[5]—in which I responded to four defenses of the official story, published in August 2006, that explicitly sought to debunk the claims of the 9/11 truth movement—led me to speak even more strongly, saying in that book's first sentence: "The evidence that 9/11 was an inside job is overwhelming."[6]

My first 2008 book, *9/11 Contradictions: An Open Letter to Congress and the Press*,[7] showed the case against the official story to be even stronger. That is because any theory, to be credible, must exemplify two main characteristics: self-consistency and adequacy to the relevant facts. NPH and most of my other books have, like the 9/11 truth movement in general, focused primarily on the many ways in which the official theory fails to be adequate to the empirical facts (about steel-frame high-rise buildings, standard operating procedures for flight interception, photographs of the Pentagon damage and the Flight 93 crash site, and so on). In *9/11 Contradictions*, however, I emphasized the fact that the official story is also riddled with internal contradictions—I described 25 of them.

In the present volume, which is organized as a chapter-by-chapter commentary on those issues discussed in NPH about which there is something new to say, I mention some of these contradictions as well as several recent developments in the discussion of the official theory's inadequacy to the empirical evidence. I now begin the commentary on the introduction of NPH.

The use of 9/11 to promote the "war on terror" and various other policies enacted by the Bush administration, discussed in the introduction to NPH, has continued. It is widely acknowledged that 9/11 has been constantly invoked to justify dubious, even illegal, policies. It is also widely acknowledged that the Bush administration has repeatedly lied to the American people and that these lies include the basis for the war in Iraq, which has cost hundreds of billions of dollars and thousands of American lives, as well as—occasionally acknowledged—probably over a million Iraqi lives.[8] It is even acknowledged that the Bush administration lied about the safety of the air at the World Trade Center site after the attacks,[9] and this lie, which has already led to debilitating illness in thousands of rescue and clean-up workers, may result in more premature deaths than occurred on 9/11 itself.[10] Nevertheless, the possibility that the official story about 9/11 might itself be a lie is a topic that, as this book went to press, still had not been explored in Congress or the mainstream press.

THE FAILURE OF THE PRESS

One newspaper writer asked on the second anniversary of 9/11: "[W]hy after 730 days do we know so little about what really happened that day?"[11] Now at the seventh anniversary, someone could equally well ask: Why after 2,557 days do we still know so little? A large part of the answer would be that the failure of the mainstream press to do its job has continued. Indeed, far from investigating the evidence provided by the 9/11 truth community, the press has attacked and ridiculed this community, thereby defending the official account. I have briefly discussed the press's irresponsible behavior in the introduction and conclusion of D9D. A much more extensive discussion can be found in a 2006 book, *Towers of Deception: The Media Cover-Up of 9/11*, by Canadian journalist Barrie Zwicker.[12] Also, in the Summer 2007 issue of *Global Outlook* ("The Magazine of 9/11 Truth"), Zwicker reprinted and critiqued 45 mainstream news articles and TV shows that appeared in 2006 and 2007, showing that, with only a few exceptions, they were aimed at creating a negative impression of the 9/11 truth movement, not at engaging in objective journalism about a controversial subject.[13]

As I pointed out briefly in NPH and then more fully in a lecture entitled "9/11: The Myth and the Reality,"[14] one way the Bush administration prevented public questioning of the official account of 9/11 was by presenting it as a sacred story, so that any questioning of it would be regarded as not only unpatriotic but also sacrilegious. For example, on the only mainstream television show in the United States on which I have appeared, the host, Tucker Carlson, said: "[F]or you to suggest. . . that the US government killed 3,000 of its own citizens" is "wrong, blasphemous, and sinful."[15] One correspondent wrote to me that Carlson, in accusing me of blasphemy, seemed to confuse Bush, Cheney, and Rice with the Holy Trinity.

I developed this theme further in another lecture, "9/11 and Nationalist Faith,"[16] in which I argued that, although America is generally regarded as a basically Christian nation, another form of faith is more pervasive and, even for many Christians, more fundamental. This is faith in the essential goodness of America and its leaders. This faith implies that, although our leaders may be incompetent and may even lie upon occasion, they would never deliberately do something horrendously evil, especially to their own citizens. Given this faith, which is usually known as the belief in "American exceptionalism," the idea that the Bush administration could have orchestrated, or even consciously allowed, the 9/11 attacks can be ruled out a priori, so that no examination of relevant evidence is necessary. Insofar as the mainstream press serves to maintain this nationalist faith in the public sphere, no public examination of relevant evidence is even permitted. When the 9/11 truth community is not simply ignored, it is defamed.

9/11 AND THE LEFT

It is not, however, merely the mainstream press that has supported the official account by treating the 9/11 truth movement with disdain. This practice has been at least equally prevalent in the left-leaning press. For example, Alexander Cockburn—writing in *The Nation*, as well as in his own publication, *Counterpunch*—referred to members of the movement as "the 9/11 conspiracy nuts."[17] These nuts, Cockburn assured his readers, have no knowledge of military matters, no conception of evidence, and no grasp of the real world.[18]

In making such charges, Cockburn revealed that he knew nothing about the actual membership of the movement—that it contains people such as Colonel Robert Bowman, who flew over 100 combat missions in Vietnam and earned a Ph.D. in aeronautics and nuclear engineering before becoming head of the "Star Wars" program during the Ford and Carter administrations;[19] Andreas von Bülow, formerly state secretary in the German Federal Ministry of Defense, minister of research and technology, and member of the German parliament, where he served on the intelligence committee;[20] General Leonid Ivashov, formerly chief of staff of the Russian armed forces;[21] former CIA analyst Ray McGovern, who was the chairman of the National Intelligence Estimates and provided the president's daily brief for Ronald Reagan and George H.W. Bush;[22] Colonel George Nelson, formerly an airplane accident investigator for the US Air Force;[23] Colonel Ronald D. Ray, a highly decorated Vietnam veteran who became deputy assistant secretary of defense during the Reagan administration;[24] Robert David Steele, who had a 25-year career in intelligence, serving both as a CIA clandestine services case officer and as a US Marine Corps intelligence officer;[25] Captain Russ Wittenberg, a former Air Force fighter pilot with over 100 combat missions, after which he was a commercial airlines pilot for 35 years;[26] and many other people with knowledge of the "real world" in general and military matters in particular.

Another charge leveled by Cockburn against members of the 9/11 truth movement was that "their treatment of eyewitness testimony. . . is whimsical. . . . [T]estimony that undermines their theories. . . is contemptuously brushed aside."[27] However, besides revealing his unawareness of the fact that the movement contains many scientists and other intellectuals who deal regularly with evidence, Cockburn also, by his own ignorance, contradicted first-hand testimony. At the time Cockburn wrote his statement, I had published a widely circulated essay entitled "Explosive Testimony,"[28] which showed that dozens of members of the Fire Department of New York, along with journalists and World Trade Center employees, testified that explosions had been going off in the Twin Towers during and prior to their collapses. Cockburn, however, wrote: "People inside who survived the collapse didn't hear a series of explosions."[29]

Cockburn also said that the 9/11 truth movement represented "the ascendancy of magic over common sense [and] reason."[30] But then, after acknowledging that the Twin Towers fell rapidly, he claimed that the collapses did not require preplaced explosives, because, he said: "High grade steel can bend disastrously under extreme heat."[31] Cockburn, in other words, suggested that the fires, by bending the steel on a few floors, caused these 110-story buildings to collapse symmetrically, at virtually free-fall speed, into piles of rubble only a few stories high. If that is not magical thinking, what would be? The hundreds of professionals who have joined Architects and Engineers for 9/11 Truth certainly do not believe that Cockburn's scenario is even remotely possible.[32] But thus far Cockburn has evidently remained unaware of, or indifferent to, the fact that his view runs counter to the growing weight of professional opinion.

Not only Cockburn's *Counterpunch* but also most of the other major left-leaning publications, such as *The Nation*, *The Progressive*, and *In These Times*,[33] have remained impervious to the fact that, as more and more people with professional expertise examine the evidence, they reject the official story. A case in point is former senior CIA official Bill Christison, who wrote in the summer of 2006: "I spent the first four and a half years since September 11 utterly unwilling to consider seriously the conspiracy theories surrounding the attacks of that day. . . . [I]n the last half year and after considerable agony, I've changed my mind."[34] On the basis of that change of mind, Christison wrote an essay entitled "Stop Belittling the Theories about September 11," in which he said: "I now think there is persuasive evidence that the events of September did not unfold as the Bush administration and the 9/11 Commission would have us believe."[35]

Robert Baer is another former CIA official who changed his mind. Late in 2004, he wrote a review of NPH for *The Nation*, in which he faulted me for "recycl[ing] some of the wilder conspiracy theories." The attacks, Baer assured his readers, were best explained in terms of "a confluence of incompetence, spurious assumptions and self-delusion on a grand scale."[36] By 2006, however, a closer examination of the evidence had led him to question his former position. Asked by interviewer Thom Hartmann whether "there was an aspect of 'inside job' to 9/11 within the US government," Baer replied: "There is that possibility, the evidence points at it."[37]

These changes of mind by Christison and Baer have, however, apparently not led *The Nation* or any of the other left-leaning magazines to reconsider their stances on 9/11. It was, in fact, months after Baer's public statement that *The Nation* published Cockburn's "9/11 Conspiracy Nuts." These magazines have also thus far seemed unfazed by the large number of scientists, pilots, architects, engineers, and military and intelligence officers who have publicly rejected the official conspiracy theory in favor of the view that 9/11 was, at least in part, an inside job. While recognizing that the Bush administration has lied about almost everything else, they continue to accept on faith the fantastic tale about 9/11 told by this administration—while, without irony, referring to the growing rejection of that tale as "The 9/11 Faith Movement."[38]

I keep hoping, however, that the press will finally get empirical about this issue, rather than continuing to dismiss the alternative theory on a priori grounds—a plea that I made in a lecture called "9/11: Let's Get Empirical."[39] As Christison and hundreds of other professionals have illustrated, once people actually examine the evidence, the fact that 9/11 was an inside job becomes pretty obvious.

"INCIDENTS" AND FALSE-FLAG ATTACKS

In writing the introduction to NPH, I mentioned that while studying the history of American imperialism, I had learned that "the US government had fabricated 'incidents' as an excuse to go to war several times." Having later learned more about a type of such incidents known as "false-flag attacks," I wrote at some length about them.[40] Originally, a false-flag attack was one in which the attackers, perhaps in ships, literally showed the flag of an enemy country, so that it would wrongly be blamed for the attack. But the expression has come to be used for any attack made to appear to be the work of some country, party, or group other than that to which the attackers themselves belong.

Imperial powers have regularly staged such attacks as pretexts for consolidating power or going to war. When Japan's army in 1931 decided to take over Manchuria, it blew up the tracks of its own railway near the Chinese military base in Mukden, then blamed Chinese solders. This "Mukden incident," which occurred on September 18 and is still known in China as "9/18," began the

Pacific part of World War II.[41] In 1933, after the Nazis took power, they started a fire in the Reichstag (the German parliament building), blamed the Communist Party, then used the event as a pretext to imprison enemies, to annul civil liberties, and to consolidate power.[42] In 1939, when Hitler wanted a pretext to attack Poland, he had Germans dressed as Poles stage raids on German outposts on the Polish–German border, in some cases leaving dead German convicts dressed as Polish soldiers at the scene. The next day, referring to these "border incidents," Hitler attacked Poland in "self-defense," thereby starting the European part of World War II.[43]

The United States itself has used lies to start many wars: the Mexican–American war, based on President Polk's false claim that Mexico had "shed American blood on the American soil";[44] the Spanish–American war, started on the basis of the false claim that Spain had sunk the US battleship *Maine*;[45] the war in the Philippines, based on the false claim that Filipinos had fired first;[46] and the full-scale part of the Vietnam war, based on the Tonkin Gulf hoax.[47]

Although those deceptive claims did not involve false-flag attacks, such attacks were sponsored after World War II by the United States in Western European countries in order to dissuade their citizens from voting for Communists and other leftists. NATO, working with right-wing organizations and guided by the CIA and the Pentagon, organized terrorist attacks, then planted evidence to implicate leftists.[48] In Italy, where the terrorist campaign was known as Operation Gladio, one of these attacks— a massive explosion in the waiting room of the railway station in Bologna—killed 85 people and wounded another 200.[49]

The best-known example of a Pentagon-planned false-flag attack within the United States was one that was planned but not carried out—Operation Northwoods, which was discussed in Chapter 7 of NPH.

It is of utmost importance to realize that America's political and military leaders have planned and sometimes put into effect such deceitful operations, because this knowledge overcomes what is probably the main a priori reason for rejecting the idea that 9/11 was a false-flag operation: the assumption that our political and military leaders simply would not do such a heinous thing. Also, being aware that such operations invariably involve the planting of false evidence makes it easier to see the planted 9/11 evidence, to be discussed in Chapters 3 and 6, for what it was.

"CONSPIRACY THEORIES"

In spite of the fact that members of the 9/11 truth community have repeatedly pointed out the illogic and even dishonesty involved in using the "conspiracy theory" label to discredit the alternative account of 9/11, this practice has continued unabated. For example, when the editors of *Popular Mechanics* put out their book in 2006, they called it *Debunking 9/11 Myths: Why Conspiracy Theories Can't Stand Up to the Facts*[50]—thereby implying that the official account, which they were defending, was *not* a conspiracy theory. Jim Dwyer wrote a *New York Times* article entitled "2 US Reports Seek to Counter Conspiracy Theories About 9/11,"[51] although a more accurate title would have been: "2 US Reports Say Government's Conspiracy Theory is Better than Alternative Conspiracy Theory." Matthew Rothschild, the editor of *The Progressive*, published an essay entitled "Enough of the 9/11 Conspiracy Theories, Already,"[52] although he was not calling on the government to stop espousing its own conspiracy theory. Rothschild spoke pejoratively of my books as writings in which "Griffin has peddled his conspiracy theory," but he did not characterize *The 9/11 Commission Report* as a book in which the Zelikow-led Commission "peddled the government's conspiracy theory." The conceit that it is only the alternative account of 9/11 that is a conspiracy theory was also expressed in the title of a *Time* magazine article, "Why the 9/11 Conspiracies Won't Go Away."[53]

While illegitimate, this one-sided use of the term can be effective, because it allows defenders of the official story to exploit the fact that "conspiracy theory" is used in two ways: in a generic sense and in a pejorative sense. A conspiracy, according to my dictionary,[54] is "an agreement to perform together an illegal, treacherous, or evil act." To hold a conspiracy theory in the generic sense, therefore, is simply to believe that some event resulted from such an agreement. Given this generic meaning, the official account of 9/11 is obviously a conspiracy theory, because it holds that the attacks resulted from an agreement between Osama bin Laden and fellow members of al-Qaeda.

But conspiracy theories in the generic sense can either be rational theories, based on good evidence and logical inferences, or irrational theories, based on false or cherry-picked evidence and illogical inferences. The pejorative use of the term "conspiracy theory" falsely implies that all conspiracy theories are of this irrational type. The genus has fallaciously been equated with one of its species.

Because this pejorative usage has become widespread, however, people can discredit a theory without having to provide any evidence against it, because simply to call it a conspiracy theory is to damn it. Columnist Paul Krugman, commenting on this tactic, has written:

> The truth is that many of the people who throw around terms like "loopy conspiracy theories" are lazy bullies who [as one observer put it] want to "confer instant illegitimacy on any argument with which they disagree." Instead of facing up to hard questions, they try to suggest that anyone who asks those questions is crazy.[55]

In order for this tactic to work with regard to 9/11, the fact that the official theory is a conspiracy theory must be suppressed.

Accordingly, to get people to be empirical about 9/11, it is important to keep making this obvious but widely ignored point— that the official theory is itself a conspiracy theory. My D9D, for example, is subtitled "An Answer to *Popular Mechanics* and Other Defenders of the Official Conspiracy Theory." It is also necessary to keep reminding people of a complementary point. In the preface to our book in which "intellectuals speak out" about 9/11, Peter Dale Scott and I said that our book "demonstrates that alternative accounts of 9/11 cannot be dismissed on the grounds that they are offered only by people who fit the label of 'conspiracy theorists' in the pejorative sense."[56]

Besides making these points, moreover, I have argued that it is the official account of 9/11 that best fits the description of a conspiracy theory in the pejorative sense. In responding to

Thomas Kean and Lee Hamilton's *Without Precedent: The Inside Story of the 9/11 Commission*,[57] I pointed out that they accurately said that conspiracy theorists (in the pejorative sense) typically exemplify five characteristics: They (1) begin with their theories rather than the facts; (2) continue to hold their theories after they have been disproved; (3) ignore all evidence that contradicts their theories; (4) uncritically accept any evidence that supports their theories; and (5) have disdain for open and informed debate.

The only flaw in Kean and Hamilton's discussion was their failure to acknowledge that these characteristics are exemplified most fully by supporters of the official theory about 9/11, such as themselves. Take the first characteristic: Besides the fact that the 9/11 Commission began with the assumption that the 9/11 attacks were orchestrated by Osama bin Laden and al-Qaeda, its executive director, Philip Zelikow, even prepared a detailed outline of its final report before the Commission had began its investigation (as discussed in Chapter 10). Or take the fifth characteristic: Members of the 9/11 Commission, members of the Bush administration, scientists at NIST, and the editors of *Popular Mechanics* have all refused invitations to debate leading members of the 9/11 truth movement.[58] It is advocates of the official conspiracy theory, not advocates of the alternative theory, who have disdained public debate.

The chapters to follow will show, even more clearly than did NPH, why those who have articulated the official theory avoid debating this theory in public with knowledgeable members of the 9/11 truth community.

1. FLIGHT 11, FLIGHT 175, AND THE WORLD TRADE CENTER: NEW DEVELOPMENTS

Chapter 1 of NPH requires considerable commentary, partly because it covered so many things—not only Flights 11 and 175 but also the destruction of the World Trade Center—and partly because it contained some inaccuracies.

One inaccuracy was that I spoke only of NORAD (the North American Aerospace Defense Command), not also specifically of NORAD's Northeast Air Defense Sector, known as NEADS, located in Rome, New York. All the 9/11 flights were in that sector, so the FAA's contact with the military would have been with NEADS. Whenever I wrote that NORAD was contacted by the FAA or had planes scrambled, therefore, I should have instead written "NEADS." Contacting NORAD would usually mean contacting NORAD headquarters at Peterson Air Force Base or NORAD's operations center at Cheyenne Mountain, both in Colorado, or else the headquarters of NORAD's Continental United States Region, which is at Tyndall Air Force Base in Florida. Air traffic controllers at the FAA's Boston Center would have always contacted NEADS, not NORAD as such.

AMERICAN AIRLINES FLIGHT 11

One problem in the discussion of this flight was my claim that "the loss of radio contact alone [at 8:14] would have led the flight controller to begin emergency procedures." I later learned that the momentary loss of radio contact is not uncommon and that controllers typically try for a minute or so to reestablish contact before notifying anyone. Also, although the additional loss of the transponder signal would increase the controllers' concern, it might not lead them to call the military immediately. Absolutely correct, however, was the quotation from MSNBC saying that, when a plane goes significantly off course, "It's considered a real emergency," leading the flight controllers to "hit the panic button." This is because an off-course plane might well run into another plane. Therefore, although the FAA's Boston Center might not have called the military at 8:14 or 8:15, it should immediately have done so at 8:21, after Flight 11 was observed going off course. Both Robin Hordon, who previously worked at Boston Center, and Colin Scoggins, who still works there as the military specialist, have indicated that they would have called by 8:22 at the latest.[1]

The most important problem in my discussion, however, was that I did not distinguish between two different reasons for contacting the military: hijackings and in-flight emergencies. This is important because the pre-9/11 protocols were very different.

The protocol for dealing with hijackings was quite slow, for several reasons. First, it often takes time to establish whether a plane has really been hijacked. Second, it was assumed that hijackers would not be on suicide missions but would be intent on entering into negotiations to attain something. Accordingly, a regional FAA center would contact FAA headquarters in Washington, which would have its hijack coordinator contact the military. Third, after military planes were sent up, they would not intercept the hijacked plane but would follow several miles behind it, out of sight, "escorting" it.

The protocol for an in-flight emergency was, by contrast, aimed at intercepting the plane as quickly as possible. In Robin Hordon's words:

> [T]he interceptor "launch system" is sitting in waiting for immediate reaction and launch. Interceptors are located in open-ended hangars near the ends of runways, the flight crews are located within a few feet and few moments of climbing on board the fighter, the mechanics keep the aircraft mechanically fit and warm with power sources connected for immediate start-up . . . . This is a highly skilled and highly practiced event. . . . Everyone [concerned is] prepared to launch within a few minutes of the request. . . . The "emergency scramble protocol"

[then] calls for the fighter pilots to fly at top speed to intercept the emergency aircraft.[2]

I had failed to make this distinction, saying instead that the early danger signs were evidence that American Flight 11 had been hijacked. I should have said that they were signs that the plane was experiencing an in-flight emergency and, therefore, fighters should have been scrambled immediately under the emergency protocol. Having made that distinction in D9D, I wrote:

> If standard procedure had been followed, . . . the FAA would have notified NEADS no later than 8:22, NEADS would have issued the scramble order no later than 8:23, the fighters would have been airborne no later than 8:27, and AA 11 would have been intercepted by 8:37—over nine minutes before the North Tower of the World Trade Center was struck.[3]

This conclusion does not, incidentally, depend on my inference in NPH that fighters could have been scrambled from nearby McGuire Air Force Base in New Jersey, which is only 70 miles from NYC, instead of from Otis Air National Guard Base in Cape Cod. This inference was erroneous, because McGuire was not one of the bases that kept fighters on alert. But even planes coming from Otis, if they had taken off by 8:27, could have arrived over Manhattan with several minutes to spare.[4]

Accordingly, the conclusion of my discussion of American Flight 11 stands: If standard operating procedures had been followed, it would have been intercepted before the North Tower was struck.

The reason it was not, according to NORAD, was that the FAA had not followed standard procedures. Instead of notifying the military at 8:21 (after it saw Flight 11 go off course) or even at 8:25 (when it learned that this plane had been hijacked), the FAA did not notify NEADS until 8:40. This was stated in "NORAD's Response Times," an official document put out on September 18, one week after 9/11.[5] But if FAA personnel at Boston Center had violated procedures so radically, with such disastrous consequences, they should have been fired and perhaps even charged with criminal dereliction of duty. But no one was even publicly reprimanded.

Also, the claim that Boston Center did not follow procedures has reportedly been denied by at least one of the controllers on duty that day. This controller has stated, according to Robin Hordon, that "the FAA was not asleep and the controllers. . . followed their own protocols."[6] On the basis of this testimony as well as his own familiarity with procedures, Hordon believes that the FAA had actually contacted NEADS by 8:20. Accordingly, Hordon believes: "When the very first call regarding AA 11 was initiated to any military facility is being covered up."[7]

Hordon's belief that the military was contacted by 8:20 is supported by Internet investigative journalist Tom Flocco. While attending the 9/11 Commission hearing in Washington, DC, on May 22, 2003, Flocco has reported, he learned from Laura Brown, the deputy in public affairs at FAA headquarters, that the National Military Command Center had initiated a teleconference at about 8:20 or 8:25 that morning. Flocco added that Brown, after returning to her office and conferring with superiors, sent him an e-mail revising the commencement time of the teleconference to "around 8:45AM." Flocco, however, put more stock in her original statement, before Brown's memory had been "refreshed" by her superiors.[8]

Even if we focus only on what happened after the FAA's Boston Center had received what it took to be clear evidence that Flight 11 had been hijacked—namely, when it heard a voice at 8:25, presumably from Flight 11's radio, saying: "We have some planes. Just stay quiet, and you'll be okay. We are returning to the airport"—the official timeline is problematic. According to the 9/11 Commission, NEADS was not notified until 8:38 (NORAD's timeline had said 8:40). But Colin Scoggins, who placed most of the calls from the FAA's Boston Center to NEADS, has made various statements that, when taken together, imply that *Boston Center's first call to NEADS about the hijacking must have occurred at about 8:27 or 8:28, ten minutes earlier than the Commission claims.*[9] That earlier time is made additionally plausible by the fact that it is about when it should have occurred, if Boston had received evidence of the hijacking, as we are told, at 8:25.[10]

In NPH, I suggested that the best explanation for the military's failure to intercept Flight 11 was that a stand-down order had been issued. *The 9/11 Commission Report* did nothing to weaken that suspicion. Indeed, the case against the official story about Flight 11 is even stronger today than when NPH was first published.

UNITED AIRLINES FLIGHT 175

The original official story about United Flight 175, as we saw in NPH, was even more problematic. The chief question was why, if the military learned about its hijacking at 8:43, this plane was not intercepted prior to 9:03. Twenty minutes was more than enough time. The Otis fighter jets should not have been 71 miles from Manhattan when the South Tower was struck at 9:03.

One reason they were still so far away, we were told, was that they were not airborne until 8:52. According to NORAD's own timeline, however, this was nine minutes after NEADS had been notified about Flight 175 and at least twelve minutes after it had been notified about Flight 11. Why did it take so long?

The first part of the official answer was that NEADS did not give the scramble order to Otis until 8:46, at least six minutes after NEADS had been notified of the hijacking. Why? Because, we are told, Colonel Marr, the commander at NEADS, called to get authorization from General Larry Arnold, the head of NORAD's Continental US Region, who was in a meeting and did not call back until 8:46.[11] According to the military's own manual, however, no such authorization was necessary.[12]

A second part of the reason for the delay was that even after the scramble order was given at 8:46, the planes were not airborne until 8:52. Why did it take the pilots six minutes to become airborne after they had received the scramble order? We were told that at 8:46, the pilots were merely given the green light to taxi onto the runway, where they sat "in their jets, straining at the reins."[13] This six-minute delay has never been satisfactorily explained. According to Colin Scoggins, the military has falsely tried to blame the FAA:

> They [military officials] state in several places that they were waiting on a clearance from the FAA. That is false; we asked them on several occasions why the fighters had not launched. It seemed like an eternity.[14]

FLIGHT 11, FLIGHT 175, AND THE WORLD TRADE CENTER 5

Elaborating on his statement about "several occasions," he said that he and his colleagues called NEADS and Otis several times, asking NEADS if they had given the order to launch, then asking Otis if they had received the order.[15] Scoggins clearly found the time it took to launch the Otis fighters far from normal.

However, even if the planes were not airborne until 8:52, they should have been able to intercept or shoot down Flight 175 before it reached New York City.

Some people have claimed that the pilots would not have shot the planes down. Robin Hordon, however, has said otherwise:

> [M]ake no mistake about this, should the "hijacked aircraft" appear to threaten major populations, or seem to be headed for important military or civilian targets, then the pilots can shoot them down on their own. Shootdown orders are authorized for the pilots to use under certain conditions, some of them pre-approved by higher ups, and some of them at a moment's notice. . . . If an Otis fighter . . . pilot saw the Boeing descend and head straight for NYC, he would already be considering shooting the aircraft down miles and miles away from NYC. And this is regardless of it being an airliner full of passengers. If the pilot came to the conclusion that AA 11 was going to crash into NYC, or its nuclear plant, I will guarantee that AA 11 would have been shot down prior to hitting any buildings.[16]

If what Hordon says about American 11 is true, then it would have been all the more true about United 175, after American 11 had already crashed into the World Trade Center. The Otis pilots, therefore, would not have needed to intercept Flight 175 but only to get within range to down it with a missile. This fact makes the account given by NORAD, in its timeline put out on September 18, 2001, all the more problematic.

Perhaps because it agreed that NORAD's account of Flight 175 was too problematic, the 9/11 Commission, amazingly, gave a completely new account. According to this new account, the FAA did not notify the military about United 175 at 8:43, as NORAD had said in "NORAD's Response Times," issued September 18, 2001. Rather, according to the Commission, "The first indication that the NORAD air defenders had of the second hijacked aircraft, United 175, came in a phone call from New York Center to

NEADS at 9:03," which was "at about the time the plane was hitting the South Tower."[17]

The 9/11 Commission explained this extremely late notification in terms of a number of inexplicable failures on the part of FAA controllers. Even though the New York Center controller learned of a "suspicious transmission" from this flight at 8:42, we are told, this controller did not notice when, at about 8:44, "United 175 turned southwest without clearance from air traffic control." Nor did he notice at 8:46 that the plane's transponder code was changed twice. Moreover, although New York Center knew by 8:48 that United 175 had been hijacked, it made no attempt to contact the military, even after the course and code changes were finally noticed at 8:51. Rather, the Commission claimed, controllers and other FAA personnel merely began discussing among themselves the fact that United 175 was probably hijacked. Even between 9:01 and 9:02, when word of the probable hijacking reached the FAA's Command Center in Herndon, Virginia, the military was not called. Finally, at 9:03, someone at New York Center called NEADS.[18]

To believe the 9/11 Commission's account, we must not only believe that the controllers at the FAA's New York Center could have acted so irresponsibly. We must also believe that they could have done so without being fired or even reprimanded.

The basis for this wholly implausible account was a set of tape recordings of telephone conversations in NORAD's air traffic monitoring stations on 9/11. These NORAD tapes, which were obtained by the Commission in late 2003, were said by it to contain the "true story of the military's response on September 11."[19] In D9D, however, I argued that the more plausible view, for various reasons, is that the tapes were doctored before they were turned over to the Commission, so that they presented a falsified history.[20] Although my full argument for this conclusion can be found only in D9D, some reasons for this conclusion will be mentioned here and in subsequent chapters.

One of those reasons is the very fact that the Commission's tapes-based account of the FAA's behavior in relation to United 175 is wholly implausible. Another reason is the fact that the 9/11 Commission's new story about United 175 also contradicts many previous reports.

One of those reports was, of course, "NORAD's Response Times," issued September 18, 2001. If the military had really not been notified about Flight 175 until 9:03, as the 9/11 Commission claims, why would NORAD have reported, one week after 9/11, that it had been notified at 8:43? The Commission concluded that the military, in preparing this timeline, had lied.[21] However, although we can understand that the military might lie to cover up its own incompetence, we cannot imagine that, if the failure to stop Flight 175 was entirely the FAA's fault, the military would have lied to make it seem as if the fault had been at least partly its own.

Even before the publication of this NORAD document, moreover, CNN had published a timeline, derived from "informed defense officials," that included this entry: "8:43 AM: FAA notified NORAD that United Airlines flight 175 has been hijacked."[22]

The FAA's early notification of the military about Flight 175 was also stated in many other news reports. For example, an Associated Press story in 2002, after saying that the FAA had notified NORAD about the possible hijacking of American 11 at 8:40, said: "[T]hree minutes after that, NORAD was told United Airlines 175 had been hijacked."[23] In an NBC program on the first anniversary of 9/11, Tom Brokaw said that NORAD, after being "alerted to a second hijacking," scrambled "two F-15 fighter jets from Otis air force base in Massachusetts to potentially intercept the United plane."[24]

The 9/11 Commission's later claim that the military was not notified about United 175 also ran counter to the testimony of several military officers. One of these was Captain Michael Jellinek, a Canadian who was overseeing NORAD headquarters in Colorado that day. According to a story in the *Toronto Star*, Jellinek was on the line with personnel at NEADS while they watched United 175 crash into the South Tower. Jellinek then asked: "Was that the hijacked aircraft you were dealing with?" They replied: "Yes, it was."[25] NEADS could hardly have been "dealing with" United 175 if it had not learned about its troubles until after it crashed.

Another officer whose testimony was contradicted by the 9/11 Commission's new story was Brigadier General Montague

Winfield, who on 9/11 was the deputy director of operations at the Pentagon's National Military Command Center (NMCC). In 2002, he said on an ABC special about 9/11:

> When the second aircraft flew into the second tower, it was at that point that we realized that the seemingly unrelated hijackings that the FAA was dealing with were in fact a part of a coordinated terrorist attack on the United States.[26]

Although the Commission would later claim, on the basis of the tapes that it received from NORAD, that the military prior to 9:03 was aware of only one hijacking—that of AA 11, which had already crashed—Winfield, in speaking of the military's awareness prior to 9:03, referred in the plural to the "seemingly unrelated *hijackings*."

Another report of prior notification was contained in a 2003 book by Pamela Freni entitled *Ground Stop: An Inside Look at the Federal Aviation Administration on September 11, 2001*. After the Otis pilots had taken off at 8:52, Freni reported, "Word of the hijacking of UA175 was passed up to them."[27]

The 9/11 Commission's tapes-based claim that the FAA did not notify the military about United 175 until it had crashed is also contradicted by a memo, "FAA Communications with NORAD on September 11, 2001," which was sent to the 9/11 Commission on May 22, 2003 by Laura Brown, the deputy in public affairs at FAA headquarters. This memo, in seeking to clarify how the FAA responded to the events of 9/11, said:

> Within minutes after the first aircraft hit the World Trade Center, the FAA immediately established several phone bridges [telephone conferences] that included FAA field facilities, the FAA Command Center, FAA headquarters, DOD [meaning the NMCC in the Department of Defense], the Secret Service. . . . The US Air Force liaison to the FAA immediately joined the FAA headquarters phone bridge and established contact with NORAD. . . . The FAA shared real-time information on the phone bridges about the unfolding events, including information about loss of communication with aircraft, loss of transponder signals, unauthorized changes in course, and other actions being taken by all the flights of interest.[28]

"Within minutes" after the first attack would mean about 8:50. "[A]ll flights of interest" at that time would have definitely included United 175, because even if people at FAA headquarters had not yet learned about this flight, they would have been quickly informed by the Boston and New York "field facilities." This memo implied, therefore, that NORAD and the NMCC would have learned about United 175's situation from this teleconference.

How did the 9/11 Commission deal with the fact that all these reports contradicted its explanation as to why the military did not intercept United Flight 175? By simply failing to mention them, thereby implicitly admitting that it could not explain why, if its new story were true, all those reports existed. This is a serious problem. To believe the Commission's tapes-based account, one would need to assume that Captain Jellinek, General Winfield, and the authors of the NORAD's timeline as well as the authors of the FAA memo had lied. We can understand that the authors of the FAA memo might have lied to make their personnel look better. But what possible motivation would the military people have had for lying?

In sum, the 9/11 Commission's new explanation of why United 175 was able to strike the World Trade Center is no more successful than the story that the military had told from 2001 until the Commission constructed, on the basis of the NORAD tapes, its new story in 2004. I will present more reasons in later chapters for believing this tapes-based account to be false. For now, the point to emphasize is that when all the evidence is taken into account, we can only conclude that Flight 175 could not have hit the World Trade Center unless there had been a stand-down order, canceling standard operating procedures.[29] In the next chapter, moreover, I will quote the testimony of a man who reports having learned, from conversations involving security officials at LAX, that a White House-ordered stand down had in fact occurred.

THE COLLAPSE OF THE TWIN TOWERS

With regard to the destruction of the World Trade Center, two very important developments have occurred since NPH was published. First, in 2005, NIST (the National Institute of Standards and Technology) issued what was billed as the definitive official report on the collapse of the Twin Towers. (Although this report was originally intended to deal with WTC 7 as well, this part of NIST's report has been repeatedly delayed, as discussed below.) Second, a large number of people with academic and professional qualifications to evaluate this report—including physicists, architects, and structural engineers—have joined the 9/11 truth movement. As a result, even though the official theory of the World Trade Center, according to which the three buildings came down without the aid of explosives, was endorsed by NIST, the case against it is even stronger now than it was in 2004.[30]

NIST AS POLITICAL AGENCY

By way of preparing readers for how shockingly bad NIST's report is, I will point out that NIST is not a neutral, independent organization; it is an agency of the US Department of Commerce. While NIST was writing its report, therefore, it was an agency of the Bush administration, which, according to a statement signed by over 12,000 scientists (including 52 Nobel Laureates and 63 recipients of the National Medal of Science), has been guilty of engaging in "distortion of scientific knowledge for partisan political ends."[31]

A former NIST employee has, in fact, reported that in recent years this agency has been "fully hijacked from the scientific into the political realm." As a result, scientists working for NIST "lost [their] scientific independence, and became little more than 'hired guns.'" With regard to 9/11-related issues, this whistleblower said:

> By 2001, everyone in NIST leadership had been trained to pay close heed to political pressures. There was no chance that NIST people "investigating" the 9/11 situation could have been acting in the true spirit of scientific independence. . . . Everything that came from the hired guns was by then routinely filtered through the front office, and assessed for political implications before release.[32]

In fact, this whistleblower said, all reports, besides being examined by the front office, were also scrutinized by three external oversight groups: the National Security Agency, "the HQ staff of the Department of Commerce" ("which scrutinized our work very closely and frequently wouldn't permit us to release papers or give talks without changes to conform to their way of looking at things"), and the Office of Management and Budget (which is "an arm of the Executive Office of the President" and "had a policy person specifically delegated to provide oversight on our work").[33]

NIST's report on the WTC must, accordingly, be viewed as a political, not a scientific, document[34]—a fact that will be illustrated in the following discussion.

NIST'S FIVE CRUCIAL CLAIMS

NIST's theory of the collapse of the Twin Towers is in one respect the same as that of MIT Professor Thomas Eagar, which was discussed in NPH: Both theories have tried to explain the collapses totally in terms of the impact of the airplanes, the resulting fires, and gravity. Otherwise, however, NIST's theory is significantly different, partly by giving more importance to the impact of the planes. According to NIST, the towers collapsed primarily because of five factors: (1) the towers were not constructed to withstand the impact of a plane as large as a Boeing 767; (2) the planes sliced several core columns and stripped the fireproofing insulation from many more;[35] (3) the subsequent fires weakened these susceptible columns; (4) the fires produced sagging floors, which pulled perimeter columns inward, thereby reducing their support capacity; and (5) the upper portion of each building, above the impact zone, fell down on the lower portion, exerting such downward momentum that this lower portion collapsed at virtually free-fall speed.

NIST's theory is clearly inadequate, because each of these five claims is unsupported by the relevant evidence.

(1) *The Alleged Unanticipated Impact of the Airliners*: NIST's *Final Report*, put out in 2005, said that building codes for buildings to be used by the general population "do not require building designs to consider aircraft impact."[36] NIST thereby implied that the Twin Towers had not been designed to withstand the impact of a large airliner.

However, a 1964 document, which was in the files of the Port Authority of New York and New Jersey, summarized a structural analysis of the Twin Towers carried out by the firm of

Worthington, Skilling, Helle & Jackson. One of the points said:

> The buildings have been investigated and found to be safe in an assumed collision with a large jet airliner (Boeing 707–DC 8) traveling at 600 miles per hour. Analysis indicates that such collision would result in only local damage which could not cause collapse.[37]

In January 2001, Frank De Martini, who had been the on-site construction manager for the World Trade Center, said of one of the towers: "The building was designed to have a fully loaded 707 crash into it, that was the largest plane at the time. I believe that the building could probably sustain multiple impacts of jet liners."[38]

Those two statements led to one of the questions to which NIST responded in a 2006 document, "Answers to Frequently Asked Questions," namely: "If the World Trade Center (WTC) towers were designed to withstand multiple impacts by Boeing 707 aircraft, why did the impact of individual 767s cause so much damage?"[39]

NIST, failing to acknowledge that the question was based partly on De Martini's statement, replied that the Port Authority "indicated that the impact of a [single, not multiple] Boeing 707 aircraft was analyzed during the design stage of the WTC towers."[40] By ignoring De Martini's statement, NIST implied, with its bracketed words, that the question was based on faulty information.

Then, in seeking to refute the idea that if a 707 would not have induced collapse, neither would a 767, NIST said that "a Boeing 767 aircraft. . . is about 20 percent bigger than a Boeing 707." That fact alone, however, would not necessarily mean that a 767 would do more damage: As NIST itself acknowledged, the damage on 9/11 "was caused by the large mass of the aircraft [and] their high speed and momentum." In other words, speed as well as mass had to be considered. This point is crucial, because the 1964 analysis spoke of a Boeing 707 traveling at 600 mph, whereas the 767s that hit the North and South Towers were reportedly traveling at only 440 and 540 mph, respectively.[41] As a result, the kinetic energy of the envisaged Boeing 707 would actually have been greater than the kinetic energy of the 767s, especially the one that hit the North Tower, which was reportedly going only

440 mph.[42] There was, accordingly, no justification for NIST's insinuation that the 767s, because of their greater weight, would have caused more damage than the envisaged 707s.

Another problem with NIST's argument was that it failed to acknowledge a statement by John Skilling, who was responsible for the structural design of the Twin Towers. In 1993, after the bombing of the World Trade Center, he said that, according to his analysis, if one of these buildings were to suffer a strike by a jet plane loaded with jet fuel, "there would be a horrendous fire" and "a lot of people would be killed," but "the building structure would still be there."[43] If NIST had been a truth-seeking body, it would not have ignored this important statement.

In sum: NIST claimed that "the structural damage to the towers was due to the aircraft impact and not to any alternative forces," such as pre-set explosives. But it failed to provide any good reason to conclude that the impact of a 767 would have caused sufficient structural damage to help initiate collapse.

(2) *The Alleged Cutting and Stripping of Columns*: NIST, nevertheless, made very strong claims about the kind of damage caused by the impact of each 767. This alleged damage was of two types: many core columns (as well as peripheral columns) were severed, and fireproofing insulation was stripped from many other core columns.

To begin with the severing: NIST claimed that six of the North Tower's core columns and ten of the South Tower's were severed. The claim that the South Tower's core was more severely damaged was then used by NIST to explain why it collapsed more quickly.[44] (As we saw in NPH, this was a serious problem: If the buildings collapsed because the fire weakened the steel, the North Tower, which was struck first, should have collapsed first.)

However, even if we grant, for the sake of argument, that core columns could have been severed, the idea that more of the South Tower's core columns would have been severed is extremely implausible, for two reasons. First, whereas the North Tower was struck at approximately the 95th floor, the South Tower was struck near the 80th floor, where the core columns were considerably thicker. They would have been less, rather than more, likely to be severed. Second, NIST's own discussion, besides suggesting that the engines were the only parts of the planes likely to sever core columns, also suggested that an engine would sever a column only if it struck it directly.[45] Yet the plane that hit the North Tower struck the building in the center, so that both engines would have been headed toward its core, whereas the South Tower was struck near the right corner, so only the plane's left engine could have struck a core column. Accordingly, if there were severed columns in both towers, there should have been fewer, not more, in the South Tower.[46]

As architect Eric Douglas has pointed out, NIST's estimates were based entirely on computer simulations.[47] In coming up with estimates, it began, in the words of NIST's own scientists, with "a 'base case' based on a best estimate of all input parameters." But it also provided "more and less severe damage estimates based on variations of the most influential parameters."[48] NIST then chose the most severe estimates. Why? "NIST selected the more severe cases because," Douglas says, "they were the only ones that produced the desired outcome."[49] The more severe estimates were needed, in other words, to produce collapse. In dealing with the South Tower, for example, NIST first estimated that from three to ten core columns were broken, then chose the most severe estimate, because only with it would the tower, in the computer simulation, collapse.[50]

That Douglas's description of NIST's method is no misrepresentation can be seen from the following statement in NIST's *Final Report*:

> The Investigation Team . . . defined three cases for each building by combining the middle, less severe, and more severe values of the influential variables. Upon a preliminary examination of the middle cases, it became clear that the towers would likely remain standing. The less severe cases were discarded after the aircraft impact results were compared to observed events [meaning the fact that the buildings collapsed]. The middle cases . . . were discarded after the structural response analysis of major subsystems were [sic] compared to observed events. . . . The more severe case . . . was used for the global analysis of each tower.[51]

It appears, moreover, that collapse was not generated even by the most extreme variables, so an adjustment was necessary. In NIST's own words: "Complete sets of simulations were then performed for [the extreme variables]. . . . To the extent that the simulations deviated from the photographic evidence or eyewitness reports, the investigators adjusted the input."[52]

Steven Jones, having quoted this passage, commented: "How fun to tweak the model like that, until one gets the desired result!"[53] Douglas, spelling out Jones's implicit criticism, said:

> [A] fundamental problem with using computer simulation is the overwhelming temptation to manipulate the input data until one achieves the desired results. Thus, what appears to be a conclusion is actually a premise. We see NIST succumb to this temptation throughout its investigation. . . . NIST tweaked the input until the buildings fell down.[54]

The fact of the matter is that no one really has any idea how many, if any, of the core columns in the Twin Towers were severed by the planes. All we know is that the numbers given by NIST (six in the North Tower and ten in the South) must be posited if the towers were to collapse in NIST's computer simulations—on the assumption, of course, that explosives were not used. NIST's (circular) logic ran like this:

(1) If explosives were not used, then all those core columns had to have been severed by the planes.

(2) Explosives were not used.

(3) Therefore, all those core columns were severed by the planes.

NIST then cited this conclusion as evidence that explosives were not used.

Equally problematic was NIST's claim that the planes also stripped the fireproofing insulation from many of the unsevered core columns on several floors. This claim was an essential part of its theory, as NIST clearly stated, saying:

> The WTC towers would likely not have collapsed under the combined effects of aircraft impact damage and the extensive, multifloor fires that were encountered on September 11, 2001, if the thermal insulation had not been widely dislodged or had been only minimally dislodged by aircraft impact.[55]

Quantifying its claim that the insulation was "widely dislodged," NIST estimated that the airplanes stripped the insulation from 43 of the North Tower's 47 core columns and from 39 of the South Tower's.

The method reportedly used by NIST to reach those figures does not inspire confidence. Former Underwriters Laboratories scientist Kevin Ryan discovered that NIST's "test for fireproofing loss. . . involved shooting a total of fifteen rounds from a shotgun at non-representative samples in a plywood box. Flat steel plates were used instead of column samples."[56]

From this description, we can infer that NIST's real method for determining how many of the columns were stripped was the same method it used for determining how many core columns were severed: a computer simulation, in which NIST tweaked the variables until collapse was produced.

(3) *The Alleged Weakening of the Core Columns*: According to NIST, once some of the core columns were severed and others lost their fireproofing insulation on the impact floors, fire heated these columns to a point where they lost so much of their strength that they buckled, allowing the top portion of the building to fall down on the lower portion.

Were the fires really hot enough to heat the core columns to a temperature at which they would lose much of their strength? Besides claiming that the fires reached 1,000°C (1,832°F),[57] NIST even gave the impression that some of the steel columns themselves reached this temperature, saying: "[W]hen bare steel reaches temperatures of 1,000 degrees Celsius, it softens and its strength reduces to roughly 10 percent of its room temperature value."[58] NIST led the reader to believe, in other words, that some of the core columns lost 90 percent of their strength.

However, for a fire to heat even a portion of a column to a point where it would even begin to approximate the gas temperature (the fire's own temperature), the fire would need to maintain that temperature for a long time. A single piece of steel can, to be sure, heat up quite quickly. But, as Mark Gaffney has written:

> The columns in each tower were part of an interconnected steel framework that weighed some 90,000 tons; and because steel is

known to be at least a fair conductor of heat, on 9/11 this massive steel superstructure functioned as an enormous energy sink. The total volume of the steel framework was vast compared with the relatively small area of exposed steel, and would have wicked away much of the fire-generated heat. . . . The fires on 9/11 would have taken many hours. . . to slowly raise the temperature of the steel framework as a whole to the point of weakening even a few exposed members.[59]

Moreover, NIST itself said: "At any given location, the duration of the temperatures near 1,000°C was about 15 min to 20 min. The rest of the time, the calculated temperatures were near 500°C or below."[60] So even if the fires had occasionally risen to 1,000°C here and there, no steel columns would have reached that temperature, by NIST's own calculations.

NIST also admitted, most significantly, that its analysis of recovered steel found "no evidence that any of the samples had reached temperatures above 600°C [1,112°F]." This was, it should be noted, a statement about recovered steel of every type, not simply steel from columns.[61]

With regard to steel from columns in particular, NIST reported that, having examined 16 *perimeter* columns, it found that "only three columns had evidence that the steel reached temperatures above 250°C [482°F]." What about *core* columns? NIST reported that it found no evidence that any of the core columns had reached even that temperature.[62] In other words, although NIST insinuated that some core columns had "reached temperatures of 1,000 degrees Celsius," it had no empirical evidence from its own scientists that any of them had even reached 250 degrees Celsius (482 degrees Fahrenheit)!

NIST's own scientists, therefore, provided no evidence to support the contention of NIST's *Final Report* that the core columns had been weakened by fire. "[S]tructural steel," MIT's Thomas Eagar has pointed out, "begins to soften around 425°C [797°F]."[63] *NIST had no empirical evidence, therefore, that any of the core columns had reached the temperature at which they would even begin to weaken*, let alone a temperature at which they would become so weak that they might buckle.

NIST's report was, however, replete with statements that the fires did weaken the core columns, such as this one: "As the structural temperatures continued to rise, the columns thermally weakened and consequently shortened." Here is another example: "Under high temperatures... in the core area, the remaining core columns with damaged insulation were thermally weakened."[64]

NIST made these claims in spite of the fact that its own tests found only a few perimeter columns that had "reached temperatures above 250°C" and *no* core columns that had reached 250°C. How could NIST justify its claim in light of these results? It simply said that it "did not generalize these results, since the examined columns represented only... 1 percent of the core columns from the fire floors."[65] NIST claimed, in other words, that the pieces it tested could not be assumed to be representative. But there are two problems with this claim.

First, although it is true that the tests did not prove that no columns got hotter than those tested, they also provided no evidence that any of them did get hotter than those tested. Any claim that some columns became hot enough to begin losing strength (425°C; 797°F) would be pure speculation, devoid of empirical support. Such speculation would be especially unwarranted in light of the fact that the fires in the cores, where there was an oxygen deficiency (as shown by the black smoke emanating therefrom), would most likely have been cooler than the fires by the peripheral columns near the holes made by the planes.

The second problem with NIST's rationale is that it contradicts what NIST itself had previously said. In a December 2003 report, it wrote:

NIST has in its possession about 236 pieces of WTC steel. ....
NIST believes that this collection of steel from the WTC Towers is adequate for purposes of the Investigation [emphasis NIST's]. Regions of impact and fire damage were emphasized in the selection of steel for the Investigation.

It also wrote:

These pieces represent a small fraction of the enormous amount of steel examined at the various salvage yards where the steel was sent as the WTC site was cleared. In addition, NIST has examined additional steel stored by the Port Authority at JFK airport and has transported 12 of those specimens to NIST.[66]

Given NIST's threefold statement that it had examined an "enormous amount of steel," that "[r]egions of impact and fire damage were emphasized in the selection of steel for the Investigation," and that this selection was deemed to be "adequate for purposes of the Investigation," how could it later claim that it need not be bound by the results of this investigation because the pieces it analyzed were not representative?

When challenged on this point in a "Request for Correction" sent by Steven Jones, Kevin Ryan, and other members of the 9/11 truth movement,[67] NIST replied: "NIST has stated that, 'the steel recovered is sufficient for determining the quality of the steel and… for determining mechanical properties.'"[68] NIST thereby implied that it had never assumed that the recovered steel would be sufficient for *determining the temperatures reached by the steel* in the towers.

But after NIST had emphasized in its December 2003 report that its collection of steel was "adequate for purposes of the Investigation," it added: "The NIST analysis of recovered WTC steel includes: . . . Estimating the maximum temperature reached by available steel."[69] NIST *had*, therefore, clearly stated that it had selected its steel partly to make a judgment about the maximum temperature reached by the steel in the towers.

It is hard to avoid the suspicion that NIST started describing its steel as unrepresentative and insufficient only after it realized that, if the towers in its computer simulations were to collapse, the steel in the core columns would have needed to attain temperatures far greater than those for which NIST had physical evidence.[70] Accordingly, the only recourse for the authors of NIST's *Final Report* was to dismiss the empirical evidence provided by its own scientists as unrepresentative.

It must be emphasized that NIST's claim that the core columns were heated to a temperature at which they would have lost a significant amount of strength—whether 90 percent, 50 percent, or even 20 percent—is pure speculation. Besides not being warranted by any physical evidence, it even runs counter to the evidence presented by NIST's own scientists. NIST has failed, therefore, to provide credible support for its claim that the core columns, having been stripped of their fireproofing insulation, would have been greatly weakened by the fires.

(4) *The Alleged Floor Sagging*: Another essential part of NIST's theory is its claim that the fires, by heating some of the floors, caused them to sag so much that they pulled on perimeter columns, causing them to bow inward. This claim differentiates NIST's theory from the "pancake" theory proposed by Thomas Eagar and presupposed by the 9/11 Commission, according to which the floors fell because they became disconnected from the columns. NIST said, by contrast, that the floors that were caused to sag by the fires "remain[ed] connected to the columns and pull[ed] the columns inwards."[71]

In order to make this claim, however, NIST had to fudge the data enormously. For example, NIST's physical tests showed that the fires, even if they had been as hot as NIST claimed, would have caused the floors to sag less than 4 inches. But in NIST's computer simulations, the floors sagged some 42 inches! (See "Request for Correction" and a follow-up "Appeal").[72]

(5) *The Alleged Irresistible Downward Momentum of the Top Section*: NIST's assigned task, as it pointed out, was to "[d]etermine why and how WTC 1 and WTC 2 collapsed following the initial impacts of the aircraft."[73] NIST completed its explanation of these collapses by saying that, after the towers had been weakened by the developments discussed in the preceding points, "the massive top section of [each] building at and above the fire and impact floors" fell down on the lower section, which "could not resist the tremendous energy released by [the top section's] downward movement."[74] The statement that it "could not resist" means that it provided virtually *no* resistance: "Since the stories below the level of collapse initiation provided little resistance to the tremendous energy released by the falling building mass, the building section above came down essentially in free fall, as seen in videos."[75]

But NIST thereby at best gave a description, not an explanation. This fact is illustrated by NIST's statement that, once the top portion of the building started falling, the "story immediately below the stories in which the columns failed was not able to arrest this initial movement as evidenced by videos from several vantage points."[76] As the aforementioned "Request for Correction" pointed out, this statement describes what happened "but gives the reader absolutely no idea why it occurred."[77]

Such an explanation was required, because the description—"the building section above came down essentially in free fall, as seen in videos"—runs counter to basic physical principles, most obviously the conservation of momentum (assuming, as NIST did, that steel supports for the lower section had not been removed by explosives). William Rice, who has both practiced and taught structural engineering, has made this point, saying:

> [E]ach of these 110-story Twin Towers fell upon itself in about ten seconds at nearly free-fall speed. This violates Newton's Law of Conservation of Momentum that would require that as the stationary inertia of each floor is overcome by being hit, the mass (weight) increases and the free-fall speed decreases. Even if Newton's Law is ignored, the prevailing theory would have us believe that each of the Twin Towers inexplicably collapsed upon itself crushing all 287 massive columns on each floor while maintaining a free-fall speed as if the 100,000, or more, tons of supporting structural-steel framework underneath didn't exist.[78]

Another structural engineer, Edward Knesl, has written:

> It is impossible that heavy steel columns could collapse at the fraction of the second within each story and subsequently at each floor below. . . . The engineering science and the law of physics simply doesn't know such possibility. Only very sophisticated controlled demolition can achieve such result, eliminating the natural dampening effect of the structural framing huge mass that should normally stop the partial collapse.[79]

NIST's theory is, in other words, *physically impossible*. The authors of the "Request for Correction" made this same point, writing:

> Basic principles of engineering (for example, the conservation of momentum principle) would dictate that the undamaged steel structure below the collapse initiation zone would, at the very least, resist and slow the downward movement of the stories

above. There is, indeed, a good chance that the structural strength of the steelwork below would arrest the downward movement of the stories above. NIST must explain why the intact structure below the impact zone offered so little resistance to the collapse of the building.[80]

NIST gave the appearance of offering an explanation by saying:

> The structure below the level of collapse initiation offered minimal resistance to the falling building mass at and above the impact zone. The potential energy released by the downward movement of the large building mass far exceeded the capacity of the intact structure below to absorb that through energy of deformation.[81]

However, the question that NIST needed to answer, with some quantitative analysis, was *why* the lower structure, if it truly was "intact," did not have the capacity to absorb the energy exerted on it by the upper structure. The lower structure should have had far more than enough capacity to do this, especially given the fact that, as Gaffney points out, the columns in the lower part of the towers, being "untouched by the plane impacts and fires. . . suffered no loss of strength."[82]

According to an analysis of the North Tower by mechanical engineer Gordon Ross, so much energy would have been absorbed by the lower structure that "vertical movement of the falling section would [have been] arrested . . . within 0.02 seconds after impact. A collapse driven only by gravity would not continue to progress beyond that point."[83] Ross's analysis perhaps explains why NIST provided no quantitative analysis to support its claim.

The statement in the "Request for Correction" about the conservation of momentum was only one of many criticisms of NIST's theory for violating this principle.[84] In a December 2007 document, NIST responded to these criticisms by, incredibly, pretending that the question was whether "basic principles of conservation [were] satisfied in NIST's analysis of the structural response of the towers to the aircraft impact." But as physicist Crockett Grabbe has pointed out, "There was *never* any issue of the energy and momentum the plane impacts had on the towers!"[85] All the questions raised about conservation principles have involved whether these principles were satisfied by NIST's claims about the collapses of the towers. By pretending to be embarrassingly stupid, however, NIST's "hired guns" were able to evade the question.

Determined not to let them continue to evade this question, Steven Jones and several colleagues raised it again in an article published in the (peer-reviewed) *Open Civil Engineering Journal*. They wrote:

> NIST evidently neglects a fundamental law of physics in glibly treating the remarkable "free fall" collapse of each Tower, namely, the Law of Conservation of Momentum. This law of physics means that the hundreds of thousands of tons of material in the way must slow the upper part of the building because of its mass. . . . [T]his negligence by NIST (leaving the near-free-fall speeds unexplained) is a major flaw in their analysis. NIST ignores the possibility of controlled demolitions, which achieve complete building collapses in near free-fall times by moving the material out of the way using explosives. So, there is an alternative explanation that fits the data without violating basic laws of physics. . . . [W]e are keen to look at NIST's calculations of how they explain near-free-fall collapse rates without explosives. We await an explanation from NIST which satisfies Conservation of Momentum.[86]

In addition to the conflict between the conservation-of-momentum principle and the virtually free-fall speed of the collapses, there is another major fact that is inconsistent with NIST's claim that the lower sections of the towers collapsed because of the downward force exerted by the top sections. The top section of the South Tower (WTC 2), as the "Request for Correction" points out,

> did not fall as a block upon the lower undamaged portion, but instead disintegrated as it fell. Thus, there would be no single large impact from a falling block . . . [but only] a series of small impacts as the fragments of the disintegrating upper portion arrived.[87]

In other words, the empirical evidence provided by videos of the South Tower's destruction completely undermines NIST's claim about the "tremendous energy" that would have been released by the "downward movement" of the "massive top section." The top section was not massive, because it disintegrated as it fell.

This issue has been explored in a paper by Graeme MacQueen and Tony Szamboti dealing with the North Tower. Observing that NIST's theory of its collapse requires that the top 12 stories constituted a rigid block that fell down on the building's lower structure, they pointed out that—as Zdenek Bazant, a defender of NIST's theory, has said—this fall would have needed to produce "one powerful jolt" to the lower structure in order to initiate its collapse: "Without it the required work could not have been done." Then, noting that "if there was a powerful jolt to the lower structure there must also have been a powerful jolt to the upper, falling structure," they added that, by the law of the conservation of momentum, "a jolt entails deceleration." They then studied videos of the collapse to see if the requisite deceleration could be observed. Focusing on a feature of the upper block that could be easily tracked—its roof—they found that the requisite deceleration did not occur. To quote their conclusion:

> We have tracked the fall of the roof of the North Tower through 114.4 feet, and we have found that it did not suffer severe and sudden impact or abrupt deceleration. There was no jolt. Thus there could not have been any . . . mechanism to explain the collapse of the lower portion of the building, which was undamaged by fire. The collapse hypothesis of Bazant and the authors of the NIST report has not withstood scrutiny.[88]

For all of these reasons, the fifth factor in NIST's theory, like the other four factors, is inconsistent with the relevant evidence.

NIST'S IGNORING OF RELEVANT EVIDENCE

Besides the fact that its crucial claims are unsupported by evidence, NIST's theory is inadequate for a second major reason. Whereas NIST claimed that it "found no corroborating evidence for alternative hypotheses suggesting that the WTC towers were brought down by controlled demolition using explosives,"[89] the truth is that it simply ignored all such evidence. I will give four examples.[90]

(1) *Explosions in the Towers:* According to NIST, "there was no evidence (collected by . . . the Fire Department of New York) of any blast or explosions in the region below the impact and fire floors."[91]

Although in this statement NIST limited its claim to the denial of any explosions "in the region below the impact and fire floors," it wrote as if there were no explosions reported anywhere in the towers before or during their collapses. Insofar as NIST implicitly made this statement, it was a falsehood of enormous proportions.

Readers of NPH might well have missed the fact that explosions were reported. I had only one sentence about it in the text, and witnesses were quoted only in the accompanying note in the back of the book. In that note, moreover, I quoted only one firefighter and three WTC employees.

Since then, however, there has been an explosion of evidence for explosions. The most important event was the public release of 503 oral histories that were recorded shortly after 9/11 by the Fire Department of New York (which includes emergency medical workers as well as firefighters). The City of New York, which (under Mayor Michael Bloomberg) had long refused to release these testimonies, was finally forced by a court order to do so in August 2005. The *New York Times*, one of the plaintiffs, then made these oral histories publicly available.[92] Shortly thereafter, I published an essay entitled "Explosive Testimony," which quoted statements from 31 of these oral histories, along with many testimonies from journalists, police officers, and WTC employees.[93]

A few months later, Graeme MacQueen published an essay entitled "118 Witnesses," in which he reported that 118 of the 503 oral histories referred to the occurrence of phenomena in the towers clearly suggestive of explosions.[94] Here are three examples:

> [Y]ou just heard explosions coming from building two, the South Tower. It seemed like it took forever, but there were about ten explosions. . . . We then realized the building started to come down.[95]
>
> [T]here was what appeared to be at first an explosion. It appeared at the very top, simultaneously from all four sides, materials shot out horizontally. And then there seemed to be a momentary delay before you could see the beginning of the collapse.[96]
>
> [W]e were standing there watching the North Tower and not even paying attention to the South Tower. Then you look up and it's like holy shit, the building didn't come down, it shot straight out over our heads, like straight across West Street.[97]

The fact that NIST did not discuss these testimonies cannot be explained by ignorance. Although MacQueen's essay as well as mine appeared after NIST's *Final Report* was published, NIST had been given access to the oral histories prior to their public release.[98] NIST might claim, to be sure, that these testimonies did not provide evidence that explosives had been placed in the towers. By denying that the FDNY had collected any evidence of "explosions in the region below the impact and fire floors," NIST seemed to be claiming that any explosions that did occur could be explained away as resulting from the impact of the planes and the resulting fires.

That claim, however, would be implausible with regard to many of the testimonies, such as this one: "[T]here was just an explosion. It seemed like on television [when] they blow up these buildings. It seemed like it was going all the way around like a belt, all these explosions."[99]

Random explosions could not explain this pattern, which in the demolition industry is known as a "demolition ring."

Moreover, even if we accepted NIST's criterion, according to which only explosions "occurring in the region below the impact and fire floors" would count as evidence of pre-set explosives, NIST's denial that any such explosions were reported is false, as the following examples show:

> [T]he South Tower. . . actually gave at a lower floor, not the floor where the plane hit. . . [W]e originally had thought there was like an internal detonation, explosives, because it went in succession, boom, boom, boom, boom, and then the tower came down.[100]
>
> I saw low-level flashes. . . . I didn't know what it was. I mean, it could have been as a result of the building collapsing, things exploding, but I saw a flash flash flash and then it looked like the building came down. . . . [It was at] the lower level of the building. You know like when they demolish a building, how when they blow up a building, when it falls down? That's what I thought I saw.[101]
>
> I was distracted by a large explosion from the South Tower and it seemed like fire was shooting out a couple of hundred feet in each direction. . . . [This fire] appeared . . . [m]aybe twenty floors below the impact area of the plane.[102]

[T]hen there was an explosion in the South Tower. . . . Floor after floor after floor. One floor under another after another and when it hit about the fifth floor, I figured it was a bomb, because it looked like a synchronized deliberate kind of thing.[103]

Then the building popped, lower than the fire. . . . I was going oh, my god, there is a secondary device because the way the building popped. I thought it was an explosion.[104]

Somewhere around the middle of the World Trade Center, there was this orange and red flash coming out. . . . Then this flash just kept popping all the way around the building and that building had started to explode. The popping sound, and with each popping sound it was initially an orange and then a red flash came out of the building and then it would just go all around the building on both sides as far as I could see. These popping sounds and the explosions were getting bigger, going both up and down and then all around the building.[105]

In its *Final Report*, NIST failed to mention any of these testimonies.

The authors of the "Request for Correction" confronted NIST on this matter by mentioning several of the FDNY oral histories that referred to phenomena suggestive of explosions. In its letter of reply, NIST said:

> NIST reviewed all of the interviews conducted by the FDNY of firefighters (500 interviews) and in addition conducted its own set of interviews with emergency responders and building occupants. Taken as a whole, the interviews did not support the contention that explosives played a role in the collapse of the WTC Towers.[106]

This was an incredible response. As we have seen, almost 25 percent (118 out of the 503) of the members of the FDNY gave testimony suggestive of explosions. This is a very high percentage, especially given the fact that these men and women had not been asked whether they had witnessed phenomena suggestive of explosions; they simply volunteered this information. Yet NIST claimed that, "taken as a whole," the interviews did not support the idea that explosives played a role.

What did NIST's statement mean? Evidently, that the interviews could be ignored because phenomena suggestive of explosions were not mentioned in all of them, or at least a *majority* of them. The authors of the "Request for Correction," in their later "Appeal," said: "The Requesters wonder how many firefighters reporting explosions it would have taken for NIST to seriously consider the explosive demolition hypothesis for the collapses."[107] This was, however, a rhetorical question, because the authors of the "Request" knew the answer: NIST had a cover-up to carry out, so it would not have considered this hypothesis no matter how many FDNY personnel had reported phenomena suggestive of explosions.

This cynical view of NIST's approach is supported by the fact that the "Request for Correction" had specifically included three testimonies referring to explosions that occurred below the impact zones in the towers. In its letter of reply, NIST gave the same response: "taken as a whole, these first person accounts do not support the assertion of blasts occurring below the impact zone."[108] NIST had previously claimed, it should be recalled, that the Fire Department of New York had collected "no evidence. . . of any. . . explosions in the region below the impact and fire floors." "No evidence" would mean no testimonies. But after the "Request for Correction" showed this to be untrue by quoting three such testimonies, NIST simply upped the ante, implying that there were *not enough* such testimonies.

It should be noted, moreover, that there were dozens of credible testimonies beyond those supplied by members of the Fire Department. For example, *Wall Street Journal* reporter John Bussey said: "I. . . looked up out of the [WSJ] office window to see what seemed like perfectly synchronized explosions coming from each floor. . . . One after the other, from top to bottom, with a fraction of a second between, the floors blew to pieces."[109]

Some of these other testimonies referred specifically to explosions far below the impact zone. North Tower employee Teresa Veliz, who had been on the 47th floor, said that after she got out of the building and onto the street: "There were explosions going off everywhere. I was convinced that there were bombs planted all over the place and someone was sitting at a control panel pushing detonator buttons."[110] Employee Genelle Guzman reported that when she got down to the 13th floor of the North Tower some 20 minutes before it came down, she heard a "big explosion," after which "[t]he wall I was facing just opened up, and it threw me on the other side."[111] Janitor William Rodriguez, also in the North Tower, reported that he and others felt an explosion below the first sub-level office at 8:46AM, just before the building was hit by the plane, after which co-worker Felipe David, who had been in front of a nearby freight elevator, came into the office with severe burns on his face and arms yelling, "explosion! explosion! explosion!"[112]

Rodriguez, moreover, gave additional evidence of NIST's determination to ignore all such testimony, stating:

> I contacted NIST. . . four times without a response. Finally, [at a public hearing] I asked them before they came up with their conclusion. . . if they ever considered my statements or the statements of any of the other survivors who heard the explosions. They just stared at me with blank faces.[113]

As "hired guns," of course, they could do little else—a fact that probably made some of the NIST employees uncomfortable.

Indeed, the previously quoted NIST whistleblower reported that he has some "friends who are still there and who have been closely, though unhappily and often unwillingly, involved in some of the politicization [of NIST] and its effects."[114] To understand the situation is, however, not to excuse the behavior, in which people, in order to keep their jobs, have contributed to the cover-up of the crime of the century—a crime involving mass murder and treason.

In any case, can anyone, in light of NIST's cavalier dismissal of evidence for explosions, doubt that its report is a political, not a scientific, document? Can anyone doubt that its mission was to conceal, not to reveal, the truth about the destruction of the World Trade Center? This judgment is further confirmed by NIST's treatment of additional evidence.

(2) *Horizontal Ejections*: As one of the testimonies quoted above stated, when the towers exploded near the top, "materials shot out horizontally." From reading NIST's documents alone, one might infer that these "materials" were limited to what NIST calls "puffs of smoke," which it explained as air that was compressed when the buildings started collapsing.[115]

NIST failed to mention, however, that some of the materials ejected horizontally were massive sections of perimeter columns, weighing hundreds of tons, and that some of them traveled 500 or 600 feet and implanted themselves in neighboring buildings, as can be seen in videos and photographs.[116]

If NIST's assigned task was to defend the official account—according to which the only energy available, beyond that supplied by the airplane impacts and the resulting fires, was gravitational energy, which pulls things straight down—NIST needed to pretend that these horizontal ejections had not occurred. To acknowledge these ejections would be to admit the falsity of the official account. For example, Dwain Deets, the former director of the research engineering division at NASA's Dryden Flight Research Center, has mentioned the "massive structural members being hurled horizontally" as one of the factors that "leave no doubt" in his mind that "explosives were involved."[117]

These horizontal ejections also included human bone fragments. In 2005 and 2006, over 700 bone fragments were found on the roof of the nearby Deutsche Bank building.[118] Unless explosives were going off, what could have shattered human bones into tiny fragments and then ejected them out far enough to fall on nearby buildings?

These bone fragments were, incidentally, only part of a more general phenomenon, namely, that about half of the victims could not be identified. Dr. George Bauries, a former FBI evidence expert, said: "The problem with the trade center is that when the pieces are that small, [they] can get mixed in with other debris. . . and it creates an incredibly difficult task to separate things out."[119] Why, if the only sources of energy were fire and gravity, would the body pieces have been so small?

(3) *Evidence that Steel Had Melted*: If some of the steel in the towers melted, this would be strong evidence that explosives had been used. The fires could not have melted steel, because steel does not begin to melt until it reaches about 2,700°F (1,480°C),[120] and an open, diffuse fire fed by hydrocarbon material (including jet fuel) could never, even under the most ideal conditions, get much above

1,832°F (1,000°C). Accordingly, if steel melted, explosives must have been used. (In this discussion, I am using the term "explosives" very broadly to refer not only to explosives in the technical sense but also to incendiary mixtures, such as thermite and thermate, and any other substances or devices that can be used to produce explosions that would cut steel.)

One of the major problems for the official account, accordingly, was the fact that several reports indicated that steel had indeed melted. Leslie Robertson, a member of the engineering firm that designed the Twin Towers, said: "As of 21 days after the attack, the fires were still burning and molten steel was still running."[121] Dr. Keith Eaton, the chief executive of the London-based Institution of Structural Engineers, reported after a tour of the site that he was shown slides of "molten metal, which was still red hot weeks after the event."[122] Dr. Alison Geyh of the Johns Hopkins School of Public Health, who led a scientific team that went to the site shortly after 9/11 on behalf of the National Institute of Environmental Health Sciences, said: "Fires are still actively burning. . . . In some pockets now being uncovered they are finding molten steel."[123] FDNY Captain Philip Ruvolo said: "You'd get down below and you'd see molten steel, *molten* steel, running down the channel rails, like you're in a foundry, like lava."[124] Herb Trimpe, an Episcopalian deacon who served as a chaplain at Ground Zero, said: "I talked to many contractors and they said. . . beams had just totally been melted because of the heat."[125]

Some witnesses spoke of seeing steel beams that were molten at the end. Joe O'Toole, a Bronx firefighter who worked on the rescue and cleanup efforts, said of a beam that was lifted from deep below the surface: "It was dripping from the molten steel."[126] According to Greg Fuchek, vice president of a company supplying computer equipment to identify human remains: "[S]ometimes when a worker would pull a steel beam from the wreckage, the end of the beam would be dripping molten steel."[127] Tom Arterburn, writing in *Waste Age*, said: "[F]or about two and a half months after the attacks, . . . NYDS [New York Department of Sanitation] played a major role in debris removal—everything from molten steel beams to human remains."[128]

One of the most important witnesses was Abolhassan Astaneh-Asl, a professor of civil engineering at the University of California at Berkeley. Immediately after 9/11, he received a National Science Foundation grant to spend two weeks at Ground Zero studying steel from the buildings. In speaking about what he learned in October 2001, he reported that steel flanges "had been reduced from an inch thick to paper thin."[129] He also reported seeing 10-ton steel beams that "looked like giant sticks of twisted licorice" and also steel that was smoothly warped at connection points, which could happen, he said, only if the steel had become yellow or white hot—"perhaps around 2,000 degrees."[130]

In 2007, after a tanker truck fire caused an overpass near the San Francisco Bay Bridge to collapse, Astaneh-Asl received an NSF grant to study its steel. Shortly thereafter, he was interviewed about the overpass collapse on PBS's *NewsHour* with Jim Lehrer. Saying that "the fire was the reason why the steel got soft and weak and collapsed," he then—alluding to the fact that some reports had said that steel girders in the overpass had melted— cautioned: "the word 'melting' should not be used for [the] girders, because there was no melting of girders." Having made that distinction between melting and merely softening, he underlined the distinction by adding: "I saw melting of girders in [the] World Trade Center."[131] So, whereas steel in the overpass fire was merely softened, not melted, Astaneh-Asl said, some steel in the World Trade Center *was* melted.

As the previous paragraphs show, there was evidence of many types, coming from many credible people, that steel in the Twin Towers had melted. How did NIST deal with this evidence?

On the one hand, NIST pointed out that the fires could not have melted the structural steel. Dr. Frank Gayle, a metallurgist who led NIST's team dealing with the steel forensics of the collapses, said: "Your gut reaction would be the jet fuel is what made the fire so very intense, a lot of people figured that's what melted the steel. Indeed it didn't, the steel did not melt."[132]

So how did NIST respond to the reports indicating that steel had, nevertheless, melted? In its *Final Report*, issued in 2005, NIST simply ignored the issue. In its 2006 publication, "Answers to Frequently Asked Questions," NIST admitted that one of these questions was: "Why did the NIST investigation not consider reports of molten steel in the wreckage from the WTC towers?"[133] Its answer: "NIST investigators and [other] experts. . . found no evidence that would support the melting of steel in a jet-fuel ignited fire in the towers prior to collapse."[134] The question, however, was: Given the fact that steel could not have been melted by "jet-fuel ignited fire," why did steel melt anyway? Did NIST not understand the question at issue, or was it simply playing dumb in order to evade a question it did not dare answer?

In any case, NIST then said that, even if some steel had melted, this would not prove that explosives had gone off, because there would be a better explanation:

> Under certain circumstances it is conceivable for some of the steel in the wreckage to have melted after the buildings collapsed. Any molten steel in the wreckage was more likely due to the high temperature resulting from long exposure to combustion within the pile than to short exposure to fires or explosions while the buildings were standing.[135]

The idea that combustion in an oxygen-starved pile could produce temperatures hot enough to melt steel is absurd in relation to an ordinary structure fire. It would, however, be possible if the pile contained quantities of chemical energetic materials, such as thermite, which provide their own fuel and oxygen (see note on page 57).

But NIST, being unable to mention that possibility, adopted as its main approach simply denying the evidence. This was shown not only by its silence about the issue in its report but also by a statement of John L. Gross, one of NIST's principal scientists. Having been asked during a public presentation to explain the "pools of molten steel beneath the towers," Gross challenged the premise that "there was a pool of molten steel," saying: "I know of absolutely no. . . eyewitness who has said so."[136]

Given all the eyewitness testimony quoted above, Gross's statement suggests that unless he was inexcusably ignorant of evidence with which he should have been familiar, he was simply lying. Moreover, the existence of pools of molten metal, which was widely identified as molten steel—although it may have been molten iron, which is produced when certain substances, such as thermite, are used to cut steel—was not the only evidence that steel had melted.

Three science professors from Worcester Polytechnic Institute (WPI), all of whom were involved in the school's Fire Protection Engineering program, reported that they had made a very surprising discovery while analyzing two sections of steel—a section from WTC 7 and another section from one of the Twin Towers. This surprising discovery was reported in a 2002 *New York Times* story by James Glanz and Eric Lipton, which said:

> Perhaps the deepest mystery uncovered in the investigation involves extremely thin bits of steel collected from the trade towers and from 7 World Trade Center. . . . The steel apparently melted away, but no fire in any of the buildings was believed to be hot enough to melt steel outright.[137]

This story brought out the threat to the official account: *Although the fire could not have melted steel, steel had melted.*

This finding by these WPI professors appeared not only in the *New York Times*. When FEMA put out its report on the WTC collapses that same year (2002), it included, as an appendix, a report by these professors, in which they emphasized that the steel had thinned as the result of sulfidation, and then added: "No clear explanation for the source of the sulfur has been identified."[138] This is significant because when sulfur is added to cutter charges—as when it is mixed with thermite to make thermate—it greatly lowers the temperature at which steel melts.[139]

The significance of the report by these WPI professors was made more understandable to laypeople by an essay entitled "The 'Deep Mystery' of Melted Steel," which said:

> [S]teel—which has a melting point of 2,800 degrees Fahrenheit—may weaken and bend, but does not melt during an ordinary office fire. Yet metallurgical studies on WTC steel brought back to WPI reveal that a novel phenomenon—called a eutectic reaction—occurred at the surface, causing intergranular melting capable of turning a solid steel girder into Swiss cheese. . . . The *New York Times* called these findings "perhaps the deepest mystery uncovered in the investigation." The significance of the work on a sample from Building 7 and a structural column from one of the twin towers becomes

apparent only when one sees these heavy chunks of damaged metal. A one-inch column has been reduced to half-inch thickness. Its edges—which are curled like a paper scroll—have been thinned to almost razor sharpness. Gaping holes—some larger than a silver dollar—let light shine through a formerly solid steel flange. This Swiss cheese appearance shocked all of the fire-wise professors, who expected to see distortion and bending—but not holes.[140]

(One of the phenomena reported here—a "one-inch column. . . reduced to half-inch thickness," with edges "thinned to almost razor sharpness"—had been anticipated by Astaneh-Asl's report in 2001 of a piece of steel that "had been reduced from an inch thick to paper thin." But Astaneh-Asl's report, contained only in a local publication in Berkeley, California, went virtually unnoticed at the time.[141])

How did NIST deal with this evidence, which was contained not only in the *New York Times* but also in FEMA's WTC report, the predecessor of NIST's report? *By simply not mentioning it.* This silence provided the clearest possible example of the fact that, when the authors of NIST's report said that they *found no evidence* that the towers were brought down by explosives, what they meant was that they *turned their eyes away from all such evidence.* This deliberate ignoring of evidence pointing to the use of explosives is also illustrated in the next issue to be examined.

(4) *Residues of Explosives:* One of the "frequently asked questions" to which NIST replied in 2006 was worded thus: "Was the [WTC] steel tested for explosives or thermite residues? The combination of thermite and sulfur (called thermate) 'slices through steel like a hot knife through butter.'" NIST replied:

> NIST did not test for the residue of these compounds in the steel. . . . Analysis of the WTC steel for the elements in thermite/thermate would not necessarily have been conclusive. The metal compounds also would have been present in the construction materials making up the WTC towers, and sulfur is present in the gypsum wallboard that was prevalent in the interior partitions.[142]

There are two big problems with NIST's claim that it did not test for these residues because such a test "would not necessarily have been conclusive." In the first place, as the "Appeal" to NIST pointed out:

> NIST conducted many tests that were "not necessarily conclusive." . . . Clearly NIST thought [its] physical temperature and fire resistance tests. . . *might have been* instructive on some aspect of the collapses. Why then would NIST not conduct a very simple lab test for the presence of explosive residue?[143]

In the second place, to say that a test *would not necessarily* have been conclusive entails that it *might possibly* have been conclusive. As the "Request for Correction" stated: "A chemical analysis for explosive residue on the steel or in the dust. . . could put to rest. . . the theory that explosives were responsible for the collapses of the Twin Towers." Why would NIST not have run a simple test that might have conclusively disproved the theory that the towers were brought down by explosives? Can we avoid the conclusion that those in charge of NIST's investigation did not run this test because they knew that it would *not* provide this negative result?

Of course, in saying that the tests would not necessarily be conclusive, NIST's argument was that the tests might not conclusively prove that thermite or thermate was used, because, it said: "metal compounds also would have been present in the construction materials making up the WTC towers, and sulfur is present in the gypsum wallboard that was prevalent in the interior partitions." However, if explosives using these compounds had in fact been used, these compounds would surely have been present in much higher quantities than could be explained by NIST's alternative hypothesis. This alternative hypothesis, moreover, seems to assume, implausibly, that the WPI professors, in finding the sulfidation so mysterious, did not realize that gypsum wallboard contains sulfur. Also, as the "Appeal" points out (quoting a passage from Materials Engineering, Inc.): "When thermite reaction compounds are used to ignite a fire, they produce a characteristic burn pattern."

It is hard to avoid the suspicion, therefore, that NIST's real reason for not performing the tests was its knowledge that the results would have supported the view that explosives *had been* used.

This suspicion is supported by findings of Steven Jones, who performed the tests in spite of not having NIST's funding and facilities. By using an electron microscope, he discovered that dust from Ground Zero contained large numbers of microspheres that were rich in both iron and aluminum, with the shape indicating that "these metals were once molten, so that surface tension pulled the droplets into a roughly spherical shape." This was a significant discovery, Jones pointed out, because iron-aluminum-rich microspheres are "produced in thermite-control reactions."[144] In a lecture in December 2007, Jones described his discovery of "red chips" with thermite's chemical signature in World Trade Center dust—a discovery that he called "the last nail in the coffin."[145]

In January 2008, Jennifer Abel of the *Hartford Advocate* reported a remarkable conversation she had about this issue with Michael Newman, the spokesman for NIST's Department of Public and Business Affairs. Abel asked: "[W]hat about that letter where NIST said it didn't look for evidence of explosives?" Newman replied: "Right, because there was no evidence of that." That puzzling answer led Abel to ask: "But how can you know there's no evidence if you don't look for it first?" Newman responded with a still stranger statement: "If you're looking for something that isn't there, you're wasting your time. . . and the taxpayers' money."[146]

Although Newman's answer was obviously circular, clearly illustrating NIST's refusal to follow the scientific method's empirical dimension when it would lead to politically unacceptable results, there was really little else he could say— assuming, as seems evident, that NIST's assigned task was to cover up the fact that explosives had been used.

Conclusion: NIST's report did nothing to strengthen the case for the official theory about the destruction of the Twin Towers. Indeed, it actually weakened it. Previously, people could have assumed that good scientists, like those at NIST, would be able to answer all the criticisms of the official theory. When NIST's report actually appeared, however, that assumption was no longer possible. When compared with the relevant evidence, all of the pillars of NIST's theory crumble. Also, NIST's report could deal with many phenomena—such as the explosions, the horizontal ejections of steel columns, the sulfidation and melting of steel, and the thermite residue—only by ignoring them. NIST thereby showed that the official theory can be defended only through unscientific reasoning, including the omission and distortion of evidence.

NIST's distortions have been noted by Edward Munyak, a mechanical and fire protection engineer who long worked in the US departments of energy and defense. Munyak has said:

> The aircraft impact and fire severity effects were magnified in the NIST reports. . . . The official reports and conclusions had many technical distortions and obfuscations of the excellent research input in arriving at a flawed, politically driven conclusion.

As to what really happened, Munyak added: "The concentric nearly free-fall speed exhibited by each building was identical to most controlled demolitions. . . . Collapse [was] not caused by fire effects."[147]

With regard to the alternative explanation—that the towers were victims of controlled demolition—a common question is how the explosives could have been planted. In NPH's Afterword, I suggested possible answers by pointing out that two of President Bush's relatives—a brother and a cousin—had been principals of a company that handled security for the World Trade Center and also by citing Scott Forbes's report that, during the weekend prior to 9/11, the South Tower's power had been down while "many 'engineers' [were] coming in and out of the tower."[148] More recently I learned that Nancy Cass, who worked for the New York Society of Security Analysts on the 44th floor of the North Tower, stated on 9/11: "The passenger elevators on the west side of the building had been out of order for the past five or six weeks and the elevator company had a crew of men working on the scene."[149] None of these facts have been mentioned by NIST.

If the NIST scientists who wrote the report were, as suggested earlier, working simply as "hired guns," paid to put out a report that concealed the truth, we would expect that they would refuse to engage in any public debate with knowledgeable critics. And this has indeed been the case. Ed Haas, the editor of the *Muckraker Report*, reported a conversation he had with NIST spokesman Michael Newman (whose explanation for NIST's decision not to search for explosives residue was quoted above). After pointing out that "more than half of all Americans now believe the US government has some complicity if not culpability regarding 9/11," Haas suggested to Newman "a possible method to reconcile the division in the United States between the government and its people": have a series of televised debates between the NIST scientists and some scientists who have criticized its report. But Newman replied emphatically that none of the NIST scientists would participate in any public debate.[150]

I will conclude this discussion of NIST's treatment of the Twin Towers by discussing one more piece of evidence that it ignored: Mayor Giuliani's statement to Peter Jennings, quoted in the Afterword to NPH, that while he and his people were operating out of the building at 75 Barclay Street (I had wrongly said that it was WTC 7), he was told that "the World Trade Center was gonna collapse." This information came from the Office of Emergency Management, which was staffed by Giuliani's own people. Given the fact that there was no historical precedent for steel-frame high-rise buildings collapsing except through controlled demolition, it is hard to imagine how Giuliani's people could have known that the towers were going to collapse unless they knew that explosives had been planted. Giuliani later tried to claim that he did not think that the towers would collapse immediately but only that they would do so "over a long period of time, the way other buildings collapsed. . . over a 7, 8, 9, 10-hour period." That interpretation, however, is not suggested by Giuliani's statement to Jennings. ("[W]e were operating out of there [75 Barclay Street] when we were told that the World Trade Center was gonna collapse. And it did collapse before we could actually get out of the building.") Also, there had been no previous steel-frame high-rise buildings that had collapsed after 7 to 10 hours—or even 18 hours—because of fire.[151]

NIST faced an even more formidable task in trying to construct an explanation of the collapse of WTC 7 that, while avoiding any mention of explosives, would appear at least superficially plausible. NIST's explanation for the Twin Towers, as we saw, relied on the impact of the airplanes combined with the fires ignited by their fuel. WTC 7, however, was not hit by a plane, and fires were reported, according to NIST itself, on only six of this building's 47 floors.[152] (New York magazine reporter Mark Jacobson, describing what WTC 7's condition had been a few minutes before it collapsed, said: "It wasn't a 47-story building that was engulfed in flames. The whole building wasn't on fire. . . . There was a lot of fire coming out of a few floors."[153])

The special difficulty of explaining the collapse of this building was acknowledged not only by FEMA, which admitted that the best explanation it could provide had "only a low probability of occurrence,"[154] but also implicitly by the 9/11 Commission, which simply omitted any mention, in its 571-page report, of the fact that this building had collapsed.[155]

Perhaps not surprisingly, therefore, NIST has repeatedly delayed publishing a report on WTC 7. In 2003, NIST said that this report would be issued along with its report on the Twin Towers, the draft of which was to be provided in September 2004.[156] However, when NIST's reports (both the draft and the final report) on the Twin Towers actually appeared, which was not until 2005, it announced that the WTC 7 report was being delayed until 2006. Then in August 2006, NIST said: "It is anticipated that a draft report will be released by early 2007."[157] At the end of 2007, NIST's "projected schedule" called for it to "release draft reports for public comment" on July 8, 2008.[158] By the end of July, when this book went to press, no such reports had appeared.

How has NIST explained these repeated delays? In 2006, its excuse was that it had insufficient staff.[159] Any such problem, however, would have been self-inflicted: NIST admitted that it chose not to hire additional staff when it took on this task. Also, given NIST's issuance of a preliminary report on WTC 7 in 2005 (see next paragraph), the continued delay of its final report probably had less to do with personnel problems than with a political agenda—to delay this report until near the end of the Bush administration (perhaps at the insistence of the aforementioned oversight person from the Office of Management and Budget).

NIST's Probable Explanation: In any case, the nature of NIST's eventual report was likely indicated by a preliminary report, issued in 2005, which announced NIST's "working collapse hypothesis for WTC 7," according to which the "initiating event" was an "initial local failure at the lower floors. . . due to fire and/or debris induced structural damage to a critical column."[160]

This reference to debris-induced structural damage suggested that NIST planned to argue that debris from the collapse of the North Tower caused damage to WTC 7 analogous to that inflicted on the towers by the airplanes. NIST's preliminary report cited extensive damage to the lower part of its south side (which faced the North Tower), especially the southwest corner between floors 8 and 18. A photograph showing damage to the southwest corner was provided.[161] And NIST's lead investigator, Shyam Sunder, said about WTC 7's south face: "On about a third of the face to the center and to the bottom—approximately ten stories—about 25 percent of the depth of the building was scooped out."[162] It appears, therefore, that NIST will argue that this damage plus the fires in the building suffice to explain its collapse.

This argument, however, faces three problems of increasing severity. The first problem is the difficulty of trying to imagine how debris from the collapse of the North Tower could have caused the alleged damage to the southwest face. The second problem is the existence of a photograph that does not show the damage to the southwest face seen in NIST's photograph, which suggests that the photograph used by NIST may have been doctored.[163] The third and most serious problem is that, even if debris from the North Tower really did cause the damage shown in NIST's photograph, this damage would provide little if any help in explaining why WTC 7 collapsed in the manner it did. I will mention several features of the collapse for which this alleged damage plus the fires could not begin to account.

Vertical, Symmetrical Collapse: One difficulty is the fact that the building, as videos show, came straight down, meaning that the collapse was perfectly symmetrical. For this to have occurred, all 81 of the building's steel columns had to fail simultaneously. . . . had to fail simultaneously. As structural engineer Kamal Obeid said on a BBC documentary about WTC 7, for this to occur as alleged by the official theory—namely, without the use of explosives—would be an "impossibility."[164] Even if 20 floors on the southwest side of the building were indeed scooped out, that damage would not begin to explain the building's symmetrical collapse. The fires also cannot explain it, because they were spread unevenly (asymmetrically) throughout the building on only a few floors.

Melted Steel: A second difficulty is the fact that WTC 7's rubble, like that of the Twin Towers, contained evidence that steel had been melted. Pools of molten steel or iron were found under it, as well as under the Twin Towers. Professor Abolhassan Astaneh-Asl, speaking of a horizontal I-beam from WTC 7, reported that parts of the beam, which had been five-eighths of an inch thick, had vaporized; WTC 7 was also the source of one of the pieces of steel that, according to the three WPI professors, had been sulfidized and melted.[165] Steel in WTC 7 had, therefore, been exposed to temperatures far above the highest possible temperature of the fires in the building.

Virtually Free-Fall Speed: A third difficulty is created by the fact that the building came down in under seven seconds and hence at virtually free-fall speed. NIST explained the rapid collapse of the Twin Towers by claiming that it was caused by the top section of each building falling on the lower section. That explanation is physically impossible, to be sure, because it violates the law of the conservation of momentum, but at least it was an explanation. But no plane hit WTC 7, so NIST cannot offer even that explanation for this building's rapid collapse.

Same As Classic Implosion: Still another difficulty is provided by the fact that the collapse of WTC 7 perfectly exemplified the classic type of induced implosion, in which the collapse starts from the bottom and the building folds in on itself. One of the main arguments used to reject the idea that the Twin Towers were demolished with explosives has been the claim that controlled demolitions must start from the bottom. NIST itself employed this argument, saying: "Video evidence [of each of the Twin Towers] showed unambiguously that the collapse progressed from the top to the bottom."[166] This argument was false, because a collapse can be initiated at various places, depending "on the order in which explosives are detonated," as Steven Jones has pointed out.[167] But the fact that controlled implosions almost always do begin at the bottom allowed NIST, along with other defenders of the official theory, to argue that the towers were not victims of controlled demolition. NIST cannot, however, make this argument with regard to WTC 7, because it clearly exemplified the usual pattern.

Expert Testimony: This fact, along with the other points mentioned above, has led several experts to declare that WTC 7 was indeed brought down by explosives. Hugo Bachmann, emeritus professor of structural analysis and construction at the Swiss Federal Institute of Technology, has said: "In my opinion the building WTC 7 was, with great probability, professionally demolished." Jörg Schneider, who also taught structural engineering at this institute, has said virtually the same thing.[168] Jack Keller, emeritus professor of engineering at Utah State University (who has been named by *Scientific American* as one of the world's leaders in using science and technology to benefit society), said of the demise of WTC 7: "Obviously it was the result of controlled demolition."[169]

The most dramatic demonstration of this obviousness was provided when Danny Jowenko, a controlled demolition expert in the Netherlands, was asked to comment on a video of the collapse of WTC 7, without knowing what it was—he had not realized that a third building had collapsed on 9/11. After viewing it, he said: "They simply blew up columns, and the rest caved in afterwards. . . . This is controlled demolition." When he was asked if he was certain, he replied: "Absolutely, it's been imploded. This was a hired job. A team of experts did this." When he was told that this happened on September 11, he was at first incredulous, repeatedly asking, "Are you sure?" When he was finally convinced, Jowenko said: "Then they've worked very hard."[170] When asked in

2007 whether he stood by his original statement, he replied: "Absolutely. . . . I looked at the drawings, the construction and it couldn't be done by fire. . . absolutely not."[171]

Testimony about Explosions by Hess and Jennings: Of course, the assigned task of the NIST scientists was to make a plausible case that WTC 7 came down the way it did—straight down at virtually free-fall speed—even though it was not demolished with explosives. Its preliminary report said, very prominently: "NIST has seen no evidence that the collapse of WTC 7 was caused by bombs . . . or controlled demolition."[172] Another problem for NIST is that this claim is contradicted by considerable testimonial evidence.

Two New York City officials—Michael Hess, the city's corporation counsel, and Barry Jennings, the deputy director of the Emergency Services Department of the New York City Housing Authority—have testified that there was an explosion in WTC 7 quite early in the morning. Shortly after the attack on the North Tower, which occurred at 8:46AM, both Jennings and Hess went to the Office of Emergency Management Command Center on the 23rd floor of WTC 7, assuming that Mayor Rudy Giuliani would be there. But upon arriving there, Jennings has reported,

> we noticed that everybody was gone. I saw coffee that was on the desks still, the smoke was still coming off the coffee. I saw half-eaten sandwiches. And after I called several individuals, one individual told me to leave and to leave right away.[173]

Finding that the elevator would not work—all the power had gone out, Hess reported[174]—they started down the stairs, but when they got to the sixth floor, Jennings said, "the landing that we were standing on gave way—there was an explosion and the landing gave way." Clarifying, Jennings added: "The explosion was beneath me." After they went back up to the eighth floor, Jennings said (explicitly rejecting the idea that what he felt might have been effects from the collapse of the North Tower), he looked out the window and saw that "both buildings [the Twin Towers] were still standing."[175]

Using a fire extinguisher to break a window, Jennings caught someone's attention with his cries for help.[176] But he and Hess were not rescued immediately because, although the firefighters came to the window twice, they ran away both times:

> The fire department came and ran. They came twice. Why? Because Building Tower One fell, and then Tower Two fell. I was trapped in there several hours. I was trapped in there when both buildings came down. All this time I'm hearing explosions.[177]

After the fire department finally came and rescued them, Hess was interviewed by Frank Ucciardo of UPN 9 News "on Broadway about a block from City Hall," which is almost a half mile from the WTC site. This interview began before noon (either at 11:34 or 11:57AM).[178]

How long had Hess and Jennings been trapped? In the statement just quoted, Jennings said "several hours"; in an earlier statement, he had said "an hour."[179] Hess estimated "an hour and a half." The actual duration must have been between 90 minutes and two hours, given the following facts: Jennings said that, having "received the call [to go to WTC 7] shortly after the first plane hit"—which would have meant shortly after 8:46—he "had to be inside in the twenty-third floor when the second plane hit,"[180] which was at 9:03. If we allow six minutes for Hess and Jennings to learn that they should leave and six more minutes for them to get down to the sixth floor, the explosion they felt when they reached that floor would have been at about 9:15. If the firefighters reached them 90 minutes to two hours later, Hess and Jennings would have been found at about 10:45 or 11:15 and outside the building by about 11:00 or 11:30—which is about the time it must have been if by 11:34 or 11:57, Hess was being interviewed almost a half-mile away.[181]

How did NIST, which interviewed Hess and Jennings, deal with their reports? By distorting them. One element in this distortion was NIST's claim that these two men were rescued "[a]t 12:10 to 12:15PM."[182] Given the fact that Hess was being interviewed almost a half mile away before noon, this claim was obviously false. Why would NIST have made this claim?

Although it would have been shortly after 9:03 when Hess and Jennings learned that the elevator did not work, NIST claimed that it did not work because WTC 7's electric power was lost when the South Tower collapsed at 9:59. NIST then claimed that the "explosion" that the two men reported when they got down to the sixth floor was really the collapse of the North Tower, which did not occur until 10:28.[183] If they were trapped for roughly 90 minutes after that, as Hess said, they could not have been rescued much if any before noon. NIST's claim that they were rescued at "12:10 to 12:15," therefore, supported its claim that the two events reported by Hess and Jennings—the loss of power and the apparent explosion in WTC 7—were caused by the collapses of the South and North Towers, respectively.

But in order for NIST to make these claims, it needed to ignore the fact that Hess gave an interview about a half-mile away before noon, which means that he and Jennings must have been rescued more than 30 minutes earlier than NIST claimed. NIST also had to contradict Jennings, who said that after the explosion in WTC 7 occurred, "both [towers] were still standing." The afore-mentioned BBC special on WTC 7 continued and even increased NIST's distortion of Jennings's testimony.[184]

Having distorted the two men's testimony about this explosion, NIST completely omitted another part of Jennings's testimony, in which he reported what he experienced when the firefighters took him downstairs:

> When they finally got to us and they took us down to what they called the lobby—'cause I asked them "Where are we?" He said, "This *was* the lobby." And I said, "You got to be kidding me." It was total ruins, *total* ruins. Now keep in mind, when I came in there, the lobby had nice escalators, it was a huge lobby, and for me to see what I saw, it was unbelievable. And the firefighter that took us down kept saying, "Don't look down." I asked, "Why?" And he said, "Do not look down." We were stepping over people, and you know you can feel when you're stepping over people. They took us out through a hole in the wall. . . . And this big giant police officer came to me, and he says, "You have to run," and I said, "I can't run, my knees are swollen." He said, "You'll have to get on your knees and crawl, then, because we have reports of more explosions."[185]

Given the fact that Jennings reported that the huge explosion he and Hess felt when they reached the sixth floor was *beneath* them, it could well have been the explosion that destroyed the lobby. But it was, he said, not the only explosion: Speaking of the period that they were trapped, he said: "All this time I'm hearing explosions." He also said that, according to the "big giant police officer," there were "reports of more explosions."

Besides saying nothing about these additional explosions, NIST's summary contains not a word about Jennings's testimony about the destroyed lobby containing bodies he had to walk over. If and when NIST finally produces a report about WTC 7, this silence will probably continue.

Was WTC 7 Supposed to Collapse in the Morning? WTC 7 did not come down until 5:20 in the afternoon. If that was when it was scheduled to be demolished, why would there have been a massive explosion at about 9:15 in the morning? As mentioned earlier, janitor William Rodriguez reported a massive explosion in the basement of the North Tower at 8:46AM (just before the building was hit by the plane), 102 minutes before it came down. This explosion was probably for the sake of removing some of the core columns, so that not all of the core columns would need to be destroyed at the same time. The explosion reported by Hess and Jennings in WTC would have likely been for the same purpose. But why would it have been set off about eight hours before the building was destined to be destroyed?

Two 9/11 researchers—Matthew Everett and Jeremy Baker— have independently suggested that WTC 7 was probably intended to go down in the morning, shortly after the collapse of the North Tower. Its collapse at that time would have been less suspicious, as it more plausibly could have been portrayed as resulting from the collapses of the two previous buildings, especially the North Tower.[186]

Support for this hypothesis has been provided by the discovery that a premature announcement of the building's collapse was made that morning. As we will see in the text below, premature announcements of WTC 7's collapse were begun in the afternoon at about 4:15 by CNN. However, a recent discovery by Matthew Everett (one of the editors of *The Complete 9/11 Timeline*) shows that there had been a previous premature announcement at 11:07

that morning by CNN correspondent Alan Dodds Frank, who reported by phone from Lower Manhattan:

[J]ust two or three minutes ago there was yet another collapse or explosion. . . . [A]t a quarter to 11, there was another collapse or explosion following the 10:30 collapse of the second tower. And a firefighter who rushed by us estimated that 50 stories went down. The street filled with smoke.[187]

After quoting that statement, Everett said:

What could have led Frank to make his incorrect report? Surely, even in the chaos of that morning, it would have been quite difficult for a mistaken report of another massive skyscraper coming down to have emerged out of nothing. Could the reason be that WTC 7 had originally been scheduled to be brought down (with explosives) at 10:45AM? . . . However, something— as yet unknown to us—happened that meant the demolition had to be delayed, and so Building 7 was not ready to be brought down until late that afternoon.[188]

Jeremy Baker made a suggestion as to what that "something" was. With an allusion to "Murphy's law," he wrote: "Murphy was working overtime that day. Incredibly, the demolition system in WTC 7 simply did not respond as intended and the building defiantly remained intact." The building could be brought down only after "the conspirators . . . scrambled to bring the demolition system in WTC 7 back online."[189]

More recently, Baker made a discovery that led him to refine his hypothesis. The discovery was of a short video clip from ABC News showing "an enormous gash that extends down the center of WTC 7's facade from its roofline all the way to the ground." Pointing out why this discovery is so important, Baker writes:

The force required to gouge the straight, clean, cavernous gash in WTC 7 represents a source of destructive power far greater than anything that was present that day and simply could not have been caused by falling debris.[190]

Then, connecting this discovery with his previous hypothesis, Baker asks:

Could the straight, clean gouge in WTC 7's south face be an indication that a line of explosives running up the center of the building detonated but then stalled? Buildings typically have their centers blown out first when they are being demolished and this kind of failure is certainly not without precedent. Though this theory is surely speculative, is it unreasonable to ask the question: *What else could have caused such a bizarre wound in the south face of WTC 7?*

Larry Silverstein, Baker points out, did suggest an alternative cause. In explaining what caused WTC 7 to collapse, he said:

> [One cause was] the falling antenna from the roof of the North Tower. That antenna came crashing down and sliced through the façade in the front of 7. As it did so, it ruptured fuel lines in the building. . . [which] caught fire. That fire started to burn and burned intensively the rest of the day.[191]

Although Baker was unimpressed by this explanation for the gash, saying that "this ridiculous claim. . . is easily refuted by video evidence," it is interesting that Silverstein did thereby show awareness of this vertical gash down the front of WTC 7, which evidently had not previously been publicly acknowledged.

In any case, Baker's discovery of this video led him to an alternative suggestion about the firefighter's report that a third building, this one 50 stories, had collapsed at 10:45. Baker writes:

> Could this uncanny description from a firefighter be a hasty reference to the botched *attempt* to demolish Building 7? The time frame is perfect. The few explosives that did detonate would certainly have sounded like a "collapse or explosion". . . . A vertical column of explosives blasting out the full height of the building could very well have given someone the impression that "fifty stories" were going down.[192]

If, as Everett and Baker have suggested, WTC 7 was intended to go down at 10:45 that morning, that would have been about 90 minutes after the explosion reported by Hess and Jennings. The interval would, therefore, have been about the same as that between the collapse of the North Tower and the explosion in the basement of that building reported by William Rodriguez.

Further Testimonies of Explosions: In addition to these testimonies by Hess and Jennings about explosions in the morning, there were also several reports of explosions much later in the day, just before WTC 7 collapsed at 5:20. A *New York Daily News* reporter, for example, said:

> [T]here was a rumble. The building's top row of windows popped out. Then all the windows on the thirty-ninth floor popped out. Then the thirty-eighth floor. Pop! Pop! Pop! was all you heard until the building sunk into a rising cloud of gray.[193]

According to a reporter for WINS NYC News Radio: "People started to run away from the scene and I turned in time to see what looked like a skyscraper implosion—looked like it had been done by a demolition crew."[194] A New York University medical student, who was serving as an emergency medical worker that day, said:

> [W]e heard this sound that sounded like a clap of thunder. . . . [T]urned around—we were shocked. . . . [I]t looked like there was a shockwave ripping through the building and the windows all busted out. . . . [A]bout a second later the bottom floor caved out and the building followed after that.[195]

A former NYPD officer said:

> I was real close to Building 7 when it fell down. . . . That didn't sound like just a building falling down to me . . . . There's a lot of eyewitness testimony down there of hearing explosions. . . . [A]ll of a sudden. . . I looked up, and . . . [t]he thing started pealing [sic] in on itself. . . . I started running . . . and the whole time you're hearing "boom, boom, boom, boom, boom."[196]

Foreknowledge of the Collapse: These reports, according to which explosions were going off just before and during the collapse of WTC 7, were complemented by reports that it was known in advance that this building was going to collapse. As a result, a collapse zone was established several hours before the building collapsed. NIST even admitted this, saying:

> According to the FDNY first-person interviews, . . . firefighting was never started in [WTC 7]. When the Chief Officer in charge of WTC 7 got to Barclay Street and West Broadway,

numerous firefighters and officers were coming out of WTC 7. These firefighters indicated that several blocks needed to be cleared around WTC 7 because they thought that the building was going to collapse.[197]

Why did they think this? According to Captain Michael Currid, who was the sergeant at arms for the Uniformed Fire Officers Association, "Someone from the city's Office of Emergency Management" had told him that WTC 7 was "basically a lost cause and we should not lose anyone else trying to save it."[198] The Office of Emergency Management (OEM) was directly under Mayor Rudy Giuliani (it was the OEM Command Center in WTC 7 to which Hess and Jennings had gone to find Giuliani, only to discover that everyone had already left). It is especially significant that it was Giuliani's OEM that reportedly spread the word that WTC 7 was going to collapse, because this same office had been the source of the advance knowledge, reported earlier in terms of an exchange between Giuliani and Peter Jennings, that the Twin Towers were going to come down.[199]

NIST's intention to defend the official account is made still more difficult by the fact that this foreknowledge, according to some reports, reflected awareness that the building was to be brought down. One such report was provided by Indira Singh, a senior consultant for JP Morgan Chase. On 9/11, she served as a volunteer emergency medical worker and was asked to set up triage sites. In 2005, while being interviewed on Bonnie Faulkner's *Guns and Butter* radio show, Singh said:

> [P]retty soon after midday on 9/11 we had to evacuate [the site where we had been working] because they told us Building 7 was coming down. . . . I do believe that they brought Building 7 down because I heard that they were going to bring it down because it was unstable because of the collateral damage. That I don't know; I can't attest to the validity of that. All I can attest to is that by noon or one o'clock, they told us we need to move from that triage site. . . because Building 7 was gonna come down or be brought down.

Faulkner then asked: "Did they actually use the word 'brought down' and who was it that was telling you this?" Singh replied:

"The fire department. And they did use the words 'we're gonna have to bring it down.'"[200]

After playing footage showing Singh's statement, a video entitled "Seven is Exploding" shows footage taken on 9/11 in which some police officers say: "Keep your eye on that building, it'll be coming down. . . . This building is about to blow up; move it back."[201] We then hear the sound of loud explosions, after which a firefighter says: "We gotta get back. Seven is exploding."[202]

The Media's Premature Reports: News media provided further evidence suggestive of foreknowledge of WTC 7's collapse by providing premature reports of this collapse. These reports evidently began "at about 4:15," when CNN's Aaron Brown said: "We are getting information now that. . . Building 7. . . has either collapsed or is collapsing."[203] At 4:53, the BBC's Radio Five Live said it had reports "that another large building has collapsed just over an hour ago." At 4:54, BBC's domestic television news channel announced the collapse. Then at about 5:10, BBC World repeated this announcement and even provided an explanation of why the building had collapsed ("this wasn't the result of a new attack but because the building had been weakened during this morning's attack"). Finally, at 5:14, BBC reporter Jane Standley was seen announcing the collapse of the Salomon Brothers building—the other name for WTC 7—while it could still be seen standing in the background.[204]

In February 2007, a video containing some of this news footage, especially of the BBC's premature reporting, was placed on the Internet. After it had evoked an enormous amount of discussion on the Internet and "lots of e-mails" to the BBC, Richard Porter, the head of news for the BBC's international channel, BBC World, responded on his blog, writing:

> We're not part of a conspiracy. Nobody told us what to say or do on September 11th. We didn't get told in advance that buildings were going to fall down. We didn't receive press releases or scripts in advance of events happening. . . . If we reported the building had collapsed before it had done so, it would have been an error—no more than that.[205]

This was a manifestly inadequate response (as shown by viewers' responses to it, which numbered almost 600 by the end of 2007). The fact that the BBC's announcement was "an error" was obvious. The question was how such an error—announcing the collapse almost 30 minutes before it happened—could have occurred. Rather than offering some explanation, Porter simply exclaimed that the BBC was not part of any conspiracy.

The suspicion that the BBC's premature announcement reflected something more than simply an inexplicable "error" was not entirely unreasonable, given some of the BBC's previous coverage of 9/11. On September 13, 2001, it published an article on its website entitled "How the World Trade Center Fell," which quoted two experts making the obviously false assertion that the buildings collapsed because the jet-fuel-fed fires had melted their steel columns.[206] Then in February 2007, just over a week before Porter's blog entry was published, the BBC aired what is probably the worst, most biased, television program ever produced on the subject, *The Conspiracy Files: 9/11*.[207]

In March 2007, Porter wrote another blog entry on the subject in which he said that, on the afternoon of 9/11, there had been "a fairly consistent picture being painted of Building 7 in danger of collapse." But how did the transition get made to the declaration that the building had collapsed? Referring to the fact that three BBC channels reported the collapse "in quick succession," Porter was "inclined to believe that one or more of the news agencies was reporting this, or at least reporting someone saying this." But why would such agencies have been reporting the collapse some 30 or even—in the case of CNN—60 minutes before it happened? Porter's only explanation was to "point to [the] confusing and chaotic situation on the ground."[208] This second blog entry by Porter evoked over 600 responses, most of which found his explanation wanting.

Porter could have offered a somewhat plausible explanation. He could have suggested that the rumor that WTC 7 was *going to* collapse, which had been circulating for several hours, at some point became changed, through misunderstanding, into the rumor that it had *already* collapsed. It might be concluded, therefore, that the BBC's premature announcement of the collapse adds nothing more to what we have already established, namely, that Giuliani's Office of Emergency Management had spread the word several hours in advance that WTC 7 was going to collapse.

Even with that interpretation, however, the premature announcements were not insignificant, because they revealed in a dramatic, unforgettable fashion the fact that *someone* knew in advance that Building 7 was going to collapse. This is important because, given the salient facts—that WTC 7 had not been hit by a plane, that no steel-framed high-rise building had ever collapsed because of fire and external damage alone, that WTC 7 had fires on only a few floors, and that some of the other still-standing WTC buildings had been damaged far worse—there should have been no reason to expect it to collapse.

Of equal importance was the fact, not addressed by Porter, that the BBC's announcement was accompanied by a premature explanation of why WTC 7 had collapsed, even though, unlike the Twin Towers, it was not struck by a plane: "because the building had been weakened during this morning's attack." Was this explanation provided by someone trying to prevent news reporters from saying the obvious, as did Dan Rather[209]—that the collapse looked just like a controlled demolition?[210]

In April 2008, Phil Hayton, the BBC anchor who was on screen while Jane Standley was prematurely reporting the collapse of WTC 7, was questioned about the event by We Are Change UK. Expressing surprise that there was no official explanation for the premature report, Hayton, who by then was no longer with the BBC, said to his questioners: "I sense that you think there's a conspiracy here—but you might be right."[211]

Silverstein's Statement: The suspicion that WTC 7 was brought down by explosives was also increased by WTC leaseholder Larry Silverstein's 2002 statement about this building, which I quoted in NPH's Afterword, that he and the fire commander had made the decision to "pull it."[212] This statement generated considerable controversy involving what the meaning of "it" was. The US State Department, citing a "clarification" put out by a Silverstein spokesperson, claimed that "it" referred not to the building but to "the contingent of firefighters remaining in the building."[213]

Popular Mechanics, citing the same "clarification," said that Silverstein was "referring to his desire to pull the squadron of firefighters from the building."[214]

To see if this is plausible, we need to look again at Silverstein's statement: "I said, 'We've had such terrible loss of life, maybe the smartest thing to do is pull it.' And they made that decision to pull and we watched the building collapse." If he had meant the firefighters, would he not have said so in a more straightforward way—such as, "pull the firefighters out of the building"? And did not the final sentence, in which "decision to pull" was followed by "and we watched the building collapse," suggest that he was talking about pulling *the building*?

Popular Mechanics also argued that "*pull it* is not slang for controlled demolition."[215] It supported this claim by citing several experts, including Mark Loizeaux, the president of Controlled Demolition, Inc., and then saying: "Firefighters contacted by *Popular Mechanics* confirm that *pull it* is a common firefighting term for removing personnel from a dangerous structure."[216] However, a member of the 9/11 truth movement took the initiative to call Loizeaux's company. Reaching the receptionist, the caller asked, "if you were in the demolition business and you said the term 'pull it,' I was wondering what exactly that would mean?" After asking the caller to hold for a moment, the receptionist returned and said, "'Pull it' is when they actually pull it down."[217]

One issue that had been unclear was the time at which Silverstein and the fire commander reportedly made this decision. If it had been made early in the day, before the firefighters had been pulled out of the building, then the "clarification" of Silverstein's statement could at least possibly be true. But in March 2008, Silverstein, in response to a question about his statement from a "We Are Change" group, said that the decision was made around 3:30 or 4:00PM, after it was clear (he said) that the fire was going to bring the building down.[218] This was several hours after all the firefighters had been taken out, so Silverstein undermined the proffered "clarification" of his "pull it" remark.

Conclusion: With regard to WTC 7: There are still many mysteries about it, such as why it collapsed so late in the day (although, as we have seen, a reasonable hypothesis is available). But *why* it collapsed at all is not one of the mysteries: It was clearly brought down with explosives. Of course, if a report on WTC 7 is ever issued by NIST, it will probably maintain otherwise, however implausibly.

With regard to the Twin Towers and WTC 7: The conclusion that they were all destroyed by explosives is now beyond reasonable doubt. That this is so is illustrated by the fact that NIST, tasked to provide explanations without invoking explosives, has been unable to do so. The conclusiveness of the evidence is also illustrated by the growing number of architects and engineers who have publicly signed the petition at Architects and Engineers for 9/11 Truth calling for a new investigation. By the first anniversary of the posting of this petition, over 400 architects and engineers had signed it. Having quoted some of them above, I will close this chapter by quoting one more, J. Marx Ayres, a nationally recognized mechanical engineer who founded one of the largest building firms in Los Angeles:

> Dr. Steven Jones. . . has provided a scientific foundation for the collapse of the three World Trade Center (WTC) towers. . . . [T]he Jones 2006 paper, "Why Indeed Did the WTC Buildings Completely Collapse?" . . . is a rational step-by-step study that meets the accepted standards for scientific building research. His critical reviews of the FEMA, NIST, and 9/11 Commission reports are correct.[219]

Last-Minute Note: One phenomenon not discussed above is that, in spite of all attempts to suppress them, very hot fires continued to burn in the Ground Zero debris piles for months. New information from the EPA has now revealed that, long after all normal combustible materials would have been consumed, violent fires occasionally flared up, releasing rare toxic substances. "Environmental Anomalies at the World Trade Center: Evidence for Energetic Materials," by Kevin R. Ryan, James R. Gourley, and Steven E. Jones (*The Environmentalist*, August 4, 2008), shows that these and related phenomena point to the presence of energetic materials, such as thermite.

2. FLIGHT 77 AND THE PENTAGON:
NEW DEVELOPMENTS

S ince the appearance of NPH in 2004, there have been many developments regarding both American Flight 77—mainly because the 9/11 Commission created a completely new explanation as to why it was not intercepted—and the Pentagon attack.

WERE THE SOURCES FOR THE IDENTIFICATION CREDIBLE?

One of the problems in the official story, as we saw in NPH, involved the credibility of people who identified the cause of the damage to the Pentagon as American Flight 77, or at least a Boeing 757. The 9/11 Commission, perhaps in response to this problem, claimed that a pilot in the air also made this identification. After examining this claim, I will discuss new developments that have undermined Ted Olson's claim about calls from his wife.

The 9/11 Commission's Claim about a C-130 Pilot: According to the 9/11 Commission, the fact that the Pentagon was struck by a Boeing 757 was confirmed by a pilot. "At 9:32, . . . [s]everal of the Dulles controllers observed a 'primary radar target tracking eastbound at a high rate of speed.'" However, "[t]he aircraft's identity or type was unknown." Accordingly, said *The 9/11 Commission Report*: "Reagan National controllers then vectored an unarmed National Guard C-130 H cargo aircraft. . . to identify and follow the suspicious aircraft. The C-130H pilot spotted it [and] identified it as a Boeing 757."[1]

However, the pilot of the C-130, Steve O'Brien, has recently said that he was about a minute away from the Pentagon, so he could not see whether the plane that approached it actually hit it.[2] If he was too far away to see that, he was too far away to identify the kind of plane it was.

Ted Olson's Claim about Calls from His Wife: As we saw in NPH, Theodore "Ted" Olson, the solicitor general for the Department of Justice, reported that his wife, Barbara Olson, had called him from Flight 77 shortly before the Pentagon was struck. This report supported the claim that Flight 77 struck the Pentagon by virtue of being the only evidence that this flight, which had disappeared from the FAA radar screen at 8:56, was still aloft and headed back toward Washington. But this report has now completely disintegrated.

Olson's claim that he received two phone calls from his wife was problematic from the first, I mentioned in NPH, because it was "vague and self-contradictory." The contradictions involved the type of phone used. On September 11, he told CNN that she had used a cell phone.[3] On September 14, he told Fox News's *Hannity & Colmes* that she had reached him by calling the Department of Justice collect, so she must have been using the "airplane phone"—because, he surmised, "she somehow didn't have access to her credit cards."[4] However, this second version of Olson's story, besides contradicting his first version, was even self-contradictory, because a credit card is needed to activate a passenger-seat phone.

Later that same day on CNN's *Larry King Show*, moreover, Olson said that the second call from her suddenly went dead because "the signals from cell phones coming from airplanes don't work that well."[5] After this return to his first version, he finally settled on his second account, saying that his wife had called collect and therefore must have used "the phone in the passengers' seats" because she did not have her purse.[6]

By settling on this story, Olson avoided a technological pitfall. Given the cell phone system in use in 2001, as will be discussed in Chapter 3, high-altitude cell phone calls from airliners were impossible, or at least virtually so (Olson's statement that "the signals from cell phones coming from airplanes don't work that well" was a considerable understatement). Olson avoided this problem by settling on the claim that his wife had used an onboard phone. However, this second version of Olson's story, besides being self-contradictory, was also contradicted by American Airlines.

A 9/11 researcher, knowing that AA Flight 77 was a Boeing 757, noticed that AA's website showed that its 757s do not have passenger-seat phones. In 2006, he wrote to ask if this had been true on September 11, 2001, and an AA customer service representative replied: "That is correct; we do not have phones on our Boeing 757. The passengers on flight 77 used their own personal cellular phones to make out calls during the terrorist attack."[7]

Defenders of the official story might argue, in response to this revelation, that Ted Olson was evidently right the first time: his wife had used her cell phone. However, this possibility, besides being rendered unlikely by the cell phone technology of 2001, has been contradicted by the FBI.

In 2006, the FBI, in presenting evidence at the trial of Zacarias Moussaoui, the so-called 20th hijacker, submitted a report on phone calls from all four 9/11 flights. In its report on American Flight 77, the FBI report attributed only one call to Barbara Olson, and it was an "unconnected call," which (of course) lasted "0 seconds."[8] According to the FBI, therefore, Ted Olson did not receive a single call from his wife using either a cell phone or an onboard phone.

Back on 9/11, the FBI itself had interviewed Olson. A report of that interview indicates that Olson told the FBI agents that his wife had called him twice from Flight 77.[9] And yet the FBI's report on calls from Flight 77, presented in 2006, indicated that no such calls occurred. This was an amazing development: The FBI is part of the Department of Justice, and yet it undermined the well-publicized claim of the DOJ's former solicitor general that he had received two calls from his wife on 9/11.

Ted Olson's story has also been quietly rejected by the historians who wrote Pentagon 9/11, a treatment of the Pentagon attack put out by the Department of Defense. According to Olson, his wife had said that "all passengers and flight personnel, including the pilots, were herded to the back of the plane by armed hijackers."[10] This was an inherently implausible scenario. We were supposed to believe that 60-some people, including the two pilots, were held at bay by three or four men—one or two of the hijackers would have been in the cockpit—with knives and boxcutters. This scenario becomes even more absurd when we realize that the alleged hijackers were all small, unathletic men (the 9/11 Commission pointed out that even "[t]he so-called muscle hijackers actually were not physically imposing, as the majority of them were between 5'5" and 5'7" in height and slender in build"[11]), and that the pilot, Charles "Chic" Burlingame, was a weightlifter and a boxer, who was described as "really tough" by one of his erstwhile opponents.[12] Also, the idea that he would have turned over the plane to hijackers was rejected by his brother, who said: "I don't know what happened in that cockpit, but I'm sure that they would have had to incapacitate him or kill him because he would have done anything to prevent the kind of tragedy that befell that airplane."[13] The Pentagon historians, in any case, did not accept the Olson story, according to which Burlingame and his co-pilot did give up their plane and were in the back with the passengers and other crew members. They instead wrote that "the attackers either incapacitated or murdered the two pilots."[14]

This official rejection of Ted Olson's story is a development of utmost importance. Without the alleged Olson calls, there is no evidence that Flight 77 returned to Washington. Also, if Ted Olson's claim was false, as the accounts given by the FBI and the Pentagon historians indicate, then there are only two possibilities: Either Olson lied or he was duped. In either case, the official story was based on deception.

Incidentally, my statement in NPH that Barbara Olson was reportedly the only person to have made a call from Flight 77 was incorrect. Flight attendant Renee May reportedly made a cell phone call to her parents.[15] However, the idea that only two people made calls is hardly more credible than the idea that only one did. Moreover, the 2006 FBI report contradicted Renee May's parents' belief that she had used a cell phone—just as it contradicted, as we will see in the next chapter, the belief of relatives of people on other planes that they had been called from cell phones.

I have organized the commentary in this section under seven headings: damage, debris, videos, time-change parts, flight data recorder, seismic signal, and C-ring hole.

Damage: My statement in NPH that the hole in the facade was only "between 15 and 18 feet in diameter" was incomplete. Beneath that small hole was a damaged area approximately 90 feet wide, which had been obscured by water from fire hoses in most of the photographs.

This fact, however, does little to support the view that the Pentagon was struck by a Boeing 757. The *Popular Mechanics* book, holding otherwise, stated: "When Flight 77 hit the Pentagon it created a hole in the exterior wall of the building approximately 90 feet wide."[16] However, the photographs used to support this view do not warrant this description. *Popular Mechanics* came closer to an accurate description of this "hole" in calling it a "messy 90-foot gash." But even this description suggested something more continuous than what we see in the photographs.[17] Another problem is that some of the remaining structure appears to be bending outward, suggesting that the damage was caused by a blast from inside rather than an aircraft from outside. The most serious problem, however, is the fact that this gash was at ground level. How could a Boeing 757, with its engines extending beneath its wings, have struck the Pentagon so low without damaging the lawn and destroying the large cable spools on the ground in front of the damaged area?

Debris: The debris problem remains. Dean Eckmann, one of the F-16 pilots who was sent to Washington from Langley Air Force Base, was asked by NEADS to fly over the Pentagon and report on the extent of the damage. He reported that he suspected that the damage had been caused by "a big fuel tanker truck because of the amount of smoke and flames coming up and. . . there was no airplane wreckage off to the side."[18] Karen Kwiatkowski, who was then an Air Force Lieutenant Colonel employed at the Pentagon, has written of "a strange lack of visible debris on the Pentagon lawn, where I stood only moments after the impact. . . . I saw. . . no airplane metal or cargo debris."[19] Her observation was confirmed by CNN's Jamie McIntyre. After inspecting the area near the strike zone shortly after the attack, McIntyre said that all he saw were "very small pieces of the plane. . . , small enough that you can pick up in your hand. There are no large tail sections, wing sections, fuselage, nothing like that anywhere around."[20] Registered Nurse Eileen Murphy said:

> I knew it was a crash site before we got there, and I didn't know what it was going to look like. I couldn't imagine because the building is like rock solid. I expected to see the airplane, so I guess my initial impression was, "Where's the plane? How come there's not a plane?" I would have thought the building would have stopped it and somehow we would have seen something like part of, or half of the plane, or the lower part, or the back of the plane. So it was just a real surprise that the plane wasn't there.[21]

Having run to the crash site right after the strike, Engineer Steve DeChiaro, the president of a technology firm, said: "[W]hen I looked at the site, my brain could not resolve the fact that it was a plane because it only seemed like a small hole in the building. No tail. No wings. No nothing."[22] Brian Ladd, a firefighter from Fort Myer, VA, reported that, although he had expected to see pieces of the airplane's wings or fuselage, he instead saw "millions of tiny pieces of debris" spread "everywhere."[23] Likewise, according to *Pentagon 9/11*, when Captain Dennis Gilroy—the acting commander of the Fort Myer fire department—arrived, "he wondered why he saw no aircraft parts."[24] According to the same book, still another firefighter, Captain John Durrer, "had expected to see large parts of the plane and thought, 'Well where's the airplane, you know, where's the parts to it?' You would think there'd be something."[25] Former Navy and commercial pilot Ralph Kolstad has asked:

> Where are the big pieces that always break away in an accident? Where is all the luggage? Where are the miles and miles of wire, cable, and lines that are part and parcel of any large aircraft? Where are the steel engine parts?. . . Where is the tail section that would have broken into large pieces?[26]

This lack of debris outside the Pentagon, along with the lack of other signs that an airliner had hit the Pentagon, even led one person to make a film. Filmmaker Paul Cross had been doing post-production work in Washington when he heard about the attack on the Pentagon. On the basis of his observation of the scene about five hours later, he has said: "There was no passenger jet wreckage; the lawn wasn't scorched; lamp posts, fences and construction materials in the path of the jet were untouched." Although he had been a "flag-waving patriot" who had "voted Republican all [his] life," he made a feature film, *Severe Visibility*, to alert fellow Americans about the "hoax" that had been perpetrated on them by their political and military leaders.[27]

Having quoted in NPH some people who reported a similar lack of debris *inside* the Pentagon, I will here add a few more. Army officer April Gallop, who was seriously injured in the attack along with her two-month-old son, said:

> I was located at the E ring. . . . And we had to escape the building before the floors, debris et cetera collapsed on us. And I don't recall at any time seeing any plane debris. . . . I walked through that place to try to get out before everything collapsed on us . . . . [S]urely we should have seen something?[28]

Sgt. Reginald Powell said:

> I was. . . impressed. . . with how the building stood up, after they told me the size of the plane. And then I was in awe that I saw no plane, nothing left from the plane. It was like it disintegrated as it went into the building.[29]

Two journalists who managed to get inside gave similar testimonies. Judy Rothschadl, a documentary producer, reported: "There weren't seats or luggage or things you find in a plane."[30] ABC's John McWethy reported: "I got in very close, got a look early on at the bad stuff. I could not, however, see any plane wreckage." McWethy added that the plane "had been, basically, vaporized."[31] In offering this explanation, McWethy was evidently repeating what he had been told by Pentagon officials.

In Chapter 2 of NPH, I wrote: "[T]he more-or-less official story was that the fire was so hot that all this metal not only melted but was vaporized." In putting it this way, I was reflecting the two-fold fact that, on the one hand, this claim was evidently never publicly stated by any Pentagon official or in any official document, and yet, on the other hand, it was widely thought to be the government's position and was defended by advocates of that position. As I mentioned in a note, French author Thierry Meyssan quoted French defenders of the official theory to this effect. One of them wrote: "The intensity of the heat caused by the conflagration can easily pulverize the aircraft. Meyssan does not know it perhaps, but at 5,400° F, aluminum transforms into a gas!"[32]

As I pointed out in NPH, this explanation was absurd. For one thing, ordinary, diffuse hydrocarbon fires can at best get to 1,800°F and hence nowhere close to the temperature needed to vaporize aluminum. Also, it has been claimed that the bodies of the plane's occupants were later identified by their DNA, and fire hot enough to vaporize aluminum would have left no human remains with identifiable DNA.

The absurdity of the argument did not, however, keep it from being defended, and not only by French authors. Recent stories in the *Lone Star Iconoclast* reported an event involving this issue that eventually led Sergeant First Class Donald Buswell, who had been in the US Army some 20 years and had won a Purple Heart in Iraq, to leave the service.

In 2006, Buswell was working as a military analyst at Fort Sam Houston. One day he, along with all the other military personnel in the intelligence facility where he worked, received an e-mail letter arguing against the idea that the absence of debris at the Pentagon crash site contradicted the claim that "a Boeing airliner hit the Pentagon." Using a video clip purportedly showing that when an F-4 hits a concrete wall it "turns to vapor," this e-mail writer suggested that the same thing happened when the Boeing airliner hit the Pentagon. Hitting the "reply to all" key, Buswell replied that this was nonsense and that the Pentagon had no "tell-tale signs of a jumbo-jet impacting [it]." Adding that the benefits from 9/11 came not to the Arab world but to the Military Industrial Complex, he said: "We must demand a new independent investigation into 9/11 and look at all options."[33]

Military superiors responded swiftly. Charging that Buswell "used his Government issued e-mail account to send messages disloyal to the United States with the intent of engendering disloyalty or disaffection for the United States in a manner that brought discredit upon the United States Army,"[34] they took away his security clearance, ordered him to take a mental health examination, and planned an investigation. Although the case against Buswell was then suddenly dropped,[35] the experience made him rethink whether he wanted to remain in the military. By April 2008, Buswell had become a civilian, a status that allowed him to work openly to expose what really happened on 9/11.[36] One of the fruits of his new freedom was the co-authorship of an article warning us about the possibility that terror drills will be used to fabricate another false-flag attack.[37]

I have told Buswell's story to emphasize the fact that the claim that Flight 77 vaporized, which was evidently suggested to John McWethy in the first hours after the attack on the Pentagon, was still being stated several years later by people intent on defending the official account of the damage to the Pentagon. Although the claim is absurd, these people have little choice, given the lack of 757 debris at the site, but to defend some version of it. According to the *Pentagon Building Performance Report*, for example, the effects of the plane's impact "may be represented as a violent flow through the structure of a 'fluid' consisting of aviation fuel and solid fragments."[38] *Popular Mechanics*, apparently quoting Mete Sozen, one of the authors of that report, says that the plane's exterior crumbled up "like a sausage skin," after which the rest of the plane "flowed into the structure in a state closer to a liquid than a solid mass."[39] Defenders of the 757 theory are forced into such absurdities by the absence of 757 debris reported by both cameras and eyewitnesses.

Various photos, to be sure, reveal wheel and engine components that, according to some people, are 757 parts.[40] But Dave McGowan, recalling the fact that an empty Boeing 757 weighs well over 100,000 pounds, has written: "Even if all of the photos did actually depict debris from a 757, and if all that debris was actually found inside the Pentagon, then a few hundred pounds of Flight 77 has been accounted for." The official story, therefore, "cannot account for . . . 99.9% of the wreckage."[41] Former airline pilot Russ Wittenberg has made the same point, saying: "It's roughly a 100 ton airplane. An airplane that weighs 100 tons all assembled is still going to have 100 tons of disassembled trash and parts after it hits a building."[42]

Videos: If a Boeing 757 had really hit the Pentagon, that would have been easy for authorities to prove. In NPH, I mentioned the video taken from the Citgo gas station. In the meantime, a FOIA request to release the relevant videos led the Department of Justice to admit that it has 85 videos that were confiscated from cameras on or near the Pentagon. The DOJ denied the request, however, saying that these videos were "exempt from disclosure."[43] The 9/11 Commission, far from using its subpoena power to obtain these videos, did not even mention their existence. Brief segments of a few videos have been released, but they have shown nothing definitive.[44] Is it believable that of the 85 videos, none would give a clearer idea of what did and did not hit the Pentagon than the few frames that have been released? Can we believe that the government would not release them if they supported its story?

Time-Change Parts: There would be an even more definitive way for the government to prove that American 77 hit the Pentagon, if it really did. Retired Air Force Colonel George Nelson, who had specialized in the investigation of aircraft mishaps, has pointed out that every plane has many "time-change parts," which must be changed periodically because they are crucial for flight safety. Each time-change part has a distinctive serial number. These parts, moreover, are virtually indestructible, so an ordinary fire resulting from an airplane crash could not possibly "destroy or obliterate all of those critical time-change parts or their serial numbers."[45] By identifying some of those numbers, investigators can determine the make, model, and registration number of a crashed aircraft. Accordingly, if Flight 77 did indeed hit the Pentagon, the FBI, which took charge of the investigation, could have proven this to the press within hours.

Flight Data Recorder: Still another sure-fire way for authorities to have proved that American Flight 77 struck the Pentagon, if it did, would have been to show the press the serial number of the plane's flight data recorder (FDR), which Pentagon authorities claimed to have found in the wreckage. As Aidan Monaghan has shown with extensive documentation, when the NTSB (National Traffic Safety Board) issues a report on a crashed airplane, it almost always lists the serial number of the FDR.[46] Indeed, the only exceptions between 1991 and 2006—excluding planes with no FDRs—have evidently been the reports about the four planes that allegedly crashed on 9/11.[47] How can we avoid suspecting that the reason the NTSB's report on American Flight 77's FDR does not mention its serial number is that no FDR with the serial number for that flight was found at the Pentagon?

In 2007, Monaghan sent a FOIA request to the FBI for "documentation pertaining to any formally and positively identified debris by the FBI, from all four civilian commercial aircraft used in the terrorist attacks of September 11, 2001." The FBI replied that "any potentially responsive records were located in a pending file of an ongoing investigation, and [are] therefore. . . exempt from disclosure." Monaghan then asked the FBI for

> documentation revealing the process by which wreckage recovered by defendant [the FBI]. . . was positively identified by defendant (with the aid of the National Transportation Safety Board), . . . presumably though the use of unique serial number identifying information.

The FBI responded that no such documentation existed because "the identity of the three [sic] hijacked aircraft has never been in question by the FBI, NTSB or FAA."[48] According to the FBI itself, therefore, it has no documentation to prove that the aircraft that hit the Pentagon was American Flight 77.[49]

The Pentagon's failure to show the serial number was not the only problem with the Pentagon's claim to have found Flight 77's flight data recorder. Another problem was that the Pentagon's file on this FDR, based on information downloaded from it, was created over four hours before this FDR was reportedly found. According to a widely published report, the FDR from Flight 77 was found Friday, September 14, 2001, at 4:00 in the morning. *USA Today*, for example, wrote:

Searchers on Friday found the flight data and cockpit voice recorders from the hijacked plane that flew into the Pentagon and exploded, Department of Defense officials said. The two "black boxes," crucial to uncovering details about the doomed flight's last moments, were recovered at about 4AM, said Army Lt. Col. George Rhynedance, a Pentagon spokesman. Rhynedance said the recorders were in the possession of the FBI, and that officials from the National Transportation Safety Board were providing technical assistance in reading any data they contain.[50]

This story also reported that despite some damage to the boxes, "the FBI still was confident the data can be recovered from both."[51] However, according to a file released by the NTSB in response to a FOIA request from Aidan Monaghan, the flight data file for American Flight 77, which was based on this FDR, was created at 11:45PM on Thursday.[52]

Here is a serious contradiction within the official story. According to the Pentagon, the NTSB, and the FBI, the FDR was found on Friday morning and authorities later in the day were hoping that information on it could be recovered. And yet the file based on it had already been created the previous day. The presence of such a contradiction suggests that the story about the discovery was invented.

This conclusion is further suggested by the existence of contradictory reports as to where the FDR was found. According to the *USA Today* story just quoted, it was found "right where the plane came into the building." *Newsweek* likewise reported that it was discovered "near the impact site."[53] According to the *Pentagon Building Performance Report*, however, the FDR was found "nearly 300 ft into the structure."[54] This view was popularized by *Popular Mechanics*, which said that it "was found almost 300 feet inside the building."[55]

Given all these contradictions, it is difficult to take seriously the claim that American Flight 77's flight data recorder was found in the debris at the Pentagon.

Seismic Signal: Another count against the official story is the fact that the attack on the Pentagon did not create a strong enough seismic signal for seismologists to determine the time of impact.

Won-Young Kim and Gerald Baum, having been asked to determine the time of each airline crash (see Chapter 3), were able to determine the crash times for the other three flights. With regard to the Pentagon attack, however, they wrote:

> We analyzed seismic records from five stations in the northeastern United States, ranging from 63 to 350 km from the Pentagon. Despite detailed analysis of the data, we could not find a clear seismic signal. Even the closest station. . . did not record the impact. We concluded that the plane impact to the Pentagon generated relatively weak seismic signals.[56]

If United 93, also a Boeing 757, created a detectable signal by crashing into the soft soil in Pennsylvania, how could a detectable signal not be created by a Boeing 757 crashing into the Pentagon's steel-reinforced outer wall at several hundred miles per hour?

C-Ring Hole: In NPH, I wrote that the hole in the C ring shows "[j]ust how far the aircraft went into the Pentagon." That statement presupposed that the hole in the C-ring wall in Wedge 2 had been created by an aircraft striking the Pentagon (the claim was that it had struck Wedge 1 at an angle, so that by the time it reached the C ring, it was in Wedge 2). But it may have been created by something else, such as "a shaped charge warhead or device," as mechanical engineer Michael Meyer believes. "The hole is circular," explains Meyer, and "cleanly cut, . . . as would be expected from the extremely localized and focused energy from the shaped charge warhead."[57]

In any case, whatever created this hole, the view that it was *not* caused by the nose of a Boeing 757 is now widely accepted. Although the official report on the Pentagon damage—the *Pentagon Building Performance Report*—accepted the view that the Pentagon was struck by American 77, it said that "the front of the aircraft disintegrated essentially upon impact."[58] This report did not provide any explanation for the C-ring hole.

Such an explanation was proffered, however, by the *Popular Mechanics* book, which said that the plane's landing gear "was responsible for puncturing the wall in Ring C."[59] This conclusion was evidently based on a misreading of the *Pentagon Building*

Performance Report, but that report did at least agree with *Popular Mechanics*'s conclusion that "the hole was not made by. . . the nose of Flight 77 pushing through the building's interior."[60]

This conclusion created a problem, because it contradicted what officials had said shortly after the attacks. Secretary of Defense Donald Rumsfeld, appearing on ABC's *Good Morning America* four days after 9/11, had said the plane "came in. . . between about the first and second floor. . . . And it went in through three rings. I'm told the nose is—is still in there, very close to the inner courtyard, about one ring away."[61]

Lee Evey, the program manager for the Pentagon Renovation Project, said at a news briefing two days later: "The plane actually penetrated through the. . . E ring, D ring, C ring. . . . The nose of the plane just barely broke through the inside of the C ring, so it was extending into A-E Drive a little bit."[62]

But now the Rumsfeld–Evey claim has been abandoned. In a book on the history of the Pentagon, *Washington Post* reporter Steve Vogel wrote: "the nose came to an almost immediate stop."[63] Even the book *Pentagon 9/11*, written in 2007 by historians employed by the Office of the Secretary of Defense, did not support the story told by their former boss. Just before mentioning "the so-called 'punch out hole' in the C-ring wall," they said that, when the plane struck the building, "the front part of the relatively weak fuselage disintegrated."[64]

Defenders of the official story certainly should be troubled by the fact that both *Pentagon 9/11* and the *Pentagon Building Performance Report*, the two official reports on the Pentagon strike, imply that Rumsfeld and Evey were not telling the truth. Should not Congress and the press try to discover if they deliberately told a falsehood and, if so, why?

WHAT ABOUT THE REPORTED SIGHTINGS OF AN AMERICAN AIRLINER?

The testimony of alleged eyewitnesses still provides the main support for the official view. *Popular Mechanics*, for example, claimed that "hundreds of witnesses saw a Boeing 757 hit the building."[65] There are severe problems, however, with using this testimony as proof for the truth of the official account.

Problems with the Alleged Eyewitness Accounts: One problem is that no firm conclusion can be drawn from the testimonies taken as a whole. The most extensive list of alleged witnesses contains 152 people.[66] Whereas some of these people did claim to have seen an airliner crash into the Pentagon, others gave very different reports, as we saw in the introductory section of NPH's second chapter.

Moreover, when Jerry Russell, who has advanced degrees in both engineering and psychology, examined these testimonies, he found that only 31 of them provided "explicit, realistic and detailed claims" about an airliner striking the Pentagon. He then examined these 31 alleged witnesses in light of the hypothesis that, if the official story was false, "'eyewitness' sources strongly linked to the US corporate and media elite might [have] provide[d] false testimony." He found that 24 of the 31 alleged witnesses "worked for either the Federal Government or the mainstream media." His suspicions were further justified by the fact that 21 of these 31 testimonies contained "substantial errors or contradictions."[67] For example, Steve Anderson, director of communications for *USA Today*, said that the plane "drug it's [sic] wing along the ground" before it hit the Pentagon.[68] But this would have created a huge scar in the Pentagon lawn, which, photographs show, did not exist.

Further reasons to be suspicious of witnesses supporting the official story are provided by testimonies cited approvingly by *Popular Mechanics*. Structural engineer Allyn Kilsheimer claimed: "I held in my hand the tail section of the plane."[69] No one else, however, reported seeing the tail section of a 757, and no photograph has shown it. Retired Army officer Frank Probst, supporting the idea that an American airliner came toward the Pentagon very close to the ground, claimed that it was flying so low that he dove to the ground for fear of being hit.[70] In part of his testimony not quoted by *Popular Mechanics*, Probst claimed that one of the plane's engines passed by him "about six feet away."[71] Dave McGowan, who has studied the effects of wind turbulence from large airliners, pointed out that if a Boeing 757 going several hundred miles an hour had come this close to Probst, he would have been a victim, not a witness.[72]

Challenges to the Official Flight Path: According to the official account, Flight 77 flew over the south side of the nearby Citgo gas station (now called the Navy Exchange). Only with this trajectory could the plane have headed toward the part of the C ring where the hole was created. And only with this trajectory could the plane have hit five light poles that were knocked over, photos of which have always been part of the evidence that an airliner struck the Pentagon[73] (one of the alleged eyewitnesses cited by *Popular Mechanics*, for example, claimed that he saw the airliner clip three of the poles[74]).

The idea that the airliner's flight path was south of the Citgo station had always been challenged by Pentagon police officer William Lagasse, who was at the station at the time. The plane actually, he maintained, passed on the north side of the station. His testimony was generally dismissed because it was not supported by other witnesses. However, in *PentaCon*, a video put out by Citizen Investigation Team (CIT), Lagasse's testimony is corroborated by three more eyewitnesses: another Pentagon police officer, an employee at the station, and an auto mechanic at a nearby shop. This combined testimony presents a strong challenge to the official story, according to which the approaching plane hit the light posts before it crashed into the Pentagon.[75]

One of the four witnesses, in fact, said that the plane, rather than hitting the Pentagon, pulled up at the last second in order to fly over the Pentagon. This flyover theory, an earlier version of which I mentioned in NPH, has been developed more fully in a second CIT video, *The Pentagon Flyover: How They Pulled It Off*.[76] According to its theory, the plane that approached the Pentagon and then flew over it was obscured from view by the smoke that billowed up from the Pentagon (which was due to an explosion in Wedge 1 just as the plane flew over it). The aforementioned C-130, which was seen flying near the Pentagon, was there to provide a cover story: If people saw the flyover plane flying away from the Pentagon, it could be said that they had seen the C-130. Whatever one thinks of that theory, the video makes a very strong case, based on testimony from many people, that the plane that approached the Pentagon had a completely different flight path than the one declared by the National Transportation Safety Board (NTSB) to have been the flight path of American 77—which will be discussed next.

In 2006, the NTSB released an animation that, it claimed, was based on American 77's Flight Data Recorder (FDR). Rob Balsamo, the founder of Pilots for 9/11 Truth, has shown that this flight path is doubly problematic from the point of view of what had until then been the official flight path—namely, the one portrayed in an animation put out by the 9/11 Commission, which is the flight path needed if the plane was to hit the light poles. One problem is that the flight path indicated by the FDR was north of the path needed to strike the poles. (In this respect, it agreed with the four eyewitnesses presented in *PentaCon*.) A second problem with the FDR flight path is that it was much too high for the aircraft to have hit either the light poles or the Pentagon. (In this respect, it differed from those witnesses.) So, Balsamo has shown, American 77 now has two official flight paths, which are mutually contradictory.[77]

Still another challenge has been presented by Scott Cook and his boss, Ray, who were in the conference room in the Portals building in Washington, which had a wide window looking directly at the Pentagon, with Reagan Airport to the left. Having learned about the attacks in New York and thinking that Washington might be attacked next, they kept their eyes on the landscape as well as the TV set. Suddenly they saw that the Pentagon had been struck. Cook later wrote:

> We didn't know what kind of plane had hit the Pentagon. . . .
> Later, we were told that it was a 757 out of Dulles, which had come up the river in back of our building, turned sharply over the Capitol, ran past the White House and the Washington Monument, up the river to Rosslyn, then dropped to treetop level and ran down Washington Boulevard to the Pentagon. I cannot fathom why neither myself nor Ray, a former Air Force officer, missed a big 757, going 400 miles an hour, as it crossed in front of our window in its last 10 seconds of flight.[78]

The alleged eyewitness support for the official account is, in sum, far too problematic to provide support for the claim that a Boeing 757 struck the Pentagon. Corroborating physical evidence would be required, and that evidence does not exist. In any case, although there is much disagreement within the 9/11 truth movement about what actually damaged the Pentagon, there is virtual unanimity on the next two points.

WHY WOULD TERRORISTS HAVE STRUCK WEDGE 1?

Although I should have referred to the damaged section of the Pentagon as Wedge 1 (rather than the West Wing), my discussion in this section of NPH has proved sound. Indeed, in their book *Firefight: Inside the Battle to Save the Pentagon on 9/11*, which supports the official story, Patrick Creed and Rick Newman wrote:

> The National Military Command Center was on the other side of the building from where Flight 77 had smashed into the Pentagon's western wall. It was located in a section of the Pentagon. . . that housed the offices of the military's Joint Staff and many top officials, including the Secretary of Defense. . . . The location of the Defense Secretary's office, on the outer E Ring, had been listed in a 1992 history of the Pentagon published by the Defense Department itself. . . . [T]he office of the Chairman of the Joint Chiefs of Staff, the nation's top military officer, [was] one deck below the Defense Secretary's suite. Many other generals and admirals worked in the same area. Had terrorists been targeting not just the Pentagon, but the senior government officials inside, there was plenty of information available to help them figure out exactly where to aim. . . . Yet the VIPs in the most prestigious part of the Pentagon were strangely immune.[79]

Likewise, in his history of the Pentagon, Steve Vogel, while accepting every detail of the official account, remarked that "the plane had hit the building in the best possible place." Besides pointing out that Wedge 1 had been reinforced, equipped with sprinklers, and only partially occupied, Vogel wrote:

> The hijackers had not hit the River or Mall sides, where the senior military leadership had been concentrated since 1942. Rumsfeld had been sitting in the same third-floor office above the River entrance as every secretary of defense since Louis Johnson in 1949, a location that had been a matter of public record all that time. The joint chiefs. . . were arrayed in various prime E-Ring offices on the River and Mall sides. All the

command centers save the Navy's were on the River or Mall sides; the National Military Command Center could have been decimated. . . , a disaster that could have effectively shut down the Pentagon.[80]

Both of these books pointed out, apparently inadvertently, that the al-Qaeda terrorists must have been very stupid—even though, paradoxically, they had been brilliant enough to outfox the most sophisticated defense system in the world.

In any case, there are two more reasons why Wedge 1 would have been the least likely spot for foreign terrorists to strike. First, given the fact that they would have been flying through prohibited airspace, in which "civilian flying is prohibited at all times,"[81] they should have feared that they would be intercepted by fighter jets. And yet executing the downward spiral to hit Wedge 1 required their plane, according to the official report, to be aloft for an additional three minutes and two seconds.[82] Why would they needlessly have taken this extra risk, through which the whole mission might have failed?

Second, Wedge 1 was the only part of the Pentagon that presented serious obstacles, including the control tower for the Pentagon's heliport plus elevated signs above the highway. As a result, the attacking 757 would have needed, after clearing these obstacles, to reduce its altitude and then level out in a very short distance in order to hit the side of Wedge 1. Why would those who planned this attack have imposed such a difficult feat on an amateur pilot?

Indeed, as recent calculations by Rob Balsamo of Pilots for 9/11 Truth have demonstrated, this would have been not merely difficult but physically impossible. As shown by photographs of American 77's alleged flight path provided by Citizen Investigation Team, there was a VDOT (Virginia Department of Transportation) antenna, 169 feet in height, in this path. According to the official account, as mentioned earlier, the plane hit five light poles before reaching the Pentagon. The distance from the VDOT antenna to the first of these light poles was 2,400 feet. To hit even the top of the pole after clearing the antenna, the plane would have needed to descend 224 feet. According to the flight data recorder, the plane was going 530 miles per hour and hence 781 feet per second. The plane, therefore, had to descend 224 feet in slightly over three seconds. That first light pole was only 1016 feet from the Pentagon. So the plane, in order to be level with the Pentagon lawn before striking Wedge 1 between the first and second floors (as allegedly shown in the Pentagon security video released in 2006[83]), would have needed to level out in 1.3 seconds after striking the light pole. Doing so would have been physically impossible. In the language used by pilots, the plane would have needed to "pull over 10 G's" (which would mean experiencing over 10 times the earth's gravitational pull). This would be much more than the plane could have endured: "10 Gs," Balsamo says, "would rip the aircraft apart."[84]

Given the fact that the official story is physically impossible, we can know that it is false. Balsamo also gives another reason for drawing this conclusion: "10 G's was never recorded in the FDR."[85]

COULD AN INEXPERIENCED PILOT HAVE FLOWN THE AIRCRAFT?

The official flight path, we have seen, could not have been executed in a Boeing 757 even by one of the best pilots in the world. Still clearer is the fact that it could not have been executed by one of the worst.

Before it was announced that Hani Hanjour had been the pilot of American 77, this plane's trajectory in its final minutes had been described as one requiring great skill. A *Washington Post* story on September 12 said:

> [J]ust as the plane seemed to be on a suicide mission into the White House, the unidentified pilot executed a pivot so tight that it reminded observers of a fighter jet maneuver. . . . Aviation sources said the plane was flown with extraordinary skill, making it highly likely that a trained pilot was at the helm.[86]

But Hani Hanjour was not that. Indeed, a CBS story reported that an Arizona flight school said that Hanjour's "flying skills were so bad. . . they didn't think he should keep his pilot's license." The manager said: "I couldn't believe he had a commercial license of any kind with the skills that he had."[87] A *New York Times* story, entitled "A Trainee Noted for Incompetence," quoted one of his instructors as saying that Hanjour "could not fly at all."[88]

I mentioned earlier that the 9/11 truth movement now contains many pilots. One thing on which they all agree is that Hani Hanjour, known to be incapable of safely flying even a single-engine plane, could not possibly have flown the trajectory allegedly taken by Flight 77 in its final minutes. Former Navy and Pan-American Airlines pilot Ted Muga, for example, has said:

> The maneuver at the Pentagon was. . . a tight spiral coming down out of 7,000 feet. . . . [I]t takes some very, very talented pilots to do that. . . . I just can't imagine an amateur even being able to come close to performing a maneuver of that nature.[89]

Russ Wittenberg, who flew large commercial airliners for 35 years after serving in Vietnam as a fighter pilot, says it would have been "totally impossible for an amateur who couldn't even fly a Cessna" to have flown that downward spiral and then "crash into the Pentagon's first floor wall without touching the lawn."[90] Ralph Omholt, a former 757 pilot, has bluntly said: "The idea that an *unskilled* pilot could have flown this trajectory is simply too ridiculous to consider."[91] Ralph Kolstad, who was a US Navy "top gun" pilot before becoming a commercial airline pilot for 27 years, has said: "I have 6,000 hours of flight time in Boeing 757's and 767's and I could not have flown it the way the flight path was described. . . . Something stinks to high heaven!"[92] (These statements were made, moreover, before there was awareness of the additional problem posed by the VDOT antenna, discussed above.)

This problem is so insurmountable that defenders of the official story have typically ignored it. For example, the *Popular Mechanics* authors, while acknowledging that Hanjour and the other pilots "may not have been highly skilled," claimed that they could have, using Global Positioning System units, simply put their planes on autopilot.[93] With regard to Hanjour in particular, they said: "He steered the plane manually for only the final eight minutes of the flight."[94] They thereby simply ignored that fact that it was during these eight minutes that Hanjour had allegedly done the impossible.

The 9/11 Commission dealt with the problem by saying contradictory things. On the one hand, it admitted that a flight instructor in Arizona had described Hanjour as "a terrible pilot."[95] It also reported that in the summer of 2001, just months before 9/11, a flight instructor in New Jersey, after going up with him in a small plane, "declined a second request because of what he considered Hanjour's poor piloting skills."[96]

On the other hand, the Commission made two comments in its notes suggesting that perhaps Hanjour was not such a terrible pilot. One comment involved repeating an assertion reportedly made by KSM (Khalid Sheikh Mohammed), the alleged mastermind of 9/11: "KSM claims to have assigned the Pentagon specifically to Hanjour, the operations' most experienced pilot."[97] The Commission distanced itself from this statement by saying "KSM claims." And well it should have: Given what we have learned about Hanjour's abilities, KSM's reported statement, by suggesting that Hanjour was highly experienced, provided one more example of the fact (to be discussed in Chapter 8) that KSM's reported testimony is completely untrustworthy. In another note, the Commission wrote:

> Hanjour successfully conducted a challenging certification flight supervised by an instructor at Congressional Air Charters of Gaithersburg, Maryland, landing at a small airport with a difficult approach. The instructor thought Hanjour may have had training from a military pilot because he used a terrain recognition system for navigation.[98]

How could an instructor in Gaithersburg have had such a radically different view of Hanjour's abilities from that of all the other flight instructors who worked with him? Who was this instructor? How could this report be verified?

The 9/11 Commission provided no answer to these questions. Its sole reference for its claim was: "Eddie Shalev interview (Apr. 9, 2004)." Extensive searches, however, turned up no evidence of a flight instructor of that name and no evidence of Hanjour's having attended Congressional Air Charters.[99] Did the 9/11 Commission, out of desperation, simply invent a witness?

In any case, I have elsewhere devoted an entire chapter to the conflict between the official account and the evidence about Hani Hanjour's abilities—a conflict that by itself disproves the official account about the attack on the Pentagon.[100]

Why Was the Strike Not Prevented by Standard Operating Procedures?

Given NORAD's timeline of September 18, 2001, which said that the FAA notified the military about Flight 77 at 9:24, the military should have intercepted it, as I pointed out in NPH, before it could have struck the Pentagon. (This would have been true even if there had really been no fighters on alert at Andrews, requiring the interceptors to come from Langley.) This was the claim of the 9/11 truth movement at the time NPH was written.

The 9/11 Commission recognized the validity of this argument, saying that NORAD's account had "made it appear that the military was notified in time to respond."[101] The co-chairmen of the 9/11 Commission, Thomas Kean and Lee Hamilton,[102] made this point even more clearly in their 2006 book, saying that, "if the military had had the amount of time they said they had," they should have been able to shoot the plane down.[103]

Not surprisingly, therefore, the 9/11 Commission, on the basis of the NORAD tapes (discussed in the previous chapter), told a new story, labeling the military's earlier story, reflected in NORAD's timeline of September 18, 2001, "incorrect."[104] According to this new story, the military "never received notice that American 77 was hijacked" until after the Pentagon was struck.[105] This new story, however, was contradicted by many prior reports.

Contradictory Reports: In the FBI section of the Arlington County "After-Action Report" on the Pentagon attack, we read: "At about 9:20AM, the [FBI's] WFO [Washington Field Office] Command Center was notified that American Airlines Flight #77 had been hijacked shortly after takeoff from Washington Dulles International Airport."[106] Can we believe that the FBI learned this but the military did not?

Also, as we saw in the previous chapter, Laura Brown, the FAA's deputy in public affairs, sent the 9/11 Commission a memo on May 22, 2003, about FAA–NORAD communications. According to this memo, the 9:24 notification time given by NORAD was wrong not by being too early, as the Commission would later claim, but by being too late. The FAA, this memo explained, had established phone bridges that connected the FAA with NORAD and the Pentagon's NMCC, immediately after the first strike on the World Trade Center, hence about 8:50. In this teleconference,

> The FAA shared real-time information. . . about. . . all the flights of interest, including Flight 77. NORAD logs indicate that the FAA made formal notification about American Flight 77 at 9:24AM, but information about the flight was conveyed continuously during the phone bridges before the formal notification.[107]

After reading this memo into the record, Commissioner Richard Ben-Veniste commented on its point that "there was an informal real-time communication of the situation, including Flight 77's situation, to personnel at NORAD."[108] However, when the Commission's report appeared in 2004, it contained no mention of this memo. This omission suggests a deliberate cover-up of the truth.

In any case, the Commission, in claiming that the FAA had failed to notify the military about Flight 77, had to explain this failure. Its explanation was that, although the air traffic controller in Indianapolis lost this flight's transponder signal, its radar track, and its radio at 8:56 AM, he did not notify the military because he concluded that "American 77 had experienced serious electrical or mechanical failure," after which it had crashed.[109] But why would the controller have made this inference after two planes had already been hijacked, one of which had already crashed into the World Trade Center? The Commission claimed that the controller had been unaware of all this—that no one at Indianapolis Center "had any knowledge of the situation in New York." It was not until 9:20, the Commission claimed, that the FAA controllers in Indianapolis "learned that there were other hijacked aircraft."[110] But this is unbelievable.

For one thing, television networks had started broadcasting images of the World Trade Center at 8:48. Are we to believe that while much of America had some idea of what was going on by 8:50, the Indianapolis controllers—whose business it is to know what is happening in the skies—were insulated from all such information for another 30 minutes?

Also, Indianapolis, like all the other air traffic control centers, would have been directly notified. General Mike Canavan, the former associate administrator of Civil Aviation Security, told the 9/11 Commission: "[A]s soon as you know you had a hijacked aircraft, you notify everyone. . . . [The notification] gets broadcast out to all the regions."[111]

There were, moreover, reports that this occurred. On an NBC program, Tom Brokaw said that, immediately after controllers at the FAA's Boston Center determined that Flight 11 had been hijacked (which would have been at about 8:26), "Boston Center supervisors notif[ied] the FAA and other air traffic centers about the hijacking of American Flight 11."[112] In a book about the FAA's activities that day, Pamela Freni said that at 9:07, the Command Center at Herndon sent a message "to every air traffic facility in the nation, announcing the first hijacking."[113]

The Commission's claim that Indianapolis did not know about the hijackings until 9:20 was, therefore, surely false. And without that claim, the Commission would be left with no explanation as to why Indianapolis would not have made sure that the military was told about Flight 77's troubles—as Laura Brown's memo said it was.

To make its claim that the military was not aware of Flight 77's troubles, the Commission also had to ignore information it had been given about military liaisons. According to the Commission's report, the FAA Command Center in Herndon, Virginia, and FAA headquarters in Washington, DC, knew by 9:25 that Flight 77 was lost, but they did not pass this knowledge on to the military. However, Ben Sliney, the operations manager at the Command Center, told the 9/11 Commission that the Command Center had military liaisons who were "present at all of the events that occurred on 9/11," after which he added: "If you tell the military you've told the military. They have their own communication web."[114] Monte Belger, the FAA's acting deputy administrator on 9/11, told the Commission that the same was true at FAA headquarters.[115]

These reports undermined in advance, therefore, the 9/11 Commission's later claim that, although Flight 77's troubles were known at Herndon and FAA headquarters, they were not known by the military. The Commission, in making its claim, had simply ignored what it had been told by Sliney and Belger.

The claim that no one but the FAA knew about Flight 77 was also contradicted by Barbara Riggs, who was in the Secret Service's Washington office on 9/11.[116] In 2006, having just retired as the Service's deputy director, she said: "Thru monitoring radar and activating an open line with the FAA, the Secret Service was able to receive real time information about. . . hijacked aircraft. We were tracking two hijacked aircraft as they approached Washington, D.C."[117] Can we believe that the Secret Service, knowing that hijacked aircraft were headed toward the capital, would not have notified the military?

Where Were Rumsfeld and Myers? A central element in the 9/11 Commission's claim that the military was unaware of Flight 77 and any danger to the Pentagon was its account of the location of Secretary of Defense Donald Rumsfeld and General Richard Myers, the acting chairman of the Joint Chiefs of Staff. The Commission based its accounts on statements provided by these two men themselves.

According to the Commission, Rumsfeld, after learning about the second attack on the World Trade Center, remained in his office, where he was meeting with a CIA briefer, until the strike on the Pentagon, after which he went down to the attack site to see what had happened. He returned to his office at about 10:00, where he talked by telephone to President Bush, after which he went to the Executive Support Center, "where he participated in the White House video teleconference." Having been out of the loop, he did not gain "situational awareness" until almost 10:40.[118]

General Myers, according to the Commission, was on Capitol Hill, meeting with Senator Max Cleland in preparation for Myers's confirmation hearing. Having assumed that the first attack on the World Trade Center was an accident and having not been informed about the second one, Myers did not emerge from Cleland's office until the Pentagon was attacked, at which time he rushed back to the Pentagon, arriving just before 10:00.[119]

These accounts, besides being inherently implausible, were contradicted in advance by Richard Clarke's book *Against All Enemies*,[120] which came out while the Commission's hearings were still going on. Clarke had run a video conference on the morning of 9/11 from the White House Video Teleconference Center. In describing the beginning of this conference, which according to his account started at about 9:10,[12] Clarke wrote:

As I entered the Video Center, . . . I could see people rushing into studios around the city: Donald Rumsfeld at Defense and George Tenet at CIA. . . . Air force four-star General Dick Myers was filling in for the Chairman of the Joint Chiefs, Hugh Shelton, who was over the Atlantic.[122]

Then, shortly before 9:28, after Clarke had received a report from FAA head Jane Garvey, who said that both planes that hit the World Trade Center had been hijacked and that perhaps a total of eleven planes had been hijacked, he had, he reported, this exchange with Myers:

"JCS [Joint Chiefs of Staff], JCS. I assume NORAD has scrambled fighters and AWACS. How many? Where?"

"Not a pretty picture Dick. . . . We are in the midst of Vigilant Warrior, a NORAD exercise, but. . . Otis has launched two birds toward New York. Langley is trying to get two up now." . . .

"Okay, how long to CAP over D.C.?" . . . .

"Fast as we can. Fifteen minutes?" Myers asked, looking at the generals and colonels around him. It was now 9:28.[123]

Although Clarke reported no interaction with Rumsfeld during this period, he did write that, after first hearing that "there had been an explosion in the Pentagon parking lot, maybe a car bomb," and then being told that a "plane just hit the Pentagon," he replied: "I can still see Rumsfeld on the screen."[124] Then, describing an interaction that occurred at about the same time that the president's plane took off from Sarasota, and hence at about 9:55, Clarke wrote:

Rumsfeld said that smoke was getting into the Pentagon secure teleconferencing studio. Franklin Miller urged him to helicopter to DOD's alternate site. "I am too goddam old to go to an alternate site," the Secretary answered. Rumsfeld moved to another studio in the Pentagon and sent his deputy, Paul Wolfowitz, to the remote site.[125]

Richard Clarke's account, therefore, completely contradicts that of the 9/11 Commission. According to Clarke, both Rumsfeld and Myers were in the Pentagon participating in his video conference from about 9:10 until after the Pentagon attack. They both, therefore, had "situational awareness" all along. According to the 9/11 Commission, by contrast, both Rumsfeld and Myers were occupied with other matters until after the Pentagon was struck. Rumsfeld did not participate in Clarke's video conference until after 10:00, and Myers evidently never did. Although *The 9/11 Commission Report* did not directly challenge Clarke's account—indeed, it never even acknowledged the existence of Clarke's book—it implied the falsity of his account by stating: "We do not know who from Defense participated, but we know that in the first hour none of the personnel involved in managing the crisis did."[126] This statement fit with the Commission's claim that Rumsfeld did not participate until several minutes after 10:00.

Deciding which of these accounts is closer to the truth is not difficult, as all of the relevant considerations favor Clarke's account. First, if Myers and Rumsfeld did not participate in Clarke's video conference, it is hard to imagine what motive he would have had to lie about it; whereas if they did participate, Rumsfeld and Myers, by claiming that they did not and were therefore unaware of what was happening, could avoid questions as to why they had not prevented the attack on the Pentagon. Second, if it were Clarke's account that was the lie, the 9/11 Commission could have proved this by simply producing the videotape of his teleconference. Third, Rumsfeld's story—according to which he, after learning about the second strike on the World Trade Center, continued receiving a CIA briefing about other matters for another 35 minutes, until the Pentagon was struck—is completely implausible. Fourth, the same is true of Myers's story, according to which he was not informed about the second strike on the World Trade Center and hence remained in Senator Cleland's office with no idea of what was going on until the Pentagon was struck. Fifth, although Senator Cleland has supported Myers's story, his accounts, as I have shown elsewhere, contradict various crucial details in Myers's accounts.[127]

Moreover, the account given by Rumsfeld and the 9/11 Commission has been contradicted in 2004 by Robert Andrews, a former Green Beret and CIA liaison to the White House and Department of Defense, who on 9/11 was the acting assistant secretary of defense for special operations and low intensity conflict. While being interviewed by military affairs journalist Barbara Honegger, Andrews supported, perhaps unwittingly, Richard Clarke's position, saying that, after the second attack on the World Trade Center at 9:03, Rumsfeld went across the hall from his office to the Executive Support Center (ESC) and joined Clarke's teleconference.[128] In a lecture at the Naval Postgraduate School in Monterey, California, Andrews stated:

> The moment I saw the second plane strike "live," I knew Secretary Rumsfeld would need the most up-to-date information, and ran down to our counterterrorism center to get maps of New York and other data to take to him in the Executive Support Center.[129]

It was while he and his aide were in the counterterrorism center, Andrews explained to Honegger, that the Pentagon attack happened (at about 9:32, as discussed below). As soon as it did, they rushed to the ESC to join Rumsfeld.[130] "I was there in the Support Center with the Secretary," Andrews added, "when he was talking to Clarke on the White House video-teleconference, and to the President."[131]

As can be seen, Andrews's account completely agrees with Clarke's, according to which Rumsfeld went to the ESC shortly after 9:03 and participated in Clarke's video conference until after the Pentagon was struck. If there was any doubt before, we can take the testimony by Andrews as settling the issue: The account given by Rumsfeld and the 9/11 Commission was false. Given that conclusion, moreover, we can assume that Clarke's account of General Myers was also essentially correct, meaning that the account given by Myers and the 9/11 Commission was false.

Accordingly, if both Rumsfeld and Myers were participating, along with FAA head Jane Garvey and other officials, in Clarke's video conference, the 9/11 Commission's claim that the FAA failed to transmit information to the military is absurd. With regard to Flight 77 in particular, the FAA, Laura Brown's memo had reported, had been communicating with the military about it even before 9:24 (the time at which NORAD had said it had been notified about Flight 77 by the FAA back before the 9/11 Commission declared that it had never been notified). Accordingly, if Myers and Rumsfeld had been participating in the video conference with FAA head Jane Garvey, they surely would have heard something about this flight.

What about Andrews Air Force Base? In explaining why no planes were available to protect Washington, the military, as I reported in NPH, claimed that Andrews had no fighters on alert. The military then altered a website that had indicated otherwise. The military's claim about Andrews was highly implausible, especially given the fact that, as a National Guard spokesman said on 9/11: "Air defense around Washington is provided mainly by fighter planes from Andrews Air Force Base."[132] If Andrews had the primary responsibility for protecting the White House, the Pentagon, the Congressional office buildings, the Supreme Court, and the US Treasury, the claim that it did not keep fighters on alert at all times cannot be taken seriously.

This a priori reasoning is also supported by evidence. In 9/11CROD, I summarized a telephone conversation that Kyle Hence, the co-founder of 9/11 Citizens Watch, reported having had with Donald Arias, the Chief of Public Affairs for NORAD's Continental Region. Hence first asked Arias if any alert fighters had been available at Andrews, to which Arias replied that Andrews was not part of NORAD. Hence then asked if "there were assets at Andrews that, though not technically part of NORAD, could have been tasked." Rather than answer, Arias hung up.[133]

The suspicion that Hence had articulated the truth of the matter was later confirmed by Colin Scoggins, the military expert at the FAA's Boston Center. Speaking of the fact that Andrews and several other bases—at Atlantic City, Toledo, Selfridge, Burlington, and Syracuse—all had fighters flying that morning, Scoggins said: "NEADS's authority doesn't necessarily extend to them, but under the circumstances, they could have grabbed all those aircraft."[134] The significance of Scoggins's statement, incidentally, extends beyond the question about Andrews. It shows the falsity of the oft-repeated claim that on 9/11, the military had at its disposal only four fighter jets to defend the entire North Eastern region of the United States.[135] To say that NORAD had only four fighters on alert status, which may be true, is not to say that there were only four fighters that could have been tasked. According to Scoggins, there were at least sixteen.

In any case, *Washington Post* military reporter Steve Vogel (whose history of the Pentagon was quoted earlier) has provided additional information about Andrews, writing: "Unlike other Guard units, the D.C. Guard reports to the president, not a governor. And the 113th Wing works closely with Secret Service agents across the runway in the Air Force One hangar."[136] This makes sense: If one of the main purposes of the Air National Guard at Andrews is to protect the White House and Air Force One, then the Guard would take orders to scramble from the Secret Service. The 9/11 Commission, in fact, stated that at 10:42 that morning, fighters were "scrambled out of Andrews, at the request of the Secret Service and outside the military chain of command."[137]

Accordingly, the claim that fighters did not need to come all the way from Langley, made in NPH, has been confirmed.

When we combine this fact with Barbara Riggs' statement, according to which the Secret Service was tracking two planes headed toward Washington, the idea that the Pentagon could not have been protected from Flight 77—assuming here, for the sake of argument, the claim that it was 77 that hit the Pentagon— becomes especially ludicrous. The fighters from Langley were 150 miles from Washington when the Pentagon was struck, the 9/11 Commission claimed, because they were sent out over the ocean by mistake. But even if this story, which I have questioned,[138] were true, the Secret Service could have simply had planes scrambled from Andrews, only about 10 miles away.

The idea that fighters should have been launched from Andrews has, moreover, been explicitly stated by someone who should know—Paul Hellyer, the former minister of national defense of Canada, which shares control of NORAD with the United States. Speaking out of this background, Hellyer asked: "Why did airplanes fly around for an hour and a half without interceptors being scrambled from Andrews? . . . [T]hey should have been there in five minutes or ten minutes."[139]

Still more evidence that Washington had its own defenses, rather than being dependent solely on the fighter jets at distant Langley, is provided by the description of the "principal missions" of Davison Army Airfield:

> [T]o operate a "Class A" Army Airfield on a 24-hour basis, maintain a readiness posture in support of contingency plans, provide aviation support for the White House, US government officials, Department of Defense, Department of the Army, and other government agencies . . . ; and exercise operational control of this airspace.[140]
>
> Davison, which is about 12 miles south of the Pentagon, is equipped with both fixed-wing aircraft and UH1 and UH60 military helicopters [Hueys and Black Hawks].[141]

Inherent Implausibility: Besides being contradicted by many prior reports, the 9/11 Commission's new story about Flight 77, based on the NORAD tapes, is inherently implausible. Implicit in this new story is the claim that NORAD, in reporting that it had been notified about Flight 77 at 9:24, had lied. Kean and Hamilton explicitly made this claim in their 2006 book, speaking of "willful concealment" and adding: "Fog of war. . . could not explain why. . . NORAD officials advanced an account of 9/11 that was untrue."[142] But this charge implied that the military had told a completely irrational lie.

According to the 9/11 Commission, the blame for the attack on the Pentagon belonged entirely to the FAA, because it failed to notify the military about Flight 77's hijacking. If that were indeed the truth, the military would have had absolutely no reason to lie about it. If the military really had not been notified until after the Pentagon was hit, why would its officers, in issuing "NORAD's Response Times" on September 18, 2001, have said that it had been notified at 9:24, thereby inviting the charge that it had, whether through criminal complicity or merely massive incompetence, failed to prevent the attack on the Pentagon? That would have been a completely unmotivated lie. We can imagine that the military would have lied to protect itself from charges of incompetence or complicity. We cannot imagine that it would have told a lie that would needlessly invite such charges.

For these and other reasons discussed elsewhere,[143] the 9/11 Commission's new story about Flight 77 must be considered false. Insofar as this story was based on the tapes the Commission received from NORAD, those tapes must have been doctored. We will see further grounds for this conclusion in the following chapter.

WHY WAS THE PENTAGON NOT EVACUATED?

Pentagon officials, as we saw in NPH, claimed that they did not have the building evacuated because they had no idea that an aircraft was headed their way. Damning evidence to the contrary was provided not only in reports summarized above but also by Secretary of Transportation Norman Mineta's report, quoted in NPH's Afterword, that Vice President Cheney had been informed, prior to the Pentagon attack, that an aircraft was headed toward Washington. Can anyone believe that if Cheney knew this, Rumsfeld did not?

The Commission's Treatment of Mineta's Report: It is instructive to see what the 9/11 Commission did with this report. Mineta said that he had arrived in the PEOC at about 9:20AM, at which time Cheney was already there, and that the conversation about the incoming flight occurred at about 9:25 or 9:26. The 9/11 Commission, however, claimed that Cheney did not arrive until almost 10:00, "perhaps at 9:58."[144] Mineta's testimony to the contrary was simply ignored in *The 9/11 Commission Report.* It was also removed from the 9/11 Commission's video archive.[145] Mineta's testimony can, nevertheless, be viewed on the Internet.[146] Also available is an informal 2007 interview in which Mineta reaffirmed that Vice President Cheney was already there when he arrived in the PEOC and then added, "so was Mrs. Cheney."[147] (He thereby contradicted the Commission's claim about her quoted in the following paragraph.)

The Commission claimed that it had evidence for its assertion that Cheney did not arrive in the PEOC until almost 10:00. Referring to the Secret Service timeline, it said that Cheney did not enter the underground corridor leading to the PEOC until

9:37, after which Cheney paused in the corridor to telephone President Bush and then, learning that the Pentagon had been hit, "saw television coverage of the smoke coming from the building." The Commission then said: "The Secret Service logged Mrs. Cheney's arrival at the White House and she joined her husband in the tunnel. According to contemporaneous notes, at 9:55 the Vice President was still on the phone with the President. . . . After the call ended, Mrs. Cheney and the Vice President moved from the tunnel to the shelter conference room."[148]

However, after having made these claims, the Commission admitted, in a note in the back of the book, that the Secret Service told it in 2004 that "the 9:37 entry time in their timeline was based on alarm data, which is no longer retrievable."[149] Furthermore, in 2008, in response to a FOIA request for information about the arrival time of Cheney into the PEOC, the Secret Service said: "A review of the Secret Service's systems of records indicated that there are no records or documents pertaining to your requests in Secret Service files."[150] According to official sources, in short, there is no documentation for the 9/11 Commission's claim that Cheney did not enter the corridor until 9:37 and did not reach the PEOC until almost 10:00.

In making this claim, moreover, the Commission ignored other evidence, besides that provided by Mineta, that Cheney had arrived much earlier. Richard Clarke reported that Cheney, Condoleezza Rice, and he himself had a brief meeting shortly after 9:03, following which the Secret Service wanted Cheney and Rice to go down to the PEOC. Rice, however, first went with Clarke to the White House's Video Teleconferencing Center, where Clarke was to set up a video conference, which began at about 9:10. After spending a few minutes there, Rice said, according to Clarke: "You're going to need some decisions quickly. I'm going to the PEOC to be with the Vice President. Tell us what you need." At about 9:15, Norman Mineta arrived and Clarke "suggested he join the Vice President."[151] Clarke thereby implied that Cheney was in the PEOC by 9:15.

Additional testimony was provided in an ABC News program on the first anniversary of 9/11. Cheney's White House photographer, David Bohrer, reported that Secret Service agents had come into Cheney's office shortly after 9:00 and said, "Sir, you have to come with us." During this same program, Rice said: "As I was trying to find all of the principals, the Secret Service came in and said, 'You have to leave now for the bunker. The Vice President's already there. There may be a plane headed for the White House.'" ABC's Charles Gibson then said: "In the bunker, the Vice President is joined by Rice and Transportation Secretary Norman Mineta."[152] As this program illustrated, it was common knowledge that Cheney had gone to the bunker quite early, before Mineta arrived.

The 9/11 Commission's account was even contradicted by Cheney himself five days after 9/11. Speaking to Tim Russert on NBC's *Meet the Press*, Cheney said: "[A]fter I talked to the president. . . I went down into. . . the Presidential Emergency Operations Center. . . . [W]hen I arrived there within a short order, we had word the Pentagon's been hit."[153] Cheney himself, therefore, indicated that he had entered the PEOC prior to the Pentagon attack, not 20 minutes after it, (assuming that it happened at 9:38) as the Commission would later claim.

It might be thought, to be sure, that Cheney's statement did not contradict what the 9/11 Commission said, because he did not explicitly say that the Pentagon attack occurred after he had entered the PEOC—he said only that *news of the strike* reached him after he had entered it. However, to use this point to defend the Commission's account would require the implausible assumption that no one had informed Vice President Dick Cheney, the former secretary of defense, about this momentous event until 20 some minutes after it occurred. More important, the 9/11 Commission's account was directly contradicted by Cheney's statement to Russert. As we saw earlier, the Commission said: "He [Cheney] learned in the tunnel that the Pentagon had been hit, and he saw television coverage of the smoke coming from the building."[154] According to the Commission, therefore, *Cheney learned about the Pentagon strike while he was still in the corridor*, but Cheney had told Russert that he learned about it *after he entered the PEOC*. So the Commission, besides contradicting Mineta, Clarke, Bohrer, and Rice, also contradicted Cheney himself.

Finally, besides ignoring all of this contradictory testimony, the Commission also took several other steps to counter Mineta's testimony, which is most naturally construed as his inadvertent report of Cheney's confirmation of a stand-down order. The most important of these steps was the creation of an alternative version of the incoming flight story. According to Mineta, as we saw in the Afterword to NPH, a young man came into the PEOC three times, telling Cheney how far out the plane was. After the third report, the young man asked, "Do the orders still stand?" Cheney replied, "Of course the orders still stand. Have you heard anything to the contrary?" This confirmation was given, Mineta reported, at about 9:25 or 9:26. When we consult *The 9/11 Commission Report*, however, here is what we find:

> At 10:02, the communicators in the shelter began receiving reports from the Secret Service of an inbound aircraft. . . . At some time between 10:10 and 10:15, a military aide told the Vice President and others that the aircraft was 80 miles out. Vice President Cheney was asked for authority to engage the aircraft. . . . The Vice President authorized fighter aircraft to engage the inbound plane. . . . The military aide returned a few minutes later, probably between 10:12 and 10:18, and said the aircraft was 60 miles out. He again asked for authorization to engage. The Vice President again said yes.[155]

According to the 9/11 Commission, therefore, the incoming aircraft story ended with an order for a shoot down, not a stand down. By placing it after 10:10, moreover, the Commission, besides disassociating it from the Pentagon strike, also ruled out the possibility that Cheney's shootdown authorization might have led to the downing of United Flight 93, which had crashed, according to the Commission, at 10:03. (This latter point is discussed more fully in the next chapter.)

Accordingly, the Commission's treatment of Norman Mineta's testimony provides one of the clearest examples of its attempts to cover up the truth, which in this case involved Cheney's presence in the PEOC during a crucial 45-minute period, during which he apparently confirmed a stand-down order.[156]

Ear-Witness Testimony of a Stand-Down Order from the White House: Charles E. Lewis, who had worked on security systems at Los Angeles International Airport (LAX) shortly before 9/11, has provided a written statement saying that, on the morning of 9/11, he overheard LAX Security officials discussing a stand-down order.[157] Lewis wrote:

> Although I was no longer employed at LAX on September 11, 2001, I had worked there until about two months before as the Quality Control Manager for Kiewit Pacific Construction on the Taxiway "C" project. A large part of my work involved security in the Air Port Operations, or APO (but now called the "Airport Operations Area," or "AOA"), which is where the planes are. . . .
>
> On the morning of 9/11, I was working. . . only a few minutes by car from where I had worked at LAX. When I realized, after the second strike on the WTC, that the country was under attack, I decided that I should return to the APO, because I was one of only a few persons who would know how to fix certain parts of the new security systems if problems developed. Especially crucial were the systems at Guard Post II, for which I had managed the design changes and construction. So, after [closing down the job where I was working], I rushed to LAX Guard Post II. Arriving at about 6:35AM (PDT), I explained my purpose for being there to the Security Guards. I then heard some very interesting things.
>
> As on other days, there was "chatter" on LAX Security walkie-talkies and I could easily hear what Security was saying. . . . On some of the walkie-talkies, I could hear both sides of the conversations, on others only one. I do not know who was at the other end of the walkie-talkies, but I assumed that it was LAX Security dispatch or command.
>
> At first, LAX Security was very upset because it seemed to Security that none of the FAA's Air Traffic Controllers (ATCs) tracking the hijacked airliners had notified NORAD as required. More chatter revealed that ATCs had notified NORAD, but that NORAD had not responded, because it had been "ordered to stand down."
>
> This report made Security even more upset, so they tried to find out who had issued that order. A short time later the word came down that the order had come "from the highest level of the White House." Security was puzzled and very upset by this

and made attempts to get more details and clarification, but these were not forthcoming while I was still there.[158]

The "highest level of the White House" would probably have meant Cheney, especially given the fact that, with Bush away, he was clearly in charge.

Although Lewis had, at my request, written up this statement in 2005, I did not publish it because he was not willing to have his name revealed.[159] He was planning to return to work at LAX and feared that, if his authorship of this statement became known, he would lose his security clearance and hence his ability to work there. And I felt that his account, if given anonymously, would be widely dismissed, because there would be no way for anyone to check his credentials and otherwise corroborate his story. By 2008, however, Lewis had decided that it was so important to make the truth about 9/11 known that he should openly tell his story, even though this might prevent future employment.[160]

Lewis's statement points to several people and other sources of information that could corroborate his account of what he overheard. The most interesting of these involves a private conversation he had in 2006 with Captain LaPonda Fitchpatrick of the Los Angeles Airport Police (LAWAPD), head of security in the Airport Operations Area. Lewis wrote: "I told her that I heard everything Security was discussing on 9/11 at Guard Post II and that I did not see how the attacks could have succeeded without inside participation. She replied that LAX security was well aware that 9/11 was an inside job."[161]

Lewis's testimony about what he heard LAX Security officials saying provides support for the most natural inference to draw from Mineta's statement about the conversation that he heard between Cheney and the young man, namely, that although Washington officials knew that an aircraft was approaching the capital, there were orders, confirmed by Cheney, not to shoot it down.

The E-4B: The claim that the Pentagon was not aware of an approaching aircraft has been further undermined by a recent revelation that, during the attack on the Pentagon, an E-4B, which is a US Air Force plane with extraordinary command and communication capacities, was flying over Washington. According to the official story, Flight 77 executed a 330-degree downward spiral before crashing into the Pentagon, and the execution of this spiral, as mentioned earlier, took 3 minutes and 2 seconds.[162] If it were generally known that an E-4B was flying over the White House, only a few miles away, the claim that no one in the Pentagon knew that an aircraft was approaching would become completely implausible.

Perhaps unsurprisingly, therefore, the Pentagon has denied that the plane seen over the White House was a military plane. In 2006, Congressman Adam Schiff (D-CA), having been made aware of the reported aircraft over Washington by one of his constituents, wrote a letter to the Pentagon on behalf of this constituent, who had requested information about the aircraft. A letter of reply to Schiff from the US Air Force, dated November 8, 2006, said:

> This is in reply to your inquiry on behalf of [your constituent] regarding his request for information relating to an unidentified aircraft that may have been in restricted airspace near the White House on September 11, 2001 between the hours of 9:30–10:30AM.
>
> Air Force officials have no knowledge of the aircraft in question.[163]

Close to a year later, that denial was shown to be false. On September 12, 2007, John King gave a report on CNN's *Anderson Cooper 360°* featuring a video clip with a clear image of the airplane flying over the White House. Pointing out that the plane was "a four-engine jet banking slowly in the nation's most off-limits airspace," King said that "still today, no one will offer an official explanation of what we saw."[164] However, King added: "Two government sources familiar with the incident tell CNN it was a military aircraft. They say the details are classified." Next, confirming what Congressman Adam Schiff had learned ten months earlier, King added: "Ask the Pentagon, and it insists this is not a military aircraft."[165]

King then presented decisive evidence to the contrary. Showing two pictures side by side, King said:

This comparison of the CNN video and an official Air Force photo suggests the mystery plane is among the military's most sensitive aircraft, an Air Force E-4B. Note the flag on the tail, the stripe around the fuselage, and the telltale bubble just behind the 747 cockpit area.[166]

CNN then played footage showing retired US Air Force Major General Don Shepperd endorsing this identification.[167]

Given the identification of the plane as an E4-B, the crucial question becomes: Was it over the White House before the attack on the Pentagon? Evidence suggests that it was.

The full video, from which CNN played brief segments during its report, is 18 minutes long. At 6 minutes 20 seconds into the video, the camera, panning upward, caught the E-4B in the sky and stayed focused on it for 29 seconds. Over two minutes later, at 8 minutes and 40 seconds into the video, smoke is suddenly seen behind the White House, and the conversations of some men talking on cell phones show that they have just been informed of the strike on the Pentagon. This video shows, therefore, that the E-4B was already flying above Washington about two minutes and 20 seconds before the Pentagon attack.[168]

Additional evidence was provided in a CNN report that appeared two days after 9/11. According to this report, Brig. General Clyde Vaughn of the US Army, director of military support, said that the attack on the Pentagon occurred a few minutes after he had seen an airplane "loitering over Georgetown, in a high, left-hand bank."[169]

Furthermore, a report that same day (September 13) on England's Channel 4 television station stated: "Just before the crash [of AA 77], . . . there were reports of a military plane circling the US capital. Moments later, the Department of Defense was hit."[170]

It seems undeniable, therefore, that one of the US Air Force's E-4Bs was flying over Washington prior to the attack on the Pentagon. The fact that Pentagon officials have tried to deny this shows that something very threatening to the official story is being covered up.

The Helicopter: The idea of Pentagon ignorance is also undermined by a credible report that a helicopter was flying over the Pentagon just before the fireball erupted. Speaking from the Pentagon at 9:42 that morning, Chris Plant, a CNN producer, said that many people had reported an explosion. He then added:

> I was told by one witness, an Air Force. . . senior enlisted man, that he was outside when it occurred. He said that he saw a helicopter circle the building. He said it appeared to be a US military helicopter, and that it disappeared behind the building where the helicopter landing zone is. . . and he then saw a fireball go into the sky.

Later, indicating that more than one person reported seeing the helicopter, he said:

> [I]nitial reports from witnesses indicate that there was in fact a helicopter circling the building, contrary to what the AP reported, according to the witnesses I've spoken to anyway, and that this helicopter disappeared behind the building, and that there was then an explosion.[171]

It would appear that Pentagon officials have not been forthcoming about aircraft they had in the air prior to the attack on the Pentagon.

A Warning to Fairfax Hospital: The claim that the Pentagon had no idea of an approaching aircraft becomes still more impossible to believe in light of the following report in *Pentagon 9/11*:

> Even before the plane hit the Pentagon, in accordance with established procedure the Dulles Air Traffic Control Tower notified Fairfax Hospital, the largest in Northern Virginia, that a hijacked aircraft was missing, alerting Dr. Thomas Mayer, chair of the Department of Emergency Medicine and medical director for Fairfax County Fire and Rescue. Mayer recalled: "We knew that something was headed towards the national capital area. We didn't know where. But we knew we needed to get ready. So we immediately went on disaster planning mode."[172]

It would be difficult to believe that the Pentagon would have remained ignorant while the hospital was informed.

If we must conclude that the official account of what happened at the Pentagon is false, do we have any basis for saying what really did happen? Given the contradictory evidence, no complete answer will likely be possible until there is a genuine investigation. But a window into what really happened has perhaps been provided by April Gallop, whose testimony about seeing no airplane debris was quoted earlier.

April Gallop's Testimony: Gallop, who was a US Army executive administrative assistant with top security clearance, had just returned to work on the morning of September 11 after a two-month maternity leave. Having brought her baby son, Elisha, with her, she was planning to take him to the day-care center. She was told, however, that there was some paper work she needed to take care of immediately, and she was allowed to take him with her to her work station, which was in the secure area, without getting him cleared.

Her work station was in the Army administrative offices in the E ring of Wedge 2.[173] Her desk, she was later told, was only 35 to 45 feet from the impact site. (According to the official story, it should be recalled, Flight 77 entered Wedge 1 at an angle, so that it quickly entered Wedge 2.) As soon as Gallop pushed the button to start her computer, she said, she heard a huge "boom," which "sounded like a bomb." Whatever it was, it made the ceiling cave in, covering her and her son with debris, which caused several injuries to them.[174]

After she regained consciousness and found her son, she picked him up and, with some help from others, got outside. Although she went out the so-called impact hole, she found no evidence that a plane had hit the Pentagon.

> I had no jet fuel on me. . . . I didn't see any airplane seats. I didn't see any plane parts. . . . I didn't see anything that would give me any idea that there was a plane. . . . I didn't see anything on the lawn. . . . I didn't see luggage, metal pieces.[175]

Later, knowing that she had had a traumatic experience, including an injury to her head, Gallop checked with other people who had been there, but "they did not see anything of this nature as well." Indeed, she added: "I have not talked to anyone yet who said that [they saw evidence of a plane]."[176]

Asked by Barbara Honegger—who conducted the interview on which this account is based—if she saw any fire, Gallop said: "Coming out of the computers. There were flames coming out of . . . the computers." (A woman in the D ring named Tracy Webb, interestingly, reported that her "computer burst into flames."[177]) Gallop was certain, however, that there was no fire on the floor. Pointing out that she had lost one of her shoes, she said that she did not feel anything hot with her bare foot.[178]

This account is difficult to reconcile, of course, with the view that an airliner with thousands of gallons of jet fuel crashed into the Pentagon and exploded. But it is consistent with photographs showing that in the first few minutes after the attack, there was no big fire at the alleged crash site.[179]

While Gallop was in the hospital, she added, a team of representatives from the various services came to see her. When they asked what she thought had happened, she replied that she thought that her computer had triggered a bomb. The Army representative, stating that he was going to let her know what really happened, told her that a plane had hit the Pentagon.[180]

Support for Gallop's View: Whether or not Gallop's belief that her computer triggered an explosion is true, her conviction that one or more bombs had gone off in the Pentagon was shared by other people who were there. Army Lt. Colonel Victor Correa said: "We thought it was some kind of explosion. That somehow someone got in here and planted bombs because we saw these holes."[181] Steve Vogel, while supporting the official view, wrote that there was much confusion: "Some thought a bomb had exploded; almost no one understood the building had been hit by a plane."[182] According to *Pentagon 9/11*, when Lt. Nancy McKeown heard an explosion and saw ceiling tiles coming down, she yelled "Bomb!"[183] Moreover, Michael J. Nielsen, who was a civilian auditor for the Department of the Army on temporary assignment at the Pentagon, told Barbara Honegger that, after he heard an explosion and felt the building shake, hundreds of panicked Pentagon personnel ran down the corridor outside his office toward the south entrance yelling "Bombs!" and "A bomb went off!"[184]

The conclusion that the explosions really were caused by bombs is supported by the fact that some witnesses said they smelled cordite, a substance that is used in bombs and has a very distinctive smell, completely different from that of jet fuel. One such witness was Gilah Goldsmith, an attorney at the Pentagon. After hearing an "incredible whomp noise," she saw a "huge black cloud of smoke," adding that it smelled like cordite or gun smoke.[185] Don Perkal, the deputy general counsel for the secretary of defense, wrote:

> People shouted in the corridor outside [my office] that a bomb had gone off. . . . Even before stepping outside I could smell the cordite. Then I knew explosives had been set off somewhere.[186]

The conclusion that bombs went off is also supported by reports of death and destruction in the B and A rings, which were further inside the building than the C ring, beyond which the airliner reportedly did not go. (As we saw earlier, Donald Rumsfeld had claimed that Flight 77's nose cone, after creating the hole in the C ring, was still there.) A *Washington Post* story the day after the event said:

> The attack destroyed at least four of the five "rings" that spiral around the massive office building. . . . A 38-year-old Marine major. . . said he and dozens of his colleagues rushed to the area in the Pentagon that appeared most heavily damaged—the B ring between the 4th and 5th corridors.[187]

If all the damage was due to an airliner, which crashed into the E ring and did not travel past the C ring, why would the B ring have suffered severe damage? Why, moreover, would there have been deaths in the A ring? But such deaths there were, according to Robert Andrews, the then acting assistant secretary of defense for special operations, whose statement to Barbara Honegger about Rumsfeld's participation in the White House video conference was mentioned earlier. Andrews also told Honegger that after he and his aide felt the effects of some violent event while they were in the counterterrorism center and started rushing back to the other side of the Pentagon to join Rumsfeld, they entered the corridor on the A ring and found that they "had to walk over dead bodies."[188]

As to *when* the bombs exploded, April Gallop reports that her watch, which she still has, stopped just after 9:30.[189] Roughly this time—as opposed to almost 9:38 (9:37:46), the official time of the Pentagon attack—is supported by other people and other time-pieces. Robert Andrews reported that the violent event that occurred while he was in the counterterrorism center was at about 9:32. (Although his watch actually said 9:35, he kept it a few minutes fast in order to get to meetings on time.[190] It is likewise possible that Gallop's watch was a minute or two slow.) The caption of a photograph taken by the Pentagon Renewal (PENREN) project reads: "The Pentagon after it was attacked by a hijacked jet at 9:30AM."[191] An FAA timeline put out six days after 9/11 placed the Pentagon attack at 9:32.[192] Even Alberto Gonzales, who was then the White House counsel, said during an August 2002 lecture: "The Pentagon was attacked at 9:32."[193] Finally, two clocks—one that was placed in the Smithsonian Museum of American History and one that is shown on the US Navy website[194]—stopped at about 9:32.

The conclusion that bombs went off says nothing one way or the other about the idea that this part of the Pentagon was struck by an aircraft of some sort. As discussed below, there were reports that it was hit by a missile. Some researchers point to evidence that it was hit by a Global Hawk or an A3 Skywarrior, and some believe it was hit by one of those plus a missile. The point at hand, however, is simply that the evidence for internal explosions at about 9:32 is not necessarily in conflict with the idea that the Pentagon was attacked from the outside. Indeed, if the attack at the Pentagon involved both explosives and an aircraft of some sort, it would parallel the attacks on the Twin Towers.

Why the First Floor of Wedges 1 and 2? If, as the evidence suggests, the Pentagon attack was self-inflicted, the question arises as to why the attack was where it was: Wedge 1 and Wedge 2, especially the first floor (92 of the 125 people inside the Pentagon who were killed were on the first floor).[195] As we saw, Wedge 1 was the only part of the Pentagon that would have presented physical obstacles to an attacking airliner. As we also saw, the first floor would have been the most difficult floor for an airliner to hit, especially by an amateur pilot. The official trajectory was, in fact, impossible to execute, given the VDOT antenna. So why would Pentagon officials have chosen to explode bombs in that part of the Pentagon and then claim that it was struck by a hijacked airliner? There must have been some motive other than simply wanting to claim that the Pentagon had been struck.

One suggested answer puts together two facts: First, the day before 9/11, Secretary of Defense Rumsfeld stated at a press conference that the Pentagon was missing $2.3 trillion dollars.[196] Second, one of the most damaged areas was the Army's financial management/audit area. This combination of facts has led Barbara Honegger to ask: "Were the auditors who could 'follow the money,' and the computers whose data could help them do it, intentionally targeted?"[197]

According to Honegger, she discussed this issue with Michael Nielsen, the aforementioned civilian auditor for the Army—who in fact was working in the Operations Office of the Army's Financial Management Branch and probably survived only because he had gone back to his own (temporary) office shortly before the attack, which killed most of the people in the Operations Office. When she asked Nielsen whether he believed that the Operations Office might have been targeted because of the missing money, he replied in the affirmative, according to Honegger, adding that the records there were, in fact, destroyed.[198] In any case, this hypothesis is one that should be considered if and when a true investigation takes place.

The idea that the Pentagon attack was "self-inflicted," I should add, requires qualification. If the Pentagon attack was engineered by General Richard Myers and other Air Force officers, they did not attack their own personnel: All the victims were either in, or worked for, the Army or the Navy.[199]

In any case, the suspicion that Pentagon officials did want people in that area to die has been increased—unintentionally, I assume—by Steve Vogel. On the same page of *The Pentagon* on which he pointed out that, after people at the Pentagon learned about the New York attacks, they realized that, "if there were more attacks, the Pentagon was an obvious target," he wrote: "The

National Military Command Center learned at 9:31AM that a hijacked airplane was reported to be Washington-bound. But no steps were taken to alert Pentagon employees or evacuate the building."[200]

In saying this, Vogel was presupposing the official story, according to which the Pentagon was attacked only by an airplane and that this attack did not occur until almost 9:38. Within the framework of that story, the fact that no alarms went off before the attacks creates a big problem.

But whenever the attacks occurred, the absence of alarms is suspicious. It has been mentioned by several people. For example, Don Perkal, whose testimony about smelling cordite was quoted above, said that even after people started shouting that a bomb had gone off, "[n]o alarms sounded."[201] The absence of alarms has been especially emphasized by April Gallop, who said there were "no alerts, no warnings, no alarms."[202] This was strange, she observed, because prior to 9/11 there had been random "drill exercises utilizing an alarm for us to evacuate the building." She had, in fact, become "disgusted at the frequency of [these] random drill exercises." And yet, "on that particular day, no alarm." This was especially odd, she added, "considering the fact of what had already taken place at the World Trade Center."[203]

MEYSSAN'S THEORY

Thierry Meyssan's belief that the Pentagon was hit by a missile has been widely, almost universally, rejected and ridiculed. But it has not been completely devoid of support. Having quoted Lon Rains, the editor at *Space News*, in NPH, I will here give his more complete statement. As he was headed north on I-395, he wrote:

> [T]he traffic slowed to a crawl just in front of the Pentagon. . . [which was] to the left of my van. . . . At that moment I heard a very loud, quick whooshing sound that began behind me and stopped suddenly in front of me and to my left. In fractions of a second I heard the impact and an explosion. The next thing I saw was the fireball. I was convinced it was a missile. It came in so fast it sounded nothing like an airplane.[204]

Second-hand testimony in support of this view has come from David E. Edwards, professor of anthropology at Salisbury University in Maryland. He has written that on the morning of 9/11, he was going to Capitol Hill for a 10:00AM meeting. Just after he transferred to an Orange Line subway car at L'Enfant Station, a young couple burst in and started shouting: "We saw a missile fly into the Pentagon! We saw it, we saw it!" They then kept repeating their claim (saying things such as: "A missile, we saw it, a missile, it flew right into the Pentagon. I can't believe it. Now it's on fire, there's smoke!"), Edwards reported, until he got off the train at Capitol South Station.[205]

Still another second-hand report has come from Charles Lewis, whose statement about hearing LAX Security officials learn that there had been a stand-down order, issued by the White House, was quoted earlier. Having explained that it was about 6:35AM (9:35 EDT) when he arrived at the place where the Security officials were, Lewis also wrote:

> Another piece of information that I heard, shortly after my arrival, was that the Pentagon had been "hit by a rocket." It's possible that the word was "missile," although I'm quite certain it was "rocket." I was, in any case, quite surprised when I later got home and learned that the media were reporting that an *airliner* had hit the Pentagon.[206]

Whatever be the truth of the matter, the essential part of Thierry Meyssan's theory, as I emphasized in NPH's Afterword, was not the claim that the Pentagon was struck by a missile. It was the two-fold claim that the striking aircraft could not have been a Boeing 757 and that it must have instead been a military aircraft of some sort.

Anti-Aircraft Batteries? Part of the reason for the latter claim was that unless the aircraft had a military transponder, it should have been shot down by the Pentagon's anti-aircraft system. When I asked Meyssan about the source of his information that the Pentagon did indeed have an anti-aircraft system prior to 9/11, he replied: "The presence of these anti-missile batteries was testified to me by French officers to whom they were shown during an official visit to the Pentagon. This was later confirmed to me by a

Saudi officer."[207] Evidence for such an anti-aircraft system has also been supplied by other people familiar with the Pentagon.[208]

The Pentagon has, to be sure, denied that it had any anti-aircraft batteries at that time. "Unlike the White House," said a Pentagon official on 9/11 itself, "the Pentagon has no anti-aircraft batteries to defend against attacks from the air." Why? Because the Pentagon had thought them "too costly and too dangerous to surrounding residential areas."[209] But can anyone seriously believe that Pentagon officials would have let such considerations prevent them from protecting themselves? If such considerations did not prevent anti-aircraft missiles from being installed at the White House, why would they have prevented their installation at the Pentagon?

In another story published that same day, Rear Admiral Craig Quigley, serving as a Pentagon spokesman, reportedly said that the Pentagon had no anti-aircraft defense system *that he was aware of*.[210] But can we believe that a senior officer in the Pentagon, qualified to serve as a spokesman, could have been uncertain about such a crucial matter?

One more consideration is the fact that the Pentagon has regularly been described as an exceptionally safe building. For example, April Gallop has reported that while taking a classified tour after being assigned to the Pentagon, she was told that it was the safest and best-defended building in the world.[211] On 9/11 itself, Paul Gonzales, a supervisor in the comptroller's office, "had confidently declared that the Pentagon was probably the safest building in the world."[212] How could people have considered the Pentagon the best-defended building in the world if it, unlike the White House, did not have anti-aircraft missiles?

A 9:32 Strike? In any case, if some sort of military aircraft did hit the Pentagon, and if this occurred at about 9:32 instead of 9:38, this would resolve another anomaly. As we saw earlier, Norman Mineta estimated that the conversation in the PEOC, in which Cheney was told by a young man that an aircraft was "10 miles out," occurred at about "9:25 or 9:26." That is also about the time that a fast-moving blip was originally said to have been spotted by Danielle O'Brien and other air traffic controllers at Dulles Airport (as mentioned in NPH). If this aircraft was going over 500 miles an hour and hence almost 10 miles a minute, why would it have not struck the Pentagon until almost 9:38? The downward spiral taken by the aircraft did, to be sure, reportedly take 3 minutes and 2 seconds. But factoring in that time would not bring us close to 9:38.

The 9/11 Commission avoided this problem by stating, as mentioned at the outset of this chapter, that the Dulles air traffic controllers spotted the fast-moving aircraft at 9:32. But how did the Commission arrive at this time? News reports shortly after 9/11 said that the aircraft was spotted at 9:25, or at least prior to 9:30.[213] The 9/11 Commission cited no contemporary news reports to support the 9:32 time but merely a single interview.[214]

It would appear that the Commission reached the 9:32 time by starting with the official strike time of 9:37:46 and then subtracting 5 minutes and 46 seconds, thereby allowing 2 minutes and 44 seconds for the aircraft to reach Washington plus the 3 minutes and 2 seconds for the downward spiral. The only support for the 9:32 time, in other words, seems to be the fact that it makes plausible the idea that the aircraft spotted by the Dulles controllers struck the Pentagon shortly before 9:38.

What happens if we accept the Commission's calculations while returning to the time at which the aircraft was originally said to have been spotted—a few minutes before 9:30? If we, for example, took Mineta's estimated time of "9:25 or 9:26" and then added the Commission's 5 minutes and 46 seconds, we would get a strike time of 9:30:46 or 9:31:46—the latter of which is virtually the time of one of the stopped clocks.[215]

To suggest that the Pentagon was struck by an aircraft at about this time, and hence at about the same time as bombs exploded, would, of course, be merely a speculative suggestion. Whether it is true could be determined only through a genuine investigation. In the meantime, this suggestion provides a possible way of fitting together the Dulles radar evidence, Mineta's testimony, and the evidence that the Pentagon attack(s) occurred shortly after 9:30.

SUMMARY

As the above discussion shows, the case against the official account of Flight 77 and the Pentagon has become considerably stronger since the publication of NPH. This case now includes the following points:

(1) The absence of damage, debris, and a seismic signal consistent with the crash of a Boeing 757.

(2) The government's failure to provide security camera videos or the serial numbers from time-change parts and the flight data recorder to prove that the Pentagon was struck by Flight 77.

(3) The fact that the purported eyewitness support for the Boeing 757 theory, including the 9/11 Commission's claim about the C-130 pilot, lacks credibility.

(4) The fact that the government's claims about many issues— the Barbara Olson phone calls, the C-ring hole, the whereabouts of Donald Rumsfeld and General Myers and other claims supporting the military's ignorance of FAA reports about Flight 77, the lack of alert fighters at Andrews, the failure to evacuate the Pentagon, the denial of the military ownership of the white plane over the White House, the time of Dick Cheney's entrance into the underground bunker, and evidently even the time of the attack—have proven to be false.

(5) Norman Mineta's testimony and its suppression by the 9/11 Commission.

(6) The fact that foreign hijackers would not have chosen to attack Wedge 1.

(7) The evidence that bombs went off inside the Pentagon.

(8) The fact that the official story is simply impossible for the twofold reason that Hani Hanjour could not have flown a Boeing 757 into the Pentagon's first floor and that Flight 77's alleged trajectory would have been impossible even for an expert pilot.

The case against the official story of the Pentagon attack is, therefore, now about as strong as that against the official accounts of Flights 11, 175, and the World Trade Center—which is very strong indeed. The 9/11 truth community's exposé of the falsity of these accounts is now so compelling that it can be disputed only by ignoring this community's evidence and arguments.

3. Flight 93: Additional Evidence against the Official Story

Although most of the material in NPH's third chapter has stood the test of time, especially the discussion of the crash site and the witness testimony, additional evidence has forced a reconsideration of the overall thrust of that chapter, which was based on the assumption that phone calls from the plane gave us insight into what happened on board. Additional evidence has made that assumption doubtful.

Cell Phone Calls from United 93?

Many of the passengers on United Flight 93 were reported to have made cell phone calls to relatives. The idea that these calls gave us some understanding of what happened on Flight 93 was stated five days after 9/11 in a *Washington Post* article by David Maraniss, who said:

> The plane was at once a lonesome vessel, the people aboard facing their singular fate, and yet somehow already attached to the larger drama, connected again by cell phones. People on the plane learned about what had happened in New York and sent word back the other way about what was happening to them.[1]

These cell phone calls provided the most widely publicized evidence for the existence of hijackers on this flight. Maraniss wrote:

> Thomas E. Burnett Jr., a California businessman, called his wife, Deena, four times. In the first call, he described the hijackers and said they had stabbed a passenger and that his wife should contact authorities. In the second call, he said the passenger had died and that he and some others on board were going to do something about it.[2]

An earlier *Washington Post* story, published September 13, had said:

> As United Airlines Flight 93 entered its last desperate moments
> in the sky, passenger Jeremy Glick used a cell phone to tell his
> wife, Lyzbeth, . . . that the Boeing 757's cockpit had been taken
> over by three Middle Eastern-looking men wielding knives and
> a red box they claimed was a bomb. The terrorists, wearing red
> headbands, had ordered the pilots, flight attendants and
> passengers to the rear of the plane. . . . Glick said he and others
> aboard the plane had decided to rush the cockpit and try to
> subdue the terrorists.[3]

A few days later, a story in the *Pittsburgh Post-Gazette* about
passenger Marion Britton said:

> She called longtime friend Fred Fiumano, from whom she had
> borrowed a cell phone. She said the plane had been hijacked,
> they had slit the throats of two people and the plane had made
> a U-turn.[4]

One of the flight attendants was also reported to have made a cell
phone call. A story entitled "Flight Attendant Helped Fight
Hijackers," discussing a "cellular phone conversation" between
Sandra Bradshaw and her husband, said:

> Bradshaw said he took his wife's call about 9:30 AM. . . . "Have
> you seen what's happening? Have you heard?" Sandy asked her
> husband in a calm voice. "We've been hijacked.". . . She said
> the plane had been taken over by three men with knives. She
> had gotten a close look at one of the hijackers. . . . "He had an
> Islamic look," she told her husband.[5]

From these press reports, therefore, the American people were
informed that Flight 93 had been hijacked by men who looked not
only "Middle Eastern" but even "Islamic."

According to these press reports, as we have seen, much of
this information came from cell phone calls. But were these
reported cell phone calls really made? Could they have been made?

Cell Phone Technology: When I wrote NPH, I had not taken into
account the evidence that, given the technology available in 2001,
high-altitude cell phone calls from airliners would have been
impossible, or at least virtually so (most of the reported calls from

United 93 would have definitely been high-altitude calls, as they were reportedly made when the plane was between 34,300 and 40,700 feet[6]). There were three problems. First, a cell phone had to complete a "handshake" with a cellsite, and this took several seconds, so cell phones in high-speed planes would have had trouble staying connected to a cellsite long enough to complete a call. Second, the signals were sent out horizontally, from cellsite to cellsite, not vertically. Although there was some leakage upward, the system was not designed to reach cell phones at high altitudes.[7] Third, receiving a signal was made even more difficult by the insulation provided by the large mass of an airliner.

Canadian mathematician and scientist A. K. Dewdney, who had long written a column for *Scientific American*, conducted some experiments with single- and double-engine airplanes to test the likelihood of successful cell phone calls from high altitudes. He found that in a single-engine plane, successful calls could be counted on only under 2,000 feet. Above that altitude, they became increasingly unlikely. At 20,000 feet, Dewdney concluded, "the chance of a typical cellphone call making it to ground and engaging a cellsite there is less than one in a hundred. . . . [T]he probability that two callers will succeed is less than one in ten thousand." The likelihood of nine successful calls at that altitude, he concluded, would be "infinitesimal."[8] And yet there had allegedly been, according to one count, nine cell phone calls from Flight 93 while it was above 30,000 feet.[9]

In later experiments using a twin-engine plane, which has greater mass and hence provides greater insulation from electronic signals than a single-engine plane, Dewdney found that the success rate decayed to 0 percent at 7,000 feet.[10] A large airliner, having much greater mass, would provide far greater insulation—a fact, Dewdney added, that "is very much in harmony with many anecdotal reports. . . that in large passenger jets, one loses contact during takeoff, frequently before the plane reaches 1000 feet altitude."[11] Dewdney concluded, therefore, that numerous successful cellphone calls from airliners flying above 30,000 feet would have been "flat out impossible."[12] Many passengers and flight attendants have provided anecdotal evidence that supports this conclusion.[13]

In 2004, Qualcomm announced a successful demonstration of a fundamentally new kind of cell phone technology, involving a "picocell," that would allow passengers "to place and receive calls as if they were on the ground." American Airlines announced that this new technology was expected to be commercially available in 2006.[14] This technology in fact first became available on commercial flights (in European planes) in March 2008.[15]

The evidence is very strong, therefore, that most if not all of the alleged cell phone calls from Flight 93 would have been impossible.

Voice Morphing Technology: When I wrote NPH, I was also unaware of the fact that another technology, voice morphing, was sufficiently advanced to explain the alleged cell phone calls from passengers and flight attendants. In a 1999 *Washington Post* article, William Arkin wrote: "By taking just a 10-minute digital recording of [anyone's] voice," voice morphing experts can "clone speech patterns and develop an accurate facsimile," causing people to appear to have said things that they "would never otherwise have said." To illustrate, Arkin described a demonstration in which the voice of General Carl Steiner, former Commander-in-Chief of the US Special Operations Command, said: "Gentlemen! We have called you together to inform you that we are going to overthrow the United States government."[16]

Pointing out that this new technology could be used equally by Hollywood and by military and intelligence agencies, Arkin wrote: "For Hollywood, it is special effects. For covert operators in the US military and intelligence agencies, it is a weapon of the future." One agency interested in this weapon of the future, Arkin reported, was "the Information Operations department of the National Defense University in Washington, the military's school for information warfare." Adding that video and photo manipulation had already "raised profound questions of authenticity for the journalistic world," teaching it that "seeing isn't necessarily believing," Arkin pointed out that the addition of voice morphing means that "hearing isn't either." He meant, of course, that hearing *shouldn't* be believing, because one now needs to be aware that the voices could have been morphed.

Discussing both of these issues in D9D, I concluded that the reported cell phone calls from passengers on Flight 93 must have been faked.[17]

The FBI Telephone Report: This conclusion was reinforced by the report on phone calls from the four 9/11 airliners provided at the Moussaoui trial in 2006. Although it was widely believed that there had been at least eleven cell phone calls from Flight 93, the FBI reported—both orally at the trial[18] and in an online graphics presentation[19]—that of the thirty-seven calls made from Flight 93, only two of them could confidently be called cell phone calls.[20]

These two calls were said to have been made by passenger Ed Felt calling 911 and flight attendant CeeCee Lyles calling home, both at 9:58AM, when the plane was said to have descended to 5,000 feet. With this declaration, the FBI avoided committing itself to the dubious claim that any high-altitude cell phone conversations had occurred. Although even at 5,000 feet, two successful cell phone calls from an airliner would have been quite unlikely, they would not have been as completely ruled out as nine such calls from over 30,000 feet.

In light of information provided in *The 9/11 Commission Report*, it appears that the FBI's report on phone calls from the airliners submitted as evidence to the Moussaoui trial was partly identical with a report that the FBI had completed by September 20, 2001.[21] But the two reports clearly were not completely identical. For one thing, as we will see in Chapter 6, the FBI changed its report about a reported call from Flight 11 by flight attendant Madeline ("Amy") Sweeney. Having said in 2001 that it was a cell phone call, the FBI in 2004 declared it to have been made from an onboard phone. This change, moreover, was part of a more sweeping change, after which the only two calls from any of the four flights still designated as cell phone calls were the just discussed calls by Felt and Lyles from Flight 93, when it was down to 5,000 feet. The evidence that these changes were made in 2004 is provided by a 9/11 Commission staff report dated August 26, 2004, which I only recently learned about. In this report, the only two calls from Flight 93 referred to as cell phone calls were those 9:58 calls by Felt and Lyles.[22]

In saying this, I am correcting an assertion I had made in previous books, especially in *9/11 Contradictions*, in which I wrote:

> It was passengers on United Flight 93 who were most explicitly said to have made cell phone calls. Even the 9/11 Commission, which had not specifically referred to any of the calls from other flights as cell phone calls, said, in discussing United 93: "Shortly [after 9:32], the passengers and flight crew began a series of calls from GTE airphones and cellular phones."[23]

Although the Commission's statement did not specifically say that some of the calls made at that time, when the plane would have been at a high altitude, were made from cell phones, it did seem to imply it, so my inference was not an unreasonable one. In light of the aforementioned staff report, however, the Commission's statement appears to have been deliberately ambiguous, allowing the Commission to avoid affirming any high-altitude cell phone calls without drawing attention to the fact that the FBI report no longer affirmed any such calls. The press was thereby allowed to continue reporting that passengers had reached loved ones by means of cell phone calls.

In any case, given the fact that the FBI had made this change in 2004, it was prepared, when it had to present evidence in a court of law in 2006, to avoid claiming that any high-altitude cell phone calls had been completed.

Ironically, the FBI presented this report to the Moussaoui trial at about the same time that the film *United 93*, which portrayed several passengers making cell phone calls, came out. This FBI report was also submitted at about the same time that *Popular Mechanics* published its book, *Debunking 9/11 Myths*, which argued that "cell-phone calls from airplanes were possible in 2001—even from extremely high altitudes."[24] *Popular Mechanics* had rushed in where the FBI feared to tread. Both the dramatization in *United 93* and the claim in *Debunking 9/11 Myths* were undermined by the report presented by the FBI at the Moussaoui trial.

Moreover, this FBI report, by avoiding the problem of claiming in court that technologically impossible cell phone calls had been made, created another problem: Why were several people who reported receiving calls from Flight 93 convinced that these calls had been made on cell phones? In some cases, it was evidently because the callers had specifically said that they were using cell phones. In those cases, one might assume that there had been misunderstandings.

But in one case, the reason was evidently more compelling: Deena Burnett, who reported receiving four calls from her husband, Tom Burnett, said that she had recognized his cell phone number on her phone's Caller ID. Besides telling this to journalists and writing it in her book,[25] she said it to FBI interviewers on 9/11 itself. The FBI's recently declassified report of this interview said: "Burnett was able to determine that her husband was using his own cellular telephone because the caller identification showed his number. . . . Only one of the calls did not show on the caller identification as she was on the line with another call."[26]

There were other discrepancies. Whereas Deena Burnett had told the press that she had received four calls from her husband, the FBI report presented at the Moussaoui trial said that Tom Burnett made only three calls.[27] Also, the times she reported for the calls differed somewhat from the times given by the FBI's report to the Moussaoui trial. But these are minor matters, easily accounted for by imperfect memory. Indeed, the FBI summary of its interview with her on 9/11 indicated that she had reported "a series of three to five cellular phone calls from her husband."[28] If she could not remember whether there had been three, four, or five calls, she certainly would not have remembered exactly when the calls occurred. Faulty memory cannot, however, account for the discrepancy with regard to the kind of phone that was used, given her repeated observation of her husband's cell phone number on the caller ID.

Deena Burnett's firm belief that her husband had used his cell phone to call her several times from Flight 93 is contradicted by both the cell phone technology of the time and the FBI report to the Moussaoui trial. But we surely cannot accuse her of either lying or being mistaken with regard to what she experienced. The only possible explanation would seem to be that the calls were faked—an explanation that becomes especially plausible once we know that there are devices that allow deceitful callers to fake other people's Caller ID numbers as well as their voices.[29]

CALLS FROM ONBOARD PHONES?

According to the FBI's report to the Moussaoui trial, we have seen, there were 37 phone calls made from Flight 93, 35 of which were made from onboard phones. Why should we not say that, even if the reported cell phone calls did not occur, the reported calls from these onboard phones, which were entirely possible from a technological point of view, really occurred and hence gave us reliable information about what occurred on Flight 93?

One reason is that, if the reported cell phone calls were faked— a conclusion that is least disputable with regard to the reported cell phone calls to Deena Burnett—this fact provides strong evidence that the reported onboard calls, which were similar in nature and content, were likewise fabricated. Why would any calls have been fabricated if the official story about what happened on Flight 93 were otherwise accurate?

The nature and content of some of the reported calls provide additional reasons for doubting their authenticity. For example, Jack Grandcolas, referring to a call he believed to be from his wife, Lauren Grandcolas, said: "It was really quiet in the background. There wasn't screaming. She sounded calm."[30] Lyz Glick, speaking about the calls she believed to be from her husband, Jeremy, said:

> He was so calm, the plane sounded so calm, that if I hadn't seen what was going on on the TV, I wouldn't have believed it. . . . I was surprised by how calm it seemed in the background. I didn't hear any screaming. I didn't hear any noises. I didn't hear any commotion.[31]

Kathy Hoglan, the aunt of passenger Mark Bingham, said that he sounded "calm, matter-of-fact." His mother, Alice Hoglan, said: "His voice was calm. He seemed very much composed," adding that the passengers' discussion about trying to take control of the plane, which she could hear in the background, sounded like a "calm boardroom meeting."[32] Esther Heyman, referring to a call she believed to be from her stepdaughter, Honor Elizabeth Wainio, said that Elizabeth had been "remarkably calm throughout our whole conversation." According to *New York Times* reporter Jere Longman: "Esther could not hear another person. She could not hear any conversation or crying or yelling or whimpering. Nothing."[33]

In addition to the fact that in some cases both the callers and the cabin seemed too calm, the statements made by some of the callers reeked of inauthenticity. The most notorious case is that of the call purportedly from Mark Bingham, mentioned above. According to Longman's account, after Kathy Hoglan, Mark's aunt, spoke briefly with the caller, she said to her sister-in-law, Alice Hoglan: "Talk to Mark, he's been hijacked," after which Alice said: "Hi, Mark." The caller replied: "Mom, this is Mark Bingham."[34] Would any of us, even in the most stressful situation, identify ourselves to our own mothers by giving our first and last names—especially after our mother had already addressed us by our first name?

Another example is provided by the calls to Deena Burnett, which she believed to be from her husband, Tom Burnett. One suspicious fact is that, except for uttering Deena's name a few times, "Tom" never mentioned a name. For example, when he, in his final call, asked about the children, he simply called them "the kids." That was not terribly surprising, but then when Deena told him that the kids were asking to talk to him, he said: "Tell them I'll talk to them later." This was 20 minutes after he had purportedly realized that the hijackers were on a suicide mission, planning to "crash this plane into the ground," and 10 minutes after he and other passengers had allegedly decided that they must, as soon as they were "over a rural area," try to gain control of the plane.[35] Given the reported fact that the hijackers had already killed one person, the real Tom Burnett would have known that there was a good chance that he would die in the next few minutes, one way or another. Is it believable that, rather than taking this perhaps last opportunity to speak to his children, he would instruct his wife to tell them that he would "talk to them later"? Is it not more likely that this statement was made so that "Tom" would not need to demonstrate that he knew anything about them, even their names?

The conclusion that none of the reported calls to the relatives of passengers on Flight 93 were authentic is of utmost importance, because it undermines the primary reason for believing that there had been hijackers on this plane. The question of the existence of hijackers on *any* of the planes will be discussed in Chapter 6.

THE CRASH SITE(S)

The falsity of the official story about Flight 93 is further suggested by descriptions of the (alleged) crash site. One problem is the fact that there was little evidence to suggest that an airliner had crashed there. One television reporter said:

> There was just a big hole in the ground. All I saw was a crater filled with small, charred plane parts. Nothing that would even tell you that it was the plane. . . . You just can't believe a whole plane went into this crater. . . . There were no suitcases, no recognizable plane parts, no body parts.[36]

A newspaper photographer said: "I didn't think I was in the right place. . . . I was looking for anything that said tail, wing, plane, metal. There was nothing."[37] A paramedic said: "[T]here weren't normal things going on that you would have expected. When a plane crashes, there is a plane and there are patients."[38]

Debris, instead, was spread over a wide area. *Popular Mechanics* tried to debunk the claim that it was found several miles away by saying that, although Indian Lake was indeed 6 miles from the crash site by car, it was only 1.5 miles as the crow flies. The debris at Indian Lake, therefore, could have blown there after it was "blasted skyward by the explosion from the crash."[39] But John Fleegle, an employee at Indian Lake Marina, reported that the debris that washed ashore included "pieces of seats, small chunks of melted plastic and checks."[40] Does *Popular Mechanics* seriously believe that such items could have been propelled over a mile through the air by the blast and the wind?

Moreover, Indian Lake was not the most distant place where debris was reported. A Pittsburgh newspaper said that the plane left "a trail of debris five miles long."[41] Other newspapers reported that debris was found in New Baltimore, which was over a mountain ridge more than eight miles from the alleged crash site.[42]

Another problem is that, although Flight 93 reportedly would have had over 37,000 gallons of fuel left when it crashed, tests of the soil and groundwater found no evidence of contamination.[43] People at the crash site, moreover, reported that there was no smell of jet fuel.[44]

Finally, one of the strangest features of the crash site was that evidently there were two of them. According to CNN reporter Brian Cabell, speaking from the official crash site, the FBI had "cordoned off a second area about six to eight miles away from the crater." He then asked: "Why would debris from the plane—and they identified it specifically as being from this plane—why would debris be located 6 miles away?"[45]

THE FLIGHT PATH(S)

Parallel to this report of two crash sites was evidence that there were two flight paths. According to the flight data recorder— which Pilots for 9/11 Truth obtained from the NTSB by means of a FOIA request—the plane came in from the north. This flight path was confirmed by some witnesses in the Shanksville area. But other residents reported that the plane came from the east.[46] Indian Lake, mentioned earlier, was east of the crash site. Jim Stop, who was fishing at the Indian Lake Marina, and other local residents reported that the plane flew right over the lake.[47]

Given these reports of two crash sites and two flight paths, we can say one thing with certainty: The official story is certainly not the full truth about what happened near Shanksville that morning.

THE TIME OF THE CRASH

According to the government, as we saw in NPH, Flight 93 crashed at 10:03, although a US Army-authorized seismic study, which was carried out by Won-Young Kim of Columbia University's Lamont-Doherty Earth Observatory and Gerald R. Baum of the Maryland Geological Survey, determined that it occurred at 10:06.[48] This three-minute difference was important to the claim that the flight was not shot down, because the cockpit voice recording went silent at 10:03. If the 10:06 time were accepted, then someone would need to explain why the final three minutes of this recording were missing.

When *The 9/11 Commission Report* appeared, it supported the official view. Although it mentioned the seismic study by Kim and Baum, it dismissed its conclusions by alleging that the seismic data on which it was based were "far too weak in signal-to-noise ratio and far too speculative in terms of signal source" to be considered definitive.[49] But that claim contradicted what Kim and Baum themselves had said. According to their report, only the signal from the Pentagon crash was too weak for a definite time to be determined. Putting the crash time of UA 93 at 10:06:05, they based this conclusion on seismic records from three nearby stations, saying: "Although seismic signals across the network are not as strong and clear as the WTC case, three component records. . . are quite clear."[50]

Besides being contradicted by this seismic study, the government and 9/11 Commission's crash time was also contradicted by the reported phone call from Jeremy Glick to his wife, Lyzbeth Glick, which was mentioned above. According to the Commission, the passenger revolt began at 9:57, six minutes before the plane crashed. According to Lyzbeth Glick, however, she told her husband about the collapse of the South Tower, which occurred at 9:59. Their conversation then continued for several minutes, after which "Jeremy" reported that the passengers were taking a vote about whether to attack the hijackers. So much time went by that this attack could not have begun much, if any, before 10:03, making a crash time of 10:03:11 impossible.[51]

Supporters of the official account, therefore, have a difficult choice to make. If they insist on the 10:03 crash time, they must cast doubt on the authenticity of the phone call received by Lyzbeth Glick. If they take this route, they raise the question of the authenticity of all the phone calls. But if they accept the authenticity of the call to her, then they must accept the 10:06 crash time, and this alternative raises the question of why the final three minutes of the tape are missing. In either case, the official story is in trouble.

THE CLAIM OF MILITARY IGNORANCE

The 9/11 Commission's main response to the allegation that United 93 was shot down by the US military—evidence for which was given in NPH—was to say that this was impossible for two reasons. One reason was that, "By the time the military learned about the flight, it had crashed."[52] But this explanation, which was based on the tapes the Commission had obtained from NORAD, was multiply problematic.

One problem was that the Commission's explanation as to why the military was not notified required a completely implausible account of FAA behavior. To accept this account, we would need to believe that, although the FAA knew by 9:32 that Flight 93 had been taken over by hijackers with a bomb, its officials could not bring themselves to notify the military about the plane's troubles until 10:07, after it had crashed.[53]

Besides containing an inherently implausible account of FAA behavior, the Commission's account, according to which the military was not notified about Flight 93 until after it had crashed, was also contradicted by several prior reports, which indicated that the FAA had notified the military about this flight much earlier.

One such report was the aforementioned memo sent to the Commission by the FAA's Laura Brown, which was read into the Commission's records on May 23, 2003. This memo stated that, in an FAA-initiated teleconference that began "minutes after the first aircraft hit the World Trade Center," the FAA had "shared real-time information. . . about. . . all the flights of interest."[54] Those flights would have included United Flight 93, at least by 9:32, the time at which, according to the Commission, the FAA had realized that Flight 93 had been hijacked.[55]

The FAA's report that it had told the military about United 93 was confirmed by General Larry Arnold, the commander of NORAD's US continental region. Having been asked by the 9/11 Commission in 2003 what NORAD was doing at 9:24, Arnold replied: "Our focus was on United 93, which was being pointed out to us very aggressively I might say by the FAA."[56] He explicitly contradicted, therefore, the Commission's later portrait of an FAA reluctant to disturb the military. Besides telling the Commission that the military had been tracking Flight 93, Arnold also stated this in a book. Referring to a time before the flight had turned around, hence before 9:36AM, he stated: "[W]e watched the 93 track as it meandered around the Ohio-Pennsylvania area and started to turn south toward D.C."[57]

Arnold's testimony, moreover, fit with that of Brigadier General Montague Winfield, the deputy director of the National Military Command Center in the Pentagon, who said in 2002: "We received the report from the FAA that Flight 93 had turned off its transponder, had turned, and was now heading towards Washington, DC."[58]

Consistent with these testimonies was a 2002 article in *Aviation Week and Space Technology* about the 121st Fighter Squadron of the Air National Guard at Andrews Air Force Base. This article reported that this squadron, having learned that the FAA and NEADS were tracking the hijacked United Flight 93, feared it was coming toward Washington. Lt. Col. Marc Sasseville, who was the air operations officer, was quoted as saying: "We all realized we were looking for an airliner—a big airplane. That was Flight 93; the track looked like it was headed toward D.C. at that time." Once Sasseville was airborne, "He swept the northwest area of Washington—where the hijacked United Flight 93 was expected to be."[59]

In claiming that NORAD's tapes prove that the military had lied in its testimony to the Commission, as well as in its timeline of September 18, 2001, the Commission was thinking primarily about the military's claim that it had been tracking United Flight 93. According to John Farmer, who was in charge of the team tasked to determine what happened in the skies on the morning of 9/11, the military told a false story in order "to obscure mistakes on the part of the FAA and the military, and to overstate the readiness of the military to intercept and, if necessary, shoot down UAL 93."[60]

When examined, however, this claim is highly implausible. We can understand that the military might have lied to avoid criticism by foisting blame onto the FAA. But the idea that the military would have lied to protect the FAA, as Farmer suggested, is most unlikely. This fact becomes especially important when we see that, according to the NORAD tapes given to the Commission, the mistakes were made almost entirely by the FAA, rather than by the military. The lies of which Arnold and the other military figures were accused by Farmer would have been entirely unmotivated. This fact evidently bothered Farmer somewhat, because he could not understand why the military had lied: "The information they got [from the FAA] was bad information, but they reacted in a way that you would have wanted them to. The calls [they made] were the right ones."[61] Farmer himself admitted, therefore, that there would have been no reason for the military to have told the lies of which he was accusing them.

Moreover, the military officers who, if the NORAD tapes are correct, must have lied include, besides General Arnold, also, as we have seen, Brigadier General Montague Winfield and Lt. Col. Marc Sasseville. As we will see in the next section, moreover, they also include NEADS commander Colonel Robert Marr and a pilot, Lt. Anthony Kuczynski.

And still more officials, beyond those in the FAA and the military, must have lied, if the tapes given to the Commission were accurate. One of these officials would have been counterterrorism czar Richard Clarke. In his description of his White House video conference, Clarke stated that at about 9:35AM, while both Secretary of Defense Rumsfeld and General Richard Myers were participating, FAA Administrator Jane Garvey reported a number of "potential hijacks," which included "United 93 over Pennsylvania."[62] According to Clarke, in other words, the Pentagon's two highest officials were informed about the possible hijacking of Flight 93 almost a half hour before it crashed.

Those who participated in giving a false account of Flight 93, if the 9/11 Commission's account is accepted, must also have included Karl Rove and Vice President Cheney, both of whom indicated, in an ABC News television program on the first anniversary of 9/11, that they had known about Flight 93 shortly after the Pentagon strike. Narrator Charles Gibson reported that Cheney, in the bunker under the White House, was compiling a list of possible threats. David Bohrer, Cheney's photographer, then recalled: "Eventually it narrowed to Flight 93. That was the biggest threat at that point." Karl Rove added: "If you take the trajectory of the plane, of Flight 93 after it passes Pittsburgh and draw a straight line, it's gonna go to Washington, DC." Cheney himself, asked by Gibson "whether he had any thoughts at the time as to what the target of that airplane might be," replied: "I thought probably the White House or Capitol. We found out later. . . that

. . . the fourth plane was intended for the White House."[63] It is not, of course, beyond the realm of possibility that Rove and Cheney might have lied about various things. But it is hard to imagine what conceivable motivation they would have had for telling this particular alleged lie, thereby opening Cheney to the charge of having ordered Flight 93 to be shot down and then lying about it (to be discussed in the next section).

In sum: The 9/11 Commission's claim that the military was unaware of Flight 93's problems until after it crashed is unbelievable for a number of reasons. It involves a wholly implausible account of the behavior of FAA officials. It implies that military officials told a completely unmotivated, irrational lie. And it contradicts the combined testimony of FAA, military, and White House figures.

THE CLAIM ABOUT SHOOTDOWN AUTHORIZATION

The Commission, to be sure, had a back-up claim. Even if the military had known about Flight 93's hijacking, it said, the military could not have shot it down. Why? Because shootdown authorization was not received until long after the flight had crashed.

This authorization was received, everyone agreed, from Vice President Cheney while he was in the Presidential Emergency Operations Center (PEOC) below the White House, and Cheney, the Commission claimed, did not arrive in the PEOC until "shortly before 10:00, perhaps at 9:58."[64] Then at "some time between 10:10 and 10:15," on the basis of a false report that United 93 was still headed toward Washington, Cheney issued the shootdown authorization. Richard Clarke, who had asked for this authorization, did not actually receive it, the Commission claimed, until 10:25, and the military did not receive it until 10:31.[65]

But every element in this timeline is contradicted by strong evidence. Norman Mineta, as we saw in Chapter 2, testified that Cheney was already in the PEOC by 9:20, and this testimony, as we also saw, was consistent with the accounts of several other people.

Also, Richard Clarke reported that he received the shootdown authorization at about 9:45 or 9:50 (not 10:25),[66] and Clarke's claim had been supported in advance by a CNN program in 2002, in which Barbara Starr, CNN's Pentagon correspondent, said:

It is now 9:40, and one very big problem is out there: United Airlines Flight 93 has turned off its transponder. Officials believe it is headed for Washington, D.C. . . . Fighter aircraft begin searching frantically. On a secure phone line, Vice President Cheney tells the military it has permission to shoot down any airliners threatening Washington.[67]

Moreover, NEADS commander Colonel Robert Marr stated that he received the shootdown authorization and "passed that on to the pilots."[68] Marr also said: "United Airlines Flight 93 would not have hit Washington, D.C. He would have been engaged and shot down before he got there."[69] The fact that this shootdown authorization was actually received by military pilots was confirmed by three of them, one of whom was Lt. Anthony Kuczynski, who reported that he and two F-16s were "given direct orders to shoot down an airliner [United 93]."[70]

CLAIMS THAT UNITED 93 WAS SHOT DOWN

In Chapter 3 of NPH, considerable evidence was provided that pointed to the conclusion that United 93 was actually shot down by the US military. There are now reports that officials have said that this is indeed what happened.

According to investigative reporter Wayne Madsen, three employees of the National Security Agency (NSA) have confirmed that United Flight 93 "was shot down over rural Pennsylvania by US Air Force jets scrambled from Andrews Air Force Base in Maryland." Madsen added:

> In fact, a number of personnel who were on watch at the Meade Operations Center (MOC), which is a floor below the NSA's National Security Operations Center (NSOC), were aware that United 93 was brought down by an Air Force air-to-air missile. Personnel within both the MOC and NSOC have reported the doomed aircraft was shot down. The 9/11 Commission. . . never interviewed the on-duty signals intelligence personnel who were aware that United 93 was brought down by Air Force jets.[71]

Another report has come from Charles Lewis, parts of whose written statement about things he heard at an LAX Security guard post on the morning of 9/11 were quoted in Chapter 2. In another part of his statement, Lewis reported that he heard a radio station reporting "that two fighter jets had been scrambled and had successfully shot down a hijacked airliner over Pennsylvania."[72]

CONCLUSION

The cumulative evidence that United 93 was shot down by the US military seems quite strong. Nevertheless, most of what really happened to this flight remains mysterious. But what we can say, on the basis of the information contained above and in NPH, is that every part of the official story about United 93 appears to be untrue. This realization is sufficient for demanding a full and genuine investigation, through which the truth could probably be quickly discovered.

4. Bush at the School in Sarasota: Cover-Up Attempts

Thanks to Michael Moore's film *Fahrenheit 9/11*, most politically aware people are now familiar with the fact that President Bush remained in the classroom for a long time after Andrew Card whispered in his ear about the second attack in New York. But most people are still unaware of the other fact that I reported in NPH: that on the first anniversary of 9/11, the White House started giving a different account of what happened. In addition to Card's telling this new account in the *San Francisco Chronicle* and to Brian Williams on MSNBC, as I reported, he and Karl Rove told it on ABC News, where they got Charles Gibson to endorse it. The segment went like this:

> *Andrew Card*: I think there was a, a moment of shock and he did stare off maybe for just a second.
>
> *Charles Gibson*: The President stays calm and lets the students finish.
>
> *Karl Rove*: The President thought for a second or two about getting up and walking out of the room. But the drill was coming to a close and he didn't want to alarm the children.
>
> *Gibson*: Instead Bush pauses, thanks the children. . . and heads for the empty classroom next door.[1]

The White House even succeeded in getting Sandra Kay Daniels, the teacher of the Sarasota classroom in which the episode occurred, to claim that Bush had left the classroom quickly. In a *Los Angeles Times* story on the first anniversary of 9/11, she wrote: "I knew something was up when President Bush didn't pick up the book and participate in the lesson. . . . He said,

'Mrs. Daniels, I have to leave now.' . . . He shook my hand and left."[2] The next day, she was quoted in a *New York Post* story as giving another version, according to which it was a Secret Service agent, not Andy Card, who came into the room, after which: "The president bolted right out of here and told me: 'Take over.'"[3]

Mrs. Daniels's new account cannot be explained by supposing that she had forgotten what really occurred. Just ten days earlier, a story in the *Tampa Tribune* based on an interview with her correctly reported that Bush had remained with the students "for eight or nine minutes." Stating that Bush, "lost in thought, forgot about the book in his lap," this story quoted Daniels as saying: "I couldn't gently kick him. . . . I couldn't say, 'OK, Mr. President. Pick up your book, sir. The whole world is watching.'"[4]

The fact that the White House not only lied, but also persuaded Mrs. Daniels to support this lie, showed its awareness that the truth—that the Secret Service agents had allowed Bush to remain at the school instead of rushing him to a safe location—was dangerous. According to the official story, these agents had just learned that terrorists were using hijacked airliners to attack high-value targets. In that situation, they should have assumed that the president might be a target and that, in fact, a hijacked airliner might have been bearing down on the school at that very moment. The fact that they allowed him to remain at the school for another half hour suggested that they knew that he was not a target—which would have been possible only if they knew who was carrying out the attacks.

This issue was raised by the Family Steering Committee for the 9/11 Commission. As Kean and Hamilton have admitted, one of the questions the Commission had been asked to address by this committee was: "Why was President Bush permitted by the Secret Service to remain in the Sarasota elementary school where he was reading to children?"[5]

The 9/11 Commission, however, provided no answer. Its only comment was: "The Secret Service told us they were anxious to move the President to a safer location, but did not think it imperative for him to run out the door."[6] In accepting this as an adequate answer, the Commission implied that the Secret Service's options were limited to (1) having Bush run out the door and (2) having him remain at the school another half hour. There, of course, was an obvious third option: The Secret Service could have simply walked Bush out of the room, put him in a limo, and whisked him away.[7]

The behavior of the Secret Service was one of the many signs that 9/11 was an inside job. The 9/11 Commission's completely inadequate treatment of this issue is one of the many signs that its task was not to discover, but to cover up, the truth about what happened that day.

5. Evidence of Advance Information: The 9/11 Commission's Treatment

NPH's fifth chapter was written from a limited perspective, namely: If there were no evidence that the Bush administration planned or at least assisted the attacks, would we at least be able to declare untrue its claim to have had no basis for anticipating the attacks? I discussed that general question in terms of two more specific ones, about which there is now additional information to mention.

Was the Very Possibility of Such Attacks not Envisioned?

Several more testimonies, beyond those I quoted in NPH, indicated that the possibility of 9/11-type attacks had indeed been anticipated. About a month after 9/11, for example, Paul Pillar, the former deputy director of the CIA's Counterterrorist Center, said: "The idea of commandeering an aircraft and crashing it into the ground and causing high casualties, sure we've thought of it."[1] The following year, former CIA Deputy Director John Gannon said: "If you ask anybody could terrorists convert a plane into a missile, nobody would have ruled that out."[2] In 2003, the Joint Congressional Inquiry reported that the intelligence community had learned in April 2001 that "bin Laden was interested in commercial pilots as potential terrorists" and that "the first World Trade Center bombing would be the type of attack that would be appealing."[3]

There were also several military exercises, beyond the one I mentioned, to prepare for attacks on the Pentagon. In May 2001, two medical clinics in the Pentagon held a training exercise involving a scenario in which an aircraft—a hijacked 757 according to some reports—was crashed into the Pentagon.[4] In

2004, USA Today published an article, "NORAD Had Drills of Jets as Weapons," discussing a series of exercises planned by the military in the two years prior to 9/11. In these exercises, "hijacked airliners [were] used as weapons" and "one of the imagined targets was the World Trade Center."[5] About a month before 9/11, moreover, the Pentagon held a mass casualty exercise involving the evacuation of the building after it was hit by an airplane[6] (a fact that underscores the question raised in Chapter 2 as to why the Pentagon was not evacuated on 9/11).

In 2004, nevertheless, the Bush administration continued to issue its false denials. Bush himself said: "Had I had any inkling whatsoever that the people were going to fly airplanes into buildings, we would have moved heaven and earth to save the country."[7] Donald Rumsfeld told the 9/11 Commission: "I knew of no intelligence during the six-plus months leading up to September 11 to indicate terrorists would hijack commercial airlines, use them as missiles to fly into the Pentagon or the World Trade Center towers."[8] Condoleezza Rice, testifying under oath to the 9/11 Commission, said: "This kind of analysis about the use of airplanes as weapons actually was never briefed to us."[9]

Military leaders made the same denials to the Commission. General Richard Myers said: "[T]he use of aircraft as a weapon, as a missile, . . . [T]he intelligence did not point to this kind of threat."[10]

The 9/11 Commission was aware that these claims made by the Bush administration and the military were false. It learned from former FBI director Louis Freeh, for example, that in 2000 and 2001, the planning for events designated "National Special Security Events" included "the use of airplanes, either packed with explosives or otherwise, in suicide missions."[11] Also, one of the Commissioners, Richard Ben-Veniste, said: "The concept of terrorists using airplanes as weapons was not something which was unknown to the US intelligence community on September 10th, 2001. . . . NORAD had already in the works plans to simulate in an exercise a simultaneous hijacking of two planes in the United States."[12]

How did The 9/11 Commission Report deal with the evidence contradicting the denials of the military and the Bush administration—some of which was supplied by one of the

Commissioners? On the one hand, pointing out that Richard Clarke had been "concerned about the danger posed by aircraft," it stated:

> In 1998, Clarke chaired an exercise [that] involved a scenario in which a group of terrorists commandeered a Learjet on the ground in Atlanta, loaded it with explosives, and flew it toward a target in Washington, D.C. . . . After the 1999–2000 millennium alerts, . . . Clarke held a meeting of his Counterterrorism Security Group devoted largely to the possibility of a possible airplane hijacking by al Qaeda. . . . [T]he possibility was imaginable, and imagined.[13]

The Commission could have hardly been more explicit in rejecting the claim, made by both the Bush administration and its Pentagon, that such attacks had not been imagined.

On the other hand, nevertheless, the 9/11 Commission's most prominent statements on this issue simply repeated the military's claim, saying:

> The threat of terrorists hijacking commercial airliners within the United States—and using them as guided missiles—was not recognized by NORAD before 9/11.[14]

> [We had] "a military unprepared for the transformation of commercial aircraft into weapons of mass destruction."[15]

In their 2006 book, Kean and Hamilton repeated this claim, writing:

> Why did NORAD fail to intercept any of the hijacked planes? . . . . [T]hose responding to the events. . . had not trained for the scenario they were facing. . . . [They] had not imagined hijacked civilian airliners being used as guided missiles.[16]

So, although such attacks were "imaginable, and imagined," according to the Commission, they were also, paradoxically, "not imagined."

The claim by the military and the Commission that such attacks had not been imagined was especially brazen in the light of two highly popular fictional accounts. In 1994, Tom Clancy, who had long been popular in military circles, published a bestselling novel, *Debt of Honor*, in which, after a short war between Japan and the United States, a Japanese commercial airline pilot deliberately crashed a Boeing 747 into the US Capitol during a joint session of Congress.[17] In March 2001, the pilot episode of *The Lone Gunmen*, which reportedly had 13 million viewers, was based on a rogue group within the US government crashing a remote-controlled 747 into the World Trade Center.[18]

WERE THERE NO SPECIFIC WARNINGS ABOUT THE ATTACKS?

In NPH, I discussed the massive purchases of put options on stocks that subsequently suffered huge losses because of the 9/11 attacks. These purchases, the *San Francisco Chronicle* pointed out, "raise[d] suspicions that the investors . . . had advance knowledge of the strikes."[19] After that suspicion was raised, Allen Poteshman, a professor of finance at the University of Illinois, published an article stating that the most straightforward analysis of these purchases "does provide evidence that is consistent with the terrorists or their associates having traded ahead of the September 11 attacks."[20]

How did the 9/11 Commission treat this issue? While admitting that "[s]ome unusual trading did in fact occur," the Commission claimed that "each such trade proved to have an innocuous explanation." Its prime example involved United Airlines. While conceding that the surge in the volume of put options purchased on this stock September 6 was "highly suspicious trading on its face," the Commission claimed that "further investigation has revealed that the trading had no connection with 9/11." Why? Because a "single US-based institutional investor with no conceivable ties to al-Qaeda purchased 95 percent of the UAL puts."[21]

This argument, providing a textbook example of circular reasoning, implicitly involved the following syllogism:

(1) The attacks of 9/11 were planned and executed solely by al-Qaeda.
(2) No other person or agency had any role in, or even advance knowledge of, the attacks.
(3) The purchaser of the put options on United Airlines stock had no connection with al-Qaeda.

(4) The purchaser, therefore, could not have had any advance knowledge of the attacks.

The Commission's argument, in presupposing the truth of the first two propositions, simply assumed the truth of two claims that the evidence about put options had thrown into doubt.

To explain: when critics said that the purchases pointed to advance knowledge of the attacks on the part of the investors, they were not assuming that those investors obtained this knowledge from al-Qaeda. For example, when these critics raised questions about Deutsche Bank and its former director A. B. "Buzzy" Krongard (who has been in the news more recently because of his involvement with Blackwater[22]), they did so because they suspected that Deutsche Bank had inside information about 9/11 because of its connection through Krongard to the CIA. The Commission could argue that the put option purchases for United Airlines were innocuous only by presupposing that no one other than al-Qaeda knew that the attacks were coming. This is one of dozens of examples showing that *The 9/11 Commission Report* cannot be trusted.[23] It worked to cover up, not to discover, the truth.

A final comment about the discussion of this topic in NPH: In light of all the evidence casting doubt on the idea that the attacks were orchestrated by Osama bin Laden and other members of al-Qaeda, we should, I believe, regard with considerable skepticism the NSA and FBI claims to have intercepted (but not translated), in the days just prior to 9/11, messages indicating that the attacks were imminent. These claims seem more likely to have been part of the propaganda offensive to convince the public that the attacks were indeed orchestrated by al-Qaeda. Alternatively, if such messages really were received, they could well have been sent by intelligence assets who had been instructed to send them.

6. CONTINUING OBSTRUCTIONS AND NEW DOUBTS ABOUT HIJACKERS

I
n this chapter, besides commenting on the 9/11 Commission's treatment of the information provided in Chapter 6 of NPH, I will discuss new developments involving Abu Zubaydah, Sibel Edmonds, and the alleged hijackers.

THE ANTI-HUNT FOR BIN LADEN AND AL-QAEDA

The 9/11 Commission could have easily investigated the report that in July 2001 Osama bin Laden was in Dubai's American Hospital, where he was treated by Dr. Terry Callaway and visited by Terry Mitchell, the local CIA agent. The Commission could have used its subpoena power to force these two men to testify under oath. But the Commission did not even mention this story. The names of Callaway and Mitchell—like that of Richard Labeviere, the highly respected investigative journalist who wrote the story—are missing from the Commission's report.

HIDDEN CONNECTIONS BETWEEN BUSH, BIN LADEN, AND SAUDI ROYALS

Two new developments related to this section involved Abu Zubaydah and Saudi funding.

Abu Zubaydah: In December 2007, the name of Abu Zubaydah became more prominently discussed than ever before. On December 5, Director Michael Hayden announced that the CIA had destroyed videotapes of interrogations of al-Qaeda prisoners, specifically mentioning Zubaydah (sometimes written Zubaida). This announcement made the question of the truth of Gerald Posner's account of Zubaydah's testimony to US interrogators even more important: If Posner's account of what Zubaydah said is accurate, that would provide a very understandable motive for the destruction of the videotapes.

After discussing Posner's account of Zubaydah's testimony in NPH, I discussed it more fully in 9/11CROD.[1] I there cautioned that there were reasons to doubt the truth of his account, in which Zubaydah contended that some members of the Saudi royal family supported al-Qaeda and had known in advance that America would experience terrorist attacks on September 11, 2001. Besides the fact that, because of his past works, Posner's honesty is in doubt, his story would be useful to prepare the American public for a future invasion of Saudi Arabia to gain control of the world's richest oil reserves. (And indeed, I learned later, a *Newsweek* story in 2002 reported that Bush advisors had Saudi Arabia on a list of countries to be attacked.[2]) But I also added a reason, beyond those offered by Posner, to give credence to his story. This additional reason, provided by Craig Unger, involved Prince Ahmed bin Salman, the founder of the Thoroughbred Corporation.

According to Unger, there was virtually nothing more important to Prince Ahmed in 2002 than winning the Triple Crown. War Emblem, the horse for which he had paid almost a million dollars, had in May 2002 already won the Kentucky Derby and the Preakness. If War Emblem were then to win the Belmont Stakes on June 8, Ahmed would become the first Triple Crown Winner in 25 years. But May was also the month in which, according to Posner, CIA agents informed their counterparts in Saudi intelligence about Zubaydah's claims, and on June 8, Ahmed did not even show up for the Belmont Stakes, citing "family obligations."[3] By July 22, he was dead, the official explanation being that Ahmed, who was only 43, had died of a heart attack in his sleep. When combined with the fact that all three Saudis reportedly named by Zubaydah died within an eight-day period, the fact that Ahmed had not shown up for the Belmont Stakes provided an additional reason to believe that he and the others were killed to prevent any possibility that they might confirm the truth of Zubaydah's reported allegations.

If some members of the Saudi royal family with official capacities knew about the 9/11 attacks in advance, that would certainly be an important part of the "events surrounding 9/11" about which the Commission was to give "the fullest possible account." The Commissioners, moreover, should have had no a priori reason to distrust Posner, because in the past he had supported the official view on controversial stories. In his book *Case Closed*, most famously, he supported the view that President Kennedy was assassinated by Lee Harvey Oswald working entirely alone.[4] With regard to 9/11 in particular, Posner on most issues supported the official view, including the Commission's view that the attacks succeeded because of various kinds of breakdowns and bureaucratic impediments, especially the failures of agencies to share information.[5] And yet the Commission did not refer to Posner's book or otherwise mention the claims made, according to Posner, by Abu Zubaydah.

The Commission did discuss Zubaydah. He was, in fact, one of the major characters in its narrative, being mentioned in 39 paragraphs. And yet not one of those paragraphs mentioned his reported claim that three members of the Saudi royal family, including Prince Ahmed, had foreknowledge about the attacks of 9/11. Indeed, although Prince Ahmed was one of the best-known Saudis in America, his name is not even to be found in the Commission's report.

If Posner's account of Zubaydah is true, we can certainly understand why the 9/11 Commission, one of whose tasks was evidently to cover up any connection between 9/11 and Saudi Arabia, would not have mentioned Posner's account of Zubaydah's testimony. We can also understand why the CIA, having the same task, would have destroyed the tapes of Zubaydah's interrogation: Many officials would not have wanted to risk the possibility that a copy of this tape might be leaked to the press or placed on YouTube. But is Posner's account credible? More reasons have emerged both to believe it and to doubt it.

On the one hand, *New York Times* reporter James Risen, in his well-regarded book *State of War*, supported it, writing: "In addition to the incidents described by Posner, a senior former American government official said that the United States has obtained other evidence that suggests connections between al-Qaeda operatives and telephone numbers associated with Saudi officials."

On the other hand, Risen gave a reason to doubt the truth of Zubaydah's testimony as described by Posner, saying: "Some officials believed that Abu Zubaydah's recitation of the Saudi telephone numbers may have been part of a well-rehearsed disinformation campaign, to be employed in the event of capture and designed to sow discord between America and. . . the Saudi royal family [which bin Laden hated]."[6]

Another possible reason to be suspicious of Posner's account is simply the fact that it disagrees with other, more widely discussed, accounts. In these accounts, Zubaydah's testimony is controversial, but the controversy revolves merely around two issues on which FBI and CIA spokespersons disagree: whether Zubaydah was a central member of al-Qaeda with important information, and whether torture was effective in inducing him to reveal information.

Whereas the dominant CIA view, publicly supported by President Bush, is that Zubaydah was a central member of al-Qaeda with important information to share, the dominant FBI view, we have been told, is that he was a mentally disturbed man with little information about al-Qaeda operations. And whereas the dominant CIA view is that his most important information was produced by torture, the dominant FBI view is that his valuable information came through traditional interrogation.[7] Of these two views, Posner's account agrees with the CIA view on the importance of Zubaydah and with the FBI view that Zubaydah produced the most important information when not being tortured. But in both the FBI and the CIA accounts, the most important names given by Zubaydah were Khalid Sheik Mohammed and José Padilla: No Saudi officials were mentioned. However, if Posner's account is true, we would not expect either the FBI or the CIA to admit it. We would, in fact, expect accounts that would make Posner's account seem improbable, such as characterizations of Zubaydah as mentally disturbed and ill informed.

In sum: Given the information that is publicly available, it is probably impossible to determine whether Zubaydah's testimony as described by Posner was true. This determination could be made only by a genuine investigation—the kind the 9/11 Commission did not provide. The announcement that Zubaydah's interrogation

tapes were destroyed makes this question even more important—
as Posner himself has suggested by saying: "[N]ow the [Bush
administration's] cover-up [of information about Saudi and
Pakistani involvement in 9/11] is enhanced by the CIA's
destruction of Zubaydah's interrogation tapes."[8]

Saudi Funding of al-Qaeda: According to Posner, Zubaydah claimed
that the Saudis regularly sent money to al-Qaeda.[9] The
Commission, besides failing to mention this reported claim,
explicitly denied having found any evidence of Saudi funding,
saying:

> Saudi Arabia has long been considered the primary source of al
> Qaeda funding, but we have found no evidence that the Saudi
> government as an institution or senior Saudi officials
> individually funded the organization.[10]

A *Los Angeles Times* story by Josh Meyer provided evidence
from inside the Commission that this statement was politically
motivated. Meyer's story was based on interviews with "several
senior members" of the 9/11 Commission, one of whom, Bob
Kerrey, was named. These members reportedly said that the
Commission had uncovered evidence that "Saudi Arabia provided
funds and equipment to the Taliban and probably directly to Bin
Laden."[11] "Now," wrote Meyer, "the bipartisan commission is
wrestling with how to characterize such politically sensitive
information in its final report, and even whether to include it."[12]
The result of this "wrestling" was the decision to tell the lie quoted
above—that the Commission had "found no evidence that the
Saudi government as an institution or senior Saudi officials
individually funded the organization."

The issue of hidden connections with Saudi Arabia will be
discussed further in Chapter 8.

IGNORING THE FBI IN PHOENIX

Explaining why FBI headquarters was not blameworthy for failing
to respond to the "Phoenix Memo" sent by Ken Williams, the 9/11
Commission simply said: "No managers at headquarters saw the
memo before September 11." As support for this (implausible)

claim, it merely cited the report issued by the Congressional Joint Inquiry. The Commission supplied no explanation as to how the Joint Inquiry had reached this conclusion.[13]

BLOCKING THE FBI IN MINNEAPOLIS

Coleen Rowley, because of her whistle-blowing memo, was named one of *Time* magazine's three "persons of the year" for 2002.[14] With such publicity, we would assume, the 9/11 Commission would have reported her charges that various facts had been "omitted, downplayed, glossed over and/or mis-characterized" by FBI headquarters, "perhaps. . . for improper political reasons."[15] But although a note in *The 9/11 Commission Report* mentioned Rowley, it referred merely to an interview of her by the Department of Justice's Inspector General.[16] In spite of the Commission's stated intention "to provide the fullest possible account of the events surrounding 9/11,"[17] its report contained no mention of Rowley's memo.

I had, incidentally, misidentified the role of Marion "Spike" Bowman at FBI headquarters. He was the chief of the National Security Law Unit and, as such, the one who refused to forward the request to FISA. The person who edited out the information about Moussaoui's connection to al-Qaeda, before the request was officially forwarded to Bowman, was Mike Maltbie of the Radical Fundamentalist Unit.[18]

BLOCKING THE FBI IN CHICAGO

Although FBI agent Robert Wright's charges against FBI headquarters were reported in the mainstream press, his charges were not reported nearly as prominently as those of Coleen Rowley. So, given the fact that her charges were not reported in *The 9/11 Commission Report*, it is not surprising that Wright's name was not even mentioned.

In the meantime, his troubles continued. In April 2005, Wright—whose lawsuit against the FBI for blocking the publication of his book was still pending—was notified that he was being fired.[19] That October, the Department of Justice ordered him reinstated, but he was downgraded and placed on a year's probation. "His supporters have long suspected," reported the *Chicago Tribune*, "that the FBI retaliated against him for his public criticism of the bureau."[20]

JUSTICE FOR A SPY: THE SAGA OF SIBEL EDMONDS

Although my discussion of Sibel Edmonds in NPH focused on the fact that the Department of Justice (DOJ) sided with the spy reported by Edmonds, rather than with Edmonds herself, it soon became apparent that there was much more to the Sibel Edmonds story, as indicated by my discussion in NPH's Afterword. The most important development mentioned in that discussion was her suit challenging the DOJ's use of the state secrets privilege to prevent her from telling what she learned while working for the FBI. I updated this story, which becomes increasingly interesting as the years go by, still further in 9/11CROD.[21]

Edmonds's Suit Thrown Out: One new development reported in 9/11CROD was the fact that, in 2004, Judge Reggie Walton ruled in favor of the DOJ's request that Edmonds's suit be thrown out, to which she responded by writing:

> John Ashcroft's relentless fight against me, my information, and my case, . . . has been taking place under his attempt at a vague justification titled "Protecting Certain Foreign and Diplomatic Relations for National Security." On September 11, 2001, 3,000 lives were lost. Yet this administration has hindered all past and ongoing investigations into the causes of that horrific day for the sake of this vague notion of protecting "certain diplomatic and foreign relations."[22]

The Commission Confirms Edmonds's Prediction: Another development was the 9/11 Commission's confirmation of Edmonds' prediction that her 3.5-hour testimony "behind closed doors" to the Commission's staff "will stay there and will never get out." *The 9/11 Commission Report* contains only two bits of information about Edmonds (and these are buried in its tiny endnotes): first, she was one of four people who had spoken of the need for the FBI's translation program to "maintain rigorous security and proficiency standards" and to "ensure compliance with its quality control program"; and second, the DOJ's inspector general had issued a document entitled "A Review of the FBI's Actions in Connection with Allegations Raised by Contract Linguist Sibel Edmonds."[23] From the Commission's report, however, one would not learn that this review had supported Edmonds's claim that she was terminated for whistle-blowing. Nor would one learn anything about the nature of the allegations she had raised.

In response to this blackout by the 9/11 Commission's report, Edmonds wrote an open letter to Chairman Thomas Kean, in which she said:

> I find your report seriously flawed in its failure to address serious intelligence issues that I am aware of, which have been confirmed, and which as a witness to the commission, I made you aware of. Thus, I must assume that other serious issues that I am not aware of were in the same manner omitted from your report. These omissions cast doubt on the validity of your report and therefore on its conclusions and recommendations.[24]

Edmonds then summarized eight charges she had made. One of these was that, although she had reported that her direct supervisor, Mike Feghali, "took hundreds of pages of top-secret sensitive intelligence documents outside the FBI to unknown recipients," he was not fired but instead promoted. In her most important charge, she spoke of "intentional blocking of intelligence," saying:

> If Counterintelligence receives information that contains money laundering, illegal arms sales, and illegal drug activities, directly linked to terrorist activities; and if that information involves certain nations, certain semi-legit organizations, and ties to certain lucrative or political relations in this country, then, that information is not shared with Counterterrorism, regardless of the possible severe consequences. In certain cases, frustrated FBI agents cited "direct pressure by the State Department." . . . After almost three years the. . . victims' family members still do not realize that information and answers they have sought relentlessly for over two years has been blocked due to the unspoken decisions made and disguised under "safeguarding certain diplomatic relations." Your report did not

even attempt to address these unspoken practices, although, unlike me, you were not placed under any gag.[25]

Further Developments 2004–2005: There were also some other significant developments. In 2004, Edmonds founded the National Security Whistleblowers Coalition.[26] In a hearing in April 2005, which an article in *Vanity Fair* described as "bizarre" because the DOJ lawyers were allowed to address the judge in secret,[27] a federal appeals court dismissed her appeal, with no reason provided. The ACLU then petitioned the US Supreme Court to review the lower court's application of the state secrets privilege. While awaiting a decision, Edmonds gave an interview, during which she said about the "so-called war on terror":

> We go for the Attas and Hamdis—but never touch the guys on the top. . . . [T]his would upset "certain foreign relations." But it would also expose certain of our elected officials, who have significant connections with high-level drugs—and weapons-smuggling—and thus with the criminal underground, even with the terrorists themselves.[28]

In another interview, she said:

> [T]he issue here is [not] about whistleblowing, being fired, being wronged. . . . The most important issue is: What were these criminal activities, and why instead of pursuing these our government chooses to cover it up and actually issue classification and gag orders so the American public will not know about what is going on within these agencies within their government—and even within the Congress? That is my focus point. . . . I'm not saying, "Look, they did wrong to me, and this is not fair." I'm saying, "I came forward because criminal activities are taking place—have been taking place—some of them since 1997." Some of these activities are 100 percent related to the 9/11 terrorist attacks in the United States, and they are giving this illusion that they are pursuing these cases, but they are not.[29]

In November 2005, the Supreme Court declined, without comment, to hear her case.[30] Edmonds, who had learned, she said, that she was "the most gagged person in United States history,"[31] would remain gagged. In 2006, she won the First Amendment Award given by the Pen American Center and Newman's Own.[32]

TV Networks Ignore Edmonds's Tell-All Promise: Near the end of October 2007, Edmonds announced that, having "exhausted every channel," she was prepared to talk, in spite of the gag order: "If any one of the major networks—ABC, NBC, CBS, CNN, MSNBC, FOX—promise to air the entire segment, without editing, I promise to tell them everything that I know."[33] None of these networks, however, accepted her offer, and no major US newspaper or magazine interviewed her.

London Sunday Times Stories: On January 6, 2008, however, London's *Sunday Times* published a story based on an interview with Edmonds (which came about after she approached the *Times* following its publication of a story regarding an al-Qaeda operative, Louai al-Sakka, who claimed to have trained some of the 9/11 hijackers while he was in Turkey[34]). Pointing out that Edmonds had been assigned to listen to tapes relevant to an FBI investigation into links between Turkish, Pakistani, Israeli, and US targets, the *Times* reported her claim that the US targets included "senior Pentagon officials—including household names" (meaning, others have pointed out, Richard Perle and Douglas Feith[35]). The *Times* also reported her astounding claim that US officials were accepting bribes to help Turkey and Israel plant "moles" in military and academic institutions in order to acquire nuclear technology. It also reported her claim that Turks, being less likely to arouse suspicion than Pakistanis, often acted as conduits for Pakistan's ISI.[36]

The *Times* then added that the Pakistani operation was led by then ISI chief General Mahmoud Ahmad, that Ahmad had been accused of sending $100,000 to Mohamed Atta before 9/11, and that the stolen secrets were surely passed to Pakistani nuclear scientist A. Q. (Abdul Qadeer) Khan, who had become rich by selling nuclear secrets to other countries. The *Times* also mentioned that Khan was close to both Ahmad and the ISI and that his aides had met with Osama bin Laden.

With regard to 9/11 in particular, the *Times* reported Edmonds's allegations about a "high-ranking State Department official" (whom Edmonds had elsewhere identified as Marc

Grossman, the US undersecretary of state for political affairs from 2001 until 2005, who had formerly been the US ambassador to Turkey). Paraphrasing Edmonds, the *Times* wrote: "Following 9/11, a number of the foreign operatives were taken in for questioning by the FBI on suspicion that they knew about or somehow aided the attacks." It then quoted Edmonds's statement about the way in which Grossman proved useful:

> A primary target [of the FBI investigation] would call the official [Grossman] and point to names on the list and say, "We need to get them out of the US because we can't afford for them to spill the beans." . . . The official said that he would "take care of it."

As a result, the *Times* added: "The four suspects on the list were released from interrogation and extradited."[37]

Justin Raimondo, discussing this story in an online article, quoted Luke Ryland, "the world's foremost expert on the Edmonds case," as writing: "Let me repeat that for emphasis: The #3 guy at the State Dept. facilitated the immediate release of 911 suspects at the request of targets of the FBI's investigation."[38]

As pointed out by Raimondo and other writers on the Internet, the *Sunday Times* story about Edmonds was of utmost importance. Chris Floyd called it "one of the most important stories of the last quarter-century."[39] Dave Lindorff wrote: "[T]here is enough in just this one *London Times* story to keep an army of investigative reporters busy for years."[40] Such an important story, we would assume, would surely be covered by the press around the world. And it was, indeed, reported by mainstream outlets in many countries, even the three countries accused of buying nuclear secrets: Israel, Pakistan, and Turkey.[41] In the United States, however, the mainstream media completely ignored the story. As blogger Brad Friedman said:

> Apparently *American* nuclear secrets, stolen by 'moles' at *America's* most sensitive nuclear installations, sold on the black market with the help and protection of highly placed *American* officials, which then found their way into the hands of *America's'* enemies, is not notable news to Americans.[42]

The Valerie Plame Wilson Connection: On January 20 and 27, 2008, the *Sunday Times* published two more stories based on its interview with Sibel Edmonds.[43] It reported that, according to Edmonds, the same State Department official—meaning Marc Grossman, although the paper still did not identify him by name—had thwarted a CIA covert operation intended to infiltrate the nuclear black market ring discussed in the previous *Sunday Times* stories.

This operation involved Brewster Jennings, ostensibly an energy consultation company but in reality a CIA front organization. One of the Turkish groups in the nuclear ring had been introduced to Brewster Jennings and was planning to hire it. But Grossman, knowing it to be a CIA front, warned one of the targets, who then warned others. One of the members of the Brewster Jennings team was Valerie Plame Wilson, who after the warning was transferred to a different operation. (This was two years before she and Brewster Jennings were publicly outed in 2003 after her husband, Joseph Wilson, had undermined the Bush administration's claim that Saddam Hussein's Iraq had tried to buy uranium from Niger.)

Edmonds told the *Sunday Times* that the FBI had also been investigating this nuclear black market activity and had a file, numbered 203A-WF-210023, with documents and recordings that incriminated Grossman.

Edmonds's claim, the *Times* found, was corroborated by a letter from an anonymous correspondent to the Liberty Coalition, a US human rights organization. This letter mentioned FBI file 203A-WF-210023 and suggested that the Liberty Coalition make a FOIA request for it. When the Liberty Coalition did so, the FBI replied that no such file existed. Edmonds, calling the FBI denial an "outright lie," added: "I can tell you that that file and the operations it refers to did exist from 1996 to February 2002. The file refers to the counterintelligence program that the Department of Justice has declared to be a state secret to protect sensitive diplomatic relations."[44] The *Times* then found that this claim by Edmonds was corroborated by "a document, signed by an FBI official, showing that the file did exist in 2002."[45] Insofar as the FBI's response to the FOIA request implied that the file had never existed, Edmonds was clearly right: It lied—and for a government agency to lie in response to a FOIA request is unlawful.

Now that Sibel Edmonds has managed to get part of her story out, it has become even clearer that when her freedom of speech is thwarted in the name of "state secrets," these secrets have less to do with national security than with the security of various persons who have engaged in criminal activities while serving as officials of the American government. I close this section by reminding readers of what Sibel Edmonds has said from the outset—that the issues involved in these stories—smuggling, bribery, and corruption of government officials—are intimately connected to 9/11. Exactly how they are related, if they are, is one of those many things that we may learn only if we have a genuine and thorough investigation.

THE QUESTION OF THE TRUE IDENTITY OF THE HIJACKERS

After briefly discussing problems associated with the government's account of the alleged hijackers in NPH's sixth chapter, I discussed them more fully in its Afterword. I here discuss the issue still more fully on the basis of additional information.

Still Alive? In the Afterword, I emphasized the evidence that some of the accused men were still alive after 9/11. I then devoted the first chapter of 9/11CROD to this issue. Indeed, my first shock upon reading *The 9/11 Commission Report* was seeing, in its first few pages, the names of the 19 men who had been identified as hijackers by the FBI shortly after 9/11, followed later in the book by the FBI's photographs of them,[46] without any suggestion that there might be doubts about whether all of these men had died in hijacked airliners on 9/11.

The Commission's brazen disregard of contrary evidence was shown most clearly by its treatment of alleged hijacker Waleed al-Shehri. In a September 22, 2001, article entitled "Hijack 'Suspect' Alive in Morocco," David Bamford of the BBC had made clear that the man of that name identified by the FBI as one of the hijackers was still alive:

His photograph was released by the FBI, and has been shown in newspapers and on television around the world. That same Mr Al-Shehri has turned up in Morocco, proving clearly that he was not a member of the suicide attack. He told Saudi journalists in Casablanca that. . . he has now been interviewed by the American authorities, who apologised for the misunderstanding.[47]

Nevertheless, the 9/11 Commission endorsed the FBI's inclusion of al-Shehri on the list of hijackers and even said he was probably responsible for stabbing one of the flight attendants on American 11.[48]

A 2003 article in *Der Spiegel* tried to debunk Bamford's story, along with a related BBC story of September 23, 2001 ("Hijack 'Suspects' Alive and Well"[49]), which *Der Spiegel* characterized as "nonsense about surviving terrorists." It claimed that the reported still-alive hijackers were all cases of mistaken identity, involving men with "coincidentally identical names." This claim by *Der Spiegel* depended on its assertion that, at the time of the reports, the FBI had released only a list of names: "The FBI did not release photographs until four days after the cited reports, on September 27th."[50] This, however, was not true. Bamford's BBC story of September 22, as we saw, had reported that Waleed al-Shehri's photograph had been "released by the FBI" and "shown in newspapers and on television around the world."

In 2006, the BBC withdrew its support for its own stories of September 22 and 23, 2001, on the same basis. Steve Herrmann, the editor of the BBC News website, claimed that confusion had arisen because "these were common Arabic and Islamic names." Accordingly, he said, the BBC changed its September 23 story ("Hijack 'Suspects' Alive and Well") in one respect: "Under the FBI picture of Waleed al Shehri we have added the words 'A man called Waleed Al Shehri...' to make it as clear as possible that there was confusion over the identity." However, Bamford's BBC story of September 22, which Herrmann failed to mention, had made it as clear as possible that there *was* no confusion.

The attempts by *Der Spiegel* and the BBC to discredit the reports that Waleed al-Shehri and other men on the FBI's list of hijackers were still alive after 9/11 have been refuted by Jay Kolar. He shows, among other things, that FBI photographs had been published by Saudi newspapers on September 19[51]—a fact that fits with Bamford's statement that Waleed al-Shehri had seen his published photograph prior to September 22.

Devout Muslims? Another question raised in NPH was whether, given reports of these young men's drinking and sexual habits, we can believe that they were really devout Muslims, ready to meet their Maker. The threat that these reports posed to the official account of 9/11 was brought out in an article published in a Florida newspaper five days after 9/11. Entitled "Suspects' Actions Don't Add Up," it said:

> Three guys cavorting with lap dancers at the Pink Pony Nude Theater. Two others knocking back glasses of Stolichnaya and rum and Coke at a fish joint in Hollywood the weekend before committing suicide and mass murder. That might describe the behavior of several men who are suspects in Tuesday's terrorist attack, but it is not a picture of devout Muslims, experts say. Let alone that of religious zealots in their final days on Earth. . . . [A] devout Muslim [cannot] drink booze or party at a strip club and expect to reach heaven, said Mahmoud Mustafa Ayoub, a professor at Temple University in Philadelphia. The most basic tenets of the religion forbid alcohol and any sex outside marriage. "It is incomprehensible that a person could drink and go to a strip bar one night, then kill themselves the next day in the name of Islam," said Ayoub. "People who would kill themselves for their faith would come from very strict Islamic ideology. Something here does not add up."[52]

Although this reported behavior by the alleged hijackers should have led the press to investigate why the official account did "not add up," the press instead began modifying and eliminating such reports.

An example was provided by the evolution of the most repeated story about Atta's drinking, which involved a place called Shuckums (the "fish joint" mentioned in the story quoted above). According to articles published by the *New York Times* and other papers immediately after 9/11, Atta and his constant companion, Marwan al-Shehhi, were drinking heavily there on September 7, just four days before 9/11. Atta drank vodka and orange juice, while al-Shehhi drank rum and Coke, and the bartender described the two men as "wasted."[53] Soon, however, this story was transformed in the press so that Atta had no longer drunk alcohol.[54] Rather, he had merely played games and, if he drank anything, it was cranberry juice.[55] The Atta-drank-cranberry-juice version of the Shuckums story was even carried by *Time* magazine,[56] although it had, only a week earlier, published the vodka-and-orange-juice version and quoted the bartender's statement that Atta had been "wasted."[57]

Even though the press had helpfully cleaned up the Shuckums story so that it was consistent with the official portrayal of Atta as a devout Muslim, the 9/11 Commission refused the gift. In line with its claim that Atta had become very religious, even "fanatically so,"[58] the Commission simply pretended that Atta had not even gone to Shuckums that night. Rather than doing something so frivolous four days before 9/11, Atta was all business: "On September 7, he flew from Fort Lauderdale to Baltimore, presumably to meet with the Flight 77 team in Laurel."[59] Although dozens of newspapers had reported the Shuckums episode, not one of them, to my knowledge, has challenged the 9/11 Commission's revisionist account, according to which that well-reported episode never happened.

The Commission extended this pretense to the stories about the sexual proclivities of Atta and other alleged hijackers, which were mentioned in NPH. These stories were in mainstream newspapers. The *San Francisco Chronicle* described trips to Las Vegas, during which Atta and other "self-styled warriors for Allah. . . engaged in some decidedly un-Islamic sampling of prohibited pleasures," including lap dances. The *Chronicle* then emphasized the importance of this revelation by quoting Dr. Osama Haikal, president of the board of directors of the Islamic Foundation of Nevada, as saying: "True Muslims don't drink, don't gamble, don't go to strip clubs."[60] The *Boston Herald*, after reporting that two of the hijackers had hired a prostitute just two nights before 9/11, commented that this was "just the latest link between the Koran-toting killers and America's seedy sex scene," after which it referred to reports that the hijackers, including Mohamed Atta and Marwan al-Shehhi, spent hundreds of dollars on lap dances in strip clubs in Florida and Las Vegas.[61] These reports were even pointed out in a *Wall Street Journal* editorial entitled "Terrorist Stag Parties,"[62] which referred to the stories in the *Boston Herald* and the *San Francisco Chronicle*. The Commission handled the threat posed by these reports by simply pretending to be unaware of them, claiming that it had seen "no credible evidence explaining why. . . the operatives flew to or met in Las Vegas."[63]

The Commission also covered up the fact—which I mentioned in a note to the Afterword of NPH and then discussed at some length in *9/11 Contradictions*[64]—that Atta, as documented by investigative reporter Daniel Hopsicker, had lived with a stripper named Amanda Keller in Venice, on the west coast of Florida, in the early months of 2001. Although this fact was well known in the area, having been reported by local newspapers shortly after 9/11 and verified by many witnesses, the Commission simply followed the FBI's timeline, which claimed Atta left the Venice area late in 2000, never to return.[65]

An especially dangerous part of the covered-up story was that, according to Keller, Atta regularly used cocaine, which he obtained from Huffman Aviation, where he was taking flying lessons.[66] Atta's first date with Keller, in fact, reportedly involved what Hopsicker described as a "very un-Islamic three-day drug-and-booze-fueled party in Key West."[67] Although the mainstream press has not asked the 9/11 Commission about such reports, one member of the alternative press, interviewing Commissioner Richard Ben-Veniste, asked: "If Mohamed Atta is technically a fundamentalist Muslim, what is he doing doing cocaine and going to strip bars?" Ben-Veniste replied, "You know, that's a heck of a question."[68] It was a question, however, that the 9/11 Commission, when it issued its report, did not address.

By thus ignoring all evidence to the contrary, the Commission could portray the alleged hijackers as devout Muslims ready to meet their Maker: a "cadre of trained operatives willing to die."[69]

Atta to Portland? As I suggested in NPH, the information reportedly found in Atta's luggage, which had failed to get loaded onto Flight 11, appears to have been planted. Additional evidence, unknown to me at that time, suggests an even more radical conclusion.[70]

According to the official story, partially told on the first page of *The 9/11 Commission Report*, Atta and another hijacker, Abdul al-Omari, rented a blue Nissan Altima in Boston on September 10 and drove up to Portland, Maine, where they stayed overnight at the Comfort Inn. Early the next morning, they drove the Nissan to the Portland airport, left it in the parking lot, and caught the 6:00AM commuter flight to Boston. They arrived there at 6:45, with time to spare to catch American Flight 11, which was not scheduled to depart until 7:45.[71] For some reason, however, Atta's luggage did not make the connection. When authorities later discovered and opened this luggage, they found a treasure trove of information, which seemed to leave no doubt about al-Qaeda's responsibility for the hijackings.

There have always been two mysteries about this story. First, why would Atta, after he was already in Boston, have gone to Portland and stayed overnight, making his arrival back at the Boston airport in time to catch American Flight 11 contingent on the commuter flight, which might have been late? Atta was (allegedly) the designated pilot for Flight 11 and the ringleader of the whole operation, which, after years of planning, he might have had to call off. Why would he have taken such a risk? Both the 9/11 Commission and the FBI admitted that they had no answer for this question.[72] The second mystery is based on the fact that the commuter flight arrived an hour before Flight 11's scheduled departure time, as the 9/11 Commission admitted.[73] Why, then, did Atta's bags not get loaded onto Flight 11? (A careless ground crew cannot be blamed, since the bags of all the other passengers reportedly made it.[74])

The reason for these mysteries appears to be that the whole Atta-went-to-Portland story was a late invention.

In the first few days after 9/11, news stories reported that the treasure trove of information, rather than being found in Atta's luggage inside the airport, was found in a white Mitsubishi, which Atta had left in the parking lot at Boston's Logan Airport. It was two other alleged hijackers, Adnan Bukhari and Ameer Bukhari, who were said to have driven the rented Nissan to Portland and then flown back to Boston on the commuter flight the next morning.

The distinction between Atta and the men who flew from Portland to Boston was clearly made in a CNN report on September 12, which said:

> Law enforcement sources say that two of the suspected hijackers. . . are brothers that lived [in Vero Beach, Florida]. . . . One of them is Adnan Bukhari. We have a photograph of him . . . . Also living in Vero Beach, Bukhari's brother, Ameer. . . . Law enforcement sources. . . tell CNN that the Bukhari brothers were believed to have been on one of the two flights out of Boston. . . . Also we can report to you that a car impounded in Portland, Maine, according to law enforcement authorities, was rented at Boston Logan Airport and driven to Portland, Maine. Now the Maine state police confirm that two of the suspected hijackers were on a US Air flight out of [Portland Jetport][75]. . . . The FBI is also looking at two more suspected hijackers. . ., Mohammad Atta and Marwan Yusef Alshehhi.[76]

Another CNN report that same day stated that the incriminating materials were found in a car at the Boston airport and, while discussing the Nissan found at the Portland airport, made no suggestion that it had been rented by Atta:

> Law enforcement officials confirmed that a car was seized at Boston's Logan International Airport and that suspicious materials were found. The Boston Herald said there were Arabic language flight training manuals in the car. . . . Meanwhile, in Portland, Maine, police said that two individuals who traveled by plane from that city to Boston were under investigation. "I can tell you those two individuals did get on a plane and fly to Boston early yesterday morning," said Portland Police Chief Mike Chitwood. "I cannot tell you who they are, I cannot tell you where they came from. I can tell you that they are the focus of a federal investigation." He said that the two were recorded on videotape as they went through the Portland Jetport's security cameras. . . . Maine authorities said a car—a rented silver Nissan Altima with Massachusetts plates—was seized from the Portland airport Tuesday evening. Authorities believe the two men—possible hijackers—used that car to travel to the airport, where they boarded an early morning commercial flight to Boston.[77]

Both of these reports clearly distinguished between the Nissan found at the Portland Jetport and the car with Arabic materials found at the Boston airport. Also, because the first story said that CNN had a photo of Adnan Bukhari and the second story said that the two men who took the commuter flight from Portland were recorded on the videotape of the airport's security cameras, it should have been clear whether those two men were the Bukharis or not.

On the next day, September 13, CNN identified the two men as the Bukhari brothers and also identified Atta as the person who had rented the car found at Boston—now identified as a Mitsubishi—containing the Arabic materials:

> Two of the men were brothers, . . . Adnan Bukhari and Ameer Abbas Bukhari. . . . The two rented a car, a silver-blue Nissan Altima, from an Alamo car rental at Boston's Logan Airport and drove to an airport in Portland, Maine, where they got on US Airways Flight 5930 at 6AM Tuesday headed back to Boston, the sources said. . . . A Mitsubishi sedan impounded at Logan Airport was rented by [Mohamed] Atta, sources said. The car contained materials, including flight manuals, written in Arabic that law enforcement sources called "helpful" to the investigation.[78]

That same day, September 13, CNN gave an even fuller account, saying:

> Federal law enforcement in the United States was led to the Hamburg connection by way of information linked to a car seized at Logan Airport. It was a Mitsubishi. It was rented by Mohammed [sic] Atta, who lived in an apartment in Hamburg. . . . Inside was a flight manual in Arabic language material that law enforcement investigators say was very helpful. . . . [W]e are being told by [a] law enforcement source right now that. . . the FBI was on the lead to the Bukhari brothers from that Portland car that they impounded. . . . Also, we know that those two men who took that car to Portland were on a US Air flight from Portland to Logan right before the American and United planes took off.[79]

On the afternoon of September 13, however, CNN suddenly announced that neither of the Bukharis had died on 9/11: Ameer had died the year before and Adnan was still alive. CNN apologized for the "misinformation," which had been "[b]ased on information from multiple law enforcement sources."[80]

Although the story, consequently, began to change, it did not assume its final form immediately. That same article, for example, still said that a Mitsubishi sedan at Boston's Logan Airport, which "sources said was rented by Atta," contained "materials written in Arabic, including flight manuals, that law enforcement sources called 'helpful' to the investigation" and that "led investigators to. . . Mohammed [sic] Atta and Marwan Yousef Alshehhi." Even the next day, September 14, CNN said: "According to law enforcement sources, Atta was on American Airlines Flight 11. . . . A Mitsubishi sedan he rented was found at Boston's Logan Airport. Arabic language materials were found in the car."[81]

That same day, however, the story began to change more drastically. An Associated Press report, citing Portland Police Chief Michael Chitwood, said with respect to "two suspects in the terrorist attacks on the World Trade Center":

> One of the two suspects who boarded a flight in Portland was Mohamed Atta, 33. . . . The 2001 Nissan Altima used by the men came from the same Boston rental location as another car used by additional suspects that contained incriminating materials when it was seized at Boston's Logan Airport.
>
> Once in Maine, the suspects spent the night at the Comfort Inn in South Portland before boarding the plane the next morning, said Stephen McCausland, spokesman for the Maine Public Safety Department.[82]

Suddenly, the Nissan Altima had been driven to Portland by Atta and his companion, who then stayed at the Comfort Inn. But the incriminating materials were still found in a rental car left at Logan (although this car had been rented by unnamed "additional suspects," not Atta).

Finally, on September 16, the *Washington Post* published a story in which the transition to the final form of the story had been completed: Not only had Atta (with al-Omari) driven the rental car to Portland, stayed in the Comfort Inn, then taken the commuter flight back to Boston the next morning. But also, the incriminating evidence was "left in his luggage at Boston's Logan Airport."[83]

By October 5, the FBI had supplied a timeline of the visit to Portland by Atta and al-Omari, complete with witnesses and videos proving that they had been there.[84] One of the images from this video that was circulated by the FBI showed Atta and al-Omari at the Jetport gas station at 8:28:29PM. This photo, however, had been cropped to hide the date.[85] At the trial of Zacarias Moussaoui in 2006, the FBI presented an uncropped copy of this picture, and it showed the date to be 11-10-01, rather than 9-10-01.[86] Although one might regard this photo as evidence that Atta was in Portland on November 10, two months after 9/11, the video was stamped "MON," meaning Monday, and November 10 fell on a Saturday. (September 10 was, of course, a Monday.) Still another problem was that, although the video was stamped 8:28AM, the FBI timeline reported that, on September 10, Atta and al-Omari were at the Jetport station at 9:15, having been photographed at two other places at 8:31 and 8:41.[87] The video was evidently a botched forgery—unless someone at the FBI was engaged in subtle whistle-blowing.

The FBI also included in the evidence to the Moussaoui trial an affidavit, dated 9:53AM September 12 and signed by FBI agent James K. Lechner and US Magistrate Judge David M. Cohen, stating that the blue Nissan Altima found at the Portland Jetport had been rented by Mohamed Atta; that the names of Atta and al-Omari were on the passenger list for American Flight 11; that "American Airlines personnel at Logan discovered two bags [checked to passenger Atta] that had been bound for transfer to AA11 but had not been loaded onto the flight"; and that on September 11, US Magistrate Judge Lawrence P. Cohen had authorized a search of these bags, which included much incriminating material, including Atta's will.[88] (I found no evidence that these two judges, David M. Cohen and Lawrence P. Cohen, are related.)

However, if this affidavit, in its present form, was truly signed early on September 12, the media's reporting on the following days is inexplicable. The media were getting their information from the FBI and other law enforcement officials (CNN said on September 13, as we saw, that the misinformation it had received about the Bukharis had been "[b]ased on information from multiple law enforcement sources"). If the FBI affidavit in its present form had been signed on the morning of September 12, why were the media saying until the afternoon of September 13 that the blue Nissan had been rented and driven to Portland by the Bukharis, and that Atta had rented a Mitsubishi and left it, filled with incriminating materials, in the parking lot at Boston's Logan Airport? And how could we explain the fact that it was evidently not until September 16 that anyone reported that the incriminating materials had been found in Atta's luggage? We could understand all of this, however, if the affidavit, in its present form, had been back-dated.

In any case, learning the history behind the story about Atta's trip and his luggage provides a likely explanation for why this story makes no sense: it was simply invented after the original story about the Portland trip was undermined by the discovery that the Bukharis had not died on 9/11. This new story provided a way to explain why a rental car left at the Portland airport could have led authorities to two of the hijackers. But this solution created the mystery of why Atta would have taken this trip plus the problem of explaining the well-reported fact that incriminating materials had been found at Logan Airport. This latter problem was solved by saying that these materials were found in Atta's luggage, which did not make it onto Flight 11. But this solution created, in turn, the mystery as to why Atta's luggage failed to make the flight. The main problem facing the new story, however, is simply the fact that it *is* a new story, which radically contradicts what the authorities had said the first few days after 9/11.

The idea that this story was a late invention is supported not only by all the contradictions reported above but also by the fact that ticket agent Michael Tuohey, who checked in the two men at the Portland Jetport, described their attire in a way that did not fit the security video footage of Atta and al-Omari. According to a reporter who had interviewed him:

> As [Tuohey] watched the security video taken at the passenger screening area upstairs, he picked out the two men without a doubt. They were no longer wearing the coats and ties they had on when they approached the counter. Tuohey figures they must have taken them off on the way to screening and tucked them into their carry-ons.[89]

That, however, was a very unlikely explanation, especially given the fact that the two men had arrived so late that Tuohey had been worried, he said, that they might miss the flight.[90] Tuohey claimed, in fact, that after Atta started insisting on receiving boarding passes for the second flight (American 11), Tuohey told him: "Mr. Atta, if you don't go now, you will miss your plane."[91]

As that statement illustrated, Tuohey completely supported the official account, according to which the two men he checked in were Atta and al-Omari. He was even cited in *The 9/11 Commission Report* (although it misspelled his name).[92] But his support must be considered suspect, because he made a claim—that the ticket agent in Boston who completed the reservation for Atta and al-Omari committed suicide later[93]—that appears to be baseless.[94] It may be significant, nevertheless, that Tuohey, who otherwise supported the official account, gave a description of the two men's attire that undermined the claim that the security video footage of Atta and al-Omari was taken on September 11 (see the discussion of "Airport Security Videos" below).

Replacements: When it was discovered, after the FBI had prepared its initial list of hijackers, that the Bukharis had not been on Flight 11,[95] replacements were needed. Adnan and Ameer Bukhari, who were thought to be brothers (although Adnan denied it), were replaced by two (other) brothers: Wail and Waleed al-Shehri.[96] The fact that these latter two men were last-minute substitutes may help to explain why they were both reportedly still alive after 9/11.

Moreover, two other men originally on the list of Flight 11 hijackers—Amer Kamfar and Abdulrahman al-Omari—were also replaced.[97] Amer Kamfar was replaced by Satam al-Suqami, and Abdulrahman al-Omari was replaced by a man with a similar name, Abdul Aziz al-Omari. This latter al-Omari was the man who, shortly after he was added to the list, was said to have accompanied Atta to Portland on September 10. This means that, besides the fact that Atta was originally said to have left his rental car in Boston, not Portland, the man who was said to have accompanied him to Portland was not even on the FBI's original list of hijackers.

Another name not originally on the FBI's list of hijackers was that of Hani Hanjour. On September 14 at about 10:00AM, CNN correspondent Kelli Arena, reporting that CNN had "managed to grab a list of the names of the 18 suspected hijackers that is supposed to be officially released by [the Department of] Justice sometime later today," read the list aloud. Instead of Hani Hanjour, the list included a name that, based on her pronunciation, was transcribed as "Mosear Caned."[98] On a list released by CNN at 2:00PM the same day, however, that name had been replaced with Hanjour's.[99] On September 16, a *Washington Post* story, seeking to explain why Hanjour's "name was not on the American Airlines manifest for the flight," said that "he may not have had a ticket."[100] That explanation, however, would raise the question as to how he had gotten on board. In any case, the fact that Hanjour was a last-minute substitute may help explain why the official story about Flight 77 ended up with a pilot who could not fly.

Post-175 Flights for Hamza al-Ghamdi: In February 2008, the FBI released, in response to a FOIA request, a redacted version of a document entitled "Hijackers Timeline."[101] Although this document had been cited extensively (52 times) in *The 9/11 Commission Report*, it contains several items of interest that were not mentioned by the Commission. One of these items indicates that Hamza al-Ghamdi, named as one of the hijackers on United Flight 175—which was supposed to go from Boston to Los Angeles—had booked later flights. Besides having a continuation flight from Los Angeles to San Francisco that same day, al-Ghamdi had also booked flights to and within Saudi Arabia for September 20 and 29.[102] This suggests that if he was on Flight 175, he had not thought of it as a suicide mission. Would this be why the 9/11 Commission did not mention this interesting information?

THE QUESTION OF THE VERY EXISTENCE OF HIJACKERS

As we have seen, much of the evidence that there were hijackers on the planes dissipates upon examination. In Chapter 3, we saw that the phone calls reporting the presence of hijackers on Flight 93 appear to have been faked. In the present chapter, we have seen that the idea that the alleged hijackers were devout Muslims, ready to die for their faith, is contradicted by considerable evidence; that the story about incriminating evidence found in Atta's luggage appears to have been invented; that several of the names on the FBI's final list of hijackers were added after some other names on its original list proved problematic; and that some of the people on this final list appear to have still been alive after 9/11. Does any of the evidence for hijackers stand up? I will look next at six more types of evidence that have been cited: phone calls from the flights (divided into two parts), discovered passports, a discovered headband, airport videos, a hijacker's voice on the radio of Flight 11, and names on flight manifests.

Phone Calls from Flights 77, 93, and 175: In Chapter 2, we saw that, according to the FBI's report presented to the Moussaoui trial in 2006, the phone call from flight attendant Renee May to her parents was not really, as her parents had thought, made from a cell phone. In Chapter 3, we saw that the numerous high-altitude cell phone calls reported from Flight 93, besides being extremely improbable technologically, were said in the FBI's Moussaoui trial evidence to have been made from onboard phones. In light of both the technology of the time and the FBI report, therefore, either all of these calls were faked or, if they really did originate from passengers on the flights, were made from onboard phones. If one accepts the latter possibility, one can still regard these calls as providing evidence that there were hijackers on the flights.

To accept this view, however, one would need to accept the improbable view that Renee May's parents and the relatives of several people on Flight 93 shared the same confusion, mistakenly thinking that their loved ones had said that they were calling on cell phones. This belief becomes even more improbable when we bring in United Flight 175, from which two passengers, Peter Hanson and Brian Sweeney, were believed by their relatives to have called from cell phones.[103] Can we believe that so many people would have made the same mistake? Is it not more likely that they all thought they had been called on cell phones because they had been told this by people pretending, with the aid of voice morphing, to be their relatives?

The case for this conclusion becomes even stronger when we turn to Deena Burnett, who reported that her phone's Caller ID showed her husband's cell phone number. How could she possibly have been confused about that? She must have been called by someone who faked Tom Burnett's cell phone number as well as his voice. And if the calls to Deena Burnett were faked, must we not conclude that the rest of the calls were faked, too?

The case for the conclusion that the calls were faked becomes still stronger when we recall that Ted Olson's story about getting two calls from his wife on American Flight 77 is doubly ruled out, regardless of which version we consider. The cell phone version is ruled out both by the cell phone technology of the time and the FBI report on calls from Flight 77. The onboard phone version is ruled out by American Airlines—which reported that Flight 77, being a Boeing 757, had no onboard phones—and by the FBI report. We must conclude, therefore, that either Ted Olson lied or else he was fooled, like other people, by fake phone calls. Either way, the story that Barbara Olson made two calls, reporting that Flight 77 had been hijacked, was based on deceit. If deceit was involved in this all-important call, we must suspect that all the other reported calls from passengers were deceitful.

Phone Calls from Flight Attendants on American 11: To test this suspicion, we can turn to the one flight not yet discussed, American 11. Although no passenger calls were reported from this flight, there were reportedly two calls made by two of the flight attendants, Madeline ("Amy") Sweeney and Betty Ong. These reported calls have been crucial to the official story about American Flight 11. The 9/11 Commission said that they "tell us most of what we know about how the hijacking happened."[104]

Amy Sweeney reportedly made several attempts to call the American Flight Services Office in Boston and, after finally reaching the manager, Michael Woodward, spoke to him for twelve minutes (8:32 to 8:44). Stating that her plane had been hijacked, she added that the hijackers had slit a passenger's throat and stabbed two flight attendants.[105] Most important, besides reporting that the hijackers were of "Middle Eastern descent," she gave their seat numbers, from which Woodward was able to learn the identities of three of them: Mohamed Atta, Abdul al-Omari, and Satam al-Suqami.[106] Amy Sweeney's call was critical, ABC News explained, because without it, "the plane might have crashed with no one certain the man in charge was tied to al Qaeda."[107]

The story of this very important call, however, contained at least eight problems.[108]

First, the public information about this reported call—its content along with its very occurrence—rested entirely on a report constructed by the FBI. American Airlines employees were ordered by the FBI not to discuss Sweeney's reported call with the press.[109]

Second, the only publicly available document testifying to the occurrence of the call is the previously discussed affidavit by FBI agent James Lechner, dated September 12, 2001, which (dubiously) stated that the blue Nissan had been rented by Mohamed Atta and that the incriminating evidence had been found in Atta's luggage inside Boston's Logan Airport.[110] We have good reason, in other words, to be skeptical of this document.

Third, Lechner's affidavit stated that, according to Woodward, Sweeney had been "using a cellular telephone."[111] But when the 9/11 Commission discussed this reported call, it said that Sweeney had used an onboard phone—which the Commission called an "airphone."[112]

Behind that change of story was the claim, made in 2004, that a previously unreported tape recording existed. Although Michael Woodward, this story said, had not recorded Sweeney's call, because his office had no tape recorder, he had repeated what he was hearing from Sweeney to a colleague, Nancy Wyatt, who then repeated the account by telephone to Ray Howland at American headquarters in Fort Worth, who recorded Wyatt's third-hand account.[113] After Amy Sweeney's husband was informed of the existence of this recording in June 2004, he said to Gail Sheehy:

> I was shocked that I'm finding out, almost three years later, there was a tape with information given by my wife that was very crucial to the happenings of 9/11. Suddenly it miraculously appears and falls into the hands of FBI? . . . Why did it surface now?[114]

The answer to this question might have something to do with one piece of information on the tape: that Amy Sweeney, thanks to "an AirFone card, given to her by another flight attendant," had used a passenger-seat phone.[115] Given this information, there was no need to claim that Amy Sweeney had completed a high-altitude cell phone call that lasted for twelve minutes. That this was indeed the motive is supported by the evidence, reported in Chapter 3, that the FBI in 2004 also changed its report about phone calls from Flight 93, so that it no longer affirmed any high-altitude cell phone calls.

The FBI's new account of Amy Sweeney's call, however, raised the question of why Lechner's FBI affidavit had stated that, according to Woodward, Sweeney had called on a cell phone. Although stories sometimes get changed in the retelling, it is hardly conceivable that, if Woodward had told Nancy Wyatt that Sweeney was using a cell phone, Wyatt could have misunderstood him to have said that she had borrowed a calling card in order to use an onboard phone.[116]

In light of what is publicly known, in fact, it seems possible that the Wyatt recording was created, rather than discovered, in 2004 (perhaps as part of a more general transformation of most of the reported cell phone calls into calls from onboard phones, which would explain why the FBI report on phone calls presented for the Moussaoui trial in 2006 differed radically from previous reports, as discussed in Chapter 3, with regard to the number of cell phone calls made from the airliners). This supposition would be in line with Eric Lichtblau's account on September 20, 2001, which said:

> FBI officials in Dallas, where American Airlines is based, were able, on the day of the terrorist attacks, to piece together a partial transcript and an account of the phone call. American Airlines officials said such calls are not typically recorded, suggesting that the FBI may have reconstructed the conversation from interviews.[117]

The supposition that there was no recording made on 9/11 is also supported by a statement in 2002 by American Airlines spokesman John Hotard. Referring to "Woodward's original notes of his conversation with Sweeney," Hotard said: "I've never seen them. . . . But the FBI got a hold of them very quickly, and wrote a summary."[118] Why would the FBI have used Woodward's notes to write its summary if it had a tape recording in which Amy

Sweeney's statements had been repeated verbatim? (Woodward, in explaining to FBI agent James Lechner why he had not made a recording, would surely have mentioned that a recording of the word-for-word repetition of her message was available at American Airlines headquarters in Dallas.)

A fourth problem with Sweeney's reported call involves timing. The FBI document about Sweeney's call said, according to Lichtblau's article, that while she was relating details about the hijackers, they stormed the front of the plane and "had just gained access to the cockpit."[119] The 9/11 Commission said, however, that the hijacking of Flight 11 "began at 8:14 or shortly thereafter" but that Sweeney's call did not go through until 8:25.[120] The FBI report, therefore, portrayed her as describing the hijacking as beginning at least eleven minutes after it, according to the Commission, had been successfully carried out. (This timing problem is similar to the problem discussed with the Glick call, pointed out in Chapter 3, according to which the passenger revolt on Flight 93 began at least six minutes later than it did according to the Commission's timeline.)

A fifth problem with the reported call from Sweeney involves the all-important seat identifications. According to Gail Sheehy's account of this call:

> [Sweeney] gave him [Michael Woodward] the seat locations of three of the hijackers: 9D, 9G and 10B. . . . Mr. Woodward ordered a colleague to punch up those seat locations on the computer. At least 20 minutes before the plane crashed, the airline had the names. . . of three of the five hijackers. They knew that 9G was Abdulaziz al-Omari, 10B was Satam al-Suqami, and 9D was Mohamed Atta—the ringleader of the 9/11 terrorists.[121]

According to the official report, however, Atta and al-Omari were in 8D and 8G, respectively.[122] How could they have been correctly identified by Woodward if Sweeney had said that they were in Row 9 rather than Row 8?

A sixth problem is that this same divergence from the official story—putting two of the hijackers in the ninth row—was contained in the call from the voice claiming to be flight attendant Betty Ong. The recording of this call was played at a

9/11 Commission hearing in 2004 and presented at the Moussaoui trial in 2006.[123] "Ong," speaking of "the four hijackers," said that they "had come from first-class seats 2A, 2B, 9A and 9B."[124] Seats 2A and 2B agree with the official story, according to which those seats were occupied by Wail and Waleed al-Shehri, respectively. But her statement that two of the hijackers were in 9A and 9B differed from both the statement by "Sweeney" (9D and 9G) and the official view (8D and 8G).

A seventh problem is that, whereas the official view is that there were five hijackers on Flight 11, both "Sweeney" and "Ong" spoke of only four. The statement by "Ong" was quoted in the previous paragraph. The fact that "Sweeney" said the same was shown in Eric Lichtblau's *Los Angeles Times* article of September 20, 2001, which said:

> Investigators have identified five suspected hijackers on the flight. . . . But Sweeney apparently saw only four of the five men.
> . . . Investigators noted that Sweeney even had the presence of mind to relay the exact seat numbers of the four suspects in the ninth and 10th rows, although a few of those seats do not match up with the seats assigned to the hijackers on the tickets they purchased.[125]

Mentioning only four hijackers and placing two of them in the ninth row were not, moreover, the only points on which the calls by "Ong" and "Sweeney" shared an error (meaning a statement that disagreed with what became the official story). After "Ong" called an American Airlines reservations desk in Raleigh, North Carolina, to report that her flight had been hijacked, she was asked which flight she was on. In a portion of the call that was recorded and can be heard on the Internet, she replied, "Flight 12" and did not correct the error until about a minute later.[126] Also, the person who took the first call from "Amy Sweeney" reported, according to the 9/11 Commission, that she had said that she was on Flight 12 (which was indeed scheduled to fly out of Boston that morning but had not yet departed).[127] This shared error constitutes an eighth problem.

How can we explain the fact that the calls by "Sweeney" and "Ong" had three errors in common and yet disagreed on the seating of the hijackers? One possibility would be that the people who made the calls were reading from scripts that contained identical errors (about the flight number and the number of hijackers) along with some divergent errors (the hijackers' seat numbers).

The questions about "Betty Ong" became even more complex with the appearance of another version of the "Ong" transcript. This version, which says that it was transcribed by the FBI on September 12, 2001, from an American Airlines recording, was declassified March 20, 2006.[128] It differs from the transcription of the previously known "Ong" recording in many ways: It is somewhat longer and refers to many unintelligible gaps (which are mostly not audible in the previously known recording); the statements by "Ong" occur in a different order; the statements by the two American Airlines employees—Winston and Vanessa— also differ, accordingly; the mistaken reference to the plane as "Flight 12" is made only by Winston and Vanessa, not by "Ong" herself, who consistently says "Flight 11"; and she did not, unlike "Ong" in the other transcript, say, "I think we're getting hijacked." How could the two transcripts differ so radically if they were both transcribed from the same tape recording of a call from flight attendant Betty Ong calling from American Flight 11?[129]

Given all of these problems, the alleged calls from Amy Sweeney and Betty Ong are far too problematic to be regarded as authentic. They do nothing, therefore, to contradict our previous conclusion—that the reported phone calls from passengers and flight attendants do not provide credible evidence that the airliners were hijacked by Middle Eastern men.

Discovered Passports: Although Satam al-Suqami might have been a late addition to the FBI's list of hijackers on Flight 11, the fact that he was actually on this flight was said to have been proved by the discovery of his passport at the site of the World Trade Center. But this claim came in two versions. According to the first version, provided by the FBI, al-Suqami's passport was found on the ground following the collapse of the Twin Towers.[130] After this claim was ridiculed—"[T]he idea that [this] passport had escaped from that inferno unsinged," wrote one reporter, "would [test] the credulity of the staunchest supporter of the FBI's crackdown on terrorism"[131]—the 9/11 Commission modified it to the claim that al-Suqami's passport was found before the towers collapsed.[132] This modified claim was evidently thought to be less obviously absurd: Rather than needing to survive the collapse of the North Tower, the passport merely needed to escape from the plane's cabin, avoid being destroyed by the jet-fuel fire, and then find its way to the ground, landing in a place where it could be spotted. This claim is indeed less absurd—but only slightly so.

In strong competition for the most absurd passport story is the one told about Flight 93, according to which the passport of Ziad Jarrah, said to have been flying the plane, was found at the crash site.[133] It was allegedly found on the ground even though, as pointed out in NPH, there was virtually nothing at the crash site to indicate that an airliner had crashed there. The reason for this, we were told, was that the plane had been headed downwards at 580 miles per hour and, when it hit the soft Pennsylvania soil, buried itself deep in the ground.[134] We are supposed to believe, therefore, that although Jarrah's body, which was in the cockpit, was thrust dozens of feet into the ground, his passport escaped from this fast-moving plane just before it buried itself in the soil. Did Jarrah, going 580 miles per hour, have a window open?[135]

A Discovered Headband: Problematic for the same reason was the claim that investigators also found at the Flight 93 crash site one of the red headbands that, according to some of the phone calls, the hijackers were wearing.[136] This claim was problematic for an additional reason. Former CIA agent Milt Bearden, who helped train the mujahideen fighters in Afghanistan, has pointed out that it would have been very unlikely that members of al-Qaeda would have worn such headbands:

> [The red headband] is a uniquely Shi'a Muslim adornment. It is something that dates back to the formation of the Shi'a sect. . . . [I]t represents the preparation of he who wears this red headband to sacrifice his life, to murder himself for the cause. Sunnis are by and large most of the people following Osama bin Laden [and they] do not do this.[137]

We have good reason, therefore, to conclude that the headband was planted, evidently by people who did not know the difference between Shi'a and Sunni Muslims.

Airport Security Videos: People in America and around the world have seen frames from videos, purportedly taken by airport security cameras, that were said to show hijackers checking into airports. For example, photos showing Mohamed Atta and Abdul al-Omari checking into an airport "were flashed round the world and gave a kick start to the official story in the vital hours after the attacks."[138] However, although it was widely assumed that these photos were from the airport at Boston, they were really from the airport at Portland (at least purportedly). There were no photos showing Atta or any of the other alleged hijackers at Boston's Logan Airport. We at best have photographic evidence that Atta and al-Omari were at the Portland airport.

Moreover, in light of the fact that the story of Atta and al-Omari going to Portland was apparently a late invention, we might expect the photographic evidence that they were there on the morning of September 11 to be problematic, and indeed it is. I mentioned above the curious fact that Portland ticket agent Michael Tuohey, while otherwise supporting the view that Atta and al-Omari boarded the flight from Portland to Boston, described their attire in a way that did not match the security video. But also, a photo showing Atta and al-Omari passing through the security checkpoint is marked both 05:45 and 05:53.[139] Perhaps this video was fabricated by the same person who created the one of Atta at the Jetport gas station, mentioned earlier.

Another airport video was distributed worldwide on July 21, 2004, the day that *The 9/11 Commission Report* was published. The Associated Press, using a frame from it as corroboration of the official story, included this caption:

> Hijacker Khalid al-Mihdhar. . . passes through the security checkpoint at Dulles International Airport in Chantilly, Va., Sept. 11 2001, just hours before American Airlines Flight 77 crashed into the Pentagon in this image from a surveillance video.[140]

This video would seem to be the one described in *The 9/11 Commission Report* as "Metropolitan Washington Airport Authority videotape, Dulles main terminal checkpoints, Sept 11 2001."[141]

However, as Rowland Morgan and Ian Henshall have pointed out, "a normal security video has time and date burned into the integral video image by proprietary equipment according to an authenticated pattern, along with camera identification and the location that the camera covered. The video released in 2004 contained no such data."[142] It also was of much lower resolution than airport security videos usually are. In spite of what the Associated Press told the world, accordingly, there was no evidence that this video was taken on September 11 or even at Dulles.

The lack of credible video evidence that the alleged hijackers boarded the planes is matched, moreover, by the absence of credible eyewitness testimony. *The 9/11 Commission Report* admits, in fact, that "[n]one of the checkpoint supervisors [at Logan Airport in Boston] recalled the hijackers or reported anything suspicious regarding their screening."[143]

Hijacker's Voice on Radio? One piece of irrefutable evidence for the existence of hijackers on the planes, it might be thought, was provided by three transmissions from Flight 11 heard by air traffic controllers at the FAA's Boston Center, in which a hijacker said:

> We have some planes. Just stay quiet, and you'll be okay. We are returning to the airport. . . .
> Nobody move. Everything will be okay. If you try to make any moves, you'll endanger yourself and the airplane. Just stay quiet. . . .
> Nobody move please. We are going back to the airport. Don't try to make any stupid moves.[144]

The 9/11 Commission Report, besides using the first line, "We have some planes," as the title of its first chapter, stated that these transmissions came from "American 11."

The Commission failed to inform its readers, however, that there was really no proof that this had been the case. According to the FAA's "Summary of Air Traffic Hijack Events," published

September 17, 2001, each of these transmissions was "from an unknown origin."[145] Bill Peacock, the FAA's air traffic director, said: "We didn't know where the transmission came from."[146] The idea that it came from American 11 was a pure inference. This inference would be justified only if we had independent evidence that hijackers had taken over American Flight 11, which we do not.

Flight Manifests: But, it might be assumed, we do have such evidence, because the names of the hijackers were on the passenger manifests for the four flights. According to Richard Clarke, the FBI told him at about 10:00 that morning that it recognized the names of some al-Qaeda operatives on passenger manifests it had received from the airlines. CIA Director George Tenet said that he had obtained the manifests and recognized some al-Qaeda names on them.[147] With regard to the question of how the FBI itself acquired its list, Robert Bonner, the head of Customs and Border Protection, told the 9/11 Commission in 2004:

> On the morning of 9/11, through an evaluation of data related to the passengers manifest for the four terrorist hijacked aircraft, Customs Office of Intelligence was able to identify the likely terrorist hijackers. Within 45 minutes of the attacks, Customs forwarded the passenger lists with the names of the victims and 19 probable hijackers to the FBI and the intelligence community.[148]

Under questioning, Bonner added:

> We were able to pull from the airlines the passenger manifest for each of the four flights. We ran the manifest through [our lookout] system. . . . [B]y 11:00AM, I'd seen a sheet that essentially identified the 19 probable hijackers. And in fact, they turned out to be, based upon further follow-up in detailed investigation, to be the 19.[149]

Bonner's statement, however, is doubly problematic. In the first place, the initial FBI list, as we saw above, had only 18 names. In the second place, as we also saw, several of those names were subsequently replaced with other names. It would seem, therefore, that the FBI's final list of hijackers was drawn from some source other than passenger manifests received from the airlines on September 11.

This suspicion is supported by the fact that the passenger manifests that were released to the public included no names of any of the 19 alleged hijackers and, in fact, no Middle Eastern names whatsoever.[150] These manifests, therefore, supported the suspicion that there were no al-Qaeda hijackers on the planes.

It might appear that this problem has been rectified. In 2005, a photocopy of a portion of an apparent passenger manifest from American Flight 11, with the names of three of the alleged hijackers, was contained in a book by Terry McDermott, *Perfect Soldiers: The 9/11 Hijackers*.[151] McDermott reportedly said that he had received these manifests from the FBI.[152] However, these purported manifests do not appear to have been included in the evidence presented by the FBI to the Moussaoui trial in 2006.[153]

Another problem with these manifests is that they appear in some respects to be too good to be true. (Copies of these alleged manifests can be viewed on the Internet.[154]) One problem is that Ziad Jarrah's last name was spelled correctly, whereas in the early days after 9/11, the FBI was referring to him as "Jarrahi," as news reports from the time show.[155] A second problem is that the manifest for American Flight 77 contains Hani Hanjour's name. This is a problem because, as pointed out earlier, the FBI's initial list of hijackers for Flight 77 included a name transcribed as "Mosear Caned" instead of the name Hani Hanjour, leading the *Washington Post* to speculate as to why Hanjour's "name was not on the American Airlines manifest for the flight."[156] Finally, the manifest for American Flight 11 contains the names of Wail al-Shehri, Waleed al-Shehri, Satam al-Suqami, and Abdul Aziz al-Omari. As we saw earlier, however, the FBI's original list of Flight 11 hijackers instead included the names of Adnan Bukhari, Ameer Bukhari, Amer Kamfar, and Abdulrahman al-Omari. Besides problematically spelling Jarrah's name correctly, therefore, these apparent flight manifests contain five names that had not been on the FBI's first list of hijackers. How, then, could these documents possibly be the actual passenger manifests from September 11, 2001?

The Pilots Who Didn't Squawk: Having examined various kinds of evidence offered by the government for the existence of hijackers on the flights, we have seen that none of this evidence stands up to scrutiny. This absence of good evidence for the existence of hijackers is complemented by the presence of good evidence for their nonexistence. This evidence is based on the fact that, if the planes had really been taken over by men breaking into the cockpits, at least some of the eight pilots of the four flights would have used the standard method for alerting ground control that their planes were being hijacked—entering the standard hijack code (7500) into their transponders in order to "squawk" this code to controllers on the ground.[157] As the *Christian Science Monitor* wrote the day after 9/11, referring to the (alleged) hijacking of American Flight 11:

> The pilots apparently did not punch in the four-digit hijack code. . . into the transponder, the controller says, because the radar facility never received any transmitted code—which a pilot would normally send the moment a hijack situation was known.[158]

The fact that neither of the Flight 11 pilots squawked this code, which they "normally" would do, constitutes a big problem for the official story. We can see this more clearly by looking at CNN's treatment of this issue the same day, which said:

> Flight 11 was hijacked apparently by knife-wielding men. Airline pilots are trained to handle such situations by keeping calm, complying with requests, and if possible, dialing in an emergency four digit code on a device called a transponder. It transmits crucial flight data to air traffic controllers. The action takes seconds, but it appears no such code was entered.[159]

A problem with this statement is that the word "dialing" suggests that the operation would be like dialing a telephone, which might take several seconds. However, the transponder (at least on a Boeing 757 or 767) has four knobs. The pilot (or co-pilot) simply rotates the knobs until the transponder reads "7500." This action, pilots have told me, takes only two or three seconds.

In any case, the crucial issue was indicated in the CNN story by the phrase "if possible": Would it have been possible for the pilots of Flight 11 to have performed this action? Right after the above-quoted comment, CNN said:

But in the cabin, a frantic flight attendant managed to use a phone to call American Airlines Command Center in Dallas. She reported the trouble. And according to *The Christian Science Monitor*, a pilot apparently keyed the microphone, transmitting a cockpit conversation.[160]

If there was time for both of those actions to be taken, there would have been more than enough time for one of the pilots to squawk the four-digit hijack code.

The same conclusion follows from the 9/11 Commission's account, which said:

We do not know exactly how the hijackers gained access to the cockpit; FAA rules required that the doors remain closed and locked during the flight. [Flight attendant Betty] Ong speculated that they had "jammed their way" in. Perhaps the terrorists stabbed the flight attendants to get a cockpit key, to force one of them to open the cockpit door, or to lure the captain or first officer out of the cockpit.[161]

If any of those scenarios described what really occurred on Flight 11, one of the pilots would have been able to squawk the hijack code. As the *Christian Science Monitor* pointed out, the pilots' failure to send the code was an "anomaly."[162]

How did the 9/11 Commission treat this problem? It did acknowledge that sending the code would have been standard procedure, writing:

FAA guidance to controllers on hijack procedures assumed that the aircraft pilot would notify the controller via radio or by "squawking" a transponder code of "7500"—the universal code for a hijack in progress.[163]

The Commission's report, however, did not explore the question of why the pilots, given their training, failed to send the hijack code. The Commission implicitly admitted, therefore, that this was a problem that it could not solve.

Moreover, if the pilots on American Flight 11 should have had time to squawk the hijack code, that would have been all the more true of the pilots on United Flight 93, given the official story. According to a reporter's description of the (purported) tapes from this flight, which had been played at the Moussaoui trial:

The prosecutors Tuesday played two other tapes from the cockpit that were picked up by ground control. In those tapes, the pilots shouted as hijackers broke into the cockpit. "Mayday! Mayday! Mayday!" a pilot screamed in the first tape. In the second tape, 30 seconds later, a pilot shouted: "Mayday! Get out of here! Get out of here!"[164]

According to these tapes, at least one of the pilots was still alive and coherent 30 seconds after realizing that hijackers were breaking into the cockpit. And yet in all that time, neither he nor the other pilot, according to the official account, did the most important thing they had been trained to do—turn the transponder to 7500.

In addition to the pilots on Flights 11 and 93, furthermore, the four pilots on Flights 175 and 77 all, coincidentally, failed to do this as well. This is a lot of coincidences to accept.

In one of Sir Arthur Conan Doyle's most famous short stories, "Silver Blaze," Sherlock Holmes's solution to a mystery hinged on a dog that failed to bark. Silver Blaze, a famous race horse, had disappeared the night before a big race. A Scotland Yard detective believed that an intruder had stolen it. Holmes, doubting this, pointed to "the curious incident of the dog in the night-time." The inspector replied: "The dog did nothing in the night-time." Holmes explained: "That was the curious incident."[165] Had there really been an intruder, in other words, the dog would have barked. This has become widely known as the case of "the dog that didn't bark."

Just as the intruder theory was disproved by the dog that didn't bark, the hijacker theory is disproved by the pilots who didn't squawk.

In NPH, I raised the question of "the true identity of the hijackers." Now, however, it appears that there is no good evidence for hijackers at all. Although it might seem unwarranted to move from the lack of evidence for hijackers to the conclusion that there really were no hijackers on the planes, there are three good reasons to make this move. First, all of the evidence for the existence of hijackers appears to have been fabricated, and such fabrication would have made sense only if the supposed hijackers really did not exist. Second, the fact that none of the pilots used their transponders to squawk the hijack code provides powerful evidence against the view that hijackers broke into the cockpits. Third, the role assigned to the hijackers in the official narrative— that of guiding the planes to their targets—could perhaps have been performed more effectively by remote control.[166] This third reason is not, however, a subject that needs to be settled in advance of a real investigation into 9/11. All we need in order to demand such an investigation is strong evidence that the official story about the hijackers is false, and we have far more than enough of that.

THEN WHO WERE THESE MEN? EVIDENCE FROM ABLE DANGER

If the "Muslim hijackers" were not really devout Muslims and not even hijackers, then who were Atta and these other men? A clue may come from a project known as Able Danger.

Able Danger was a "data-mining" project based on techniques pioneered by the US Army's Land Information Warfare Activity (LIWA), which was set up in 1999 on behalf of the Defense Department's Special Operations Command (SOCOM). It focused on finding members of al-Qaeda by looking for people associated with Sheik Omar Abdel-Rahman, considered the mastermind of the 1993 bombing of the World Trade Center. The team soon found evidence of al-Qaeda cells in the New York City area in late 1999 and early 2000.

One of the members of the Able Danger team was US Army Colonel Anthony Shaffer of the Pentagon's Defense Intelligence Agency (DIA). He worked closely with US Navy Captain Scott Phillpott, who headed up the Able Danger operation. After finding the al-Qaeda cells, Shaffer tried, he said, to arrange a meeting between Colonel Worthington, who was Phillpott's superior, and FBI Counterterrorism agents in Washington DC, to work out a cooperative approach to tracking these cells. But three times, Shaffer said, such a meeting was prevented by SOCOM lawyers.[167]

Shortly thereafter, the Army ordered the Able Danger documents destroyed and Shaffer was ordered by his DIA superior to cease all support for Scott Phillpott and Able Danger. He was then transferred to the DIA's HUMINT (Human Intelligence) project in Latin America.[168]

The Discovery: After the 9/11 attacks, Shaffer and other members of the Able Danger team, he reported, learned that the al-Qaeda cell members included Mohamed Atta. One participant in the project, Dr. Eileen Preisser (who ran LIWA's Information Dominance Project), showed him Atta's photograph on one of the charts they had prepared in January 2000.[169] Scott Phillpott also reported seeing Atta's photo on a chart.[170] During the last week of September 2001, Dr. Preisser, along with three Republican Congressmen—Curt Weldon, Chris Shays, and Dan Burton—showed the "Atta chart" to Deputy National Security Advisor Stephen Hadley,[171] who said he would show it to President Bush.[172]

Shortly thereafter, moreover, the team realized that their data showed that three more of the (alleged) hijackers—Marwan al-Shehhi, Khalid al-Mihdhar, and Nawaf al-Hazmi—had been identified.[173]

Reports to the 9/11 Commission: Although Shaffer had been removed from the project, he got permission, after he returned to Afghanistan (where he had previously won a Bronze Star), to meet on October 23, 2003, with Philip Zelikow and some 9/11 Commission staff members, who happened to be at Bagram Air Force Base, where Shaffer was stationed. During that meeting, which lasted for over an hour, Shaffer informed Zelikow and the others of Able Danger, including the fact, he reported, that Atta had been identified.[174]

Zelikow, according to Shaffer, gave him his card and said: "What you have said here today is very important. Please contact me upon your return to the United States so we can continue this dialogue." However, when Shaffer tried to do this in January 2004, he was told that the Commission had already learned all it needed to know about Able Danger.[175]

Next, after Shaffer reported to his superiors in DIA of his offer to share Able Danger information with the 9/11 Commission, his security clearance was suspended and, his supervisor informed him, all his classified documents, including his Able Danger documents, were destroyed. DIA also started harassing him, he reported, and making accusations against him about things that had occurred 10 to 25 years earlier.[176]

On July 12, 2004, Captain Phillpott, having asked to speak to the 9/11 Commission, was interviewed by staff member Dietrich "Dieter" Snell. Phillpott informed him about Able Danger and the fact that in early 2000 it had Atta's name and photograph. However, even though Phillpott's report reinforced what the Commission had heard from Shaffer several months earlier, the Commission's report, when it was issued ten days later, contained nothing about Able Danger.[177]

Representative Weldon Gets the Story Out: In May of the following year (2005), Shaffer was asked by superiors to visit the office of Republican Congressman Curt Weldon, the vice chairman of the House Committee on Armed Services, to assist him and Captain Phillpott in setting up an Able Danger-like capability for the Navy. Weldon, who had already learned about Able Danger from Phillpott, quizzed Shaffer, who repeated what he had told Zelikow in Afghanistan. This information led Weldon, Shaffer reported, to ask the Commission (by then technically called "The 9/11 Discourse Project") why it had not mentioned Able Danger—a question to which Weldon received an answer that he found unsatisfactory.[178]

In June, Weldon revealed what he had learned about Able Danger to reporter Keith Phucas of the *Times Herald* (Norristown, PA), who published a story that began: "Two years before the Sept. 11, 2001, attacks, US intelligence officials linked Mohammed Atta to al-Qaida, and discovered he and two others were in Brooklyn."[179] In spite of the sensational nature of this allegation, the national media did not pick up the story.

Later in June, Congressman Weldon, during an address to the House, used an enlarged version of the chart that he had received from Eileen Preisser and then had shown to Stephen Hadley. Pointing out Mohamed Atta's name on the chart, he asked why the Able Danger group was not allowed to inform the FBI about its discovery and why the 9/11 Commission had not mentioned it. He then said:

> We have to ask the question, why have these issues not been brought forth before this day? I had my Chief of Staff call the 9/11 Commission staff and ask the question: Why did you not mention Able Danger in your report? The Deputy Chief of Staff

said, well, we looked at it, but we did not want to go down that direction. So the question, Mr. Speaker, is why did they not want to go down that direction? Where will that lead us? Why do we not want to see the answers to the questions I have raised tonight? Who made the decision to tell our military not to pursue Mohamed Atta?[180]

In the middle of August that year (2005), Able Danger finally became big news. Weldon, having sent the Commission a letter complaining that "[t]he 9/11 Commission staff received not one but two briefings on Able Danger from former team members, yet did not pursue the matter," made this letter public.[181] The *New York Times* published several stories about Able Danger's claims and the Commission's response.[182] Thomas Kean and Lee Hamilton published an explanation as to why the Commission's report had not mentioned Able Danger.[183] And Anthony Shaffer, because of his "frustration" with this explanation, decided to go public, allowing reporters Keith Phucas (who had written the first Able Danger story), Philip Shenon (who had co-authored the *New York Times* stories), and Fox News to reveal his name.[184]

The Commission's Explanation: Kean and Hamilton's explanation as to why the Commission's report had not mentioned Able Danger contained three major claims.[185] One was that, according to the memos and memories of the staff members who met with Shaffer in Afghanistan in 2003, he had not mentioned Mohamed Atta by name, so the July 2004 report by the Navy captain (Phillpott was not yet being identified by name) was *not* the second time the staff had been told that Able Danger had identified Atta before 9/11).[186] In response, Shaffer, who insisted that he had named Atta in the meeting with Zelikow, replied: "I kept my talking points [for the meeting]. And I'm confident about what I said."[187]

A second reason given by Kean and Hamilton for ignoring Able Danger was that, although the Commission had asked the Pentagon for all its documents relating to this operation, "None of the documents turned over to the Commission mention Mohamed Atta or any of the other future hijackers." In response, Shaffer said: "I'm told confidently by the person who moved the material over, that the Sept. 11 commission received two briefcase-sized containers of documents. I can tell you for a fact that would not be one-twentieth of the information that Able Danger consisted of during the time we spent."[188]

Giving a third reason for ignoring the claim by the Navy captain that Able Danger had discovered Atta's association with a Brooklyn al-Qaeda cell in early 2000, Kean and Hamilton said that the Commission could not find this claim credible. Why? Because "the Commission knew that. . . Atta first . . . arrived in the United States. . . on June 3, 2000." Kean and Hamilton were here relying on Dietrich Snell, who had provided the "assessment of [Phillpott's] knowledge and credibility."[189] This was clearly the Commission's main reason for dismissing the idea that Atta could have been in the New York area in late 1999 or early 2000. For example, Al Felzenberg, the Commission's spokesman, said: "The investigators knew that this was impossible. . . . There was no way that Atta could have been in the United States at that time."[190]

However, Able Danger's evidence, insofar as it did suggest that Atta was in the country before June,[191] could have been backed up by other reports. A month after 9/11, a newspaper in Portland, Maine, said:

> Portland police interviewed two employees at the Portland Public Library who are sure they saw Atta on several occasions. Spruce Whited, head of security at the library, said he first saw a man he is convinced was Atta in April 2000. He said the man came to the library several times, using the computers. "I only recognized him because he'd been here a few times," he said. Kathy Barry, a reference librarian, also reported seeing Atta, whose photograph has been distributed widely through the media.[192]

The library's executive director reported that three other employees told her that they had seen Atta about a half dozen times in the spring and summer of 2000.[193] Even the Department of Justice reportedly confirmed Atta's presence:

> Mohamed Atta. . . rented rooms in New York City in the spring of 2000 with another hijacker, a federal investigator said. . . . Investigators confirmed that Atta and the second man rented rooms in Brooklyn and the Bronx. . . . Atta's trail in Brooklyn began with a parking ticket issued to a rental car he was driving, said a senior Justice Department official.[194]

Still another report came from Johnelle Bryant of the US Department of Agriculture. Talking to Brian Ross of ABC News "in defiance of direct orders from the USDA's Washington headquarters," Bryant said that Atta came into her office "sometime between the end of April and the middle of May 2000," asking for a loan to buy a small airplane (which she refused to give). Bryant reported that when she wrote down his name, she spelled it A-T-T-A-H, leading him to say: "No, A-T-T-A, as in Atta boy!"[195]

It would seem, therefore, that although Kean and Hamilton said that the Commission knew that Atta first arrived in the United States on June 3, they did not. What they knew was that this is what the FBI had reported.[196] But as we saw earlier, the FBI timeline on Atta simply ignored a lot of evidence that contradicts it; in this case, it ignored evidence from its own department. The Commission's main reason for dismissing the Able Danger information was, therefore, unsound. The Commission should have used the reports from Shaffer and Phillpott, along with these other reports about Atta's early 2000 presence in this country, to question the FBI's claim that Atta was not here prior to June 3.

Further Developments Strengthening the Case: The plausibility of the Able Danger claim about Atta, moreover, was soon bolstered by further developments. First, Scott Phillpott publicly acknowledged that he was the Navy captain who had briefed the Commission in 2004 and then restated his main claim: "Atta was identified by Able Danger by January–February of 2000."[197]

Second, Weldon arranged for a *New York Times* interview with James D. Smith, who as an employee of Orion Scientific Systems had carried out much of Able Danger's technical work. Answering the question, which skeptics had raised, as to how Able Danger could have gotten Atta's photograph that early, Smith reported that he had obtained it from a person in California who had been paid to gather information from Middle East contacts. Smith also, reporting that he had helped create the chart with Atta's picture on it, added that it had been on his office wall at Andrews Air Force Base until 2004. Smith's coming out meant, moreover, that three credible people were publicly stating that an Able Danger chart created in late 1999 or early 2000 had Atta's name and photograph on it.[198]

A third supportive development came, surprisingly, from the Pentagon. In late August 2005, Pentagon spokesman Lawrence Di Rita had made skeptical comments, saying that the Pentagon had found no documents to support the claims by Phillpott and Shaffer and adding that, although they were respected officers, "memory is a complicated thing."[199] In early September, however, the Pentagon admitted that, by interviewing 80 people who had been involved with Able Danger, it had found three more who said they had seen the chart with Atta's name on it, two of whom also recalled seeing his picture. One of these was James Smith, who had already spoken out. The other two were Dr. Eileen Preisser and a Mr. (probably Christopher) Westphal.[200] These additions brought the total number of Pentagon employees who had seen the chart with Atta's name on it up to five—four of whom said they had seen Atta's picture.[201]

The 9/11 Commission, however, remained unimpressed. According to an Associated Press story published in mid-September:

> The commission's former chairman, Thomas Kean, said there was no evidence anyone in the government knew about Atta before Sept. 11, 2001. . . . Kean said the recollections of the intelligence officers cannot be verified by any document. "Bluntly, it just didn't happen and that's the conclusion of all 10 of us," said a former commissioner, former senator Slade Gorton.[202]

Given the fact that five people had testified to seeing the chart, how could Kean claim that there was "no evidence?" He was obviously limiting "evidence" to "documentary evidence," even though testimony by credible people is accepted as evidence in a court of law, and even though many of the claims made in *The 9/11 Commission Report* were based solely on testimonial evidence. Gorton made an even more extreme statement, moving from the absence of documentary evidence to the unwarranted assertion that the claims by these five people were false. This assertion was especially unwarranted in the light of reports, widely discussed, that Able Danger documents had been destroyed.[203]

In the next major development, members of Able Danger were scheduled to testify before the Senate Judiciary Committee but were blocked from doing so by the Pentagon.[204] The committee did hear from the attorney for Shaffer and Smith, Mark Zaid, and also from former Able Danger team member Erik Kleinsmith. (Having retired from the Army, he could not be prevented from testifying.) When asked by Senator Arlen Specter whether he was in a position "to evaluate the credibility of Captain Phillpott, Colonel Shaffer, Mr. Westphal, Ms. Preisser, or Mr. J.D. Smith, as to their credibility when they say they saw Mohammed Atta on the chart," Kleinsmith replied that he himself did not remember seeing either Atta's name or his picture on a chart. But, he said, having worked with those five people, "I believe them implicitly. When they say that they do, I believe them."[205]

The Pentagon's refusal to let Shaffer and the others testify evoked outrage. Several senators from both parties accused the Pentagon of obstruction.[206] Congressman Weldon obtained signatures from a majority of the members of the House of Representatives on a letter that formally asked Secretary of Defense Rumsfeld to allow former members of Able Danger to testify before Congress. A refusal, the petition said, would "suggest not a concern for national security, but rather an attempt to prevent potentially embarrassing facts from coming to light."[207] This letter produced a victory for Weldon: Testimony would be given at a hearing of the House Armed Services Committee on February 15, 2006.[208]

The case was further strengthened by testimony at this hearing. Weldon announced that, in spite of reports that all of the Able Danger data had been destroyed, Pentagon sources told him that some of it had been found and that computer searches for Atta's name had resulted in eight "hits."[209]

The most important new testimony came from James Smith. Explaining that he had used Arab intermediaries in Los Angeles to buy a photograph of Atta, Smith added that it was one of some 40 photos of al-Qaeda members on a chart that he had given to Pentagon officials in 2000.[210] He also said:

> I have recollection of a visual chart that identified associations
> of known terrorist Omar Abdul-Rahman within the New York
> City geographic area. . . . Mohamed Atta's picture. . . was on

the chart. . . . The particular Atta chart is no longer available, as it was destroyed in an office move that I had in 2004. [Smith later, explaining to the Pentagon's inspector general how his Atta chart was destroyed, said: "[I]t had been up there so long I had quite a lot of tape up there because it had been rolled up. In the process the tape was tearing the chart. . . . It shredded itself as I was trying to pull it off the wall . . . so I just threw it away."[211]] I have direct recollection of the chart because I had a copy up until 2004. . . . At the time, after 9/11 when the pictures were released in newspapers and I did the compare on the chart, when I saw [Atta's] picture there, I was extremely elated and, to anyone that would listen to me, I showed them the chart that was in my possession.[212]

During questioning from Weldon, the following exchange occurred:

> Weldon: How sure are you that it was Mohammed Atta's name and picture [on the chart]?
>
> Smith: I'm absolutely certain. I used to look at it every morning. . . .
>
> Weldon: And was that the chart you think that was given to me that I gave to the White House?
>
> Smith: Yes, sir. It was.
>
> Weldon: And you're aware that when I gave that chart to the White House, Dan Burton, the chairman of the Government Ops Committee, was with me and stated to the New York Times, that he actually showed the chart to Steve Hadley and explained the linkages?
>
> Smith: Yes, sir.[213]

The DOD Inspector General's Report: However, in spite of the strong case that had been made for the truth of Able Danger's claim that Atta had been identified by early 2000, this claim would be called false in a report issued in September 2006 by the Defense Department's acting inspector general (IG), Thomas F. Gimble.[214] This report's summary statement said:

> We concluded that prior to September 11, 2001, Able Danger team members did not identify Mohammed [sic][215] Atta or any other 9/11 hijacker. While we interviewed four witnesses who

claimed to have seen a chart depicting Mohammed Atta and possibly other terrorists or "cells" involved in 9/11, we determined that their recollections were not accurate. . . . LTC Shaffer testified that he told the 9/11 Commission staff members [in an October 2003 meeting in Afghanistan] that Able Danger discovered the identity of 9/11 terrorists before the attack but was prevented from sharing that information with law enforcement authorities. However, four witness [sic] also present at the meeting unanimously disputed LTC Shaffer's recollection—testifying, under oath, that LTC Shaffer made no such claims for Able Danger at that meeting.[216]

The previous October, Representative Curt Weldon had called for "a full independent investigation by the Inspector General of the Pentagon."[217] After he saw the report, however, he found it to be neither full nor independent, saying in a press release:

Acting in a sickening bureaucratic manner, the DOD IG cherry picked testimony from witnesses in an effort to minimize the historical importance of the Able Danger effort. . . . The report trashes the reputations of military officers who had the courage to step forward and put their necks on the line to describe important work they were doing to track al-Qaeda prior to 9/11. . . . I am appalled that the DOD IG would expect the American people to actually consider this a full and thorough investigation. I question their motives and the content of this report, and I reject the conclusions they have drawn.[218]

As a matter of historical fact, the press did largely accept the report as having put the case to rest.[219] The important question, however, is whether Weldon's rejection of the report's conclusions was justified.

Weldon said that he questioned the motives behind the report. In saying this, he was suggesting that the report did not reflect what an investigation by an inspector general is supposed to be: an objective, impartial search for the truth, without bias in favor of the institution being investigated.

As shown by the title of the report, "Alleged Misconduct by Senior DOD Officials Concerning the Able Danger Program and Lieutenant Colonel Anthony A. Shaffer, US Army Reserve," the question was whether senior Pentagon officials had acted improperly by, among other things, covering up the truth about

Able Danger. Would the Pentagon—Gimble had been a long-term Pentagon employee[220]—have been capable of conducting an impartial investigation into this question, especially in relation to such a potentially explosive issue as Able Danger? The claim that the official timeline about Mohamed Atta was false threatened the government's—including the Pentagon's—account of 9/11. Indeed, one news report when the story first broke was entitled "'Able Danger' Could Rewrite History."[221] Another early story said: "Mr. Weldon has accused the commission of ignoring information that would have forced a rewriting of the history of the Sept. 11 attacks."[222] If Able Danger's evidence about the early identification of Atta was true, could the Pentagon have published a report saying so? Could it, in other words, have allowed its acting inspector general to publish a report based on an objective, impartial investigation?

An examination of the report reveals, in any case, that Gimble did not conduct such an investigation. Rather, he played a double role—that of the defense attorney for the Pentagon, defending its senior officials from all charges of misconduct (including covering up the truth about Atta), and that of the prosecuting attorney, charging Lieutenant Colonel Shaffer and other Able Danger team members of giving accounts that were "not accurate"—indeed, of lying.

That Gimble played this double role can be seen in his treatment of witnesses. With regard to claims made by Able Danger members that challenge the official account of 9/11, Gimble was assiduous in finding hostile witnesses to dispute those claims. There is no sign, however, that Gimble checked the accuracy of the statements by these hostile witnesses. Rather, he seemed to accept all their claims at face value. This uncritical acceptance was illustrated by his treatment of the testimony of Dietrich Snell, who had interviewed Captain Scott Phillpott. In Gimble's report, we read:

> Mr. Snell recalled that CAPT Phillpott "described as a recollection—although not a very solid one—that Mohammed [sic] Atta had been identified. . . and actually had appeared either by photo or by name or both on a chart that Phillpott said he had seen in the early part of 2000."[223]

However, Mr. Snell considered CAPT Phillpott's recollection with respect to Able Danger's identification of Mohammed [sic] Atta inaccurate because it was "one hundred percent inconsistent with everything we knew about Mohammed Atta and his colleagues at the time." Mr. Snell went on to describe his knowledge of Mohammed Atta's overseas travel and associations before 9/11, noting the "utter absence of any information suggesting any kind of a tie between Atta and anyone located in this country during the first half of the year 2000," when Able Danger had allegedly identified him. . . .

We considered Mr. Snell's negative assessment of CAPT Phillpott's claims particularly persuasive given Mr. Snell's knowledge and background in antiterrorist efforts involving al Qaeda.

In speaking of Snell's "knowledge," Gimble was referring to Snell's statement that Phillpott's claim about Atta's identification in early 2000 was "one hundred percent inconsistent with everything we knew about Mohammed Atta." As we saw earlier, however, Snell's so-called knowledge about this matter should instead be called Snell's *claim*. And it should be treated, in fact, as a claim that is quite likely false, given the number of people who reported seeing Atta "in this country during the first half of the year 2000." But Gimble evidently carried out no investigation to determine whether Snell's claim was true. He simply labeled it "knowledge" (which means "justified true belief").

Gimble's treatment of Phillpott was very different: He interviewed him three times—evidently until he got the answer he wanted. Gimble wrote:

CAPT Phillpott testified that within "3 or 4 days" of meeting with Dr. Preisser at LIWA in January 2000, LTC Shaffer delivered three charts to him at USSOCOM headquarters. During our initial interview, CAPT Phillpott testified that he was certain that Mohammed [sic] Atta's photograph was on one of the three charts. . . which portrayed a Brooklyn cell. . . . He testified:

"I know 100 percent Mohammed Atta's image was on the chart. I pretty well recollect that there were. . . at least three [other 9/11 terrorists], but I [do not remember] who any of them were. All I know is what I originally saw on the days shortly after 9/11 and that was him."[224]

To understand the second interview, one needs to know that one of the three charts is, in Gimble's report, labeled "Figure 1," which, he says, was "obtained but not produced by the Able Danger team." Gimble describes it thus:

> That chart (Figure 1 of this report) was produced by Orion Scientific Corporation (Orion) in May 1999 and contained the names and/or photographs of 53 terrorists who had been identified. . . before 9/11, including a Brooklyn cell, but it did not identify Mohammed Atta or any of the other 9/11 terrorists.[225]

Gimble's major thesis was that "recollections concerning the identification of 9/11 terrorists were linked to [this] single chart."[226] In other words, Phillpott, Shaffer, and the others who claimed to have seen Atta on a chart were referring to this chart, mistakenly thinking that it had Atta's name and/or photograph on it. The other two charts, everyone agreed, contained nothing about Atta. Gimble's claim, therefore, was that none of the three charts contained either Atta's name or his photograph—even the one that some of them called the "Atta chart."

However, Dr. Eileen Preisser rejected Gimble's claim—that the chart to which she was referring was the one in Figure 1. Gimble reported this rejection, writing:

> [W]e interviewed [Dr. Preisser] on three occasions because of her recollection that two charts she provided to CAPT Phillpott in early January 2000 identified Mohammed Atta. She recalled that one chart was produced by Orion and allegedly [sic] contained a photograph of Mohammed Atta. However, she denied that this was the chart at Figure 1.[227]

Gimble was never able to get Preisser to accept his claim, even in the third interview.

He was, however, more successful with Phillpott. Describing his second interview with Phillpott, Gimble wrote: "After initially denying that Figure 1 was one of those charts, CAPT Phillpott eventually testified that Figure 1 was one of the original charts."[228]

By submitting to Gimble's claim, Phillpott had put himself in conflict with his earlier statement that he was "100 percent [certain] Mohammed Atta's image was on the chart." Acknowledging the resulting cognitive dissonance, Phillpott said:

[O]bviously there's a compelling amount of evidence that would make it appear that I did not see Mohammed Atta. And I will absolutely grant you that based on what you're showing me my recollection could have been wrong. But I still need to stress that if I told you that I didn't think I saw Mohammed Atta's face, that in fact would be lying. . . . I honestly believe that I saw Atta on the chart.[229]

That clearly was not satisfactory from Gimble's point of view, so Phillpott, like Preisser—but unlike Dietrich Snell—was subjected to a third interview, which went much better:

In our third interview CAPT Phillpott stated, "I'm convinced that Atta was not on that chart, the chart that we had." However, he then recalled that, in June 2000 at USSOCOM headquarters, he "saw Atta's face" on a document that an intelligence analyst on the Able Danger team was holding. CAPT Phillpott claimed he was sitting next to the intelligence analyst who was "sifting through a bunch of paperwork" and said, "Hey, look at this guy. . . This is one mean [son of a bitch]." CAPT Phillpott testified "I turned, I looked at it and I concurred with him." CAPT Phillpott explained the incident caused him to believe that the photograph of Mohammed Atta was on a chart because, "I thought he [the intelligence officer] was working on the chart and that's how it kind of played out in my head."

CAPT Phillpott. . . could not recall whether the photograph was color or black and white and testified he only viewed the photograph for "four seconds, maybe five." He added, "that was the heart of what I recalled all along, not the chart but that damn picture." CAPT Phillpott did not recall any other instances where Mohammed Atta was identified by the Able Danger team.[230]

Was this a credible explanation? In the first interview, he had said that he recalled seeing not only Atta but also three other 9/11 terrorists on the chart. Could a four-or-five second look at a photograph of Atta on a document in an analyst's hands have transmogrified into a memory of having seen Atta and three other al-Qaeda operatives on a chart?

Be that as it may, Phillpott's about-face provided Gimble with a weapon to discredit the testimony of Shaffer and the others. Gimble wrote:

In response to whether he had any thoughts as to the reason that others claimed to have seen a chart that depicted Mohammed Atta and a Brooklyn cell as well as possibly other 9/11 terrorists, CAPT Phillpott testified, "[LTC] Tony [Shaffer] was relying on my recollection, I think, 100 percent. I mean, I think a lot of people are."[231]

From what we saw earlier, however, that explanation would not begin to account for the convictions of the others. According to Shaffer's testimony, he learned that Atta's photograph was on one of their charts from Eileen Preisser. Shortly thereafter, Preisser showed the chart to Representative Weldon, who then—with her and Representatives Dan Burton and Chris Shays—showed it to Stephen Hadley, who said he was going to show it to President Bush. (Hadley, according to Gimble, recalled the meeting, which occurred two weeks after 9/11, but not "being shown a chart bearing the name or photograph of Mohammed Atta."[232] But if there had been nothing about Atta on the chart, why would it have seemed important enough to show to Hadley—the deputy national security advisor?) Phillpott was evidently the third person to report seeing Atta's photograph on the chart. How, then, could Shaffer and Preisser have been relying on his memory? Gimble, nevertheless, made that claim, writing:

> The evidence suggested that they [Shaffer and Preisser] based their claims regarding the identification of Mohammed Atta on information provided to them by CAPT Phillpott, who ultimately acknowledged to us that he did not see Mohammed Atta's picture on any chart.[233]

Why did Phillpott "ultimately" agree to this recantation of his earlier testimony? We have no way of knowing. We cannot even make an informed judgment, because no transcript of the interrogations was provided with the report. Gimble gave us only summaries. He was able, therefore, to allow us to see only selected parts of the testimony (thereby giving rise to Weldon's charge of "cherry picking"). We have no way of knowing, therefore, whether Phillpott was given certain inducements to change his testimony. Also, there were months between Phillpott's interviews (December 13, 2005, February 17, 2006, and May 24, 2006). Maybe this young Naval Academy graduate came to fear, perhaps with the aid of hints from superiors in the Pentagon, that continuing to stick with his original story would threaten his career. Such a fear would, in fact, have been quite rational, given his observation of what happened to Anthony Shaffer.

In any case, if Phillpott's late suggestion that the others had been relying on his memory could not reasonably explain the testimony of Shaffer and Presser, even more could it not explain that of James Smith. He, as we saw, reported obtaining the photograph from someone in California in late 1999 or early 2000 and then putting a chart containing this photo on his office wall. He then said that he "used to look at it every morning" until 2004, when it disintegrated while he was trying to take it down. Describing the photograph to Gimble, Smith said: "It was. . . very grainy, but it was clear enough that you could make out that stare, his high cheekbones, the very, the very pronounced. . . eyes. Yeah, definitely Atta."[234]

Gimble, being uninterested in any evidence that might corroborate the memories of Able Danger members, did not mention the fact that Eileen Preisser had also described the photograph she had seen of Atta as "grainy."[235]

In any case, not being able to dismiss Smith's account by reference to Phillpott, Gimble took a more direct approach, saying: "[W]e concluded that Mr. Smith did not possess or display a chart with Mohammed Atta's picture on it." Why? After complaining that Smith did not provide anyone to corroborate his claim, Gimble added:

> [H]e was unable to recall a single individual on the chart except for Mohammed Atta and Sheik Rahman. Further, Mr. Smith did not recall whether the photograph included Mohammed Atta's name. Finally, we found Mr. Smith's assertion that the chart disintegrated on removal implausible.[236]

Gimble, in other words, simply dismissed Smith's testimony by calling him a liar.

Moreover, in spite of Gimble's suggestion that Shaffer and Preisser had very bad memories, most of their disputed assertions could not plausibly be explained in this way. Gimble's central approach was—either by finding people who would dispute those claims or by simply saying that he could find no evidence to support them—to suggest that Shaffer and Preisser had also lied.

By virtue of being, in effect, the judge as well as the attorney for both the defense and the prosecution, Gimble could defeat every claim of the Able Danger team that could not be dismissed in terms of faulty memories by simply accusing them of lying. Gimble, in fact, primarily took this latter approach to defeat Shaffer's claims. For example, with regard to the question of whether DIA officials had acted improperly by destroying Able Danger documents in Shaffer's office, Gimble said the question did not arise because: "We determined that LTC Shaffer did not possess Able Danger related documents as he alleged."[237]

Accordingly, given the obvious fact that the main criterion for considering an Able Danger assertion false was that it disagreed with the story being told by the Pentagon and the 9/11 Commission, the official report on Able Danger, written by Acting Inspector General Thomas F. Gimble, is circular, with the argument being, essentially: These claims by Able Danger that contradict the official account are false. Why? Because they are inconsistent with the official account. Gimble followed, in other words, the approach previously taken by Dietrich Snell and the 9/11 Commission in general: These Able Danger claims are not credible because they contradict the FBI report.

Although a much more extensive analysis of Gimble's report would be required for a thorough evaluation, we have seen enough to conclude that it should not be accepted as an objective, impartial assessment of the claim that Mohamed Atta had been identified as a member of an al-Qaeda cell in the New York area over a year before 9/11. Therefore, given the fact that this claim was made by several otherwise highly credible individuals, it should be considered probably true.

The reaction of the 9/11 Commission and the Pentagon to the public's awareness of this claim, moreover, suggests that they were very intent on covering up dangerous information—information that suggested that Atta was being protected. When we combine this observation with other things we have learned about the alleged hijackers—including the money reportedly sent to Atta by the CIA-created ISI—the Able Danger evidence provides additional reason to suspect that the "hijackers" were really paid assets.[238]

7. Motives of US Officials: The Silence of the 9/11 Commission

When I wrote NPH, I did not always have firmly in mind the distinction between orchestrating the attacks and merely allowing them to happen. Much of the book's evidence, however, pointed toward orchestration. I should not, therefore, have suggested in the title of that book's seventh chapter that the attacks had merely been allowed. In any case, *The 9/11 Commission Report* contains not even a hint that the Bush administration might have had motives for orchestrating, or at least allowing, the 9/11 attacks. Accordingly, every issue discussed in Chapter 7 of NPH was ignored or greatly played down.

Pre-9/11 Plans to Attack Afghanistan

The Commission did acknowledge that the US war in Afghanistan was aimed at producing "regime change."[1] According to the Commission, however, the United States only wanted to change the regime because the Taliban, besides being incapable of providing peace by ending the civil war, was perpetrating human rights abuses and providing a "safe haven" for al-Qaeda.[2] The Commission ignored, in other words, all evidence that the United States wanted to get control of the oil of Central Asia, as Zbigniew Brzezinski had counseled in *The Grand Chessboard*, in order to maintain "American primacy."[3]

The centrality of oil had been emphasized in *Taliban: Militant Islam, Oil and Fundamentalism in Central Asia*, a widely read book by Ahmed Rashid, who dubbed the pipeline project "The New Great Game."[4] In the 1990s, the United States had hoped the Taliban would be able to provide the stability needed for Unocal to build the pipeline—an effort discussed in two chapters by Rashid with the same title, "Romancing the Taliban: The Battle for Pipelines."[5] However, although the 9/11 Commission cited Rashid's book several times, it made no reference to his discussion of the centrality of the pipelines to Washington's intentions. It mentioned the pipeline project in general and Unocal in particular only in one paragraph, and this paragraph suggested that the US State Department was interested in Unocal's pipeline project merely insofar as "the prospect of shared pipeline profits might lure faction leaders to a conference table."[6]

The Commission also failed to mention that, at a Berlin meeting in July 2001, the Bush administration, giving the Taliban one last chance, demanded that it create stability by forming a "unity government" with its opponents. It did not mention, therefore, that according to former Pakistani Foreign Secretary Niaz Naik, the Americans said that if the Taliban failed to agree, "military action against Afghanistan would go ahead. . . before the snows started falling in Afghanistan."[7] The 9/11 Commission gave a much less bellicose account of the Bush administration's attitude, saying that it was "moving toward agreement that some last effort should be made to convince the Taliban to shift position and then, if that failed, . . . the United States would try covert action to topple the Taliban's leadership from within."[8] The needed "shift," according to the Commission, seemed to involve simply turning over bin Laden (not also forming a unity government), and the Commission gave no hint that the US representatives had threatened military force (not merely covert action).

The Commission also failed to mention that President Bush's special envoy to Afghanistan, Zalmay Khalilzad, and the new prime minister after the fall of the Taliban, Hamid Karzai, had both previously been on Unocal's payroll—a fact that led Chalmers Johnson to write: "The continued collaboration of Khalilzad and Karzai in post-9/11 Afghanistan strongly suggests that the Bush administration was and remains as interested in oil as in terrorism in that region."[9] The Commission, furthermore, did not mention that by October 10, three days after the US attack on Afghanistan began, the US Department of State had informed the Pakistani minister of oil that, "in view of recent geopolitical developments," Unocal was again ready to go ahead with the pipeline project.[10]

Another significant factor in the Bush administration's plans for Afghanistan and the surrounding countries, which was implicit in Brzezinski's call to take control of Central Asia, was the intention to build permanent military bases in the region. Chalmers Johnson, seeing the desire "to establish an American presence in Central Asia" as the central concern (even more important than helping an American company build the pipeline), pointed out in 2004 that the Bush administration, besides establishing long-term bases in Afghanistan, also quickly arranged for long-term bases in Pakistan, Kyrgyzstan, and Uzbekistan.[11]

With its very selective presentation, therefore, the Commission presented a picture of the United States as having had no imperialistic or crass material interests in the area—the kind of interests that might lead a government to devise a pretext for going to war. The United States simply wanted to capture Osama bin Laden, bring an end to the Taliban's human rights abuses, and prevent Afghanistan from being a haven for terrorists.

PRE-9/11 PLANS TO ATTACK IRAQ

In relation to the attack on Iraq, the 9/11 Commission gave the appearance of being independent and critical of the Bush administration. It pointed out that certain members of the Bush administration, especially Rumsfeld and Wolfowitz, pushed for attacking Iraq immediately after 9/11.[12] The Commission also said that it found no evidence of any "collaborative operational relationship" between bin Laden and Saddam Hussein and hence no evidence "that Iraq cooperated with al Qaeda in developing or carrying out any attacks against the United States."[13] This statement, released in a staff report about a month before the publication of *The 9/11 Commission Report*, created much discussion in the press, especially after Vice President Cheney labeled "outrageous" a *New York Times* front-page story entitled "Panel Finds No Qaeda–Iraq Tie."[14] William Safire criticized Kean and Hamilton for letting themselves be "jerked around by a manipulative staff," while Joe Conason wrote an article entitled "9/11 Panel Becomes Cheney's Nightmare."[15] The 9/11 Commission was thereby portrayed as truly independent.

The press failed to point out, however, that the Commission had shielded its readers from the evidence, cited in NPH, showing how deep and longstanding the desire to attack Iraq had been among some members of the Bush administration. For example, the Commission said: "President Bush ordered the Defense Department to be ready to deal with Iraq if Baghdad acted against US interests, with plans to include possibly occupying Iraqi oil fields."[16] The Commission thereby ignored evidence that the Bush administration was determined to attack Iraq in any case, not only if it "acted against US interests," and that its first action would be to take control of the oil fields, so that this was not something that it might only "possibly" do.

The Commission, moreover, did not mention that Paul O'Neill, who had been treasury secretary and thereby a member of the National Security Council, had said—in a highly publicized interview on CBS's 60 Minutes in January 2004—that as soon as the Bush administration took office, the main topic was going after Saddam, with the question being not "Why Saddam?" or "Why Now?" but merely "finding a way to do it."[17] The Commission did not mention O'Neill's claim even though it was backed up by Richard Clarke, who said: "[H]e is right. . . . The administration of the second George Bush did begin with Iraq on its agenda."[18] Nor did the Commission mention O'Neill's report that the Defense Intelligence Agency, which worked for Rumsfeld, had begun mapping Iraq's oil fields right after the Bush administration took office and had, by March 2001, prepared a document, entitled "Foreign Suitors for Iraqi Oilfield Contracts," which suggested how Iraq's huge reserves might be divided up following an invasion.[19]

The Commission failed, furthermore, to point out that the idea that the United States should attack Iraq had been articulated in the 1990s by the Project for the New American Century (PNAC), a neoconservative organization with which many members of the Bush administration were affiliated, including John Bolton, Dick Cheney, Zalmay Khalilzad, Lewis "Scooter" Libby, Richard Perle, Donald Rumsfeld, and Paul Wolfowitz. The Commission could have mentioned that in 1997, Wolfowitz and Khalilzad published an article entitled "Saddam Must Go."[20] It could also have mentioned that in 1998, PNAC sent a letter to

President Clinton, urging him to adopt a strategy, including "military action," aimed at "removing Saddam Hussein and his regime from power."[21]

The Commission, moreover, could have pointed out that in the fall of 2000, shortly before the Bush administration took office, PNAC published *Rebuilding America's Defenses*, which stated: "While the unresolved conflict with Iraq provides the immediate justification, the need for a substantial American force presence in the Gulf transcends the issue of the regime of Saddam Hussein."[22]

By not referring to this or any similar passage, the Commission obscured the fact, as it did with regard to Afghanistan, that the Bush administration and the Pentagon planned to build several permanent military bases in Iraq. This was known before the Commission wrote its report, as shown by a *Chicago Tribune* story published in March 2004 entitled "14 'Enduring Bases' Set in Iraq; Long-Term Military Presence Planned."[23]

One more thing ignored by the 9/11 Commission was the fact that the administration's claim that Iraq possessed weapons of mass destruction was a lie, not simply a mistake. Although the absolute proof that this was a lie—the Downing Street memo revealing that the intelligence about WMD was being "fixed around the policy"—was not published until May 2005,[24] the fact that it was a lie had, to people willing to question the administration's claims, become evident long before the Commission completed its report.[25]

In sum, the 9/11 Commission's simplistic and noncontextual account of the Bush administration's reasons for attacking Iraq falsely implied that it would not have had any plans for Iraq that could have provided a motive for fabricating a false-flag terrorist attack.

How a New Pearl Harbor Would Help

Besides not referring to the Iraq statement in *Rebuilding America's Defenses*, the 9/11 Commission also did not mention this document's most notorious statement: the one indicating that PNAC's plans would be helped by "a new Pearl Harbor." This omission further illustrated how, although Kean and Hamilton said that their 9/11 Commission had sought "to provide the fullest possible account of the events surrounding 9/11," its account was in reality very selective. While discussing bin Laden's 1998 *fatwa*—which said that Muslims should kill Americans—so as to show that al-Qaeda had had a motive for planning the attacks,[26] the Commission ignored the much clearer statement of possible motives by an organization whose members included men who became the secretary of defense, the deputy secretary of defense, and the vice president of the militarily most powerful nation on earth.

The Commission's selectivity was also illustrated by its failure to mention that 9/11 was described as an "opportunity" by several members of the Bush administration, with Bush himself saying that the attacks provided "a great opportunity" and Rumsfeld saying that they created "the kind of opportunities that World War II offered, to refashion the world."[27]

The great extent to which the Bush administration had planned to refashion the world was indicated, at least partly, by the *Newsweek* article cited in NPH, which stated that some of Bush's advisors wanted to attack not only Iraq but also Saudi Arabia, Iran, North Korea, Syria, Egypt, and Burma.[28] This same intention was reported, in slightly different form, by General Wesley Clark, who said that a three-star general in the Pentagon told him late in 2001 that the Pentagon was "going to take out seven countries in five years," starting with Iraq and ending with Iran—with the other countries being Syria, Lebanon, Libya, Somalia, and Sudan.[29] The truth of Clark's report was confirmed in 2008 by Douglas Feith, who had been undersecretary of defense for policy at the time. Feith revealed that on September 30, 2001, Donald Rumsfeld sent a letter to President Bush saying that the United States should seek to establish "new regimes" in those seven countries.[30]

The list mentioned by Clark and advocated by Rumsfeld did not, unlike the list in the *Newsweek* story, include Saudi Arabia. But this country was on the hit list of at least some of the neocons. In 2002, a speaker invited to address the Defense Policy Board by its chairman, arch-neocon Richard Perle, said that unless Saudi Arabia does as we wish, we should seize its oil fields and confiscate its other financial assets.[31] The following year, another neocon, Michael Ledeen, wrote that "we must bring down the terror regimes," after which he named Iran, Iraq, Syria, Lebanon, and "even Saudi Arabia."[32] Although this talk about attacking Saudi Arabia was largely covered up, it is relevant to a question sometimes asked about the idea of 9/11 as a false-flag operation: If one of the goals was to have a pretext to attack Iraq, why were the alleged hijackers mainly Saudis, rather than Iraqis? Part of the answer is that their nationalities did not really matter as long as they were Muslims from the Middle East. But perhaps part of the answer is that those who planned this part of the operation were looking down the road to the biggest prize of all in terms of oil reserves, Saudi Arabia.[33]

The 9/11 Commission, however, cited none of these reports or the fact that Bush and some members of his administration had described 9/11 as an "opportunity." This is serious selectivity.

MISSILE DEFENSE AND A SPACE PEARL HARBOR

When writing NPH, I misunderstood what was meant by a "Space Pearl Harbor." In my next book, 9/11CROD, I corrected this error, writing: "In speaking of a 'Space Pearl Harbor,' the [Rumsfeld Commission's] report meant an attack on its military satellites in space. The 9/11 attacks were obviously not of this nature." Nevertheless, I added, it was interesting that "only a few months after PNAC had issued its statement about 'a new Pearl Harbor,' the Rumsfeld Commission also pointed out that a Pearl Harbor type of attack might be needed to 'galvanize the nation.'"[34]

As I mentioned in NPH, the three men who had most publicly advocated developing the capability to wage war from space— Rumsfeld, Myers, and Eberhart—were also the three men who would have been most directly involved in overseeing a military stand-down order on 9/11, if such was given. In light of the otherwise inexplicable failure of our defenses, the 9/11 Commission should have viewed these three men as suspects, whose actions that morning needed to be rigorously investigated. But the Commission instead treated their testimonies as unquestionable sources of truth as to what really happened.[35]

A PRECEDENT: OPERATION NORTHWOODS

If the 9/11 Commission had been seriously investigating who was responsible for 9/11, it would have considered relevant the fact that the US government had in previous times deceived the public in order to create pretexts for war. I alluded to one such event in NPH: the sinking of the US battleship *Maine*, exploited as a pretext to take control of Cuba in 1898. I also described a plan called Operation Northwoods, which was developed by the Pentagon in 1962 as a pretext for a war to regain control of Cuba from Fidel Castro, who had defeated the US-backed dictator Batista in 1959. Although that plan did not become operational, many other deceitful plans drawn up by the US government have been carried out—such as the pretexts for the wars against Mexico, Cuba, the Philippines, and Vietnam, and also the terrorist attacks in Western Europe generally known as Operation Gladio, which were mentioned in the introduction, above, and which I have discussed at length elsewhere.[36]

A serious investigation into 9/11, pointing out that Rumsfeld, Myers, and Eberhart belonged to an institution that had made false claims to start wars many times in the past, would have explored the hypothesis that the attacks of 9/11 might have been the latest in a series of pretexts for war created by the US government. But neither Operation Northwoods nor any of the other deceptions were mentioned.

In sum, the 9/11 Commission systematically omitted any information that would have provided reason to believe that the Bush administration might have arranged or allowed the attacks as a pretext for carrying out its pre-established agenda.

8. 9/11 Commission Falsehoods about Bin Laden, al-Qaeda, Pakistanis, and Saudis

I n this chapter, I deal with new developments related to reports discussed in Chapter 8 of NPH, especially the 9/11 Commission's response to these reports. The items discussed in this chapter illustrate especially clearly the extent to which the production of *The 9/11 Commission Report* was a cover-up operation.

Continuing the Anti-Hunt for Osama bin Laden and al-Qaeda

Bin Laden's Escape from Tora Bora: The idea that the battle for Tora Bora was, as the *Guardian* put it, a "grand charade," meaning that bin Laden was deliberately allowed to escape, was supported, albeit unintentionally, in a 2005 book called *Jawbreaker: The Attack on Bin Laden and Al-Qaeda*. It was written by Gary Berntsen, who was the CIA's field commander in the joint CIA–US Armed Forces hunt for bin Laden in Afghanistan.

According to Berntsen, this US-led operation was in a position to capture or kill bin Laden and all his followers, except for one thing: they needed to put 800 US Army Rangers behind bin Laden to block all of the possible escape routes to Pakistan.[1] However, although Berntsen repeatedly and insistently requested these Rangers, the US generals refused, saying that they were deferring to the Afghanis, who wanted to be the ones to capture bin Laden.[2] Berntsen had already told the generals, however, that the Afghan military leaders did not share his passion to get bin Laden. He believed, in fact, that at least some of them wanted bin Laden to escape.[3] "So why," he asked, "was the US military looking for excuses not to act decisively? Why would they want to leave something that was so important to an unreliable Afghan army?"[4]

Berntsen was even more perplexed when he learned that, just when it was time to make the final push, he was to be replaced. His replacement, moreover, was to be a man who had previously served on George Tenet's staff and did not inspire enthusiasm in Berntsen's men. (When they learned who the replacement was to be, the men "slapped their hands over their heads and groaned.") Berntsen said: "I couldn't believe they were doing this in the middle of the most important battle of the war."[5]

Berntsen was merely perplexed, not suspicious: He described George Bush as a great commander-in-chief and *The 9/11 Commission Report* as a great book.[6] But his account and his questions show that, if the US military leaders had really been instructed to go all out to capture Osama bin Laden "dead or alive," their subsequent decisions were irrational. If, however, the plan was to let him escape, then their decisions made perfect sense. Against his own intentions, accordingly, Berntsen has lent support to the suspicion that bin Laden's escape from Tora Bora was due to something other than incompetence.

Hard Evidence of Bin Laden's Guilt? Given the Bush administration's supposed certainty that bin Laden was responsible for 9/11, its apparent lack of interest in capturing or killing him, not only in 2001 but also in the following years, has been a great source of puzzlement. Ever since 2003, pundits have regularly excoriated the Bush–Cheney administration for focusing primarily on Iraq, which had nothing to do with 9/11, and thereby diverting resources away from the search for bin Laden, who (they assume) was responsible for 9/11. However, given a different assumption— that the Bush administration knew that bin Laden was not responsible for 9/11, its behavior would be much less perplexing. This possibility brings us to one of the most important revelations about 9/11 made by government employees. No current government employee has, to be sure, said that the Bush administration knew that bin Laden was not responsible for 9/11. A spokesman for the FBI has, however, admitted that the bureau has no hard evidence that bin Laden *was* responsible.

This development occurred after it was noticed that the FBI's "Usama bin Laden" page on its "Most Wanted Terrorists" website did not mention 9/11 as one of the terrorist acts for which bin Laden was wanted.[7] Puzzled by this omission, *Muckraker Report* editor Ed Haas contacted FBI headquarters to ask why. Rex Tomb, who was then the FBI's chief of investigative publicity, reportedly replied: "The reason why 9/11 is not mentioned on Usama Bin Laden's Most Wanted page is because the FBI has no hard evidence connecting Bin Laden to 9/11."[8]

Learning from Tomb that the FBI's pages could mention only crimes for which people had been formally indicted, Haas repeatedly contacted the Department of Justice to ask why bin Laden had never been indicted for 9/11. But, he reported, he received no reply.[9]

Rex Tomb's revelation highlighted the fact that no real evidence of bin Laden's responsibility for 9/11 had ever been provided. Two weeks after 9/11, Secretary of State Colin Powell told *Meet the Press* that he would soon put out a document describing the evidence linking bin Laden to the attack.[10] But the next day, while appearing before the press with President Bush, Powell said that the document would not be forthcoming, because most of the relevant information was classified.[11] Seymour Hersh, citing a Justice Department official, reported that the administration really withdrew the pledge "for lack of hard facts."[12]

Shortly thereafter, British Prime Minister Tony Blair tried to come to the rescue, presenting a document entitled "Responsibility for the Terrorist Atrocities in the United States." Listing "clear conclusions reached by the government," it stated: "Osama Bin Laden and al-Qaeda, the terrorist network which he heads, planned and carried out the atrocities on 11 September 2001."[13] This document begins by admitting, however, that it "does not purport to provide a prosecutable case against Osama Bin Laden in a court of law." Although its evidence might have been good enough to go to war, in other words, it was not good enough to go to court.

The issue also came up in discussions between the US government and the Taliban. A CNN report on September 21 said:

President Bush demanded Thursday night that the Taliban surrender all leaders of bin Laden's al-Qaeda organization. . . . The Taliban have defied the US demand, refusing to hand over bin Laden without proof or evidence that he was involved in last week's attacks on the United States.[14]

But the Bush administration rejected the request, saying that no proof about bin Laden's responsibility for 9/11 was necessary, because he had already been indicted for other crimes:

"There is already an indictment for Osama bin Laden," [White House press secretary Ari] Fleischer said. "There's an indictment in the case of Tanzania, Kenya, the bombings in East Africa. . . . The president. . . said there would be no discussions and no negotiations."[15]

Several weeks later, a Taliban spokesman said: "We have asked for proof of Osama's involvement [in the September 11 attacks], but they have refused. Why?"[16]

Accordingly, when Rex Tomb admitted in 2006 that the FBI had no hard evidence of bin Laden's responsibility for 9/11, he was simply stating explicitly what the Bush and Blair governments had been saying implicitly all along. The fact that an FBI spokesman did explicitly state this should, of course, have resulted in screaming headlines and extensive coverage on television news and talk shows. Instead, however, it was included in Project Censored's list of the 25 most censored stories of the year.[17]

Readers might assume that, once the absence of 9/11 on bin Laden's Most Wanted page became publicized—it was, for example, discussed in a *Washington Post* story in 2006[18]—the page would have been changed. However, when the FBI updated its "Top Ten Most Wanted" list early in 2008,[19] it did not add 9/11 to the list of terrorist attacks for which bin Laden was wanted.

The Osama bin Laden "Confession Video" of 2001: It has been widely claimed, to be sure, that the missing proof was provided by a video, released by the US government in December 2001, in which bin Laden apparently admitted responsibility for the attacks. The tape, which was evidently made on November 9, 2001, was reportedly found by US intelligence officers in a house in Jalalabad, Afghanistan. A BBC report said: "The tape is being seen by America's allies as vindicating the US-led military campaign in Afghanistan. . . . The White House hopes the video will bolster international support for the war on terrorism."[20] President Bush declared: "For those who see this tape, they'll realize that not only is he [Osama bin Laden] guilty of incredible murder, he has no conscience and no soul."[21] Rudy Giuliani called the tape "one of the most detailed descriptions of a premeditated mass murder that I had ever heard."[22]

Serious questions, however, have been raised about the authenticity of this tape, partly because the man in the video has darker skin, fuller cheeks, and a broader nose than the Osama bin Laden of other videos. He also seems much healthier than bin Laden did in a video made just six days earlier.[23] Arabist Kevin Barrett said: "[T]he big guy [in the video] clearly was not bin Laden. He was at least 40 or 50 pounds heavier, and his facial features were obviously different."[24] Also, pointed out the *Guardian*, the man in the video "appears to be wearing a ring on his right hand. In previous film of bin Laden. . . , he has worn no jewelry apart from a watch."[25]

An additional reason for considering the video inauthentic is provided by some of the statements made by its "Osama bin Laden." In speaking of the hijackers, he said:

> The brothers, who conducted the operation, all they knew was that they have a martyrdom operation. . . but they didn't know anything about the operation, not even one letter. But they were trained and we did not reveal the operation to them until they are there and just before they boarded the planes.[26]

According to the government, however, records show that the hijackers purchased their plane tickets two weeks in advance.[27] The man in the video also said: "Those who were trained to fly didn't know the others. One group of people did not know the other group." But that also is not true. The men said to be pilots and those said to be the "muscle hijackers" all mingled with each other.[28] He also said:

> [W]e calculated in advance the number of casualties from the enemy who would be killed based on the position of the tower.

. . . [D]ue to my experience in this field, I was thinking that the fire from the gas in the plane would melt the iron structure of the building and collapse the area where the plane hit and all the floors above it only. This is all that we had hoped for.[29]

Given the real Osama bin Laden's experience as a contractor, he would have known the buildings were framed with steel, not iron, and he would have known that the fire, even while being fed by jet fuel, would not have melted any steel—or any iron, for that matter.

For these reasons, many experts consider the video to be a fabrication. Professor Bruce Lawrence, who is widely regarded as America's leading academic bin Laden expert, bluntly declared: "It's bogus." According to his informants within the US intelligence community's bin Laden units, Lawrence added, everyone in those units knows that the video is a fake.[30] General Hamid Gul, a former head of Pakistan's ISI, said: "I think there is an Osama Bin Laden look-alike."[31]

This video, in which Osama bin Laden appears to boast about his role in planning 9/11, has been regarded as sufficient proof of his responsibility by some defenders of the official account (such as *New York Times* reporter Philip Shenon[32]). However, bin Laden had previously stated emphatically that he had nothing to do with 9/11. On September 16, 2001, he told Al Jazeera television: "I would like to assure the world that I did not plan the recent attacks, which seem to have been planned by people for personal reasons."[33] When asked during an interview twelve days later whether he was involved in 9/11, he replied: "I have already said that I am not involved in the 11 September attacks in the United States. . . . I had no knowledge of these attacks. . . . [W]e are against the American system, not against its people, whereas in these attacks, the common American people have been killed."[34] If the question is what bin Laden himself said, what is the justification for allowing a video of dubious authenticity to overrule statements whose authenticity is indubitable?

In any case, President Bush, in response to questions that were raised about the authenticity of the tape immediately after its release, said: "It is preposterous for anybody to think that this tape is doctored. That's just a feeble excuse to provide weak support for an incredibly evil man."[35]

Those who question the tape's authenticity, however, would seem to include the Department of Justice (DOJ) and the FBI. People who tout this "Osama bin Laden confession video" as proof of his responsibility for 9/11 should recall that, even after this tape was released, the DOJ did not indict bin Laden for 9/11 and the FBI, therefore, did not list him as wanted for 9/11. The DOJ and the FBI, in other words, evidently did not regard this video as hard evidence of bin Laden's connection to 9/11.[36]

KSM and the 9/11 Commission: The 9/11 Commission wrote as if there were no question about Osama bin Laden's responsibility for 9/11. We can imagine ways in which this fact would be consistent with the FBI's admission that it has no hard evidence to support the claim of bin Laden's responsibility. Perhaps the 9/11 Commission had evidence of which the DOJ and FBI have remained unaware. Or perhaps the DOJ and FBI, while being aware of this evidence, refused to classify it as "hard" evidence only because they use an excessively rigorous standard for this classification. But, whatever be the case with the DOJ and FBI, it has been widely assumed that the 9/11 Commission had very good evidence that bin Laden was behind the attacks. That, however, turns out not to have been the case, by the admission of the Commission's own co-chairmen, Thomas Kean and Lee Hamilton.

Whenever *The 9/11 Commission Report* spoke of evidence pointing to bin Laden's responsibility, the note in the back of the book always referred to information provided by the CIA that had (presumably) been elicited during their interrogations of al-Qaeda members. The most important of these al-Qaeda members was Khalid Sheikh Mohammed (KSM), described as the "mastermind" of the 9/11 attacks. Here, for example, are some statements made by the Commission:

> KSM arranged a meeting with Bin Ladin in Tora Bora [and] presented the al Qaeda leader with a menu of ideas for terrorist operations. . . . KSM also presented a proposal for an operation that would involve training pilots who would crash planes into buildings in the United States. This proposal eventually would become the 9/11 operation. . . . Bin Ladin . . . finally decided to give the green light for the 9/11 operation sometime in late

1998 or early 1999. . . . KSM reasoned he could best influence US policy by targeting the country's economy. . . . New York, which KSM considered the economic capital of the United States, therefore became the primary target. . . . Bin Ladin summoned KSM to Kandahar in March or April 1999 to tell him that al Qaeda would support his proposal. . . . Bin Ladin wanted to destroy the White House and the Pentagon, KSM wanted to strike the World Trade Center. . . . Bin Ladin also soon selected four individuals to serve as suicide operatives. . . . [Two of them] had already obtained US visas. . . . KSM had not met them. His only guidance from Bin Ladin was that the two should eventually go to the United States for pilot training. . . . Atta—whom Bin Ladin chose to lead the group—met with Bin Ladin several times to receive additional instructions, including a preliminary list of approved targets: the World Trade Center, the Pentagon, and the US Capitol. . . . It is clear . . . that Bin Ladin and [Mohammed] Atef were very much in charge of the operation.[37]

The note for each of these statements about al-Qaeda and Osama bin Laden says "interrogation(s) of KSM."[38]

One problem with this evidence was explained by Kean and Hamilton in their 2006 book, *Without Precedent*, subtitled *The Inside Story of the 9/11 Commission*. The greatest difficulty they had, they admitted in giving one of their inside revelations, was "obtaining access to star witnesses in custody. . . , most notably Khalid Sheikh Mohammed, a mastermind of the attacks, and [Ramzi] Binalshibh, who helped coordinate the attacks from Europe."[39] Why was such access so important?

> These and other detainees were the only possible source for inside information about the plot. If the commission was mandated to provide an authoritative account of the 9/11 attacks, it followed that our mandate afforded us the right to learn what these detainees had to say about 9/11.[40]

They were not, however, allowed by the CIA to interrogate any of these detainees. Even their request to observe the interrogations through one-way glass, so that they "could at least observe the detainee[s'] demeanor and evaluate [their] credibility," was turned down, although Kean and Hamilton believed that, without at least this much access, they "could not evaluate the credibility of the detainees' accounts."[41] The Commission, finally, "never even got to meet with the people conducting the interrogations."[42]

The closest they came to the detainees was a CIA "project manager," to whom they were allowed to submit questions for the detainees, and through whom they would receive the answers. But this meant, Kean and Hamilton pointed out, that "they were receiving information thirdhand—passed from the detainee, to the interrogator, to the person who writes up the interrogation report, and finally to our staff in the form of reports, not even transcripts."[43] As a result, they admitted: "We. . . had no way of evaluating the credibility of detainee information. How could we tell if someone such as Khalid Sheikh Mohammed . . . was telling us the truth?"[44]

With that rhetorical question, Kean and Hamilton made clear that the 9/11 Commission provided no real evidence of the responsibility of Osama bin Laden for the attacks of 9/11. Given this admission, their book *Without Precedent* would have more aptly been called "Without Evidence."

Although Kean and Hamilton's admission, which I reported in *Debunking 9/11 Debunking*, went unmentioned in the mainstream press, a second major problem with the Commission's evidence did finally get exposed in an NBC News "deep background" report early in 2008. Referring to "an extensive NBC News analysis of the 9/11 Commission's *Final Report*," authors Robert Windrem and Victor Limjoco wrote:

> The analysis shows that much of what was reported about the planning and execution of the terror attacks on New York and Washington was derived from the interrogations of high-ranking al-Qaida operatives. Each had been subjected to "enhanced interrogation techniques." Some were even subjected to waterboarding. . . .
>
> The NBC News analysis shows that more than one quarter of all footnotes in the *9/11 Report* refer to CIA interrogations of al-Qaida operatives who were subjected to the now-controversial interrogation techniques. In fact, information derived from the interrogations is central to the *Report*'s most critical chapters, those on the planning and execution of the attacks.[45]

There is no doubt, moreover, that these operatives included KSM. In February 2008, CIA Director Michael Hayden admitted that both KSM and Abu Zubaydah had been subjected to waterboarding.[46]

Windrem and Limjoco focused primarily on the fact that the 9/11 Commission, while suspecting that KSM and the other detainees were tortured, did not ask the CIA whether this was the case. But Windrem and Limjoco did point out that, if torture was in fact used, then the resulting statements could not be trusted:

> 9/11 Commission staffers say they. . . were concerned that the techniques had affected the operatives' credibility. At least four of the operatives whose interrogation figured in the *9/11 Commission Report* have claimed that they told interrogators critical information as a way to stop being "tortured." . . .
>
> Specifically, the NBC News analysis shows 441 of the more than 1,700 footnotes in the Commission's Final Report refer to the CIA interrogations. Moreover, most of the information in Chapters 5, 6 and 7 of the Report came from the interrogations. Those chapters cover the initial planning for the attack, the assembling of terrorist cells, and the arrival of the hijackers in the US.[47]

Accordingly, it is now part of the public record, supported by NBC News as well as the co-chairs of the 9/11 Commission, that most and perhaps all of the evidence in the Commission's report supporting the responsibility of bin Laden and al-Qaeda for 9/11 must be judged untrustworthy. This point has been emphasized by Michael Ratner, president of the Center for Constitutional Rights, who has said:

> Most people look at the *9/11 Commission Report* as a trusted historical document. If their conclusions were supported by information gained from torture, therefore their conclusions are suspect. . . . [A]s a matter of law, evidence derived from torture is not reliable, in part because of the possibility of false confession. . . . [A]t the very least, they [the authors of the Commission's report] should have added caveats to all those references.[48]

If the report's authors had indeed added these caveats, as they certainly should have, it would have meant that nearly a quarter of *The 9/11 Commission Report*'s notes, including most of those for the chapters dealing with Osama bin Laden and al-Qaeda, would have needed to point to a caveat such as:

> We are here simply passing on information that, according to the CIA, was derived from al-Qaeda prisoners. We do not know if the prisoners really made these statements or, if they did, whether they made them after being tortured, perhaps simply to stop the torture. But we have written our report on the assumption that this information is accurate, even though we had no evidence for this except the word of CIA officials.

Had the authors of *The 9/11 Commission Report* qualified the statements in the 441 notes in question with such a caveat, the Commission's lack of reliable evidence for the responsibility of bin Laden and al-Qaeda would have been abundantly clear, at least to readers who checked the notes. In spite of appearances to the contrary, therefore, the 9/11 Commission did not provide any reliable evidence to support the Bush administration's conspiracy theory, according to which the 9/11 attacks were planned by Osama bin Laden and other members of al-Qaeda.

KSM and the Guantánamo Trials: As this book was being readied for press, it appeared that the Bush administration was planning to bolster its claims about bin Laden and al-Qaeda, at least in the mind of the general public, by means of military trials and executions at Guantánamo Bay. In February 2008, the government announced its intention to convict KSM, along with Abu Zubaydah and other members of al-Qaeda accused of responsibility for 9/11, and to seek the death penalty, which a new law would allow to be carried out at Guantánamo.[49]

Very serious concerns have been raised about these trials. These concerns are due partly to the lax standards for the military commission trials at Guantánamo. Several problems in these standards have been laid out by Lieutenant Commander Charles D. Swift of the Judge Advocate General's (JAG) Corps of the US Navy. One problem is the fact that the prosecution can use evidence obtained through torture and other coercive methods. The way such evidence might be used can be seen by looking at how the purported evidence from KSM was used at the Moussaoui trial.

In a document entitled "Substitution for the Testimony of Khalid Sheikh Mohammed," a long list of crimes to which KSM had reportedly confessed was preceded by the following statement to the jury:

> Khalid Sheikh Mohammed. . . was a high-ranking member of al Qaeda, who served as the. . . "mastermind" of the September 11, 2001, attacks. He was appointed to that role by Usama Bin Laden. . . . Sheikh Mohammed was intimately involved in the planning and execution of the September 11 attacks.

The document began, therefore, by presupposing the truth of KSM's alleged confessions, which should have been acknowledged to be dubious, given the possibility that they had resulted from torture. The jurors were, in fact, next instructed to ignore the fact that the statements were merely hearsay and, if they were really made by KSM, might have been extracted by torture:

> Sheikh Mohammed was captured in March 2003, and has been interrogated over the course of years on multiple occasions since his capture. None of the attorneys for either the prosecution or defense have been allowed access to Sheikh Mohammed, who is not available to testify either in person or by video for national security reasons. However, the lawyers have been given numerous written summaries of Sheikh Mohammed's oral statements made in response to extensive questioning.
>
> Listed below are some of the statements Sheikh Mohammed made in response to questioning. You should assume that if Sheikh Mohammed were available to testify in this courtroom under oath and subject to perjury he would have said what is contained in these statements.
>
> Although you do not have the ability to see the witness's demeanor as he testifies, you must approach these statements with the understanding that they were made under circumstances designed to elicit truthful statements from the witness.[50]

This was said even though KSM had reportedly confessed to an unbelievable number of acts, at least one of which could not possibly have been true—namely, his purported claim that he had been responsible for planning an attack on the Plaza Bank in the state of Washington. This bank was not built until 2006—three years after KSM had been incarcerated.[51]

There will likely be even less candor in the Guantánamo trials, which will involve, beyond the allowance of statements obtained by torture, the following violations of standard judicial procedures in the United States. First, prosecutors have no obligation to inform defense lawyers of exculpatory evidence. Second, the prosecution can obtain a conviction on the basis of hearsay evidence (which means that the alleged witnesses are not available for cross-examination by the defense). Third, the presiding officer and jurors are picked by the same official who approved the charges. Fourth, this same official has the power to overrule any motion for dismissal. Fifth, defense attorneys can call witnesses only with the permission of the (hand-picked) presiding officer. Sixth, defense attorneys are not allowed to share the prosecution's evidence with their defendants.[52]

The fairness of the trials has been further thrown into doubt by evidence that they have been rigged to guarantee convictions. Some of the erstwhile prosecutors have left the military commissions for this reason. Captain John Carr, for example, wrote that the chief prosecutor had told him "the military panel will be handpicked and will not acquit these detainees."[53] Another prosecutor, Major Robert Preston (who had been nominated in 2005 for the Air Force's award for the outstanding judge advocate), left the military commissions after concluding that fair trails for the Guantánamo prisoners were impossible.[54] Preston, in fact, reported that he and other prosecutors had been "told by the chief prosecutor at the time [2004] that they didn't need evidence to get convictions."[55]

Most startlingly, a later chief prosecutor, Colonel Morris Davis, resigned after he learned that Department of Defense General Counsel William Haynes, a close associate of David Addington (Dick Cheney's chief of staff), had been put over him in the commissions' chain of command. This was a problem, Davis reported, because Haynes—in response to Davis's assertion that some acquittals would lend credibility to the process—had said:

"We can't have acquittals. If we've been holding these guys for so long, how can we explain letting them get off? We can't have acquittals, we've got to have convictions."[56] Davis had also complained about interference by Air Force Brigadier General Thomas Hartmann, the legal advisor to the convening authority, Susan J. Crawford (another close associate of David Addington). According to Davis, Hartmann's interference included pressing the lawyers to have closed-door proceedings, to use evidence obtained from torture, and to allow political considerations to determine which cases to prosecute.[57]

Davis, it has been pointed out, could by no means be characterized as a "whining civil libertarian."[58] He, in fact, had been known as the military commissions' "attack dog."[59] But he felt he could not participate in rigged trials. He had fewer problems with the procedures of the military commissions themselves than with the fact that civilian political appointees with political agendas were directing the process. "They are looking for a political outcome, not justice," said Davis, who added that "top officials in the Pentagon had discussed the 'strategic political value' of putting prominent detainees on trial before the 2008 presidential election."[60] Davis was here referring to Deputy Defense Secretary Gordon England's statement: "We need to think about charging some of the high-value detainees because there could be strategic political value to charging some of these detainees before the election."[61]

Davis, it would appear, was punished by the Pentagon for speaking out: He was denied a medal for his two years of work building the cases against the suspects because, Pentagon officials told him, he did "not serve honorably."[62] The charge that political considerations have improperly influenced the legal process has, nevertheless, been made by other military lawyers. At the end of May, 2008, defense attorneys for KSM and four other 9/11 suspects asked a military appeals court to delay the arraignments scheduled for June 5 because several of the attorneys, having not yet received security clearances, would not be allowed to participate. "It is offensive to me," said Navy Lt. Commander Brian Mizer, "[that] the government would seek to proceed in a death penalty case without all detailed counsel present." Moreover, Mizer said, the government had not "provided the defense with the [time,] attorneys, resources and facilities necessary. . . to prepare a defense in this death penalty case." Mizer and other defense attorneys, reported CNN, "have accused prosecutors of rushing their clients to trial to influence the November presidential elections."[63]

It would appear, therefore, that the Bush–Cheney administration and its Pentagon devised a sure-fire plan to "prove" that KSM and other members of al-Qaeda were responsible for the attacks of 9/11. Besides arranging to have these men convicted in kangaroo courts, the administration hoped to have their lives terminated by execution—an act that would prevent the possibility of retrials.

The complaints raised about some of the personnel had some effect. In February 2008, Williams Haynes resigned as general counsel for the Department of Defense, and in May 2008, a military judge disqualified General Hartmann from playing any role in the first case scheduled for trial (that of Salim Hamdan, Osama bin Laden's driver), saying that it appeared that Hartmann had not "retain[ed] the required independence from the prosecution" to carry out his role with neutrality.[64]

Hartmann's response was that although he would not immediately resign his position as legal advisor to the tribunals, he might do so later if questions about his neutrality stalled the other cases.[65] However, even if that were to occur, so that both he and Haynes would no longer be involved, the absence of these two especially problematic individuals would do little to rectify the basic problems, which are structural and procedural.

The mainstream press has thus far failed to face the fact that these structural and procedural defects might be based on the Bush administration's knowledge that fair trials, besides probably not resulting in convictions, might expose 9/11 as an operation planned by key members of the Bush administration itself. The *New York Times* is typical. Complaining that the military trials will betray American ideals and outrage the conscience of the world, it argued that the Bush administration will be doing "unnecessary harm" (the title of its editorial). From the point of view of the Bush administration, however, this harm probably seems not at all unnecessary. Trying the men in "ordinary federal courts," as the

Times proposes, probably seems far too risky. The *Times* can assume otherwise because it has accepted the validity of the evidence against al-Qaeda, saying: "There is good reason to believe that Khalid Shaikh Mohammed and the five others may have been responsible for horrific acts."[66] In light of the above statements by Kean and Hamilton, on the one hand, and Windrem, Limjoco, and Ratner, on the other, there is we have seen, no "good reason" to accept the official story about KSM and al-Qaeda.

Could bin Laden and al-Qaeda Have Orchestrated the Attacks? In addition to what we have seen here and in Chapter 6—that there is no good evidence that the attacks were planned by KSM and Osama bin Laden, then carried out by al-Qaeda hijackers, and there is even good evidence against the idea that hijackers took over the planes—there is a complementary point: Several political and military leaders from other countries have stated that bin Laden and al-Qaeda simply could not have carried out the attacks. Andreas von Bülow, the former state secretary of West Germany's ministry of defense, said:

> The planning of the attacks was technically and organizationally a master achievement. To hijack four huge airplanes within a few minutes and within one hour, to drive them into their targets, with complicated flight maneuvers! This is unthinkable, without years-long support from secret apparatuses of the state and industry.

Horst Ehmke, former minister of research and technology of West Germany, wrote: "Terrorists could not have carried out such an operation with four hijacked planes without the support of a secret service." General Leonid Ivashov, who on 9/11 was the chief of staff of the Russian armed forces, wrote:

> Only secret services and their current chiefs—or those retired but still having influence inside the state organizations—have the ability to plan, organize and conduct an operation of such magnitude. . . . . Osama bin Laden and "Al Qaeda" cannot be the organizers nor the performers of the September 11 attacks. They do not have the necessary organization, resources or leaders.

Mohamed Hassanein Heikal, the former foreign minister of Egypt, wrote:

> Bin Laden does not have the capabilities for an operation of this magnitude. When I hear Bush talking about al-Qaida as if it was Nazi Germany or the communist party of the Soviet Union, I laugh because I know what is there. Bin Laden has been under surveillance for years: every telephone call was monitored and al-Qaida has been penetrated by American intelligence, Pakistani intelligence, Saudi intelligence, Egyptian intelligence. They could not have kept secret an operation that required such a degree of organisation and sophistication.

General Mirza Aslam Beg, former chief of staff of Pakistan's army, said:

> Many of us in this region believe that Osama or his al-Qaeda were not responsible for [the] 11 September attacks. . . . Osama bin Laden and al-Qaeda definitely do not have the know-how and the capability to launch such operations involving such high precision coordination, based on information and expertise.

Even the Pakistani president, General Pervez Musharraf, said:

> I didn't think it possible that Osama sitting up there in the mountains could do it. . . . [T]hose who executed it were much more modern. They knew the US, they knew aviation. I don't think he has the intelligence or the minute planning. The planner was someone else.[67]

This same point was also made by veteran CIA agent Milt Bearden. Speaking disparagingly of "the myth of Osama bin Laden" to Dan Rather on CBS News the day after 9/11, Bearden said: "I was there [in Afghanistan] at the same time bin Laden was there. He was not the great warrior." With regard to the widespread view that bin Laden was behind the attacks, he said: "This was a tremendously sophisticated operation against the United States—more sophisticated that anybody would have ascribed to Osama bin Laden." Pointing out that a group capable of such a sophisticated attack would have had a way to cover their tracks, he added: "This group who was responsible for that, if they didn't have an Osama bin Laden out there, they'd invent one, because he's a terrific diversion for the rest of the world."[68]

Needless to say, the 9/11 Commission did not report any of these statements.

CONCEALING THE ROLE OF PAKISTAN'S ISI

One of the recommendations of *The 9/11 Commission Report* was that the United States should sustain "the current scale of aid to Pakistan."[69] Seeing this statement, readers might assume that the Commission would not have mentioned any of the evidence summarized in NPH pointing to Pakistani complicity in 9/11. They would be right.

The 9/11 Commission did not mention that ISI chief General Mahmoud Ahmad had been in Washington since September 4, meeting with CIA chief Tenet and also (as a response to a 2008 FOIA request revealed) with the National Security Council (in spite of Condoleezza Rice's denial, reported in NPH, that she met with him). The Commission, therefore, had no reason to mention that, immediately after this week of meetings, the leader of the Northern Alliance in Afghanistan, Ahmad Shah Masood, was assassinated— by the ISI, according to the Northern Alliance.[70] The Commission also did not mention Ahmad's "most important meeting"—as a Pakistani newspaper put it—with Undersecretary of State Marc Grossman (who was central to Sibel Edmond's allegations discussed in Chapter 6). It mentioned only that Ahmad met with Deputy Secretary of State Richard Armitage on September 13,[71] thereby suggesting that Ahmad had come to Washington only after 9/11.

The Commission also did not mention the report that General Ahmad had ordered an ISI agent to send $100,000 to Mohamed Atta. The Commission, in fact, lied, saying that it had "seen no evidence that any foreign government—or foreign government official—supplied any funding" for the 9/11 plot.[72] (We can confidently call this a lie because the *Los Angeles Times* story by Josh Meyer, mentioned in Chapter 6, reported that the Commission, according to some of its members, had found extensive evidence of assistance by Pakistan as well as Saudi Arabia.[73])

The Commission, moreover, did not mention the "shocking" report that, after the money transfer ordered by Ahmad came to light, General Musharraf dismissed Ahmad, to whom he was politically indebted, at the insistence of US authorities.[74]

The Commission also failed to point out the evidence that alleged 9/11 mastermind KSM was connected to the ISI, the statement by the Afghan interior minister that the ISI had helped bin Laden escape from Afghanistan, and the evidence that the ISI was involved in the death of Daniel Pearl.[75]

Also not mentioned by the Commission was Gerald Posner's claim that, several months prior to the suspicious death of Mushaf Ali Mir, Abu Zubaydah had claimed that Mir was connected to bin Laden and possessed advance knowledge of the 9/11 attacks.

The Commission, finally, did not mention the report that another Pakistani, Rajaa Gulum Abbas, seemed to know in 1999 that the Twin Towers were going to come down.

Having failed to mention all these things, the 9/11 Commission could recommend, with a straight face, that "the current scale of aid to Pakistan" should be sustained.[76]

The Bush administration, incidentally, did not simply maintain the amount of aid that was given to Pakistan prior to 9/11. It increased it astronomically. Pakistan had been receiving only about $3 million per year in military aid (less than Estonia and Panama). But after 9/11, it started receiving over $1.5 billion per year (more than any other country except Israel and Egypt).[77] And that was only military aid. The total US aid to Pakistan from 9/11 through 2007 was over $10 billion—perhaps even twice that amount if classified aid is included.[78]

During this period, however, the insurgency of the Taliban and al-Qaeda in Afghanistan had been growing, "as a consequence," the *Washington Quarterly* suggested, "of Pakistani weakness, if not outright complicity, with militants in the Pashtun border areas." Also, although most of the US aid was provided as Coalition Support Funds, intended to help Pakistan battle terrorism, "The vast majority of this amount has been spent on [kinds of] weapons. . . [un]likely to provide much help in rooting out al Qaeda or the Taliban."[79]

The fact that this enormous amount of military aid was indeed not rooting them out was confirmed by a *New York Times* story, published just three days before Benazir Bhutto was assassinated in December 2007, which began by saying: "[T]he United States has spent more than $5 billion in a largely failed effort to bolster the Pakistani military effort against Al Qaeda and the Taliban." Far from being rooted out, "the Qaeda leaders hiding in Pakistan's tribal areas had reconstituted their command structure and become increasingly active."[80] These developments would have been less surprising to the general public if the 9/11 Commission had not concealed the connections between the ISI, the Taliban, and al-Qaeda. (Benazir Bhutto, incidentally, had singled out the ISI for special criticism shortly before her fateful return to Pakistan, saying that it would "do anything to stop democracy."[81])

OMAR AL-BAYOUMI AND THE SAUDI CONNECTION

The question of Saudi funding for al-Qaeda was extensively discussed in a 2004 book, *Intelligence Matters*, written by former Senator Bob Graham, who revealed details he learned as co-chair of the Joint Inquiry into the 9/11 attacks carried out by the intelligence committees of the US Senate and House of Representatives. Although the Inquiry's public (unclassified) report was published in July 2003,[82] much of the material had been blacked out by the CIA, the FBI, and the NSA, with the blessing of the White House. Graham's book dealt with a 28-page section of this blacked-out material that, he said, treated "the Saudi government and the assistance that government gave to some and possibly all of the September 11 terrorists."[83] (An anonymous official who reportedly saw these pages said: "We're not talking about rogue elements. We're talking about a coordinated network that reaches right from the hijackers to multiple places in the Saudi government."[84])

At the center of Graham's narrative was the relationship of Omar al-Bayoumi to two of the alleged hijackers, Nawaf al-Hazmi and Khalid al-Mihdhar, to which I had devoted merely a paragraph in NPH. Graham's book supplied many more details.

Graham provided evidence that al-Bayoumi's meeting with the two men did not occur by chance and that, just before picking them up, al-Bayoumi met with Fahad al-Thumairy, an official at the Saudi consulate in Los Angeles suspected of terrorist connections.[85] Graham also revealed that al-Bayoumi had a "ghost job," meaning that he was paid for doing no work, and that his salary was more than doubled while al-Hazmi and al-Mihdhar were with him.[86] Furthermore, Graham reported, al-Bayoumi made an extraordinary number of calls to Saudi officials.[87] Graham, finally, quoted a CIA memo from August 2002 that, referring to al-Bayoumi as a "terrorist," spoke of "incontrovertible evidence that there is support for [him] within the Saudi government."[88]

Nevertheless, Graham reported, the FBI closed its case on al-Bayoumi, claiming that he had only "briefly lent money to two of the 19 hijackers" and that all his assistance to them was "in compliance with the Muslim custom of being kind to strangers [rather] than out of some relationship with Saudi Intelligence."[89] Amazed by this conclusion, Graham requested an interview with the FBI agents who made this report, but FBI Director Robert Mueller refused to grant it.[90]

Graham's strongest criticism was directed not at the FBI, however, but at the administration from which it took its orders. During his investigations, Graham reported, he found that "the White House was directing the cover-up" and that it was doing so "for reasons other than national security"—reasons that included protecting "America's relationship with the Kingdom of Saudi Arabia."[91]

Such a cover-up appeared to be involved in the official treatment of a story involving al-Bayoumi and his wife, on the one hand, and Prince Bandar bin Sultan (the Saudi ambassador to the United States), and his wife, Princess Haifa, on the other. According to both Graham and Craig Unger (in his book *House of Bush, House of Saud*), over $100,000 was sent by Prince Bandar and Princess Haifa—most of it from her—to the wife of Osama Basnan, who was a friend of al-Bayoumi. The money was originally for her thyroid condition. But beginning in 2000, Basnan's wife began signing over her checks to al-Bayoumi's wife, who then turned at least some of this money over to al-Hazmi and al-Mihdhar. The fact that Basnan knew what his wife was doing became clear when he later bragged to FBI agents that he had done more for the hijackers than al-Bayoumi had.[92] Unger concluded: "What had happened was undeniable: funds from Prince Bandar's wife had indirectly ended up in the hands of the hijackers."[93]

Although Unger considered this story "undeniable," the 9/11 Commission rose to the occasion, saying in a note: "We have found no evidence that Saudi Princess Haifa al Faisal provided any funds to the conspiracy, either directly or indirectly."[94] The

Commission seemed thereby to deny the truth of the story summarized by Unger, although this story was based on articles by other reporters, including one in *Newsweek* by Michael Isikoff and Evan Thomas.[95] The Commission could hardly claim ignorance of this story, because it would have known about it from the final report of the Congressional Joint Inquiry.

In light of Josh Meyer's aforementioned *Los Angeles Times* story, from which we can conclude that the Commission simply decided for political reasons not to include its evidence pointing to Saudi funding of al-Qaeda, we can suspect that political considerations again trumped the desire to provide the fullest possible account.

More has been revealed about Fahad al-Thumairy, the official that al-Bayoumi had visited at the Saudi consulate in Los Angeles, by *New York Times* reporter Philip Shenon in his 2008 book, *The Commission: The Uncensored History of the 9/11 Investigation*. According to Shenon, the White House had refused to declassify the blacked-out section "because it contained evidence suggesting that Saudi government officials, including Fahad al-Thumairy . . . were part of the support network."[96] He also reports that al-Thumairy was evidently the one who had arranged for al-Bayoumi, with whom he often talked by telephone, to provide assistance to Nawaf al-Hazmi and Khalid al-Mihdhar, but that al-Thumairy, when interviewed by members of the 9/11 Commission, denied knowing al-Bayoumi— until he was confronted by the telephone records proving otherwise.

Shenon reported, finally, that Zelikow and the leader of the team dealing with the al-Qaeda plot, Dietrich "Dieter" Snell, rewrote the team's report, "remov[ing] virtually all of the most serious allegations against the Saudis." Mike Jacobson (who had authored the section on the Saudis in the Joint Inquiry's report that got blacked out) and the other members of the plot team had to settle for a compromise, in which "much of their most damning material was moved to the report's footnotes."[97]

Still more evidence about the relation of al-Bayoumi to Nawaf al-Hazmi and Khalid al-Mihdhar became available with the release of the FBI's (redacted) "Hijackers Timeline" in February 2008. Graham had shown that al-Bayoumi's meeting with these two men was not accidental, but he had portrayed it as occurring in the last week of January 2001, which would mean that they had spent a week or more in Los Angeles, after their arrival in the United States on January 15, before moving into his place in San Diego. Graham's account on this point hence agreed with that of the 9/11 Commission, which said that al-Mihdhar and al-Hazmi "spent about two weeks [in Los Angeles] before moving to San Diego."[98] But the FBI timeline indicates that the two men started staying at al-Bayoumi's place on January 15, meaning that they had gone there directly from the airport.[99] This information indicates that al-Bayoumi was part of a support network for the two men that had been arranged prior to their arrival.

LATER DEVELOPMENTS INVOLVING MOUSSAOUI

After NPH appeared, many further developments occurred in the case of Zacarias Moussaoui. In April 2005, Moussaoui pleaded guilty to terrorism charges but "vehemently denied that he was planning to be one of the Sept. 11 hijackers," saying instead that he was to be part of a second wave of attacks.[100] During his trial in 2006, however, he claimed that he was to fly a fifth plane on 9/11, which was to have hit the White House.[101] But after the trial was over, he called his guilty plea "a complete fabrication" and filed a motion to withdraw it, but was not allowed to do so.[102]

Another significant development occurred at the trial when Harry Samit, the Minneapolis FBI agent who had prepared the application for the FISA warrant to search Moussaoui's belongings, testified that he had told the DOJ's inspector general that FBI headquarters, in its handling of the evidence about Moussaoui, was guilty of "obstructionism, criminal negligence, and careerism."[103]

But the most important development at the trial was one that has already been discussed: the FBI's report about phone calls from the flights, which contradicted not only the belief of many people that they had received cell phone calls from relatives on the airliners, especially United Flight 93, but also Ted Olson's claim that he had received two phone calls from his wife, Barbara Olson. It is puzzling, to be sure, that the FBI would have done this. But if the truth about 9/11 ever becomes part of the public record, the world may look back upon the Moussaoui trial as one of the key moments in the unraveling of the official story.

9. Complicity by US Officials:
A Summary of the Evidence

As this book was ready to go to press in the summer of 2008, the most important question before the American people and their elected representatives remained the same as it was when NPH was published: whether the overall argument for the alternative account of 9/11, according to which officials in the US government were responsible for the attacks, is convincing enough "to undertake a thorough investigation of the various consider-ations used to support it." The only difference is that these "considerations" are now, as we have seen, even stronger than they were in 2004.

Who Benefits?

The question of who would have expected to benefit the most from 9/11 should have been central to the 9/11 Commission's discussion of motive. But the Commission, avoiding this question, simply told us that al-Qaeda had a motive. As Kean and Hamilton said in their 2006 book: "The starting point [of the Commission's story about how 9/11 came about] would be Usama Bin Ladin's February 1998 fatwa instructing his followers to kill Americans, military and civilian."[1] The Commission ended up writing: "Claiming that America had declared war against God and his messenger, [bin Laden] called for the murder of any American, anywhere on earth," as the duty of all Muslims. Calling this section of its report "A Declaration of War," the 9/11 Commission said that bin Laden saw himself as organizing "a new kind of war to destroy America and bring the world to Islam."[2] This was its account of the motives for 9/11.

While telling us about "Bin Ladin's murderous ideology,"[3] however, the Commission ignored evidence that members of the

Bush–Cheney administration had, prior to 9/11, planned invasions of Afghanistan and Iraq, after which they hoped to attack five other countries. The Commission thereby shielded its readers from evidence that this administration included people with an even more murderous ideology.

The benefits that 9/11 brought to the administration with regard to its planned attacks on Afghanistan and Iraq were obvious. Indeed, Rumsfeld and Wolfowitz even told the 9/11 Commission that, without 9/11, the president could not have convinced Congress that the United States needed to invade Afghanistan and overthrow the Taliban.[4] Another member of PNAC, Kenneth Adelman, who predicted in 2002 that "liberating Iraq would be a cakewalk,"[5] said in 2003: "At the beginning of the administration people were talking about Iraq but it wasn't doable. . . . That changed with September 11."[6] The 9/11 Commission, however, did not mention these potential benefits, which might have provided motives for the Bush administration to engineer 9/11 as a pretext to invade Muslim countries.

The Commission also failed to bring up other benefits to the Bush administration that could have been anticipated. To take the most important example, the main point of PNAC's *Rebuilding America's Defenses* was that "the next president of the United States. . . must increase military spending to preserve American geopolitical leadership."[7] The 9/11 attacks led to enormous increases, as even the 9/11 Commission pointed out, writing:

> The nation has committed enormous resources to national security and to countering terrorism. Between fiscal year 2001, the last budget adopted before 9/11, and the present fiscal year 2004, total federal spending on defense (including expenditures on both Iraq and Afghanistan), homeland security, and international affairs rose more than 50 percent, from $345 billion to about $547 billion. The United States has not experienced such a rapid surge in national security spending since the Korean War.[8]

Since the 9/11 Commission wrote those words in 2004, moreover, military-related spending has continued to expand. If the wars in Afghanistan and Iraq continue, spending for them alone will soon be in the trillions of dollars, according to Nobel Prize-winning economist Joseph Stiglitz.[9]

Accordingly, if 9/11 was orchestrated partly for the purpose of escalating military spending, it has been a resounding success. However, although that point would have already been abundantly obvious when *The 9/11 Commission Report* was written, that book contains not the slightest hint that the goal of boosting military spending might have provided a motive. Only al-Qaeda had a motive.

THE EVIDENCE FOR OFFICIAL COMPLICITY: A SUMMARY

To bring the summary of evidence provided in NPH up to date requires adding many items—the numbering of which reflects the fact that they are added to the 24 items provided in Chapter 9 of NPH:

25. The fact that, after the military's stories about its response to Flights 175, 77, and 93 proved to be indefensible, the 9/11 Commission provided new stories—stories that, moreover, are inherently implausible as well as being in conflict with much prior testimony.

26. Evidence that the FAA notified the military about American Flight 11's troubles at least 10 minutes earlier than NORAD and the 9/11 Commission claim.

27. The fact that Richard Clarke's account in *Against All Enemies* contradicted the accounts by both Donald Rumsfeld and General Myers as to their locations that morning.

28. The fact that NIST, in trying to show how the Twin Towers could have collapsed solely because of the airplane impacts and resulting fires, made many empirically groundless and highly implausible speculations about core columns being stripped, severed, and heated up to very high temperatures.

29. The fact that NIST, in seeking to make its theory appear plausible, ignored several features of the collapses, such as the explosions, the horizontal ejections, and the melting of steel.

30. The fact that NIST has refused to defend its conclusions in debate with scientists who have challenged those conclusions.

31. The fact that Rudy Giuliani reported knowing in advance that the Twin Towers were going to collapse, even though, given the official account, there should have been no way for anyone to know this.

32. The fact that Giuliani's Office of Emergency Management spread the word many hours in advance that WTC 7 was going to collapse, even though, given the official account, there should have been no way for anyone to know this.

33. The fact that NIST's promised explanation of the collapse of WTC 7—which exemplified standard features of controlled implosions even more perfectly than did the collapses of the Twin Towers—was repeatedly delayed.

34. The fact that NIST distorted the testimony and rescue time of two NYC employees—Michael Hess and Barry Jennings—in order to make it appear that they had not testified to the existence of explosions in WTC 7.

35. The fact that hundreds of people with relevant kinds of professional knowledge, including physicists, architects, and engineers, have publicly stated that the Twin Towers and WTC 7 were brought down with explosives.

36. The fact that the 9/11 Commission's new story about Flight 77 is contradicted by NORAD's timeline of September 18, 2001, by testimony from several military officers, and by an FAA memo to the Commission that the Commission simply ignored when writing its final report.

37. The evidence that Andrews Air Force Base did, contrary to statements by military officials, have fighter jets that could have been deployed to protect the Pentagon.

38. The fact that Ted Olson's claim that his wife phoned him twice from Flight 77 has been contradicted by both American Airlines and the FBI, with American contradicting the final version of his claim, according to which she used an onboard phone, and the FBI saying that she did not complete even one call using either an onboard or a cell phone.

39. The lack of debris, damage, and a seismic signal consistent with the Pentagon's having been struck by a Boeing 757.

40. The fact that Donald Rumsfeld and Lee Evey testified that the hole in the C ring was made by Flight 77's nose, which would have been physically impossible—as perhaps acknowledged by the fact that this claim has not been supported by any official or semi-official report.

41. The failure of the government to supply evidence showing what actually damaged the Pentagon—evidence that could have easily been provided by releasing videos and/or serial numbers of the flight data recorder and time-change parts.

42. The fact that the reported eyewitness testimony as to what damaged the Pentagon is too diverse and otherwise problematic to support, by itself, the claim that an AA Boeing 757 struck the Pentagon.

43. The fact that Wedge 1 would have been, for many reasons, the least likely part of the Pentagon for al-Qaeda terrorists to target.

44. Evidence that Hani Hanjour could not have flown the trajectory allegedly taken by Flight 77 in order to hit Wedge 1 of the Pentagon.

45. The evidence that a 757, even with an excellent pilot, could not have flown the path allegedly taken by Flight 77 to hit the light posts and then level out to enter the first floor of Wedge 1.

46. The fact that, although the Pentagon claimed that it had no idea that an aircraft was headed its way, an E4-B, with state-of-the-art communication capacities, was flying over Washington at the time of the Pentagon strike.

47. The fact that Norman Mineta reported witnessing, prior to the Pentagon attack, a conversation in which Vice President Cheney appeared to have confirmed a stand-down order.

48. The fact that the 9/11 Commission claimed that Cheney did not enter the bunker under the White House until about 9:58, in spite of abundant evidence from Mineta and others that he was there before 9:20.

49. The fact that the 9/11 Commission claimed that Cheney did not issue the shootdown authorization until after 10:10, even though Richard Clarke and several military figures said that they had received the authorization much earlier, prior to the crash of Flight 93.

50. The fact that the 9/11 Commission's main claim about Flight 93—that the military could not have shot it down because it did not know of its hijacking until after it had crashed—is contradicted by abundant news reports and testimonies by the FAA, Richard Clarke, and various military officers.

51. The fact that, after it had long been part of the official story that several passengers on the flights, especially United Flight 93, had reported the hijacking of their planes on cell phone calls to relatives, the FBI reported in 2006 that no passengers made cell phone calls to relatives from any of the four flights.

52. Evidence that Mohamed Atta and the other alleged hijackers were not, as the official story claims, devout Muslims.

53. The fact that, after it was learned that some of the men on the FBI's first list of hijackers turned out not to have died on 9/11, the FBI simply replaced them with different men.

54. The fact that the FBI's story about the discovery of incriminating information at Boston's Logan Airport, according to which it was found in Atta's luggage inside the airport, contradicted an earlier FBI story, according to which it had been found out in the parking lot in a Mitsubishi.

55. The fact that not only this information but the other types of evidence supporting the existence of hijackers on the planes, such as photographs taken in airports and passports found near the crash sites, appear to have been planted.

56. The fact that none of the pilots on the four flights used the plane's transponder to squawk the hijack code.

57. The fact that Osama bin Laden was never indicted for 9/11 because the FBI, as it has admitted, has no hard evidence of his responsibility.

58. The fact that the Bush administration's Department of Justice has continued to enforce a gag order against Sibel Edmonds, forbidding her to tell what she knows about pre-9/11 misbehavior in the State Department and FBI headquarters.

POSSIBLE PROBLEMS FOR A COMPLICITY THEORY

I will comment on only the final paragraph of my discussion under this heading in NPH, which responded to the argument that, because there are so many problems in the official account of 9/11, to believe that members of the Bush administration arranged 9/11 would be to imply that they were incredibly incompetent. Having suggested in NPH that the truth may be that "they really were terribly incompetent," I became, while writing *9/11 Contradictions*, even more convinced of the correctness of this conclusion.

This conclusion provides, moreover, an answer to one of the most common a priori arguments against the claim that the Bush administration was behind 9/11—the argument that it was simply too incompetent to have planned and pulled off the operation. Having replied to this argument at some length elsewhere,[10] I will here simply add that I agree with this argument insofar as it is understood to mean: The Bush administration was too incompetent to have pulled off 9/11 and the resulting cover-up in a way that could not have been easily exposed, if Congress and the press had carried out even minimal investigations. A 9/11 truth movement, in other words, should never have been needed. The official story about 9/11 is so filled with implausibilities and outright impossibilities and contradictions that it should have been exposed as a big lie within weeks, if not days.

Problems for a Coincidence Theory

If I were writing the section under this heading in NPH today, I would not include point 3 (which suggested that fighters from McGuire should have been scrambled) and points 18, 20, and 21 (which were based on the assumption that we knew, mainly from cell phone calls, what was happening on Flight 93). The main change in this section, however, would be the addition of a number of further coincidences, based on the new points added above in the summary of evidence for official complicity. I have not spelled out these additional coincidences here, however, because they can easily be inferred from that summary. When those additional coincidences are added to the list of 38 contained in NPH, a coincidence (or incompetence) theory about 9/11 becomes even more improbable.

10. New Revelations about the 9/11 Commission and the Strengthened Case for a New Investigation

This chapter focuses entirely on the 9/11 Commission. The first thing to say is that my discussion in NPH should not have accepted, even verbally, the idea that it could have been called "the 9/11 Independent Commission." There was nothing independent about it.

The Commission's Mandate

One problem with the idea that the Commission was independent involved its mandate. In their preface to *The 9/11 Commission Report*, Thomas Kean and Lee Hamilton said that their mandate was to investigate "facts and circumstances relating to the terrorist attacks of September 11, 2001," in order "to provide the fullest possible account of the events surrounding 9/11."[1] However, in their later book, subtitled *The Inside Story of the 9/11 Commission*, they specified that they had the task of "gathering and presenting all of the available and relevant information *within the areas specified by our mandate*" (emphasis added).[2] What exactly was their mandate? They were "to ascertain, evaluate, and report on the evidence developed by all relevant governmental agencies regarding the facts and circumstances surrounding the attacks."[3] So they were not to provide all the 9/11-related evidence they might discover but only *the evidence provided by governmental agencies*, and there was virtually no chance that any agencies of the Bush administration would knowingly provide evidence contradicting the administration's account of 9/11. (When little pieces of evidence of this type inadvertently slipped through in the testimonies of certain individuals, such as the Norman Mineta, Coleen Rowley, and Sibel

Edmonds, they could be ignored.) The Commission's mandate, therefore, virtually ruled out any evidence pointing to complicity by the Bush administration.

THE COMMISSION'S EXECUTIVE DIRECTOR

But the most serious problem was, as I put it in NPH's Afterword, that the Commission's research was directed "by Philip Zelikow and hence, arguably, by the Bush administration itself." It later became clear, moreover, that the Commission's alleged independence was even more fully compromised by Zelikow's role than I had realized while writing NPH.

Power to Determine Report: For one thing, Zelikow appears to have had almost complete freedom to determine the content of the Commission's final report. He provided, Kean and Hamilton have told us, the report's "overarching vision," after which he "steer[ed] the direction of the Commission's investigation." This steering involved organizing the Commission's staff into various teams and telling each one what to investigate[4]—and hence, by implication, what *not* to investigate.

Although the public could reasonably have assumed that the Commission's task was to find out who was responsible for 9/11, this question was not asked. The Commission, under Zelikow's guidance, simply assumed the truth of the Bush administration's account. When the teams were set up, Kean and Hamilton explained, "the subject of 'al Qaeda' [was assigned] to staff team 1," and team 1A was told to "tell the story of al Qaeda's most successful operation—the 9/11 attacks."[5] Kean and Hamilton claimed that, unlike conspiracy theorists, they started with the relevant facts, not with a conclusion: they "were not setting out to advocate one theory or interpretation of 9/11 versus another."[6] By their own admission, however, they began with the conclusion that 9/11 was "al Qaeda's most successful operation."

The fact that the Commission's conclusion had been determined in advance was made even clearer by Kean and Hamilton's admission that an outline of the final report was prepared in advance by Zelikow and his former professor Ernest May, with whom he had previously coauthored a book. This outline, Kean and Hamilton said, was prepared by Zelikow and May at "the outset of [the Commission's] work."[7]

More was revealed about this startling fact by Philip Shenon in his 2008 book, *The Commission*, which was mentioned in Chapter 8. Pointing out that Zelikow and May had prepared this outline secretly, Shenon wrote:

> By March 2003, with the commission's staff barely in place, the two men had already prepared a detailed outline, complete with "chapter headings, subheadings, and sub-subheadings." . . . Zelikow shared the document with Kean and Hamilton, who were impressed by their executive director's early diligence but worried that the outline would be seen as evidence that they— and Zelikow—had predetermined the report's outcome.[8]

Indeed, it would have been difficult to see what *other* conclusion could be drawn. And so, Shenon continued:

> It [the outline] should be kept secret from the rest of the staff, they all decided. May said that he and Zelikow agreed that the outline should be "treated as if it were the most classified document the commission possessed." Zelikow. . . labeled it "Commission Sensitive," putting those words at the top and bottom of each page.[9]

"Commission Sensitive" meant, of course, that the Commission's staff would not be allowed to see it. The work of the 9/11 Commission began, accordingly, with Kean and Hamilton conspiring with Zelikow and May to conceal from the Commission's 80-some staff members a most important fact—that their investigative work would largely be limited to filling in the details of conclusions that had been reached before any investigations had begun.

When the staff did finally learn about this outline a year later—they were given copies in April 2004—many of them, Shenon reported, were alarmed. Some of them began circulating a two-page parody entitled "The Warren Commission Report— Preemptive Outline." One of its chapter headings read: "Single Bullet: We Haven't Seen the Evidence Yet. But Really. We're Sure."[10] Whoever wrote this parody no doubt realized that the crucial chapter of Zelikow and May's outline could have been headed: "Osama bin Laden and al-Qaeda: We Haven't Seen the Evidence Yet. But Really. We're Sure."

Besides predetermining the conclusions of the report, Zelikow also sought, and largely achieved, total control over the Commission's work. In 9/11CROD, I quoted the following statement reportedly made by a disgruntled staff member: "Zelikow is calling the shots. He's skewing the investigation and running it his own way."[11] Shenon has now described various means by which Zelikow was able to do this.

First, none of the Commissioners, including Kean and Hamilton, were given offices in the K Street office building used by the Commission's staff. As a result, Shenon says, "most of the commissioners rarely visited K Street. Zelikow was in charge."[12]

Second, even though the Commission would not have existed had it not been for the efforts of the families of the 9/11 victims, "the families were not allowed into the commission's offices because they did not have security clearances."[13]

Third, "Zelikow had insisted that there be a single, nonpartisan staff." This meant that each of the Commissioners would not, as they had assumed, "have a staff member of their own, typical on these sorts of independent commissions." This structure, Shenon points out, "would prevent any of the commissioners from striking out on their own in the investigation." Zelikow himself even admitted that this was his intention, saying: "If commissioners have their own personal staff, this empowers commissioners to pursue their own agenda."[14]

Fourth, Zelikow made it clear to the staff members that they worked for him, not for the Commissioners, and he, as much as possible, prevented direct contact between the staff and the Commissioners. "If information gathered by the staff was to be passed to the commissioners, it would have to go through Zelikow."[15] Although the Commissioners forced him to rescind his most extreme order of this nature—that the staff members were not even to return phone calls from the Commissioners without his permission[16]—he largely achieved his goal: "Zelikow's micromanagement meant that the staff had little, if any, contact with the ten commissioners; all information was funneled through Zelikow, and he decided how it would be shared elsewhere."[17]

Indeed, Shenon says, Zelikow insisted "that every scrap of secret evidence gathered by the staff be shared with him before anyone else; he then controlled how and if the evidence was shared elsewhere."[18] This meant that Zelikow had the power, if he wished, to prevent the Commissioners, including Kean and Hamilton, from learning facts discovered by the various investigative teams. Hamilton reportedly believed that Zelikow was not capable of "sneaking something" by the Commissioners, but this belief, Shenon suggests, was rather unrealistic.[19]

Finally, besides having the power, through all these means, to run the Commission's investigation his own way, Zelikow also, "more than anyone else," Shenon says, "controlled what the final report would say."[20] He could exert this control because, although the first draft of each chapter was written by one of the investigative teams, Zelikow headed up a team in the front office that revised these drafts.[21] Indeed, Shenon says, "Zelikow rewrote virtually everything that was handed to him—usually top to bottom."[22]

Because of the extraordinary power Zelikow had to shape the Commission's final report, short-hand references to it should employ his name. Such references commonly use the name of the chairman, as in the "Warren Report" or the "Rumsfeld Report." In 9/11CROD, however, I suggested that, instead of referring to the 9/11 Commission's report as the "Kean–Hamilton Report," we should call it the "Kean–Zelikow Report." But in D9D, after learning how much power Zelikow had to shape it, I suggested that we should simply call it the "Zelikow Report."[23] Shenon's book has confirmed the appropriateness of this designation.

Zelikow and NSS 2002: Besides having more power to shape the Commission's final report than I knew while writing NPH, Zelikow was also an even more inappropriate choice for executive director than I then realized. One of the most serious problems was that he had been the primary author of the 2002 version of *The National Security Strategy of the United States of America* (NSS 2002).[24] According to James Mann, a first draft of this document had been produced by Richard Haass of the State Department, but Condoleezza Rice, wanting "something bolder," decided that the document should be "completely rewritten," so she "turned the writing over to her old colleague. . . Philip Zelikow."[25] His authorship of NSS 2002 is important because this document used 9/11 to justify a new doctrine of preemptive (technically "preventive") warfare that had long been desired by neoconservatives for imperial purposes.[26]

According to international law as articulated in the UN charter, a country cannot launch a preemptive attack on another country unless it knows that an attack from that country is imminent—too imminent for the case to be taken to the UN Security Council. The Bush administration used 9/11 to adopt a doctrine that excused itself from this restriction. This change in doctrine was signaled in President Bush's address at West Point in June 2002, when the administration was starting to prepare the American people for an attack on Iraq. Having spoken of "new threats," Bush said that America's security "will require all Americans. . . to be ready for preemptive action."[27]

The new doctrine was then made official US policy in NSS 2002. Stating that "our best defense is a good offense," this document said:

> Given the goals of rogue states and terrorists, the United States can no longer rely on a reactive posture. . . . [We must take] anticipatory action to defend ourselves, even if uncertainty remains as to the time and place of the enemy's attack. To forestall or prevent. . . hostile acts by our adversaries, the United States will, if necessary, act preemptively.[28]

By virtue of articulating this new policy, which became known as the "Bush doctrine,"[29] NSS 2002 was, in the words of neoconservative writer Max Boot, a "quintessentially neo-conservative document."[30] It thereby provided a prime example of the fact that, as historian Stephen Sniegoski wrote, "the traumatic effects of the 9/11 terrorism. . . enabled the agenda of the neocons to become the policy of the United States of America."[31] Referring specifically to the new policy of preventive preemption, Andrew Bacevich wrote: "The events of 9/11 provided the tailor-made opportunity to break free of the fetters restricting the exercise of American power."[32]

Given the fact that Zelikow was one of the central players in the Bush administration's exploitation of 9/11 for this purpose, it is no wonder that the 9/11 Commission, under his guidance, gave no hint—as I pointed out in Chapter 7 and the corresponding chapter in NPH—that the Bush administration might have had imperial motives for orchestrating, or at least allowing, the 9/11 attacks. Zelikow's prior role in drafting NSS 2002 meant that, insofar as the 9/11 Commission under his leadership investigated the White House's responsibility for 9/11, this was the White House investigating itself.

Zelikow and Catastrophic Terrorism: Another troubling episode in Zelikow's background was his co-authorship of a 1998 essay on "catastrophic terrorism." In this essay, which suggests that he had been thinking about the World Trade Center and a new Pearl Harbor several years prior to 2001, Zelikow and his coauthors— one of whom, John Deutch, had been the director of the CIA in 1995 and 1996—say:

> If the device that exploded in 1993 under the World Trade Center had been nuclear. . . , the resulting horror and chaos would have exceeded our ability to describe it. Such an act of catastrophic terrorism would be a watershed event in American history. It could involve loss of life and property unprecedented in peacetime and undermine America's fundamental sense of security. . . . Like Pearl Harbor, this event would divide our past and future into a before and after. The United States might respond with draconian measures, scaling back civil liberties, allowing wider surveillance of citizens, detention of suspects, and use of deadly force.[33]

Besides the fact that this remarkable document spoke of a new catastrophe as having effects comparable to those of Pearl Harbor, it also imagined the new catastrophe as an attack on the World Trade Center. Moreover, this statement predicted with great accuracy the effects of the new catastrophe: the division into a "before and after." (The contrast between a pre-9/11 and a post-9/11 mindset became one of the mantras of the Bush administration.) The statement equally predicted the government's response with "draconian measures," namely, "scaling back civil liberties, allowing wider surveillance of citizens, detention of suspects, and use of deadly force." Zelikow and his coauthors had anticipated the effects of "the New Pearl Harbor" with remarkable accuracy.

Zelikow's Double Duplicity: These features of Zelikow's background raise the question of how he was chosen. Kean and Hamilton told us in their 2006 book that he had been recommended by one of the Commission's Republican members, Slade Gorton. They also pointed out that all of the Democrats on the Commission, except Hamilton, were "wary of Zelikow's appointment." They also revealed that, amazingly, he was the only candidate that they seriously considered.[34] Why, given all of his obvious conflicts of interest, would Kean and Hamilton have chosen him to run the Commission?[35]

The shocking truth, Shenon has now revealed, is that Zelikow concealed some of his conflicts of interest from them when he applied for the job and then, when Kean and Hamilton later learned about his deception, they decided to keep him on anyway.

When he applied for the job of executive director, Zelikow gave Kean and Hamilton a copy of his résumé. It mentioned, among other things, his co-authored article, "Catastrophic Terrorism" (which Kean and Hamilton found "remarkably prescient"), the book he had co-authored with Rice, and his appointment to the White House intelligence advisory board in 2001. Although Kean and Hamilton knew that the latter two items would raise conflict-of-interest objections, "they decided the conflict was not insurmountable."[36] Zelikow had, however, failed to mention some facts that involved even more serious conflicts of interest.

One omission was his role in the creation of NSS 2002, which had been used, Shenon points out, to "justify a preemptive strike on Iraq."[37] Shenon then adds:

> When commission staffers learned that Zelikow was the principal author [of NSS 2002], many were astounded. It was arguably his most serious conflict of interest in running the investigation. It was in his interest, they could see, to use the commission to try to bolster the administration's argument for war—a war that he had helped make possible.[38]

And indeed, Shenon reports, Zelikow did try to use the Commission for this purpose, while purportedly conducting an objective, fact-finding investigation. The witnesses who would testify to the Commission were chosen by Zelikow, and the very first outside expert on the list was Abraham Sofaer, a fellow at the Hoover Institution. Testifying one week after the US invasion of Iraq, Sofaer used his time to praise this invasion and to champion the idea of preemptive war, which NSS 2002 had articulated.[39] Shortly thereafter, Zelikow made a prominent place for the American Enterprise Institute's Laurie Mylroie. Widely considered the intellectual godmother of the invasion, Mylroie argued that Iraq and al-Qaeda were closely connected, so that Saddam should be taken out because of his role in 9/11.[40] According to Shenon:

> Zelikow surely knew that many in the Bush administration wanted her theories promoted as widely as possible. . . . At the time, few members of the commission's staff understood the full significance of Zelikow's invitation to Mylroie to testify. . . . But they would later realize how troubling it was that the 9/11 commission had suggested—early in its investigation, at one of its first substantive public hearings—that the most credible academic in the United States on possible ties between Iraq and al-Qaeda was one who believed firmly that there were such ties. . . . [I]f Zelikow was trying to give credibility to Mylroie's views, it may have worked, at least as measured by the respectful news coverage of the hearing and specifically of Mylroie's testimony.[41]

Later, when rewriting the section dealing with bin Laden's actions in the 1990s, Zelikow even "inserted sentences that tried to link al-Qaeda to Iraq—to suggest that the terrorist network had repeatedly communicated with the government of Saddam Hussein in the years before 9/11."[42] This was, according to Shenon, one of the few times that Zelikow did not get his way. But his attempt clearly illustrated his intention to use his position to advance the White House's claims about Iraq.

A second fact that Zelikow failed to mention on his résumé was that he had, at Rice's request, helped effect the transition from the Clinton White House to that of George W. Bush. This was important because, when Kean and Hamilton claimed that Zelikow's coauthorship of a book with Rice did not involve an insurmountable conflict of interest, they pointed to the fact that they had both been out of office at the time.[43] Had Zelikow revealed to them his role in making the transition to the Bush White House, they could not have made this argument. In investigating 9/11, one of the Commission's task was to inquire whether the White House had done everything it could have to prevent the attacks. This inquiry was supposed to be completely independent and non-partisan, and yet Zelikow had helped set up the Bush White House.

Zelikow also did not reveal that, while carrying out this role, he "sat in on the briefings in the White House in January 2001 in which Rice was warned by her predecessor, Sandy Berger, that the biggest national security threat facing the country was al-Qaeda" (not Iraq, Iran, and North Korea, with which Rice and Bush were preoccupied). This was a point made by Richard Clarke, who told Shenon that, when he learned of Zelikow's appointment as the Commission's executive director, he concluded that the "fix" was in: With Zelikow in charge "there was no hope that the commission would carry out an impartial investigation of the Bush administration's bungling of terrorist threats."[44]

Kean and Hamilton should also have been informed about another feature of the transition: It was at Zelikow's recommendation that Richard Clarke and his counterterrorism team had been demoted, so that they had less access to the president than they had had in the Clinton White House. This was important because of the public dispute between Clarke and Rice as to how the Clinton and Bush administrations, respectively, had responded to warnings about terrorist attacks. Would not Zelikow use his position to support Rice's account against Clarke's?[45]

Again, Zelikow's duplicity in obtaining his position was evidently followed by duplicity in leading the Commission's investigation. Many members of the Commission's staff found that Zelikow's conflicts of interest did result in a "pattern of partisan moves intended to protect the White House."[46] Shenon provides some examples: Zelikow devoted most of his attention to Team 3, which had the task of reviewing the responses of the Clinton and Bush administrations to the al-Qaeda threat, insisting on being "involved in the smallest details of their work."[47] Zelikow worked to provide support for Rice's false claim that the PDB (Presidential

Daily Brief) of August 6, 2001, was mostly "historical."[48] He even told the Team 3 investigators that Clarke's statements should not be believed. Then, after Team 3 nevertheless concluded that it was mainly Clarke, not Rice, who had told the truth, Zelikow told them that their report was too "Clarke-centric" and forced them to rewrite it.[49] Likewise, after the team reported that Clinton had often spoken about terrorism in his pubic addresses but Bush never had, Zelikow insisted that the comparison be removed.[50]

Kean and Hamilton's Treatment of the Problem: In light of the fact that Zelikow's conflicts of interest turned out to have such severe consequences for the Commission's work, it is important to see how Kean and Hamilton treated this problem. Their treatment involved four phases. We have already mentioned the first phase— their decision, based on Zelikow's incomplete résumé, that his conflicts were not serious enough to disqualify him.

The second phase was centered on January 27, 2003, when they issued a press release announcing Zelikow's appointment as executive director. This press release, besides quoting Kean's description of Zelikow as "a man of high stature who has distinguished himself as an academician, lawyer, author, and public servant," identified Zelikow as the director of the Miller Center at the University of Virginia and staff-director of the Carter–Ford electoral commission. As Shenon comments, this press release was most notable for what it did not say:

> It made no mention of the fact that Zelikow had worked [with Rice] on the NSC for the first President Bush. Nothing about the book with Rice. Nothing about Zelikow's role on the Bush transition team. Nothing about the fact that he had just written [NSS 2002].[51]

Shenon then adds: "Aides to Hamilton. . . said they wrote the press release, based on the background information that Zelikow had provided to Hamilton. Zelikow reviewed it before it was handed out to reporters."[52] Kean and Hamilton, in other words, essentially allowed Zelikow to write his own press release, one that covered up even those conflicts of interest of which they were already aware.

The third phase of their treatment of this issue occurred in October 2003, after they had become aware of those conflicts of interest that Zelikow had concealed from them: his roles in the transition and his authorship of NSS 2002. Their reaction to learning this information was that Zelikow should not be replaced, because it was too late to find a new executive director and, besides, he was by then indispensable, being the only person who knew what the various teams were doing.[53] Kean and Hamilton's solution to the conflict-of-interest problem was simply to insist that Zelikow recuse himself from all interviews with senior Bush aides and all issues involving the transition.[54]

With that solution, however, Kean and Hamilton pretended that the only dangers Zelikow might pose to the impartiality of the Commission's investigations were that he might skew the interviews with Bush aides and the investigation of the transition period. They thereby ignored the most serious problem—that Zelikow, because of his personal and ideological closeness to the Bush administration, might use his role to prevent the Commission from discovering and reporting evidence pointing to the administration's responsibility for 9/11, whether through incompetence or complicity.

The fact that the Kean–Hamilton solution to Zelikow's conflicts of interest was woefully inadequate was made clear by the Family Steering Committee (FSC). Having called for Zelikow's dismissal in 2003, as I reported in NPH, the FSC said in a press release of March 20, 2004:

> It is apparent that Dr. Zelikow should never have been permitted to be Executive Staff Director of the Commission. . . . It is abundantly clear that Dr. Zelikow's conflicts go beyond just the transition period. . . . The Family Steering Committee is calling for: 1. Dr. Zelikow's immediate resignation. . . . 4. The Commission to apologize to the 9/11 families and America for this massive appearance of impropriety.[55]

The fourth phase of Kean and Hamilton's treatment of this issue was their discussion of it in their 2006 book, *Without Precedent*, in which they wrote:

Zelikow was a controversial choice. In the 1990s, as an academic, he had co-authored, with Condoleezza Rice, a book about German unification, and he later assisted Stephen Hadley in running the National Security Council transition for the incoming Bush administration in 2000–2001. . . . The 9/11 families questioned his ability to lead a tough investigation. . . . But we had full confidence in Zelikow's independence. . . . He recused himself from anything involving his work on the NSC transition. . . . It was clear from people who worked with him that Zelikow would not lead a staff inquiry that did anything less than uncover the most detailed and accurate history of 9/11.[56]

Kean and Hamilton thereby failed to tell the whole truth and nothing but the truth. They did not mention Zelikow's authorship of NSS 2002 or his role in demoting Clarke and his counterterrorism team—even though, according to Shenon, the new commissioner, Bob Kerrey, threatened to resign when he learned about those conflicts. They did not mention that the 9/11 families, pointing out that Zelikow's conflicts were too extensive to be solved by his recusal from the investigation of the transition, demanded that he be replaced. They also did not point out that, as Shenon's book shows, many of the 9/11 Commission staff members did *not* consider Zelikow independent of the White House and did *not* believe that his first concern was to report the truth.

Zelikow's Continued Conversations with Rove and Rice: Kean and Hamilton would have had even more difficulty in credibly claiming that they "had full confidence in Zelikow's independence" if they had mentioned one of the most serious revelations contained in Shenon's book, namely: Although "Zelikow had promised the commissioners he would cut off all unnecessary contact with senior Bush administration officials to avoid any appearance of conflict of interest,"[57] he had continuing contacts with both Karl Rove and Condoleezza Rice. This information was confirmed by the executive secretary for the Commission's front office, Karen Heitkotter, who had long served as an executive secretary in the State Department. With regard to Rice, Shenon writes:

While Zelikow was telling people how upset he was to cut off contact with his good friend Rice, Heitkotter knew that he hadn't. More than once, she had been asked to arrange a gate pass so Zelikow could enter the White House to visit the national security adviser in her offices in the West Wing.[58]

With regard to Rove, Shenon reports, Heitkotter's logs reveal that he called the office "looking for Philip" four times in 2003.[59] When this continuing contact became widely known after a staff member saw Rove's name in Heitkotter's logs, Zelikow ordered her, she reported, to quit keeping logs of his contacts with the White House.[60] Zelikow later denied giving this order and insisted that there had been only one exchange of calls with Rove. However, besides the fact that the logs revealed at least four calls from Rove to Zelikow's office number, Shenon points out, the logs "do not show Zelikow's calls out, nor would they show any calls on Zelikow's cell phone."[61]

Besides falsely claiming that he had had only one exchange of calls with Rove, Zelikow also claimed that this exchange had only concerned issues involving his old job at the Miller Center at the University of Virginia.[62]

However, Zelikow's claim that he and Rove did not discuss the work of the 9/11 Commission is hard to believe, given various things Shenon reveals about Rove, indicating that his interest in the Commission was very great. First, Rove had led the White House's attempt to prevent the creation of the Commission in the first place.[63] Second, when the White House could no longer prevent its creation, Rove was involved in the selection of Henry Kissinger to be its chairman.[64] Third, after this appointment did not work out, Rove was the one who offered the chairmanship to Thomas Kean— a fact that Kean found odd: "Why had membership on the panel been shopped around by Bush's political guru?"[65] Fourth, Rove viewed the 9/11 Commission as a "mortal threat" to Bush's chance for reelection in 2004—according to John Lehman, one of the Republican members of the Commission—and was the White House's "quarterback for dealing with the Commission."[66]

Besides being hard to believe in the light of Rove's intense interest in the Commission, Zelikow's claim that he did not discuss the Commission's work with Rove was also contradicted by a senior White House official with whom Shenon talked.[67]

In light of these revelations of Zelikow's continued contact with Rice and Rove, we must judge that Kean and Hamilton were less than fully honest in proclaiming their confidence in Zelikow's independence from the White House while failing to report these contacts, of which they had been apprised.[68] Even more seriously, we must conclude that the 9/11 families' fear about a Zelikow-led Commission—that its loyalty to truth would be subordinate to its loyalty to the White House—was fully justified.

Zelikow, Cambone, and the NORAD Tapes: Although Shenon's revelation of Zelikow's ongoing relationship with Rice and Rove garnered much more attention in the press, equally important is his revelation of Zelikow's close friendship with Steven Cambone, "the undersecretary of defense for intelligence, who was Rumsfeld's most trusted aide." According to Shenon, "Dan Marcus, the [Commission's] general counsel, had found it distasteful the way Zelikow would 'flaunt' his closeness to Cambone."[69]

This closeness is important in light of the central role played by the NORAD tapes in the Commission's account of the flights, as discussed above in Chapters 1–3. In agreement with Kean and Hamilton, Shenon says that there was one—and only one—set of conspiracy theories about 9/11 that could not be easily dismissed.[70] These were theories involving the way in which the FAA and NORAD had responded to the reports of the hijackings.

"Officials at the FAA and the Pentagon had no one to blame but themselves," Shenon says, because they had "released a series of timelines that fueled the skeptics by suggesting that the government should have had time to shoot down at least. . . one or two of the of the hijacked airliners."[71] But the NORAD tapes, Shenon says—endorsing the Commission's view—showed "that NORAD's public statements about its actions on 9/11 had been wrong, almost certainly intentionally." With regard to Flight 93 in particular, "the tapes made it clear that every element of the [military's] story was wrong. NORAD knew nothing about United 93 until after it had already plunged to the ground."[72]

According to Shenon, as well as Kean and Hamilton, therefore, the NORAD tapes had conveniently removed the basis for the only seemingly plausible theory supporting the idea that the government account of the 9/11 attacks was false. Was this removal (although Shenon himself does not raise this question) perhaps *too* convenient?

In Chapters 1, 2, and 3, I suggested that the NORAD tapes had been doctored. Shenon's account of Zelikow's friendship with Steven Cambone and his actions with regard to the tapes provide the basis for a possible view of how and when this doctoring could have come about.

After John Farmer learned about the existence of the tapes and the Commission was debating whether to issue a subpoena for them, Shenon reports, Zelikow at first tried to block this move—an action that was perceived as "Zelikow's effort to protect his friends in the Defense Department."[73] This effort to prevent the subpoena from being issued would certainly have made sense if the (undoctored) NORAD tapes would have revealed, as I assume, that the FAA was less responsible, and the military more responsible, for the failures than the document of September 18, 2001, "NORAD's Response Times," had indicated. (This seems especially likely with regard to NORAD's timelines for Flights 11 and 77, which portrayed the FAA as being extremely slow in notifying the military about them.)

In any case, Zelikow's attempt to block the Commission's subpoena failed, and this failure could have led Zelikow and Cambone to decide to turn a problem into a solution. If the tapes would need to be doctored to protect the military, why not doctor them in a way that would overcome every basis for the charge that the military had had time to intercept at least some of the flights?

According to former air traffic controller Robin Hordon, who worked with audio tapes at the FAA's Boston Center, making such changes would have been easy. The simplest way to doctor tapes would be to eliminate part or all of various transmissions. A second method would be to change the times of various communications, which, Hordon says, "would pose very few difficulties":

> Either one could "write over" the time channel, adjusting it to any time one would want. Or one could transfer all the audio information on particular channels onto another tape that already has a chosen time reference impregnated upon it.[74]

A third possible method would be to employ voice morphing.

Accordingly, Cambone, as undersecretary of defense for intelligence, might have turned the tapes over to the Defense Intelligence Agency, telling them how to "fix" the tapes so as to show that the military had been completely guiltless. Rather than revealing the FAA to have been blameless, as the undoctored tapes would (by hypothesis) have shown, the doctored tapes would show the FAA to have been fully to blame, thereby removing the basis for the charge that the military had stood down its defenses.

Shenon even (inadvertently) points out that there would have been time for this doctoring to occur. After the subpoena was issued by the Commission, he says, "The tapes from NORAD showed up about a month later."[75]

My suggestion that this is what happened is, of course, speculation. But to hold that the tapes were *not* doctored is also a speculative claim. And that claim, as we saw in Chapters 1–3, is contradicted by various facts, whereas my speculative suggestion provides a way of making sense of these facts. That, in any case, is its sole role in this book: It provides a way of understanding how, if the NORAD tapes were indeed doctored, this doctoring could have come about.

THE COMMISSION'S "SUCCESS"

In their "inside story of the 9/11 Commission," Kean and Hamilton claimed that, although the Commission had been "set up to fail," it nevertheless succeeded.[76] One criterion of this self-proclaimed success was evidently indicated by Kean and Hamilton's statement that they had put out a report that "the broad majority of the American people could accept."[77]

A Zogby Poll taken in May 2006, however, indicated that 42 percent of the American public believed that evidence contradicting the official account had been covered up by the government and the 9/11 Commission. Only 48 percent expressed confidence that there had not been a cover-up.[78] Far from being accepted by a "broad majority" of the American people, therefore, the Commission's report was, already in 2006, evidently not accepted by even a bare majority. In light of the increased strength of the 9/11 truth movement since that time combined with revelations in the mainstream media that have further undermined the Commission's credibility, the percentage of Americans who accept the Zelikow Report today would probably be still lower.

Suggesting a second criterion of their success, Kean and Hamilton wrote: "As for conspiracy theorists, it is hard to say how many minds we changed."[79] Reading through the customer reviews for *The 9/11 Commission Report* on Amazon.com, I did not find any readers saying that this report had moved them away from thinking that 9/11 was an inside job.

By reading these reviews in historical order, in fact, one can see that the percentage of reviewers who accept *The 9/11 Commission Report* has declined over time. In 2004, the year it appeared, the reviews were overwhelmingly positive, with most reviewers awarding the book five stars. But in 2005 and 2006, as the public became increasingly aware of the facts revealed by the 9/11 truth movement, reviews with only one star (which is the lowest possible rating) became increasingly prevalent. This trend continued in the early months of 2008, during which almost half of the reviewers gave the report only one star. Insofar as minds have changed about 9/11, therefore, the change has been *away* from, rather than *toward*, the story told by the Commission.

Suggesting one more criterion of their success, Kean and Hamilton claimed that they "had the support of an extraordinary outside group: the 9/11 families." Although they admitted that the Commission's relations with the families "were up and down, and sometimes very difficult," they suggested that the Commission continued to have the support of the families: "Their public voice did not waver." Kean and Hamilton also suggested that their book "was a bestseller" because "it answered people's questions."[80]

But did the Commission, by answering the questions of the 9/11 families, really retain their support? Near the end of *9/11: Press for Truth*, a film about 9/11 family members who worked with the Commission, one of them, Monica Gabrielle, said: "What we're left with after our journey are no answers. . . . I've wasted four years of my life." Another family member, Bob McIlvaine, said: "I'm so pissed off at this government, because of this cover-up."[81]

Moreover, if the Commission's criteria for success included the goal of convincing the political and military leaders of other countries, at least those that have traditionally been friendly to the United States, of the truth of the official account of 9/11, they failed on that score, too. In Chapter 8, we saw that the official account has been publicly rejected by Germany's Andreas von Bülow and Horst Ehmke, Pakistan's Pervez Musharraf and Mirza Aslam Beg, and Egypt's Mohamed Hassanein Heikal. Additionally, Italy's Giulietto Chiesa, who is a member of the European Parliament's Committee on Security and Defense, has called the official account of 9/11 "entirely false." Francesco Cossiga, who had served both as Italy's president and its prime minister, has said that 9/11 was planned and executed by the CIA "to falsely incriminate Arabic countries and to persuade the Western Powers to intervene in Iraq and Afghanistan." Cossiga's interpretation is especially important, because, as a confessed organizer of Operation Gladio (which was mentioned in the Introduction), Cossiga should know a false-flag operation when he sees one.[82]

One more political leader in a friendly country who has publicly questioned the official account is Yukihisa Fujita, a member of Japan's House of Councillors—which, as the upper chamber of the Japanese Diet (parliament), is similar to the US Senate. On January 10, 2008, during a meeting of the Committee on Foreign Affairs and Defense, of which Fujita is the director, he made the following comments, fully aware that his remarks were being broadcast live on Japanese television:

> I would like to talk about the beginning of the war on terror. . . . [T]he whole start of this war on terrorism was 9/11. What I want to know is if this event was caused by al-Qaeda or not. So far, the only thing the government has said is that we think it was caused by al-Qaeda because President Bush told us so. We have not seen any real proof that it was al-Qaeda. . . .
>
> I would like to ask about the suspicious information being uncovered and the doubts people worldwide are having about the events of 9/11. Many of these doubters are very influential people. In such circumstances, I believe the Japanese government, which claims the attacks were carried out by al-Qaeda, should be providing the victims' families with this new information. In that context, I would like to ask several questions. . . .

A 757 is quite a large airplane with a width of 38 meters. . . . [E]ven though such a large plane hit the Pentagon, . . . there is no damage of the sort an airplane that large should make. . . . [Also,] there are no airplane parts on [the lawn]. . . . [Consider] how the airplane hit the building. The airplane made a U-turn, avoiding the defense secretary's office and hitting the only part of the Pentagon that had been specially reinforced to withstand a bomb attack.

[A former] US Air Force official[83] says: "I have flown the two types of airplane used on 9/11 and I cannot believe it would be possible for someone who is flying one for the first time to be able to carry out such a maneuver." . . . Also, there were more than 80 security cameras at the Pentagon but they have refused to release almost all of the footage. . . .

Can you imagine if an airplane. . . hit New York that an airplane could [later] hit the Pentagon? In such a situation, how could our allies allow such an attack to take place?

Please look at this panel [about the Twin Towers]. . . . [W]e can see large pieces of material flying a large distance through the air. Some flew 150 meters. You can see objects flying in this picture as if there was an explosion. Here is a picture. . . of a fireman who was involved in the rescue talking about a series of explosions in the building that sounded like a professional demolition. . . . [H]e is saying "it went boom boom boom like explosions were going off."

[A] Japanese research team of officials from the fire department and the construction ministry. . . interviewed a Japanese survivor who said that while she was fleeing there were explosions. . . .

Normally it is said that the Twin Towers collapsed because they were hit by airplanes. However, one block away from the Twin Towers is Building Number 7. . . . This building collapsed seven hours after the WTC buildings were attacked. . . . This is a 47-story building that fell. . . in five or six seconds. It is about the same speed as an object would fall in a vacuum. This building falls like something you would see in a Kabuki show. Also it falls while keeping its shape. Remember it was not hit by an airplane. You have to ask yourself if a building could fall in that manner due to a fire after 7 hours. Here we have a copy of *The 9/11 Commission Report*. This is a report put out by the US government in July of 2004, but this report does not mention the collapse of the building I just described. . . .

I would also like to mention the put options. Just before the 9/11 attacks, i.e., on September 6th, 7th, and 8th, there were put options taken out on the stocks of the two airlines, United and American, that were hit by hijackers. There were also put options on Merrill Lynch, one of the biggest WTC tenants. In other words, somebody had insider information and made a fortune selling put options of these stocks. The head of Germany's Bundesbank at the time, who is equivalent to the Governor of the Bank of Japan, said there are lots of facts to prove the people involved in the terror attacks profited from insider information. . . .

[T]he start of the war on terror. . . has not been properly investigated. . . . I think we need to go back to the beginning and not just simply and blindly trust the US government explanation and indirect information provided by them. . . . [E]verything I have presented are facts and confirmable evidence. . . . We need to look at this evidence and ask ourselves what the war on terrorism really is. . . . Is there really a reason to participate in this war on terror?[84]

Fujita reported that after his presentation, he received several phone calls from other members of the Diet, thanking him for having the courage to discuss 9/11. Perhaps his courage will embolden other members of the Japanese Diet, and other political leaders around the world, to speak up.

A STRONG CASE FOR A NEW INVESTIGATION

This final chapter, dealing with the 9/11 Commission as such, complements the previous chapters, insofar as they show that the Commission systematically omitted and distorted evidence that, contradicting the official story about 9/11, suggests that 9/11 was an inside job. This chapter shows how White House insider Philip Zelikow, after using deceit to become executive director of the 9/11 Commission, was able to use this position to control the Commission's investigation and the writing of its final report. Once we know about Zelikow's ideology, relationships, and methods, the fact that the 9/11 Commission did not carry out a real investigation, asking who was responsible for 9/11, is no surprise. Far from asking this question, the Commission's staff and Commissioners merely filled in the details of an outline that had been written in advance by Zelikow and May—an outline that simply assumed the attacks to have been planned and carried out by Osama bin Laden and various al-Qaeda operatives. Given that outline, any evidence that would contradict this thesis was excluded in advance.

If we take this chapter together with the discussion of NIST in the first chapter, we see that the two most important official reports about 9/11 have been prepared by people highly responsive to the wishes of the White House. This revelation would not by itself point to the need for a new investigation, of course, if there were no signs that these reports had omitted and distorted evidence for political purposes. These reports, however, show signs of such omission and distortion from beginning to end. Given this two-fold fact—that these two reports were written by people with professional motivation to protect the Bush administration and its Pentagon, not to state the truth, and that a study of the reports provides ample evidence of this partisan political purpose—we have the strongest possible grounds for demanding a new, genuine, investigation.

The 9/11 truth movement's exposé of the cover-up of the truth about what happened on 9/11 is now complete—in the sense that this exposé has shown, to those who have paid attention, virtually every dimension of the official account of 9/11 to be false beyond a reasonable doubt. It is now up to Congress and the press to bring the fact of this exposé into the public realm, so that the needed adjustments in public policy can be effected.

NOTES

AFAQs	National Institute of Standards and Technology (NIST). "Answers to Frequently Asked Questions." August 30, 2006 (http://wtc.nist.gov/pubs/factsheets/faqs_8_2006.htm).
Contradictions	David Ray Griffin. *9/11 Contradictions: An Open Letter to Congress and the Press.* Northampton: Olive Branch, 2008.
D9D	David Ray Griffin. *Debunking 9/11 Debunking: An Answer to Popular Mechanics and Other Defenders of the Official Conspiracy Theory,* revised and updated edition. Northampton: Olive Branch, 2007.
Debunking	David Dunbar and Brad Reagan, eds. *Debunking 9/11 Myths: Why Conspiracy Theories Can't Stand Up to the Facts: An In-Depth Investigation by Popular Mechanics.* New York: Hearst Books, 2006.
FAA Memo	"FAA Communications with NORAD on September 11, 2001: FAA Clarification Memo to 9/11 Independent Commission." May 22, 2003. Available in the transcript of the 9/11 Commission hearing of May 23, 2003 (www.9-11commission.gov/archive/hearing2/9-11Commission_Hearing_2003-05-23.htm) and at www.911truth.org/article.php?story=2004081200421797.
9/11CR	*The 9/11 Commission Report: Final Report of the National Commission on Terrorist Attacks upon the United States,* authorized edition. New York: W. W. Norton, 2004.
9/11CROD	David Ray Griffin, *The 9/11 Commission Report: Omissions and Distortions.* Northampton: Olive Branch, 2005.
Oral History	9/11 oral histories by members of the Fire Department of New York were recorded from September 2001 through January 2002; 503 of these are now available at a *New York Times* website (graphics8.nytimes.com/packages/html/nyregion/20050812_WTC_GRAPHIC/met_WTC_histories_full_01.html).
WP	Thomas H. Kean and Lee H. Hamilton, with Benjamin Rhodes. *Without Precedent: The Inside Story of the 9/11 Commission.* New York: Alfred A. Knopf, 2006.

INTRODUCTION

1 David Ray Griffin, *The 9/11 Commission Report: Omissions and Distortions* (Northampton: Olive Branch, 2005); henceforth 9/11CROD.

2 9/11CROD 291.

3 "The 9/11 Commission Report: A 571-Page Lie," 9/11 Visibility Project, May 22, 2005 (www.septembereleventh.org/newsarchive/2005-05-22-571pglie.php); reprinted in *Global Outlook* 11 (Spring–Summer 2006), 100–05. In the meantime, I have become aware of many more lies of omission and distortion in the Commission's report.

4 *Christian Faith and the Truth behind 9/11* (Louisville: Westminster John Knox Press, 2005), 76, 82.

5 David Ray Griffin, *Debunking 9/11 Debunking: An Answer to Popular Mechanics and Other Defenders of the Official Conspiracy Theory* (Northampton: Olive Branch, 2007; revised and updated edition, August 2007); henceforth D9D (referring always to the revised and updated edition).

6 D9D 1.

7 David Ray Griffin, *9/11 Contradictions: An Open Letter to Congress and the Press* (Northampton: Olive Branch, 2008); henceforth *Contradictions*.

8 Mark Weisbrot, "Holocaust Denial, American Style," AlterNet, November 21, 2007 (www.alternet.org/columnists/story/68568).

9 See "Insider: EPA Lied About WTC Air," *CBS News*, September 8, 2006 (www.cbsnews.com/stories/2006/09/08/earlyshow/main1985804.shtml); EPA Office of Inspector General, "EPA's Response to the World Trade Center Collapse," August 21, 2003, Executive Summary and Chapter 2 (www.mindfully.org/Air/2003/EPA-WTC-OIG-Evaluation21aug03.htm); and "White House Edited EPA's 9/11 Reports," by John Heilprin, Associated Press, *Seattle Post-Intelligencer*, August 23, 2003 (http://seattlepi.nwsource.com/national/136350_epa23.html).

10 See Anthony DePalma, "Illness Persisting in 9/11 Workers, Big Study Finds," *New York Times*, September 6, 2006 (www.nytimes.com/2006/09/06/nyregion/06health.html?ex=1315195200&en=aaf1bba2e01bc497&ei=5088&partner=rssnyt&emc=rss); Kristen Lombardi, "Death by Dust: The Frightening Link between the 9-11 Toxic Cloud and Cancer," *Village Voice*, November 28, 2006 (http://villagevoice.com/news/0648%2Clombardi%2C75156%2C2.html; also at www.911truth.org/article.php?story=20061204132809573); "Dust and Disease," *NewsHour with Jim Lehrer*, PBS, November 21, 2006, available on YouTube as "60 Percent of Ground Zero Workers Sick" (www.youtube.com:80/watch?v=2bA57ObvVLc); "Jonathan M. Samet, Alison S. Geyh, and Mark J. Utell, "The Legacy of World Trade Center Dust," *New England Journal of Medicine*, May 31, 2007 (http://content.nejm.org/cgi/content/full/356/22/2233); a documentary film, *Dust to Dust* (www.informationliberation.com/index.php?id=21627), and Jerry Mazza's review of this documentary, "9/11's Second Round of

Slaughter" (http://onlinejournal.com/artman/publish/article_2845.shtml).

11 William Bunch, "Why Don't We Have Answers to These 9/11 Questions?" *Philadelphia Daily News* online, September 11, 2003 (www.truthout.org/docs_03/091203A.shtml).

2 Barrie Zwicker, *Towers of Deception: The Media Cover-Up of 9/11* (Gabriola Island, B.C.: New Society, 2006).

3 Barrie Zwicker, "Mainstream Media Forced to Acknowledge 9/11 Truth," *Global Outlook* 12 (Summer 2007): 15–139.

4 David Ray Griffin, "9/11: The Myth and the Reality," available as a DVD on Amazon.com.

5 This appearance on MSNBC's *Tucker*, August 9, 2006, can be seen in "David Ray Griffin on Tucker Carlson" (www.youtube.com/watch?v=AxKW3EqbfRE).

6 David Ray Griffin, *9/11 and Nationalist Faith: How Faith Can Be Illuminating or Blinding*, available as a DVD on Amazon.com.

7 Alexander Cockburn, "The 9/11 Conspiracy Nuts," *The Nation*, September 25, 2006 (www.thenation.com/doc/20060925/cockburn); "The 9/11 Conspiracy Nuts: How They Let the Guilty Parties of 9/11 Slip Off the Hook," *Counterpunch*, September 10, 2006 (www.counterpunch.org/cockburn09092006.html).

8 Cockburn, "The Conspiracists, Continued—Are They Getting Crazier?" *Free Press*, September 16, 2006 (www.freepress.org/columns/display/2/2006/1433).

9 See "Dr. Robert Bowman: The Impossibility of the Official Government Story" (http://video.google.com/videoplay?docid= 6900065571556128674), and "Retired Air Force Col: They Lied to Us about the War and about 9/11 Itself," October 27, 2005 (www.benfrank.net/blog/2005/10/27/oil_mafia_treason).

20 See Andreas von Bülow, *Die CIA und der 11. September. Internationaler Terror und die Rolle der Geheimdienste* (Piper, 2003), and "Michael Meacher and Andreas Von Bülow Express Their Serious Doubts about 9/11" (http://video.google.com/videoplay?docid=8274552561914055825).

21 See General Leonid Ivashov, "International Terrorism Does Not Exist," January 2, 2006 (www.physics911.net/ivashov.htm), in which he says: "Osama bin Laden and 'Al Qaeda' cannot be the organizers nor the performers of the September 11 attacks. They do not have the necessary organization, resources or leaders."

22 See Patriots Question 9/11 (www.patriotsquestion911.com/#McGovern). McGovern wrote blurbs for two of my books, *9/11 and American Empire: Intellectuals Speak Out*, co-edited with Peter Dale Scott (Northampton: Olive Branch, 2007), and *Christian Faith and the Truth behind 9/11*.

23 George Nelson, "Impossible to Prove a Falsehood True: Aircraft Parts as a Clue to Their Identity," Physics 911, April 23, 2005 (www.physics911.net/georgenelson.htm).

24 Colonel Ray, who has called the official story "the dog that doesn't hunt," says that the evidence suggests that "the conspiracy theory advanced by

the administration is not true"; see Paul Joseph Watson, "Former Reagan Deputy and Colonel Says 9/11 'Dog That Doesn't Hunt,'" Knowledge Driven Revolution, June 29, 2006 (www.knowledgedrivenrevolution.com/Articles/200607/20060701_911_Ray.htm).

25 Steele has said: "I am forced to conclude that 9/11 was at a minimum allowed to happen as a pretext for war." Review of Webster Tarpley, *9/11 Synthetic Terror: Made in the USA*, October 7, 2006 (www.amazon.com/9-11-Synthetic-Terror-First/dp/0930852311/sr=1-1/qid=1165894073/ref=pd_bbs_sr_1/002-5158292-7064018?ie=UTF8&s=books).

26 Captain Russ Wittenberg, "The Government Story They Handed Us about 9/11 is Total B.S. Plain and Simple," July 17, 2005 (www.arcticbeacon.com).

27 Cockburn, "The 9/11 Conspiracy Nuts."

28 David Ray Griffin, "Explosive Testimony: Revelations about the Twin Towers in the 9/11 Oral Histories," January 18, 2006 (www.911truth.org/article.php?story=20060118104223192); later included in slightly revised form in *Christian Faith and the Truth behind 9/11*.

29 Cockburn, "The 9/11 Conspiracy Nuts."

30 Cockburn, "The Conspiracists, Continued—Are They Getting Crazier?"

31 "The 9/11 Conspiracy Nuts: How They Let the Guilty Parties of 9/11 Slip Off the Hook."

32 Statements by some of them can be read in the Engineers and Architects section on the Patriots Question 9/11 website.

33 I discussed these magazines in the introduction and conclusion of D9D.

34 "Letter from Bill Christison to Friends," e-mail letter sent about August 14, 2006.

35 Bill Christison, "Stop Belittling the Theories about September 11," Dissident Voice, August 14, 2006 (www.dissidentvoice.org/Aug06/Christison14.htm).

36 Robert Baer, "Dangerous Liaisons," *The Nation*, September 27, 2004 (www.thenation.com/docprem.mhtml?i=20040927&s=baer).

37 "Thom Hartmann Interviews Robert Baer," transcript at 911Blogger.com, June 9, 2006 (www.911blogger.com/2006/06/former-cia-member-robert-baer-comments.html).

38 "The 9/11 Faith Movement" is the title of an article by Terry Allen published by *In These Times*, July 11, 2006 (www.inthesetimes.com/site/main/article/2702). I have responded to this article in the introduction and conclusion of D9D, pointing out that it is Allen who is taking things on blind faith.

39 This lecture, given in Seattle in 2007, is available on a DVD on Amazon.com.

40 See "9/11 and Prior False-Flag Operations," Ch. 1 of my *Christian Faith and the Truth behind 9/11*, and "False-Flag Operations, 9/11, and the New Rome: A Christian Perspective," in Kevin Barrett, John B. Cobb Jr., and

Sandra Lubarsky, eds., *9/11 and American Empire: Christians, Jews, and Muslims Speak Out* (Northampton: Olive Branch, 2007).

41 On the Mukden incident, see Walter LaFeber, *The Clash: US–Japanese Relations throughout History* (New York: Norton, 1997), 164–66; Louise Young, *Japan's Total Empire: Manchuria and the Culture of Wartime Imperialism* (Berkeley: University of California Press, 1999), 40; or "Mukden Incident," *Encyclopedia Britannica*, 2006 (www.britannica.com/eb/article-9054193).

42 Although many historians have accepted the view that Communists were responsible, William Shirer rightly blamed the Nazis themselves in *The Rise and Fall of the Third Reich* (New York: Simon and Schuster, 1990), 191–93. Shirer's position was confirmed in a later study that leaves no doubt: *Der Reichstagbrand: Wie Geschichte Gemacht Wird*, by Alexander Bahar and Wilfried Kugel (Berlin, Edition Q, 2001). This 800-page study is summarized in Wilhelm Klein, "The Reichstag Fire, 68 Years On," World Socialist Website, July 5, 2001 (www.wsws.org/articles/2001/jul2001/reic-j05.shtml). The press and the politicians, however, seem not to have caught up with the historical scholarship. In January 2008, the *Guardian* reported that Marinus van der Lubbe, the feeble-minded Communist who was beheaded after being falsely blamed for the fire, had been exonerated by Germany's federal prosecutor. The rationale, however, was not that van der Lubbe was innocent but that he had been convicted under Nazi law, which "went against the basic ideas of justice." The *Guardian* stated, moreover: "Most historians are in agreement that Van der Lubbe was involved in the fire." See Kate Connolly, "75 Years On, Executed Reichstag Arsonist Finally wins Pardon," *Guardian*, January 12, 2008 (www.guardian.co.uk/secondworldwar/story/0,,2239610,00.html).

43 See "Nazi Conspiracy and Aggression, Vol. II: Criminality of Groups and Organizations" (www.nizkor.org/hweb/imt/nca/nca-02/nca-02-15-criminality-06-05.html); "Part I Blitzkrieg September 1, 1939: A New Kind of Warfare Engulfs Poland," *Time*, August 28, 1989.

44 See Howard Zinn, *A People's History of the United States* (1980; New York: HarperPerennial, 1990), 150, and Richard Van Alstyne, *The Rising American Empire* (1960; New York, Norton, 1974), 143.

45 Stuart Creighton Miller, *Benevolent Assimilation: The American Conquest of the Philippines, 1899–1903* (New Haven: Yale University Press, 1982), 11.

46 Ibid., 57–62.

47 George McT. Kahin, *Intervention: How America Became Involved in Vietnam* (Garden City: Anchor Press/Doubleday, 1987), 220; Marilyn B. Young, *The Vietnam Wars 1945–1990* (New York: HarperCollins, 1991), 119.

48 Daniele Ganser, *NATO's Secret Armies: Operation Gladio and Terrorism in Western Europe* (New York: Frank Cass, 2005).

49 Ibid., 5.

50 *Debunking 9/11 Myths: Why Conspiracy Theories Can't Stand Up to the Facts:*

An *In-Depth Investigation by Popular Mechanics*, ed. David Dunbar and Brad Reagan (New York: Hearst Books, 2006); henceforth, *Debunking*.

51 Jim Dwyer, "2 US Reports Seek to Counter Conspiracy Theories About 9/11," *New York Times*, September 2, 2006 (www.911review.com/reviews/nyt/markup/02conspiracy.html).

52 Matthew Rothschild, "Enough of the 9/11 Conspiracy Theories, Already," *The Progressive*, September 18, 2006 (www.alternet.org/story/41601/).

53 Lev Grossman, "Why the 9/11 Conspiracies Won't Go Away," *Time*, September 3, 2006.

54 *The American Heritage Dictionary of the English Language* (American Heritage Publishing Co., 1969).

55 Paul Krugman, "Who's Crazy Now?" *New York Times*, May 8, 2006 (http://topics.nytimes.com/top/opinion/editorialsandoped/oped/columnists /paulkrugman/index.html?inline=nyt-per).

56 Griffin and Scott, eds., *9/11 and American Empire: Intellectuals Speak Out* (see note 22, above), viii.

57 Thomas H. Kean and Lee H. Hamilton, with Benjamin Rhodes, *Without Precedent: The Inside Story of the 9/11 Commission* (New York: Alfred A. Knopf, 2006); henceforth, WP.

58 D9D, Ch. 2, "The Real 9/11 'Conspiracy Theory': A Critique of Kean and Hamilton's *Without Precedent*," esp. 101–34.

CHAPTER 1: FLIGHT 11, FLIGHT 175, AND THE WTC

1 D9D, Ch. 1, "9/11 Live or Distorted: Do the NORAD Tapes Verify *The 9/11 Commission Report?*" 27–94, at 35–36.

2 E-mail from Robin Hordon, December 20, 2006.

3 Ibid.

4 NPH 9.

5 "NORAD's Response Times," September 18, 2001 (www.standdown.net/noradseptember182001pressrelease.htm).

6 Paul Joseph Watson, "Boston Air Traffic Controller Says 9/11 An Inside Job," Prison Planet, December 14, 2006 (www.prisonplanet.com/articles/december2006/141206trafficcontroller.ht m). This article is based on a telephone interview of Hordon by Rob Balsamo, the founder of Pilots for 9/11 Truth, December 13, 2006 (http://video.google.com/videoplay?docid=- 9147890225218338952&hl=en).

7 E-mail from Hordon, December 18, 2006.

8 Tom Flocco, "Rookie in the 9-11 Hot Seat?" tomflocco.com, June 17, 2004 (http://tomflocco.com/fs/NMCCOpsDirector.htm).

9 According to the NORAD tapes (discussed below in the text), Scoggins reported to NEADS at 8:40 that AA 11 was "35 miles north of Kennedy now at 367 knots" (see Michael Bronner, "9/11 Live: The NORAD Tapes," *Vanity Fair*, August 2006 [www.vanityfair.com/politics/features/2006/08/norad200608], at 08:39:58).

However, Scoggins himself says that when he made his first call to NEADS that day, he reported that the flight was "20 [miles] South of Albany heading south at a high rate of speed, 600 knots" (e-mail December 14, 2006). By the time the plane was 35 miles north of JFK, therefore, it had traveled about 90 miles. If we estimate that the plane's average speed was 500 knots and hence 8.3 nautical miles per minute, traversing that distance would have taken almost 11 minutes. Scoggins' first call, therefore, must have occurred at about 8:29 (even though he also said that he thought he did not arrive on the floor that morning until about 8:35; he admits that he cannot otherwise explain the apparent contradiction [e-mail January 8, 2007]). Scoggins says, moreover, that before he arrived on the floor, Joe Cooper, an air traffic management specialist, had phoned NEADS about the hijacking (e-mail December 31, 2006). Cooper's call, therefore, must have occurred at about 8:28 (e-mail from Scoggins, December 31, 2006). However, Cooper's call was, according to the NORAD tapes, received at NEADS at about 8:38.

10 The fact that the first notification did not occur at 8:25 or 8:26 can be explained by the fact that a debate evidently arose between the controller and his supervisor as to whether a hijacking had really occurred (see D9D 44).

11 9/11CR 20.

12 The 9/11 Commission, arguing that authorization was needed from the top, cited a memo issued June 1, 2001, by the Chairman of the Joint Chiefs of Staff, entitled "Aircraft Piracy (Hijacking) and Destruction of Derelict Airborne Objects." The relevant statement in this document says: "[T]he NMCC is the focal point within [the] Department of Defense for providing assistance. In the event of a hijacking, the NMCC will be notified by the most expeditious means by the FAA. The NMCC will, *with the exception of immediate responses as authorized by reference d*, forward requests for DOD assistance to the Secretary of Defense for approval" (www.dtic.mil/doctrine/jel/cjcsd/cjcsi/3610_01a.pdf); emphasis added. Reference d points back to a 1997 document, Directive 3025.15, which says: "The DoD Components that receive verbal requests from civil authorities for support in an exigent emergency may initiate informal planning and, if required, immediately respond." These documents clearly entail, therefore, that Marr did not need to get authorization from Arnold or anyone else. See D9D 49–51.

13 Michael Bronner, "9/11 Live: The NORAD Tapes," *Vanity Fair*, August 2006 (www.vanityfair.com/politics/features/2006/08/norad200608), 2.

14 E-mail from Scoggins, October 27, 2006.

15 E-mail from Scoggins, January 8, 2007.

16 E-mail from Hordon, December 20, 2006.

17 *The 9/11 Commission Report: Final Report of the National Commission on Terrorist Attacks upon the United States*, authorized edition (New York: W. W. Norton, 2004), 23; henceforth 9/11CR.

18 9/11CR 21–23.

19 See Philip Shenon, *The Commission: The Uncensored History of the 9/11 Investigation* (New York: Twelve, 2008), 204.

20 "9/11 Live or Distorted."

21 Kean and Hamilton, WP, 261; Shenon, *The Commission*, 208.

22 "Officials: Government Failed to React to FAA Warning," CNN, September 17, 2001 (http://archives.cnn.com/2001/US/09/16/inv.hijack.warning).

23 Leslie Miller, "Military Now Notified Immediately of Unusual Air Traffic Events," AP, August 12, 2002 (www.wanttoknow.info/020812ap).

24 "America Remembers: The Skies over America," NBC News, September 22, 2002; available at Newsmine.org (newsmine.org/archive/9-11/air-traffic-controllers-recall-events.txt) and as a video (www.jonhs.net/911/skies_over_america.htm).

25 Scott Simmie, "The Scene at NORAD on Sept. 11," *Toronto Star*, December 9, 2001 (http://911research.wtc7.net/cache/planes/defense/torontostar_russiangame.html).

26 "9/11: Interviews by Peter Jennings," ABC News, September 11, 2002 (s3.amazonaws.com/911timeline/2002/abcnews091102.html).

27 Pamela S. Freni, *Ground Stop: An Inside Look at the Federal Aviation Administration on September 11, 2001* (Lincoln, NE: iUniverse, 2003), 33.

28 "FAA Communications with NORAD on September 11, 2001: FAA Clarification Memo to 9/11 Independent Commission," May 22, 2003. Available in the transcript of the 9/11 Commission hearing of May 23, 2003 (www.9-11commission.gov/archive/hearing2/9-11Commission_Hearing_2003-05-23.htm), and at www.911truth.org/article.php?story=2004081200421797; henceforth referred to as FAA Memo.

29 I here prescind, as I did in NPH (see 208-09, n. 32), from the question of whether Flights 11 and 175 were really the planes that hit the Twin Towers. My argument is that, even if we accept this part of the official story, that story cannot withstand scrutiny.

30 For an excellent presentation by the architect who founded Architects and Engineers for 9/11 Truth, see Richard Gage, "How the Towers Fell" (www.911blogger.com/node/10025).

31 Union of Concerned Scientists, "Restoring Scientific Integrity in Policymaking" (www.ucsusa.org/scientific_integrity/interference/scientists-signon-statement.html).

32 This former employee's written statement, dated October 1, 2007, is contained in "NIST Whistleblower" (http://georgewashington.blogspot.com/2007/10/former-nist-employee-blows-whistle.html). The perversion of NIST, this individual said, began in the mid-1990s but has "only grown stronger to the present." Although this former employee wants to remain anonymous to prevent possible retaliation, the authenticity of his self-representation has been confirmed by physicist Steven Jones (e-mail from Jones, December 3, 2007).

33 "NIST Whistleblower."

34 See Dr. Crockett Grabbe and Lenny Charles, "Science in the Bush: When Politics Displaces Physics," Information Clearing House, September 8, 2007 (www.informationclearinghouse.info/article18344.htm).

35 NIST also purportedly calculated the number of perimeter columns that were severed and stripped and estimated the amount of fireproofing that was stripped from other steel assemblies. In this brief account, however, I am focusing only on the most important claims, which involve the core columns.

36 NIST NCSTAR, Executive Summary, xlvii (http://wtc.nist.gov/pubs/NCSTAR1ExecutiveSummary.pdf).

37 This statement was quoted in James Glanz and Eric Lipton, *City in the Sky: The Rise and Fall of the World Trade Center* (New York: Times Books, 2003), 131.

38 For a video containing De Martini's statement, see "The 'Truss Theory': A Fantasy Concocted to Conceal a Demolition," What Really Happened (www.whatreallyhappened.com/trusstheory.html). De Martini can also be seen making this statement in *911 Mysteries: Demolitions* (www.911Mysteries.com).

39 NIST, "Answers to Frequently Asked Questions," August 30, 2006 (http://wtc.nist.gov/pubs/factsheets/faqs_8_2006.htm), Question 1; henceforth cited as AFAQs.

40 AFAQs, Question 1.

41 NIST, *Final Report on the Collapse of the World Trade Center Towers*, September 2005 (http://wtc.nist.gov/NISTNCSTAR1CollapseofTowers.pdf), 2.3 (p. 20), 3.2 (p. 38) and 5.3.2 (p. 55). This document, which is 247 pages long, is also known as NIST NCSTAR 1 ("NCSTAR" stands for the National Construction Safety Team Act Report). The entire report, which is some 10,000 pages long, includes 42 companion volumes containing the results of eight investigations. They are abbreviated NIST NCSTAR 1–1, NIST NCSTAR 1–2, on up to NIST NCSTAR 1-8. For the entire set of documents, see Final Reports of the Federal Building and Fire Investigation of the World Trade Center Disaster (http://wtc.nist.gov/reports_october05.htm). The abbreviated title *Final Report* (in the singular) always refers to the 247-page summary report (NIST NCSTAR 1).

42 Jim Hoffman, "Twin Tower's Designers Anticipated Jet Impacts Like September 11th's," 9-11 Research (http://911research.wtc7.net/wtc/analysis/design.html).

43 John Skilling's statement is quoted in Eric Nalder, "Twin Towers Engineered to Withstand Jet Collision," *Seattle Times*, February 27, 1993 (http://archives.seattletimes.nwsource.com/cgi-bin/texis.cgi/web/vortex/display?slug=1687698&date=19930227). It is partially quoted in Glanz and Lipton, *City in the Sky*, 138.

44 NIST, *Final Report*, xxxviii–xl.

45 Eric Douglas, "The NIST WTC Investigation: How Real Was the Simulation?" *Journal of 9/11 Studies* 6: December 2006 (www.journalof911studies.com/volume/200612/NIST-WTC-Investigation.pdf): 1–28, at 10, citing NIST NCSTAR 1–2B.

46 These points have been made in Jim Hoffman, "Building a Better Mirage: NIST's 3-Year $20,000,000 Cover-Up of the Crime of the Century," 9-11 Research, December 8, 2005 (http://911research.wtc7.net/essays/nist/index.html); see the section entitled "Shrinking the Core Columns."

47 Douglas, "The NIST WTC Investigation."

48 Ibid., 9, quoting NIST NCSTAR 1–2B: 385.

49 Ibid., 14.

50 Ibid., 9–10, citing NIST NCSTAR 1–2B: 390. NIST claimed, to be sure, that it had another criterion for choosing the most severe estimates, namely, that the less severe estimates would not result in debris exiting the towers, which was an observed fact (NIST NCSTAR 1–2, Ch. 7, sect. 7.1). However, the most severe variables also fail to produce this result, by NIST's own admission. The only operative basis for choosing the most severe cases, accordingly, is that only they could produce collapse. This was shown in Douglas, "The NIST WTC Investigation."

51 NIST, *Final Report*, 144.

52 Ibid. This additional tweaking is discussed in Mark H. Gaffney, "The NIST Report on the World Trade Center Collapse One Year Later: Still Dead On Arrival," Information Clearing House, January 4, 2008 (www.informationclearinghouse.info/article18999.htm).

53 Steven E. Jones, "Why Indeed Did the WTC Buildings Collapse?" David Ray Griffin and Peter Dale Scott, ed., *9/11 and American Empire: Intellectuals Speak Out* (Northampton: Interlink, 2006), 33–62. For visual evidence of his points, Jones refers readers to the online version of his paper, which had been posted on his BYU website. But Jones was later forced to remove his paper from that site. The online version can now be read—under the title "Why Indeed Did the World Trade Center Buildings Completely Collapse?"—in the *Journal of 9/11 Studies* 3, September 2006 (www.journalof911studies.com/volume/200609/WhyIndeedDidtheWorldTradeCenterBuildingsCompletelyCollapse.pdf): 1–48.

54 Douglas, "The NIST WTC Investigation, 3, 8, 21.

55 NIST, *Final Report*, 176.

56 Kevin Ryan, "What Is 9/11 Truth?" referring to NIST NCSTAR 1-6A, Appendix C (http://wtc.nist.gov/NISTNCSTAR1-6A.pdf). Ryan has discussed NIST's approach more fully in a letter entitled "The Short Reign of Ryan Mackey," *Journal of 9/11 Studies* 18, December 2007 (http://journalof911studies.com/letters/b/MackeyLetter.pdf).

57 NIST, *Final Report*, 28; AFAQs, Question 2.

58 AFAQs, Question 7.

59 Gaffney, "The NIST Report: Still Dead on Arrival."

60 NIST, *Final Report*, 129.

61 Ibid., 88.

62 Ibid.

63 Thomas W. Eagar and Christopher Musso, "Why Did the World Trade Center Collapse? Science, Engineering, and Speculation," *JOM: Journal of the Minerals, Metals & Materials Society* 53.12 (2001), 8–11 (www.tms.org/pubs/journals/JOM/0112/Eagar/Eagar-0112.html).

64 NIST, *Final Report*, 145, 150.

65 Ibid., 88.

66 NIST, "Public Update on the Federal Building and Fire Safety Investigation of the World Trade Center Disaster," NIST Special Publication 1000–4, December 2003 (http://wtc.nist.gov/media/PublicUpdateFinal.pdf), 8.

67 "Request for Correction Submitted to NIST," *Journal of 9/11 Studies* 12: June 2007 (www.journalof911studies.com/volume/200704/RFCtoNISTbyMcIlvaineDoyleJonesRyanGageSTJ.pdf). The letter to NIST, dated April 12, 2007, was signed by Bob McIlvaine, Bill Doyle, Steven Jones, Kevin Ryan, Richard Gage, and Scholars for 9/11 Truth and Justice.

68 NIST, "Letter of Response to Request," September 27, 2007; published in *Journal of 9/11 Studies* 17: November 2007 (www.journalof911studies.com/volume/2007/NISTresponseToRequestForCorrectionGourleyEtal2.pdf).

69 NIST, "Public Update." I learned about this document from the "Appeal Filed with NIST" (see notes 70 and 72), which quoted it to expose NIST's deceitfulness on this point.

70 For this discussion, I have drawn from two superb documents: the "Request for Correction," mentioned in note 67, and a later "Appeal Filed with NIST" mentioned in note 72.

71 AFAQs, Question 2.

72 "Appeal Filed with NIST, Pursuant to Earlier Request for Correction," by James Gourley, Bob McIlvaine, Bill Doyle, Steven Jones, Kevin Ryan, Richard Gage, and Scholars for 9/11 Truth and Justice, *Journal of 9/11 Studies* 17: November 2007 (www.journalof911studies.com/volume/2007/AppealLetterToNISTGourleyEtAl.pdf).

73 NIST, *Final Report*, xxxv.

74 AFAQs, Question 2.

75 NIST, *Final Report*, 146.

76 Ibid.

77 "Request for Correction."

78 Rice's statement is quoted at Patriots Question 9/11 (http://patriotsquestion911.com/engineers.html#Rice).

79 Edward E. Knesl, "Personal 9/11 Statement," Patriots Question 9/11 (www.ae911truth.org/supporters.php?g=_AES_#996943).

80 "Request for Correction."

81 NIST, *Final Report*, 146; repeated in AFAQs, Question 2.

82 Gaffney, "The NIST Report: Still Dead on Arrival."

83 Gordon Ross, "Momentum Transfer Analysis of the Collapse of the Upper

Storeys of WTC 1," *Journal of 9/11 Studies* 1: June 2006
(www.journalof911studies.com/articles/Journal_5_PTransferRoss.pdf): 32–
39, at 37.

84 For example, Ross, "Momentum Transfer"; Jones, "Why Indeed"; Griffin,
D9D Ch. 3.

85 See NIST, "Answers to Frequently Asked Questions—Supplement,"
December 14, 2007
(http://wtc.nist.gov/pubs/factsheets/faqs_12_2007.htm), and Crockett
Grabbe, "Response to NIST on Energy and Momentum," *Journal of 9/11
Studies*, Letter, January 29, 2008
(www.journalof911studies.com/letters.html).

86 Steven E. Jones, Frank M. Legge, Kevin R. Ryan, Anthony F. Szamboti, and
James R. Gourley, "Fourteen Points of Agreement with Official
Government Reports on the World Trade Center Destruction," *Open Civil
Engineering Journal* 2/1 (2008): 35–40 (www.bentham-open.org/pages/
content.php?TOCIEJ/2008/00000002/00000001/35TOCIEJ.SGM).

87 "Request for Correction."

88 Graeme MacQueen and Tony Szamboti, "The Missing Jolt: A Simple
Refutation of the NIST–Bazant Collapse Hypothesis," publication
pending.

89 NIST, *Final Report*, 146.

90 Several more examples could be given. For a recent discussion, see Crockett
Grabbe, "Direct Evidence for Explosions: Flying Projectiles and
Widespread Impact Damage," *Journal of 911 Studies* 14: August 2007
(www.journalof911studies.com/volume/200704/GrabbeExplosions
Evidence.pdf).

91 AFAQs, Question 2.

92 These oral histories are available at a *New York Times* website
(http://graphics8.nytimes.com/packages/html/nyregion/20050812_WTC_
GRAPHIC/met_WTC_histories_full_01.html).

93 David Ray Griffin, "Explosive Testimony: Revelations about the Twin
Towers in the 9/11 Oral Histories," 911Truth.org, January 18, 2006
(www.911truth.org/article.php?story=20060118104223192); reprinted in
Griffin, *Christian Faith and the Truth behind 9/11*.

94 Graeme MacQueen, "118 Witnesses: The Firefighters' Testimony to
Explosions in the Twin Towers," *Journal of 9/11 Studies* 2: August 2006
(www.journalof911studies.com/articles/Article_5_118Witnesses_World
TradeCenter.pdf): 49–123.

95 Oral History: Firefighter Craig Carlsen, 5–6.

96 Oral History: Chief Frank Cruthers, 4.

97 Oral History: Fire Marshal John Murray, 6.

98 NIST referred to these testimonies in its *Final Report*, 163.

99 Oral History: Firefighter Richard Banaciski, 3.

100 Oral History: Firefighter Edward Cachia, 5.

101 Oral History: Assistant Fire Commissioner Stephen Gregory, 14–16.

102 Oral History: Firefighter William Reynolds, 3–4.

103 Oral History: Firefighter Kenneth Rogers, 3–4.

104 Oral History: Firefighter Timothy Burke, 8–9.

105 Oral History: Captain Karin Deshore, 15.

106 NIST, Letter of Response to Request.

107 "Appeal Filed with NIST," by James Gourley et al.

108 NIST, Letter of Response to Request.

109 John Bussey, "Eye of the Storm: One Journey Through Desperation and Chaos," *Wall Street Journal*, September 12, 2001 (http://online.wsj.com/public/resources/documents/040802pulitzer5.htm).

110 Dean E. Murphy, *September 11: An Oral History* (New York: Doubleday, 2002), 9–15.

111 Guzman's account, which was not included in my "Explosive Testimony," is contained in Mike Kelly, "Last Survivor Pulled from WTC Rebuilds Life, Recalls Horror," *Record* (Bergen County, New Jersey), September 10, 2003. It can be found at What Really Happened (www.whatreallyhappened.com/wtc_mcmillan.html).

112 Greg Szymanski, "WTC Basement Blast and Injured Burn Victim Blows 'Official 9/11 Story' Sky High," Arctic Beacon.com, June 24, 2005 (www.arcticbeacon.citymaker.com/articles/article/1518131/28031.htm).

113 Ibid.

114 E-mail from NIST whistleblower to Steven Jones, November 30, 2007.

115 AFAQs, Question 4.

116 See "911 Eyewitness: Huge Steel Sections Ejected More than 600 Feet" (http://video.google.com/videoplay?docid=1807467434260776490); *9/11 Mysteries: Demolitions*; and *Loose Change: Final Cut* (www.loosechange911.com).

117 Stated at Architects and Engineers for 9/11 Truth (www.ae911truth.org/profile.php?uid=998819).

118 "Official: Plan to Search for Remains Under Roads near WTC Site," Associated Press, October 26, 2006 (http://newsmine.org/archive/9-11/wtc-collapse/over-750-bone-fragments-found-on-deutsche-bank-building.txt).

119 "Forensic Identification of 9/11 Victims Ends: More Than 1,000 Victims Unidentified Due to Technological Limits," ABC News, February 23, 2005 (http://abcnews.go.com/WNT/story?id=525937&page=1).

120 This is NIST's own figure (http://wtc.nist.gov/pubs/factsheets/faqs_8_2006.htm).

121 James Williams, "WTC a Structural Success," *SEAU News: The Newsletter of the Structural Engineers Association of Utah*, October 2001 (www.seau.org/SEAUNews-2001-10.pdf).

122 "New York Visit Reveals Extent of WTC Disaster," *Structural Engineer*, September 3, 2002 (http://web.archive.org/web/20031117155808/www.istructe.org.uk/about/files/president/Tour-2002-NewYork.pdf), 6.

123 "Mobilizing Public Health: Turning Terror's Tide with Science," *Johns Hopkins Public Health Magazine*, Late Fall 2001 (www.jhsph.edu/Publications/Special/Welch.htm).

124 Ruvolo is quoted in the DVD *Terror Storm*

(http://www.infowars.com/terrorstorm/index.htm). For just this segment plus discussion, see Steve Watson, "Firefighter Describes 'Molten Metal' at Ground Zero, Like a 'Foundry,'" Infowars.net, November 17, 2006 (http://infowars.net/articles/november2006/171106molten.htm).

125 "The Chaplain's Tale," *Times-Herald Record*, September 8, 2002 (http://archive.recordonline.com/adayinseptember/trimpe.htm).

126 Jennifer Lin, "Recovery Worker Reflects on Months Spent at Ground Zero," Knight Ridder, May 29, 2002 (www.whatreallyhappened.com/ground_zero_fires.html).

127 Trudy Walsh, "Handheld APP Eased Recovery Tasks," Government Computer News 21/27a, September 11, 2002 (www.gcn.com/print/21_27a/19930-1.html).

128 Tom Arterburn, "D-Day: NY Sanitation Workers' Challenge of a Lifetime," *Waste Age*, April 1, 2002 (http://wasteage.com/mag/waste_dday_ny_sanitation).

129 Robert Sanders, "Report from Ground Zero: Engineer Studies World Trade Center Collapse for Clues to Failure," Berkleyan, October 3, 2001 (www.berkeley.edu/news/berkeleyan/2001/10/03_grou.html). For the references in this paragraph, I am indebted to "Engineer Sees Evidence of Extreme Temperatures in WTC Steel," 911Bloggger.com, February 25, 2008, by Matthew Everett writing under the name "Shoestring" (http://shoestring911.blogspot.com/2008/02/engineer-sees-evidence-of-extreme.html); identity revealed with permission.

130 Jeffrey Young, "Scholars Work to Rebuild the World Trade Center Virtually," *Chronicle of Higher Education*, December 7, 2001 (http://chronicle.com/cgi2-bin/printable.cgi?article=http://chronicle.com/free/v48/i15/15a02701.htm).

131 "Collapse of Overpass in California Becomes Lesson in Construction," *NewsHour with Jim Lehrer*, PBS, May 20, 2007 (www.pbs.org/newshour/bb/science/jan-june07/overpass_05-10.html). Astaneh-Asl, I should add, was not questioning the official account of the World Trade Center, as shown by this statement: "In both of them [the overpass and the World Trade Center], basically, the fire was the reason why steel got soft and weak and collapsed." But he did state that steel girders had melted (not merely softened), which cannot be reconciled with the official account.

132 ABC News, May 7, 2004, quoted in Andy Field, "A Look Inside a Radical New Theory of the WTC Collapse," Firehouse.com, February 7, 2004, updated June 14, 2007 (http://cms.firehouse.com/content/article/article.jsp?sectionId=46&id=25807).

133 AFAQs, Question 13.

134 Ibid.

135 Ibid.

136 "NIST Engineer, John Gross, Denies the Existance [sic] of Molten Steel"

(http://video.google.com/videoplay?docid=-7180303712325092501&hl=en). Gross was one of the 13 members of the National Construction Safety Team listed at the beginning of NIST's *Final Report*.

137 James Glanz and Eric Lipton, "A Search for Clues in Towers' Collapse," *New York Times*, February 2, 2002 (http://query.nytimes.com/gst/fullpage.html?res=9C04E0DE153DF931A 35751C0A9649C8B63).

138 Jonathan Barnett, Ronald R. Biederman, and R. D. Sisson, Jr., "Limited Metallurgical Examination," FEMA, World Trade Center Building Performance Study, Appendix C (http://911research.wtc7.net/wtc/evidence/metallurgy/WTC_apndxC.htm).

139 See Steven E. Jones, "Revisiting 9/11/2001: Applying the Scientific Method," *Journal of 9/11 Studies* 11: May 2007 (www.journalof911 studies.com/volume/200704/JonesWTC911SciMethod.pdf).

140 Joan Killough-Miller, "The 'Deep Mystery' of Melted Steel," *WPI Transformations*, Spring 2002 (www.wpi.edu/News/Transformations/2002Spring/steel.html).

141 See Sanders, "Report from Ground Zero" (note 129, above).

142 AFAQs, Question 12.

143 "Appeal Filed with NIST."

144 Steven E. Jones, "Revisiting 9/11/2001: Applying the Scientific Method," *Journal of 9/11 Studies* 11: May 2007 (www.journalof911studies.com/volume/200704/JonesWTC911SciMethod.pdf).

145 "Dr. Steven E. Jones, Boston 911 Conference 12-15-07, Red Chips-Thermite" (http://video.google.com/videoplay?docid=-4186920967571123147&hl=en).

146 Jennifer Abel, "Theories of 9/11," *Hartford Advocate*, January 29, 2008 (www.hartfordadvocate.com/article.cfm?aid=5546). Abel, unfortunately, spelled Newman's name "Neuman."

147 Patriots Question 9/11 (http://PatriotsQuestion911.com/engineers.html#Munyak).

148 NPH 180–81.

149 Quoted in Damon DiMarco, *Tower Stories: An Oral History of 9/11*, 2nd edition (Santa Monica, Calif.: Santa Monica Press, 2007), 59. I am indebted to Matthew Everett for this quotation.

150 Ed Haas, "Government Spokesman Says, 'I Don't Understand the Public's Fascination with World Trade Center Building Seven,'" *Muckraker Report*, March 21, 2006 (www.teamliberty.net/id235.html).

151 Giuliani's statement to Jennings can be read and heard at "Who Told Giuliani the WTC Was Going to Collapse on 9/11?" What Really Happened, n.d. (www.whatreallyhappened.com/wtc_giuliani.html); for Giuliani's attempted explanation, see a video entitled "Activists Confront Giuliani over 9/11" (http://video.wnbc.com/player/?id=112179). For more details and discussion, see my *Contradictions*, Ch. 22, "How Did Rudy Giuliani

Know the Towers Were Going to Collapse?"

152 NIST, Appendix L: Interim Report on WTC 7
(http://wtc.nist.gov/progress_report_june04/appendixl.pdf), L–34, L–34.

153 Jacobson can be seen making this statement in Michael Berger's film,
Improbable Collapse: The Demolition of Our Republic
(www.improbablecollapse.com).

154 See FEMA, World Trade Center Building Performance Study
(www.fema.gov/rebuild/mat/wtcstudy.shtm), Ch. 5, Sect. 6.2, "Probable
Collapse Sequence," which I discussed at NPH 22.

155 For an interview with 9/11 Commission Vice Chairman Lee Hamilton
about this omission, see D9D 140–41.

156 "National Construction Safety Team Advisory Committee 2003 Report to
Congress"
(http://wtc.nist.gov/media/NCSTAC2003ReporttoCongressFinal.pdf), 4.

157 AFAQs, Question 14.

158 NIST, "WTC Investigation Overview," December 18, 2007
(http://wtc.nist.gov/media/NCSTAC_December18(Sunder).pdf).

159 AFAQs, Question 14.

160 NIST, "WTC 7 Collapse," April 5, 2005
(http://wtc.nist.gov/pubs/WTC%20Part%20IIC%20-
%20WTC%207%20Collapse%20Final.pdf), 6. This preliminary report
had been preceded by an "interim" report in 2004. Given the existence of
these reports from 2004 and 2005, it was dishonest of Shyam Sunder to
claim on a BBC special about WTC 7, which was aired July 6, 2008, that
NIST had been "at this for [only] a little over two years." See *The
Conspiracy Files: 9/11—The Third Tower* (www.911blogger.com/
node/16541).

161 Ibid., "Debris Damage from WTC 1" and "WTC 7 SW Corner after WTC
1 Collapse."

162 Cited in *Debunking* 54.

163 See Truthseeker, "Contradictory Pictures of WTC 7's Corner Damage,"
April 1, 2007 (http://wtc7corner.blogspot.com/2007/04/contradictory-
pictures-of-wtc-7s-corner.html), and truth911.net, "WTC NIST Pic Is
Fake (25% NOT Scooped Out)." See also Winston Smith, "Photographic
Analysis of Damage to WTC7 and Critical Errors in NIST's Estimations,"
StudyOf911.com, October 19, 2006
(www.studyof911.com/articles/winstonwtc701).

164 BBC News, *The Conspiracy Files: 9/11—The Third Tower* (see note 160).

165 Kenneth Change, "Scarred Steel Holds Clues, and Remedies"; Barnett,
Biederman, and Sisson, "Limited Metallurgical Examination."

166 AFAQs, Question 2.

167 Jones, "Why Indeed Did the WTC Buildings Collapse?" 46.

168 See Patriots Question 9/11: Hugo Bachmann
(www.patriotsquestion911.com/engineers.html#Bachmann) and Jörg
Schneider (http://patriotsquestion911.com/engineers.html#Schneider).
These quotations were drawn from Daniele Ganser, "Swiss Professors:

WTC 7 Most Likely Controlled Demolition," English trans. by Jesse Goplen, which has been republished as a letter to the *Journal of 9/11 Studies*, February 29, 2008 (http://journalof911studies.com/letters/d/GanserSwissProfs.pdf).

169 Architects and Engineers for 9/11 Truth (www.ae911truth.org/supporters.php?g=ENG#998929).

170 This interview can be seen at "Controlled Demolition Expert and WTC7" (www.youtube.com/watch?v=HgoSOQ2xrbI). This 2006 video clip is an excerpt from a Dutch television program entitled *Zembla Investigates 9/11 Theories* (http://cgi.omroep.nl/cgi-bin/streams?/tv/vara/zembla/bb.20060911.asf). A portion of it is contained in *Loose Change: Final Cut*.

171 Patriots Question 9/11 (http://patriotsquestion911.com/engineers.html#Jowenko).

172 NIST, "WTC 7 Collapse."

173 "Barry Jennings Uncut," Loose Change 911, July 9, 2008 (www.loosechange911.com/blog/?p=105). This is an interview that Barry Jennings granted in 2007 to Dylan Avery and the other makers of the video *Loose Change: Final Cut*. This taped interview was, at Jennings's insistence after he had become worried that it might cost him his job, not actually included in the video. However, for reasons that Avery explains in his introductory statement, he decided to make it publicly available. The title "Barry Jennings Uncut" alludes to the fact that, although certain extracts from the interview had previously been placed on the Internet, the complete interview had not before been posted.

174 Hess gave a brief interview to Frank Ucciardo of UPN9 News (WWOR-TV) that morning. It begins at the 57-minute mark on a DVD posted at WantToKnow.Info (www.wanttoknow.info/008/hessjenningswtc7explosiontvbroadcast).

175 "Barry Jennings Uncut."

176 "ABC 7 News Interview of Barry Jennings." (This was a brief on-the-street interview with Jennings conducted on 9/11 by a reporter from ABC 7 News. Avery placed a portion of it at the beginning of "Barry Jennings Uncut.")

177 "Barry Jennings Uncut."

178 According to the times given on the DVD (see note 174), the video started at 10:37AM, which would mean that the Hess interview, which occurs at the 57-minute mark, started at 11:34. Internal evidence, however, suggests that the video may have started at 11:00. At the 111-minute mark, the UPN9 program switched to live coverage by CNN of a Taliban news conference, and the only reference I have been able to find to this coverage—Michael Ventura, "9/11: American Ungoverned" (www.austinchronicle.com/gyrobase/Issue/column?oid=oid%3A83213)—indicates that it began at 12:51, which would mean that the video would have begun at 11:00 and the Hess interview, therefore, at 11:57.

179 "ABC 7 News Interview of Barry Jennings."

180 "Barry Jennings Uncut."

181 The conclusion that Hess and Jennings were rescued no later than 11:30 might seem to be ruled out by the fact that Jennings, near the end of the interview, said that he and Hess "didn't get out of there until like 1:00," after which Avery made a supporting statement, saying that the interview with Hess took place at about 1:00. There are, however, many reasons to conclude that they both misspoke. First, Avery, who supplied the tape of the Hess interview, which shows the interview to have started before noon (see notes 174 and 178), has confirmed that he misspoke (e-mail July 9, 2008). Second, Jennings had previously misspoken about another crucial matter: the floor he was on when the explosion occurred. In the interview with the ABC 7 reporter after he was rescued, Jennings said that the explosion occurred after he and Hess made it to the 8th floor. Under questioning from Avery, however, he clarified that it had happened when they were on the 6th floor, after which they went back up to the 8th floor. Third, if Hess and Jennings had not gotten out of the building until 1:00, they would have been trapped for 3½ hours, and yet in one interview, as pointed out earlier, Jennings said they had been trapped for "an hour," and it would be inconceivable that he would have used that language to describe 3½ hours. Fourth, Jennings said that the fireman came back to rescue them after the collapse of the North Tower, which occurred at 10:28, and the rescue certainly would not have taken almost another 2½ hours. Fifth, 1:00 would be about 45 minutes later than even NIST claimed that the men had been rescued.

182 The interviews are cited at NIST NCSTAR 1-8, *Federal Building and Fire Safety Investigation of the World Trade Center Disaster: The Emergency Response Operations* (http://wtc.nist.gov/NISTNCSTAR1-8.pdf), 109n380. (Although NIST refers to the interviews with numbers instead of names, the account in the text obviously describes the experiences of Hess and Jennings.) The alleged rescue time is stated in NIST, Appendix L: Interim Report on WTC 7 (http://wtc.nist.gov/progress_report_june04/appendixl.pdf), L–18.

183 NIST NCSTAR 1–8: 109n380. NIST also, of course, ignored Jennings's statement that, before he and Hess were finally rescued, the firefighters had come twice but then ran away when the two towers came down. NIST simply said: "The two men went back to the 8th floor [and] broke out a window and called for help. Firefighters on the ground saw them and went up the stairs." NIST thereby portrayed Jennings as having broken the window after 10:30, rather than, as he indicated, about 9:20.

184 *The Conspiracy Files: 9/11—The Third Tower* (see note 160), directed and produced by Mike Rudin, described Jennings as "the key witness in the controversy over what really happened inside Tower 7." It could do this, while supporting the official view, by placing his statements within NIST's timeline. For example, right after showing Jennings recounting the fact that he was told to get out of WTC 7 quickly (which, according to Jennings, occurred shortly after 9:03), the BBC narrator says: "At 9:59, the 1,300-foot South Tower collapses." Then, after showing Jennings's

account of having the staircase knocked out from under him on the sixth floor (which would have been at about 9:15), the BBC narrator says: "At 10:28, the North Tower collapses. . . . This time, Tower 7 takes a direct hit from the collapsing building." Those timeline distortions then allow the narrator to conclude: "Early evidence of explosives were just debris from a falling skyscraper." Having drawn that false conclusion, the BBC could then use Jennings's account of the destructiveness of the explosion in WTC 7—"When we got to the 8th floor, I thought of walking to one side of the building. That side of the building was gone!"—as evidence that the collapse of the North Tower had caused great damage to WTC 7. To complete the timeline distortion, the BBC, after showing Jennings describing how he finally got outside of the building, showed a clock with its hands at 12:03. How did the BBC handle the problematic fact that Michael Hess was giving an interview about a half-mile away before noon? It simply made no mention of Hess, giving the impression that Jennings experienced these events by himself (even though he sometimes used the word "we"). This documentary by Mike Rudin is, to be sure, better than the BBC's previous 9/11 offering, which was produced by Guy Smith (see note 207, below), but this is not high praise.

185 "Barry Jennings Uncut." Part of Avery's motivation for releasing the whole interview, he explained in his introductory comment, was that Jennings had later, while being interviewed for the BBC special on WTC 7, raised a quibble regarding the statement about stepping over people, saying: "They [the *Loose Change* producers] portrayed me as seeing dead bodies. I never saw dead bodies. . . . I said it *felt* like I was stepping over them but I never saw any." It is true that he had not said that he *saw* any bodies. But he *had* made clear that he had no doubt about their existence, saying, "you can tell when you're stepping over people." Although the BBC tried to make it appear that the *Loose Change* producers had distorted Jennings's statement, it was the BBC that did this, claiming: "There's no evidence that anyone died in Tower 7 on 9/11" (*The Conspiracy Files: 9/11—The Third Tower*).

186 Jeremy Baker, "Last Building Standing," Serendipity (www.serendipity.li/wot/last_building_standing.pdf); Shoestring, "Was 10:45AM the Originally Planned Demolition Time of WTC 7?" 9/11 Blogger, May 1, 2008 (http://911blogger.com/node/15318). "Shoestring's" true identity is revealed here with permission.

187 Quoted from "America Under Attack," CNN Breaking News, 11:00AM (http://transcripts.cnn.com/TRANSCRIPTS/0109/11/bn.11.html).

188 Shoestring, "Was 10:45AM the Originally Planned Demolition Time of WTC 7?"

189 Baker, "Last Building Standing."

190 Jeremy Baker, "Stunning Video of WTC 7's Damaged South Face Discovered on a 9/11 Truth Debunking Website," Darkprints, July 15, 2008 (http://drkprnts.files.wordpress.com/2008/07/stunningvideowtc7ssouthface.pdf).

191 "We Are Change Confronts Larry Silverstein 3/13/03," 911Blogger.com (www.911blogger.com/node/14361).

192 Baker, "Stunning Video."

193 Reporter Peter Demarco, quoted in Chris Bull and Sam Erman, eds., *At Ground Zero: Young Reporters Who Were There Tell Their Stories* (New York: Thunder's Mouth Press, 2002), 97.

194 This statement by reporter Al Jones is in the documentary *911 Eyewitness* (http://video.google.com/videoplay?docid= 65460757734339444) at 28:25.

195 This statement is in "911 Eyewitness" at 31:30.

196 Paul Joseph Watson, "NYPD Officer Heard Building 7 Bombs," Prison Planet, February 10, 2007 (www.prisonplanet.com/articles/february2007/100207heardbombs.htm); part of the statement by this officer, Craig Bartmer, can be seen in *Loose Change: Final Cut*.

197 NIST NCSTAR 1–8: The Emergency Response 110.

198 Murphy, *September 11: An Oral History*, 175–76.

199 This fact can be seen from reading together the FDNY oral histories of Deputy Assistant Chief Albert Turi (who reported that the information came from "an EMT person"), Fire Marshall Steven Mosiello (who reported that this "EMT person" was Richard Zarrillo), Richard Zarrillo (who reported that he got the information from Chief John Peruggia), and Chief John Peruggia (who reported that he gave the information to Zarrillo after getting it from Richard Rotanz, the deputy director of the Office of Emergency Management). See *Contradictions*, Ch. 22: "How Did Rudy Giuliani Know the Towers Were Going to Collapse?"

200 "Indira Singh: Ground Zero 911, Blueprint For Terror, Part One," *Guns and Butter*, KPFA, April 27, 2005 (http://kpfa.org/archives/index.php?arch=7814). A portion of this exchange is available in a video, "Seven Is Exploding" (www.youtube.com/watch?v=58h0LjdMry0).

201 "Seven Is Exploding."

202 Ibid.

203 "Another Smoking Gun? Now CNN Jumps the Gun," Information Liberation, February 27, 2007 (www.informationliberation.com/?id=20521).

204 See Paul Joseph Watson and Alex Jones, "BBC Reported Building 7 Had Collapsed 20 Minutes Before It Fell," Prison Planet.com, February 27, 2007 (www.prisonplanet.com/articles/february2007/260207building7.htm); "BBC's 'WTC 7 Collapsed at 4:45PM' Videos," What Really Happened (www.whatreallyhappened.com/bbc_wtc7_videos.html).

205 Richard Porter, "Part of the Conspiracy?" February 27, 2007 (www.bbc.co.uk/blogs/theeditors/2007/02/part_of_the_conspiracy.html).

206 Sheila Barter, "How the World Trade Center Fell," BBC News, September 13, 2001 (http://news.bbc.co.uk/1/hi/world/americas/1540044.stm).

207 *The Conspiracy Files: 9/11*, produced by Guy Smith, was broadcast February 18, 2007, by BBC 2. The documentary can be viewed on Live

Video (www.livevideo.com/video/
094F3DD8A30B485ABEA1313A9D50CACF/the-conspiracy-files-9-11-
p1.aspx?lastvcid=78869). I pointed out some of the failings of this show in
D9D. A more extensive, truly devastating, critique has been provided in a
documentary, *911 and the British Broadcasting Conspiracy*, produced by
Adrian Connock (http://video.google.com/videoplay?docid=
1882365905982811133).

208 Richard Porter, "Part of the Conspiracy? (2)" BBC World, March 2, 2007
(www.bbc.co.uk/blogs/theeditors/2007/03/part_of_the_conspiracy_2.html).

209 While serving as the anchor for CBS News, Rather said: "For the third
time today, it's reminiscent of those pictures we've all seen too much on
television before, where a building was deliberately destroyed by well-
placed dynamite to knock it down" (www.youtube.com/
watch?v=Nvx904dAwOo).

210 A report issued by Fox-5 News of Washington DC has been portrayed as
another premature report (www.youtube.com/watch?v=GwUJ9MhzgKI).
At some point (no time is indicated on the screen), the female anchor
reports that they were "getting word from New York right now that
another building has collapsed. . . a 47-story building." About 30 seconds
later, the TV screen in the background shows the building collapsing, at
which point the male anchor says, "Take a look at that" and the female
anchor adds, "It's going down right now." However, although it is possible
that this was a premature announcement, the anchors instead seem to be
playing footage that they had received from New York after the event,
especially because the footage is replayed a few minutes later. This
broadcast is interesting, nevertheless, because of the fact that the anchors,
like the BBC anchor, had been quickly supplied with an explanation as to
why WTC 7 collapsed. After showing the collapse, the male anchor said:
"This is not from an explosion or an aircraft. . . . The information that we
have is that this is a building that was probably incredibly structurally
damaged by the goings on right next door." The female anchor then read
from a document before her and concluded, "So, structural damage, as you
had suggested, probably led to this building going down."

211 Aaron Dykes, "BBC Anchor Who Reported on WTC7 Collapse Early
Agrees There May Be a 'Conspiracy'," Prison Planet, April 25, 2008
(www.prisonplanet.com/articles/april2008/250408_b_anchor.htm).

212 Silverstein can be seen making the statement on YouTube (www.youtube.com/
watch?v=CahEva8zQas).

213 "9/11 Revealed? New Book Repeats False Conspiracy Theories,"
Identifying Misinformation, US Department of State
(http://usinfo.state.gov/media/Archive/2005/Sep/16-241966.html).

214 *Debunking* 58.

215 Ibid., 57–58. (This claim is also made in the US State Department, "The
Top September 11 Conspiracy Theories.")

216 Ibid., 57–58.

217 This telephone call, preceded by Silverstein's statement and then the

claim by Davin Coburn of *Popular Mechanics* that "the term 'pull it' is not a demolition term," can be heard at www.pumpitout.com/audio/pull_it_mix.mp3.

218 See "We Are Change Confronts Larry Silverstein 3/13/03," 911Blogger.com (www.911blogger.com/node/14361).

219 J. Marx Ayres, "Personal 9/11 Statement," Architects and Engineers for 9/11 Truth (www.ae911truth.org/supporters.php?g=ENG#999926). For more statements by engineers, see "Numerous Structural Engineers Now Publicly Challenge Government's Explanation for Destruction of the World Trade Center," George Washington's Blog, May 27, 2008 (http://georgewashington.blogspot.com/2008/04/14-structural-engineers-have-now.html).

CHAPTER 2: FLIGHT 77 & THE PENTAGON

1 9/11CR 25–26.

2 O'Brien's statement is made in Citizen Investigation Team, *The Pentagon Flyover: How They Pulled It Off* (http://video.google.ca/videoplay?docid=-8176286327617173136&q=the+pentagon+flyover&total=6&start=0&num=10&so=0&type=search&plindex=1).

3 Tim O'Brien, "Wife of Solicitor General Alerted Him of Hijacking from Plane," CNN, September 11, 2001, 2:06AM (http://archives.cnn.com/2001/US/09/11/pentagon.olson).

4 *Hannity & Colmes*, Fox News, September 14, 2001.

5 "America's New War: Recovering from Tragedy," *Larry King Live*, CNN, September 14, 2001 (http://edition.cnn.com/TRANSCRIPTS/0109/14/lkl.00.html).

6 Toby Harnden, "She Asked Me How to Stop the Plane," *Daily Telegraph*, March 5, 2002 (http://s3.amazonaws.com/911timeline/2002/telegraph030502.html). Olson had previously given this account in his "Barbara K. Olson Memorial Lecture," delivered November 16, 2001, at a convention of the Federalist Society (www.fed-soc.org/resources/id.63/default.asp). But a year after 9/11, the idea that Barbara Olson had used a cell phone was repeated in "On September 11, Final Words of Love," CNN, September 10, 2002 (http://archives.cnn.com/2002/US/09/03/ar911.phone.calls); and in 2007, Steve Vogel repeated it in *The Pentagon: A History* (New York: Random House, 2007), 426.

7 See the submission of February 17, 2006, by "the Paradroid" on the Politik Forum (http://forum.politik.de/forum/archive/index.php/t-133356-p-24.html).

8 United States v. Zacarias Moussaoui, Exhibit Number P200054 (www.vaed.uscourts.gov/notablecases/moussaoui/exhibits/prosecution/flights/P200054.html). These documents can be more easily viewed in "Detailed Account of Phone Calls from September 11th Flights" (http://911research.wtc7.net/planes/evidence/calldetail.html). I am

indebted to Rowland Morgan for information about this FBI report. For the reason to call it an "FBI report" even though it is not specifically presented as such, see note 19 of Chapter 3.

9 FBI, "Interview with Theodore Olsen [sic]," "9/11 Commission, FBI Source Documents, Chronological, September 11," 2001Intelfiles.com, March 14, 2008, (http://intelfiles.egoplex.com:80/2008/03/911-commission-fbi-source-documents.html).

10 O'Brien, "Wife of Solicitor General Alerted Him of Hijacking from Plane."

11 9/11 Commission Staff Statement 16 (www.9-11commission.gov/staff_statements/staff_statement_16.pdf).

12 Shoestring, "The Flight 77 Murder Mystery: Who Really Killed Charles Burlingame?" Shoestring911, February 2, 2008 (http://shoestring911.blogspot.com/2008/02/flight-77-murder-mystery-who-really.html).

13 "In Memoriam: Charles 'Chic' Burlingame, 1949–2001," USS Saratoga Museum foundation (available at http://911research.wtc7.net/cache/planes/analysis/chic_remembered.html).

14 Alfred Goldberg et al., *Pentagon 9/11* (Washington, DC: Office of the Secretary of Defense, 2007), 1.

15 Natalie Patton, "Flight Attendant Made Call on Cell Phone to Mom in Las Vegas," *Las Vegas Review-Journal*, September 13, 2001 (www.reviewjournal.com/lvrj_home/2001/Sep-13-Thu-2001/news/16989631.html).

16 *Debunking*, 66.

17 According to those who believe that the Pentagon was hit by a Boeing 757, or at least a large airplane of some type, the two best photographs supportive of this view are at www.geoffmetcalf.com/pentagon/images/5.jpg and www.geoffmetcalf.com/pentagon/images/6.jpg.

18 Leslie Filson, *Air War over America: Sept. 11 Alters Face of Air Defense Mission*, Foreword by Larry K. Arnold (Public Affairs: Tyndall Air Force Base, 2003), 66.

19 Karen Kwiatkowski, "Assessing the Official 9/11 Conspiracy Theory," in David Ray Griffin and Peter Dale Scott, ed., *9/11 and American Empire: Intellectuals Speak Out* (Northampton: Olive Branch Press, 2006). For a more technical discussion of the debris, see "The Missing Wings." (www.physics911.net/missingwings.htm), in which A. K. Dewdney and G. W. Longspaugh argue that the absence of wing debris alone is sufficient to disprove the claim that a huge airliner hit the Pentagon.

20 Jamie McIntyre interviewed by Judy Woodruff. Some people have claimed that McIntyre later, in supporting the view that the building was hit by a 757, contradicted his earlier statement that all the pieces he saw were "very small." The strongest evidence for this claim seems to be his statement, "I was there on September 11, and I saw the wreckage of a plane, including large pieces" (see "Jamie McIntyre Contradiction #3" at www.youtube.com/watch?v=KV0XRVL2vrw). In his interview with Judy Woodruff on 9/11, however, he had said: "The

biggest piece I saw was about three feet long, it was silver and had been painted green and red. . . . I also saw a large piece of shattered glass. It appeared to be a cockpit windshield or other window from the plane" (http://transcripts.cnn.com/TRANSCRIPTS/0109/11/bn.35.html). There is, therefore, no contradiction as long as it is understood that the "large pieces" he saw were "small enough that you can pick [them] up in your hand." Thus understood, his later affirmation of "large pieces" does not contradict his earlier report that there were "no large tail sections, wing sections, fuselage, nothing like that anywhere around."

21 "Responding in the Pentagon," Office of Medical History (http://history.amedd.army.mil/memoirs/soldiers/responding.pdf), 96.

22 Ryan Alessi and M. E. Sprengelmeyer, "An Anniversary of Agony at the Pentagon," Scripps Howard News Service, August 1, 2002 (http://web.archive.org:80/web/20021017045944/http:/www.gomemphis. com/mca/america_at_war/article/0,1426,MCA_945_1300676,00.html).

23 Goldberg et al., Pentagon 9/11, 68.

24 Ibid., 69.

25 Ibid., 70.

26 Alan Miller, "US Navy 'Top Gun' Pilot Questions 911 Pentagon Story," OpedNews.com, September 5, 2007 (www.opednews.com/articles/ genera_alan_mil_070905_u_s__navy__top_gun__.htm).

27 Henry Makow, "Filmmaker Was at Pentagon on 911," Rense.com, May 28, 2008 (www.rense.com/general82/sevdis.htm).

28 "Interview with April Gallop," George Washington's Blog, July 13, 2006 (http://georgewashington.blogspot.com/2006/07/interview-with-april-gallop.html).

29 "Responding in the Pentagon," Office of Medical History (http://history.amedd.army.mil/memoirs/soldiers/responding.pdf), 119.

30 Randy Dockendorf, "Tyndall Native Relives 9/11," Yankton Press & Dakotan, September 11, 2003 (www.yankton.net/stories/ 091103/com_20030911017.shtml).

31 McWethy's statement is quoted in Allison Gilbert et al., Covering Catastrophe: Broadcast Journalists Report September 11 (New York: Bonus Books, 2002), 187.

32 Thierry Meyssan, Pentagate (London: Carnot, 2002), 16.

33 Stephen Webster, "Under Fire! US Army Intelligence Analyst Targeted for Suggesting New Independent 9/11 Investigation," Lone Star Iconoclast, August 21, 2006 (www.lonestaricon.com/absolutenm/ anmviewer.asp?a=426).

34 Stephen Webster, "Friendly Fire: Raising Questions about 9/11 Gets an Army Sergeant Demoted for 'Disloyalty,'" Fort Worth Weekly, May 30, 2007 (www.fwweekly.com/content.asp?article=6022).

35 The case against Buswell was dropped, he learned, because of the fear that the court martial would go into 9/11-related issues and might even require subpoenas to be issued to Secretary of Defense Donald Rumsfeld and Vice President Cheney (e-mail from Buswell, May 22,

2008).

36 Stephen C. Webster, "Free At Last: Army Intelligence Analyst Buswell, 'The 9/11 NCO,' Speaks Out," *Lone Star Iconoclast*, May 13, 2008 (www.lonestaricon.com/absolutenm/anmviewer.asp?a=2792&z=247).

37 Dr. James H. Fetzer, Major William B. Fox, Captain Eric H. May, and SFC Donald Buswell, "Mayday Alert! Terror Drills Could Go Live!" *Lone Star Iconoclast*, April 28, 2008 (www.lonestaricon.com/absolutenm/anmviewer.asp?a=2758&z=243).

38 ASCE (American Society of Civil Engineers), *Pentagon Building Performance Report*, January 2003 (http://fire.nist.gov/bfrlpubs/build03/PDF/b03017.pdf), Section 7, "Analysis."

39 *Debunking*, 69.

40 See, for example, Jim Hoffman's photographs and discussion at http://911research.wtc7.net/talks/noplane/enginerotor.html and the six following pages.

41 Dave McGowan, "September 11, 2001 Revisited: The Series: Act II" (www.davesweb.cnchost.com/nwsltr68.html).

42 Quoted on Patriots Question 9/11 (www.patriotsquestion911.com/#Wittenberg).

43 See http://flight77.info/85tapes.gif, which shows a letter requesting 85 videos that had been mentioned by an FBI agent, and www.flight77.info/00new/n85reply.jpg, which shows a DOJ letter saying: "The material you requested is located in an investigative file which is exempt from disclosure."

44 See Judicial Watch, "CITGO Gas Station Cameras Near Pentagon Evidently Did Not Capture Attack," September 15, 2006 (www.judicialwatch.org/printer_5965.shtml), and a video on YouTube (www.youtube.com/watch?v=2LJvFjsl6zk). Another video was released in November 2006 (www.youtube.com/watch?v=H285_DWX_bQ).

45 Colonel George Nelson, USAF (ret.), "Impossible to Prove a Falsehood True: Aircraft Parts as a Clue to Their Identity," Physics 911, April 23, 2005 (www.physics911.net/georgenelson.htm).

46 Aidan Monaghan, "9/11 Aircraft 'Black Box' Serial Numbers Mysteriously Absent," 911Blogger, February 26, 2008 (http://911blogger.com/node/14081).

47 For the NTSB's FDR report on American Flight 77, see www.911myths.com/AAL77_fdr.pdf; for its FDR report on United Flight 93, see www.gwu.edu/~nsarchiv/NSAEBB/NSAEBB196/doc04.pdf.

48 Aidan Monaghan, "F.B.I. Elaborates On Reportedly Absent 9/11 Aircraft Wreckage Recovery & Identification Records," 911Blogger, March 18, 2008 (www.911blogger.com/node/14422).

49 This FBI statement also indicated, of course, that it had no records proving that United 93 crashed near Shanksville, Pennsylvania (see Chapter 3, below) or that the World Trade Center was struck by American 11 and United 175 (see note 29 of Chapter 1, above).

50 "Searchers Find Pentagon Black Boxes," *USA Today*, September 14, 2001

(www.usatoday.com/news/nation/2001/09/14/pentagon-fire.htm#more). I had previously (D9D 277) quoted a similar story in *Newsweek*, "Washington's Heroes: On the Ground at the Pentagon on Sept. 11," *Newsweek*, September 28, 2003 (http://msnbc.msn.com/id/3069699), but it seems to have been completely removed from the Internet.

51 Ibid.

52 Aidan Monaghan, "Pentagon 9/11 Flight 'Black Box' Data File Created Before Actual 'Black Box' Was Recovered?" 911 Blogger, May 18, 2008 (www.911blogger.com/node/15636).

53 See the *Newsweek* story cited in note 50.

54 *Pentagon Building Performance Report*, Section 6.2.

55 *Debunking*, 70.

56 Won-Young Kim and G. R. Baum, "Seismic Observations during September 11, 2001, Terrorist Attack," Spring 2002 (www.mgs.md.gov/esic/publications/download/911pentagon.pdf).

57 Michael Meyer, "Pentagon C Ring Exit Hole Mystery," Scholars for 9/11 Truth, June 10, 2006 (www.scholarsfor911truth.org/ArticleMeyer_10June2006.html).

58 ASCE (American Society of Civil Engineers), *Pentagon Building Performance Report*, January 2003 (http://fire.nist.gov/ bfrlpubs/build03/PDF/b03017.pdf), 40.

59 *Debunking*, 70.

60 Ibid.

61 *Good Morning America*, ABC, September 13, 2001.

62 Pentagon News Briefing, September 15, 2001 (www.defenselink.mil/transcripts/transcript.aspx?transcriptid=1636).

63 Vogel, *The Pentagon*, 431.

64 Goldberg et al., *Pentagon 9/11*, 17.

65 *Debunking*, 59.

66 See "Eric Bart's Pentagon Attack Eyewitness Accounts," 9-11 Research (http://911research.wtc7.net/pentagon/evidence/witnesses/bart.html).

67 Jerry Russell, "Eyewitnesses and the Plane-Bomb Theories" (www.911-strike.com/PlaneBomb.htm).

68 See "Anderson, Steve" under "Eyewitness Accounts" in "Eric Bart's Pentagon Attack Eyewitness Accounts."

69 *Debunking*, 65.

70 Ibid., 67.

71 See Probst's testimony in Eric Bart, "Eyewitness Accounts," or in Vince Crawley, "Fortress Report," MilitaryCity.com, September 11, 2002 (www.militarycity.com/sept11/fortress1.html).

72 Dave McGowan, "September 11, 2001 Revisited: The Series: Act II," Center for an Informed America (www.davesweb.cnchost.com/nwsltr68.html).

73 See, for example, Russell Pickering, Pentagon Research: Lamp Poles (www.pentagonresearch.com/lamps.html).

74 *Debunking*, 67.

75 *The PentaCon: Eyewitnesses Speak, Conspiracy Revealed*
(http://video.google.com/videoplay?docid=4196580169348087802), a
2007 video by the Citizen Investigation Team (CIT), headed by Aldo
Marquis and Craig Ranke (www.thepentacon.com).
76 *The Pentagon Flyover: How They Pulled It Off*
(http://video.google.com/videoplay?docid=-8176286327617173136).
77 See Pandora's Black Box, Chapter 1, *Analysis of American 77 Flight Data*,
and Chapter 2, *Flight of American 77*, at Pilots for 9/11 Truth
(http://pilotsfor911truth.org). These titles, with their references to
"American 77," reflect the position of the NTSB, not Pilots for 9/11
Truth. As Balsamo has said: "The NTSB claims the Flight Data Recorder
is from AA77, but it could really be from any type of aircraft" (e-mail,
January 17, 2007).
78 Scott P. Cook, "September 11, 2001," Cloth Monkey
(www.clothmonkey.com/91101.htm). Although he wrote "missed," he
obviously meant "saw."
79 Patrick Creed and Rick Newman, *Firefight: Inside the Battle to Save the
Pentagon on 9/11* (San Francisco: Presidio Books, 2008), 171–72.
80 Vogel, *The Pentagon*, 450.
81 The distinction between prohibited airspace and merely "restricted
airspace" (which is "closed to civil aircraft at specified times") is stated in
"Pilots Notified of Restricted Airspace; Violators Face Military Action,"
FAA Press Release, September 28, 2001 (http://web.archive.org/web/
20011023082620/www.faa.gov/apa/pr/pr.cfm?id=1415).
82 According to the animation of Flight 77 produced by the NTSB
(http://video.google.com/videoplay?docid+6529691284366443405&q+A
A77+animation&total+4&start+0&num+10&so+0&type+search&plind
ex+0), the downward spiral began at 9:34AM and ended at 9:37:02; see
the discussion at the Pilots for 9/11 Truth website
(http://pilotsfor911truth.org/pentagon.html).
83 See "Judicial Watch September 11 Pentagon Video—2 of 2"
(www.youtube.com/watch?v=TAaP4Z3zls8&eurl=).
84 Rob Balsamo, "Arlington Topography, Obstacles Make American 77 Final
Leg Impossible," Pilots for 9/11 Truth, March 13, 2008
(http://pilotsfor911truth.org/descent_rate031308.html). The calculation
of just over 10 G's is, moreover, based on the assumption that the plane
just barely cleared the VDOT antenna. According to the FDR, as
mentioned earlier, the plane was much higher. So to hit the light poles
and then level off, it would have experienced an even greater
gravitational pull—over 30 G's. The problem created by the needed
descent rate has been articulated by Lt. Col. Jeff Latas, who was a combat
fighter pilot before becoming an airline pilot. What really got his
attention, he has said, was the "descent rate you had to have at the end of
the flight. . . that would have made it practically impossible to hit the
light poles" (www.patriotsquestion911.com/#Latas).
85 Balsamo, "Arlington Topography."

86 Marc Fisher and Don Phillips, "On Flight 77: 'Our Plane Is Being Hijacked,'" *Washington Post*, September 12, 2001 (www.washingtonpost.com/ac2/wp-dyn?pagename=article&node=&contentId=A14365-2001Sep11).

87 "FAA Was Alerted To Sept. 11 Hijacker," CBS News, May 10, 2002 (www.cbsnews.com/stories/2002/05/10/attack/main508656.shtml).

88 Jim Yardley, "A Trainee Noted for Incompetence," *New York Times*, May 4, 2002 (http://newsmine.org/archive/9-11/suspects/flying-skills/pilot-trainee-noted-for-incompetence.txt).

89 "Pilots and Aviation Professional Question the 9/11 Commission Report" (www.patriotsquestion911.com/pilots.html).

90 Quoted in Greg Szymanski, "Former Vietnam Combat and Commercial Pilot Firm Believer 9/11 Was Inside Government Job," *Lewis News*, January 8, 2006 (www.lewisnews.com/article.asp?ID=106623).

91 E-mail from Ralph Omholt, October 27, 2006.

92 Miller, "US Navy 'Top Gun' Pilot Questions 911 Pentagon Story."

93 *Debunking*, 6.

94 Ibid., 6.

95 9/11CR 520n56.

96 9/11CR 242.

97 9/11CR 530n147.

98 9/11CR 531n170.

99 See "August 2001: Hani Hanjour Successfully Takes Certification Flight?" History Commons (www.historycommons.org/timeline.jsp?timeline=complete_911_timeline&the_alleged_9/11_hijackers=haniHanjour). Research librarian Elizabeth Woodworth, by checking the national telephone directory and doing an extensive search using Google, could find no evidence of the existence of a flight instructor named Eddie (or even Eddy) Shalev (e-mail letter of August 23, 2007). And Matthew Everett, one of the contributors to *The Complete 9/11 Timeline*, found no such person by means of a LexisNexis search (e-mail of August 23, 2007). All he turned up was a story by a journalist named Bradley Olson who, having seen the note in *The 9/11 Commission Report* about Congressional Air Charters of Gaithersburg, had called this flight school in 2006. Olson wrote: "A man who answered the phone at Congressional Air Charters of Gaithersburg declined to give his name and said the company no longer gives flight instruction" ("Md. Was among Last Stops for Hijackers," *Baltimore Sun*, September 9, 2006 (www.baltimoresun.com/news/custom/attack/bal-te.md.terrorist09sep09,0,5567459.story).

100 Those with the authority to adjust the official story could, of course, simply claim that the identification of Hanjour as the pilot had been a mistake. Indeed, the seed for such a change may have been planted in a story, published late in 2007 by London's *Sunday Times*, about Louai al-Sakka, a member of al-Qaeda who claimed to have trained some of the 9/11 hijackers. According to al-Sakka's lawyer, the pilot of "the plane that hit

the Pentagon" was really Nawaf al-Hazmi. The authors of this *Sunday Times* story comment: "Although this is at odds with the official account, . . . it is plausible and might answer one of the mysteries of 9/11. The Pentagon plane performed a complex spiral dive into its target. Yet the pilot attributed with flying the plane 'could not fly at all' according to his flight instructors in America. Hazmi, on the other hand, had mixed reviews from his instructors but they did remark on how 'adept' he was on his first flight." See Chris Gourlay and Jonathan Calvert, "Al-Qaeda Kingpin: I Trained 9/11 Hijackers," *Sunday Times*, November 25, 2007 (www.timesonline.co.uk/tol/news/world/europe/article2936761.ece).

101 9/11CR 34.

102 Although technically Kean was the chairman and Hamilton the vice chairman, they had agreed to function as co-chairmen (Philip Shenon, *The Commission: The Uncensored History of the 9/11 Investigation* [New York: Twelve, 2008], 68).

103 WP 259.

104 9/11CR 34.

105 9/11CR 34. Some of the central reports that contradict the 9/11 Commission's account of AA 77 are presented in a video entitled *The Lost Flight: Who Knew What and When about Flight AA 77 on 9/11* (http://video.google.com/videoplay?docid= 7140292755378838617&hl=en).

106 Arlington County, *After-Action Report on the Response to the September 11 Attack on the Pentagon*, 2002 (www.arlingtonva.us/departments/Fire/edu/about/docs/after_report.pdf), C–45.

107 "FAA Communications with NORAD On September 11, 2001: FAA Clarification Memo to 9/11 Independent Commission," May 21, 2003 (www.911truth.org/article.php?story=2004081200421797).

108 9/11 Commission Hearing, May 23, 2003 (www.9-11commission.gov/ archive/hearing2/9-11Commission_Hearing_2003-05-23.htm).

109 9/11CR 24.

110 9/11CR 24.

111 9/11 Commission Hearing, May 23, 2003.

112 "America Remembers: The Skies over America," NBC News, September 11, 2002 (newsmine.org/archive/9-11/air-traffic-controllers-recall-events.txt); also available as a video (www.jonhs.net/911/skies_over_america.htm).

113 Pamela S. Freni, *Ground Stop: An Inside Look at the Federal Aviation Administration on September 11, 2001* (Lincoln, NE: iUniverse, 2003), 59.

114 9/11 Commission Hearing, June 17, 2004 (www.9-11commission.gov/ archive/hearing12/9-11Commission_Hearing_2004-06-17.htm).

115 Ibid.

116 Garth Wade, "Elmira Native Protected Ronald Reagan," *Star-Gazette* (Elmira), June 6, 2006.

117 Quoted in "Spotlight on: Barbara Riggs," President's Council of Cornell

Women, Spring 2006
(http://pccw.alumni.cornell.edu/news/newsletters/spring06/riggs.html).

118 9/11CR 37, 43–44.

119 9/11CR 38, 463n199.

120 Richard A. Clarke, *Against All Enemies: Inside America's War on Terror* (New York: Free Press, 2004).

121 Some of the support for this starting time comes from the fact that Clarke's account corresponds with that of Secretary of Transportation Norman Mineta. According to Clarke, Mineta arrived after the video conference had been going on for several minutes, and Clarke then suggested that Mineta go down to the Presidential Emergency Operations Center (PEOC) to join Vice President Cheney (*Against All Enemies*, 3). Mineta told the 9/11 Commission, as we will see in the text below, that he arrived in the PEOC "at about 9:20." Mineta elsewhere said that he went down there only after having talked with Clarke for "four or five minutes" ("Interview: Norman Mineta: From Internment Camp to the Halls of Congress," Academy of Achievement, June 3, 2006 [www.achievement.org/autodoc/page/min0int-8]). If both Clarke's and Mineta's accounts are roughly accurate, Clarke's conference must have begun by about 9:10.

122 Clarke, *Against All Enemies*, 3.

123 Ibid., 4–5.

124 Ibid., 7.

125 Ibid., 8–9. Rumsfeld claimed that he went down to the attack site and helped the wounded for a few minutes, and there are pictures that support this claim. Clarke's account is not necessarily in conflict with it. If the attack occurred at about 9:32, as will be suggested below, there would have been time for Rumsfeld to get down there and back to the studio by 9:55, and nothing in Clarke's narrative implies that Rumsfeld was seen on the screen during the intervening period.

126 9/11CR 36.

127 See Chapter 6 of my *Contradictions*, "Where Was General Richard Myers?"

128 Barbara Honegger, "The Pentagon Attack Papers," published as an appendix to Jim Marrs, *The Terror Conspiracy: Deception, 9/11, and the Loss of Liberty* (New York: Disinformation Company, 2006), 439–65, at 443. This article is also available online (http://blog.lege.net/content/Seven_Hours_in_September.pdf).

129 Quoted in Barbara Honegger, "Special Operations Policy Expert and Veteran Robert Andrews Gives Distinguished Visiting Guest Lectures at NPS." This interview was conducted on September 4, 2004, and was posted that week on the main NPS (Naval Postgraduate School) website, www.nps.edu, but it is no longer in the archives.

130 Honegger, "The Pentagon Attack Papers."

131 Quoted in Honegger, "Special Operations Policy Expert."

132 Steve Goldstein, "Focus of Training for Terrorist Attacks Has Been Chemical, Biological Warfare," Knight Ridder, September 11, 2001

(http://emperors-clothes.com/9-11backups/sd.htm); quoted in 9/11CROD 160.

133 9/11CROD 161.

134 E-mail from Scoggins, December 20, 2006.

135 This claim was made, for example, in Michael Bronner, "9/11 Live: The NORAD Tapes," *Vanity Fair*, September 2006, 262–85 (www.vanityfair.com/politics/features/2006/08/norad200608), 268. The claim is implicit in the assertion by *Popular Mechanics* that "only 14 fighter jets were on alert in the contiguous 48 states" (*Debunking*, 14).

136 Steve Vogel, "Flights of Vigilance over the Capital; Air Guard on Patrols Since Sept. 11 Attacks," *Washington Post*, April 8, 2002 (www.highbeam.com/DocPrint.aspx?DocId=1P2:342932). The statement is also in Vogel, *The Pentagon*, 445.

137 9/11CR 44.

138 9/11CROD 200–03.

139 Quoted on Patriots Question 9/11 (www.patriotsquestion911.com/#Hellyer).

140 See Jody T. Fahrig, "Davison Army Airfield Hosts Open House," *Pentagram*, May 7, 1999 (http://web.archive.org/web/20030902231146/www.dcmilitary.com/army/p entagram/archives/may7/pt_i5799.html).

141 "Davison US Army Airfield" (http://web.archive.org/web/20010414003708/www.mdw.army.mil/fs–i14.htm).

142 WP 261.

143 D9D 27, 29–30, 80–82, 91–92, and *Contradictions*, Ch. 11, "When Was the Military Alerted about Flight 77?"

144 See *Contradictions*, Chapter 1, and 9/11CR 40. The attempt to combine the 9:58 time for Cheney's arrival with the known facts about what happened in the bunker created a very awkward passage in Stephen F. Hayes's hagiographical biography, *Cheney: The Untold Story of America's Most Powerful and Controversial Vice President* (New York: HarperCollins, 2007). Hayes wrote: "Much of the response by the US government to the attacks was run from the conference room in the Presidential Emergency Operations Center. . . . Cheney consulted with Transportation Secretary Norman Mineta. . . . Mineta spent much of the morning at Cheney's side, scrawling notes on a white legal pad with a blue felt-tip pen. Together with Cheney and Rice, he spent the morning trying to track planes by their tail numbers to determine how many might have been a part of the plot. Eventually, Mineta directed that all aircraft be grounded. . . . At 9:49AM, the Federal Aviation Administration carried out Mineta's order. Cheney took his place at the center of the table. . . . Not long after he sat down, the small group in the PEOC watched as the south tower crumbled. . ." (337–38). So, after suggesting (correctly) that Mineta was by Cheney's side while he tracked planes and then gave the ground-all-planes order, which was carried out

at 9:49, Hayes then suggested (without actually saying it) that Cheney did not arrive until 9:58.

145 See Gregor Holland, "The Mineta Testimony: 9/11 Commission Exposed," 911truthmovement.org, November 1, 2005 (www.911truthmovement.org/archives/2005/11/post.php).

146 See http://video.google.ca/videoplay?docid=-3722436852417384871 and www.911truth.org/article.php?story=20050724164122860.

147 "9/11 Seattle Truth Meets Norm Mineta" (www.youtube.com/v/u-5PKQTUz5o).

148 9/11CR 40 and 446n209.

149 9/11CR 464n209.

150 Aidan Monaghan, "Secret Service: No Records of Cheney's Arrival in the Bunker on 9/11," May 7, 2008 (www.911truth.org/article.php?story=2008050770616110).

151 Clarke, *Against All Enemies*, 2–5.

152 "9/11: Interviews by Peter Jennings," ABC News, September 11, 2002 (s3.amazonaws.com/911timeline/2002/abcnews091102.html).

153 "The Vice President Appears on *Meet the Press* with Tim Russert," MSNBC, September 16, 2001 (www.whitehouse.gov/vicepresident/news-speeches/speeches/vp20010916.html). I have examined this interview more fully in "Tim Russert, Dick Cheney, and 9/11," Information Clearing House, June 17, 2008 (www.informationclearinghouse.info/article20108.htm).

154 9/11CR 40.

155 9/11CR 41.

156 Another apparent lie to cover up Cheney's role involved his activity prior to the first strike on the World Trade Center, which occurred at 8:46AM. Cheney had an appointment with his speechwriter, John McConnell, for 8:30 that morning. And yet McConnell was kept waiting while Cheney met for some 20 minutes—from 8:25 until the strike on the North Tower—with Sean O'Keefe, the deputy director of the Office of Management and Budget, who had been the Pentagon's comptroller and a close confidant of Cheney while the latter was secretary of defense during the administration of George H.W. Bush. Later, however, both Cheney and O'Keefe would claim, incredibly, that they could not recall what they had been discussing. Even Cheney's admiring biographer Stephen Hayes, who reported this episode, seemed incredulous, writing: "O'Keefe spent more than twenty minutes in Cheney's office, discussing a matter that seemed urgent at eight-thirty AM on Tuesday, September 11. In time, neither man would be able to recall what it was that had been so important" (Hayes, *Cheney*, 328).

157 Charles E. Lewis, "What I Heard LAX Security Officials Say During the 9/11 Attacks" (see following note). Clarifying his meaning, Lewis wrote: "'LAX Security' involves the Los Angeles World Police Department, the Los Angeles Police Department, and sometimes the FBI and/or the California Highway Patrol. He also added that LAX Security, of which he

has always had a high opinion, "performed very professionally on 9/11."

158 Lewis, "What I Heard." Lewis had provided me an earlier, anonymous version of this statement, entitled "My Observation of LAX APO Security Events on 9/11," in 2005, based on notes he had written in 2001. This new version was written in May 2008, after Lewis decided to attach his name to it. This revised version has been published at 911Truth.org (www.911truth.org/article.php?story=2008071025531345).

159 I did, however, allow it to be printed as an attachment to a document entitled "The September 11, 2001 Treason Independent Prosecutor Act," which has been posted on the Internet (http://peaceinspace.blogs.com/ 911/2007/04/memorandum_summ.html).

160 E-mail and telephone conversation, May 24, 2008.

161 She made this statement, Lewis reported, on June 8, 2006, while the two of them were discussing solutions to security problems he had observed while working at LAX. (This statement was not mentioned in the earlier version of Lewis's account, of course, because that account was written in 2005, before this conversation occurred.) For those wishing to check out Lewis's account of his employment at LAX, he has given several references, including Captain Larry Gray and Captain LaPonda Fitchpatrick of the LAWAPD (the former and current heads of Security for the LAX AOA); Linda Yoder, the construction inspector for Los Angeles World Airports; James Bryant, the aviation security inspector at LAX; and Stephen J. Pavoggi, the project manager for the Tutor-Saliba Corporation.

162 See note 82.

163 Letter to Congressman Adam Schiff, November 8, 2006, signed by Lt. Col. Karen L. Cook, Office of Legislative Liaison, Department of the Air Force, the Pentagon (available at http://aal77.com/faa/pinnacle_docs.pdf).

164 John King segment, *Anderson Cooper 360°*, September 12, 2007 (http://transcripts.cnn.com/TRANSCRIPTS/0709/12/acd.01.html). The John King segment is available on YouTube (www.youtube.com/ watch?v=h8mGvFzvwFM&watch_response) and elsewhere (http:// anderson-cooper-effects.blogspot.com/2007/09/mystery-plane.html).

165 Ibid.

166 Ibid. Although CNN did not give credit to any researchers for having made this identification, its three-point comparison was remarkably similar to that provided by Mark Gaffney. After learning of the plane's identity from a researcher who goes by the alias "Pinnacle," Gaffney had written in an essay entitled "The 9/11 Mystery Plane": "[T]he still-shot from the docudrama matches an official photo of the E-4B, from a USAF web site. . . . Notice . . . the US flag painted on the vertical stabilizer (i.e., the tail), and the blue stripe and insignia on the fuselage. The clincher, however, is the 'bump' directly behind the bulging 747 cockpit" (Rense.com, April 5, 2007 [www.rense.com/general76/missing.htm]). The "docudrama" to which Gaffney referred is *The Flight that Fought Back*, a made-for-TV movie

that aired on the Discovery Channel in August 2005 (http://dsc.discovery.com/convergence/flight/flight.html). Gaffney had learned from Pinnacle that this film contained a three-second video of the mystery plane, taken by some person near the White House that morning.

167 John King segment, *Anderson Cooper 360°*.

168 See Mark H. Gaffney, "Why Did the World's Most Advanced Electronics Warfare Plane Circle over the White House on 9/11?" *Journal of 9/11 Studies* 13, July 2007 (www.journalof911studies.com/volume/ 200704/911MysteryPlane.pdf), 16–18. The video, entitled "White House Evacuation," is described in note 15 of Gaffney's article. For more details about this episode, see *Contradictions*, Ch. 21, "Did a Military Plane Fly over Washington during the Pentagon Attack?"

169 "Three-Star General May Be Among Pentagon Dead," CNN, September 13, 2001 (http://archives.cnn.com/2001/US/09/13/pentagon.terrorism).

170 Mark Easton, "Aboard the Hijacked Planes," Channel 4 News, September 13, 2001 (http://s3.amazonaws.com/911timeline/2001/channel4news 091301.html).

171 "Terrorism Strikes in the United States in a Massive Attack," CNN, September 11, 2001 (http://edition.cnn.com/TRANSCRIPTS/0109/11/bn.03.html).

172 Goldberg et al., *Pentagon 9/11*, 115–16.

173 In a videotaped, under-oath interview that took place on March 11, 2007, "Barbara Honegger Interviews April Gallop," Gallop incorrectly stated that she was in Wedge 5 (perhaps thinking of Corridor 5, which her office was near). But she correctly stated her room number as 1E517. The twofold fact that this was her room number and that it was in Wedge 2 is confirmed on page 30 of *Pentagon 9/11*, which gives a brief summary of an interview with her from 2001.

174 "Barbara Honegger Interviews April Gallop."

175 Ibid.

176 Ibid. As to why these people have not spoken out, she suspects that it is because they fear reprisals—a fear that would have been increased by their seeing how the Pentagon has retaliated against her, refusing to pay for the various operations she and Elisha need and even blocking outside agencies from doing so. With regard to the blocking, she reported that an American Red Cross employee showed her a fax from a Pentagon official that said: "Do not help April Gallop."

177 Dean E. Murphy, *September 11: An Oral History* (New York: Doubleday, 2002), 212.

178 "Barbara Honegger Interviews April Gallop."

179 See Ralph Omholt, "9-11 and the Impossible: The Pentagon: Part One of an Online Journal of 9-11" (www.physics911.net/omholt.htm). Referring to a photograph of the first fire trucks to the scene, Omholt writes: "There is no suggestion of an aircraft crash and the expected fuel fire—NONE! The firemen should be in aluminum-clad suits, with hand-lines extended

to the building, to "penetrate" the fire . . . . The clue is in the background smoke; indicative of a structural fire, coming from the interior rings."

180 "Barbara Honegger Interviews April Gallop."

181 "Eric Bart's Pentagon Attack Eyewitness Account Compilation," 9-11 Research (http://911research.wtc7.net/pentagon/evidence/witnesses/bart.html).

182 Vogel, *The Pentagon*, 434.

183 Goldberg et al., *Pentagon 9/11*, 31.

184 Having reported this interview in "The Pentagon Attack Papers" without revealing Nielsen's name, Honegger later gave his name to me with permission to use it (e-mail July 4, 2008).

185 "Eric Bart's Pentagon Attack Eyewitness Account Compilation."

186 "The Works of Humankind: A Dispatch by Don Perkal," Timothy McSweeney (www.mcsweeneys.net/2001/09/19perkal.html).

187 Barbara Vobejda, "'Extensive Casualties' in Wake of Pentagon Attack," Washingtonpost.com, September 11, 2001, 4:59PM (www.washingtonpost.com/wp-srv/metro/daily/sep01/attack.html).

188 Honegger, "The Pentagon Attack Papers," 444.

189 Ibid., 440; "Barbara Honegger Interviews April Gallop."

190 Honegger, "The Pentagon Attack Papers," 444.

191 See Vogel, *The Pentagon*, photograph section after page 454.

192 FAA, "Executive Summary Chronology of a Multiple Hijacking Crisis, September 11, 2001," September 17, 2001 (www.gwu.edu/~nsarchiv/NSAEBB/NSAEBB165/faa5.pdf).

193 Alberto Gonzales, Secretary of the Navy Guest Lecture, Naval Postgraduate School, Monterey, California, August 27, 2002; cited in Honegger, "The Pentagon Attack Papers," 440–41.

194 The Smithsonian, while showing the clock from the helipad firehouse frozen at 9:32, adds: "The airplane actually struck the Pentagon at 9:38AM; apparently the clock was six minutes slow" (www.americanhistory.si.edu/september11/collection/record.asp?ID=19). The US Navy website has a clock with the hands at 9:31:40. Unlike the Smithsonian, the Navy does not try to reconcile this clock with the official position, simply saying: "clock frozen at the time of impact" (www.news.navy.mil/view_single.asp?id=2480Pentagonclock_BBC). This information, like most of the other information in this paragraph, was derived from Honegger, "The Pentagon Attack Papers." My use of certain ideas from this article does not, of course, imply agreement with all the ideas in the article.

195 Goldberg et al., *Pentagon 9/11*, 23.

196 Secretary of Defense Rumsfeld, "DOD Acquisition and Logistics Excellence Week Kickoff: Bureaucracy to Battlefield," Department of Defense, September 10, 2001 (www.defenselink.mil/speeches/speech.aspx?speechid=430). This announcement might have resulted in serious questions from Congress and the press, if it had been announced at some other time. But it was

quickly forgotten after the attacks the next morning.

197 Honegger, "The Pentagon Attack Papers," 441.

198 E-mail from Honegger, July 4, 2008.

199 See the Pentagon, "Casualties at the Pentagon: September 11th, 2001" (www.classbrain.com/artfree/publish/article_62.shtml), or Goldberg et al. *Pentagon 9/11*, Appendix A, "List of 9/11 Pentagon Fatalities."

200 Vogel, *The Pentagon*, 429.

201 "The Works of Humankind: A Dispatch by Don Perkal."

202 "Barbara Honegger Interviews April Gallop."

203 "Interview with April Gallop," George Washington's Blog, July 13, 2006 (http://georgewashington.blogspot.com/2006/07/interview-with-april-gallop.html).

204 Lon Rains, "Eyewitness: The Pentagon," *Space News*, June 20, 2005 (www.space.com/news/rains_september11-1.html).

205 David H. Edwards, "'We Saw a Missile Fly into the Pentagon!' An Account of a Personal Experience," 911truth.org, January 27, 2006 (www.911truth.org/article.php?story=20060127195417919).

206 Charles E. Lewis, "What I Heard LAX Security Officials Say During the 9/11 Attacks."

207 E-mail from Meyssan in 2005.

208 See John Judge, "Pentagon and P-56 Preparations and Defenses and the Stand-Down on 9/11," Ratville Times, January 11, 2006 (www.ratical.org/ratville/JFK/JohnJudge/P56A.html).

209 Reported in Paul Sperry, "Why the Pentagon Was So Vulnerable," WorldNetDaily, September 11, 2001 (www.wnd.com/news/article.asp?ARTICLE_ID=24426).

210 Bill Nichols, "Homeland Defense Needs Now 'Grim Reality,'" *USA Today*, September 11, 2001 (www.usatoday.com/news/nation/2001/09/11/security.htm).

211 John Judge, "Pentagon and P-56 Preparations and Defenses and the Stand-Down on 9/11," Ratville Times, January 11, 2006 (www.ratical.org/ratville/JFK/JohnJudge/P56A.html).

212 Steve Vogel, "Survivors Healed, but Not Whole," *Washington Post*, March 11, 2002 (www.washingtonpost.com/ac2/wp-dyn?pagename=article&contentId=A5516-2002Mar10&notFound=true).

213 The basis for the 9:25 time cited in NPH was Don Phillips, "Pentagon Crash Highlights a Radar Gap," *Washington Post*, November 3, 2001 (www.washingtonpost.com/ac2/wp-dyn?pagename=article&node&contentId=A32597-2001Nov2), which said: "The first Dulles controller noticed the fast-moving plane at 9:25AM. Moments later, controllers sounded an alert that an aircraft appeared to be headed directly toward the White House. It later turned and hit the Pentagon." A story the following year said that the report from the Dulles controller about the fast-moving plane was received at Herndon Command Center "just prior to 9:30," which implied that the controller (O'Brien) had seen it prior to that; see Alan Levin, Marilyn Adams, and

Blake Morrison, "Terror Attacks Brought Drastic Decision: Clear the Skies," *USA Today,* September 11, 2002 (www.usatoday.com/news/sept11/2002-08-12-clearskies_x.htm).

214 The note (9/11CR 460n146) merely says: "John Hendershot interview (Dec. 22, 2003).

215 See note 194.

CHAPTER 3: FLIGHT 93: ADDITIONAL EVIDENCE

1 David Maraniss, "September 11, 2001," *Washington Post,* September 16, 2001 (www.washingtonpost.com/ac2/wp-dyn/A38407-2001Sep15).

2 Maraniss, "September 11, 2001."

3 Charles Lane and John Mintz, "Bid to Thwart Hijackers May Have Led to Pa. Crash," *Washington Post,* September 13, 2001 (www.highbeam.com/doc/1P2-459249.html).

4 Jim McKinnon, "13-Minute Call Bonds Her Forever with Hero," *Pittsburgh Post-Gazette,* September 22, 2001 (www.post-gazette.com/headlines/20010922gtenat4p4.asp).

5 Kerry Hall, "Flight Attendant Helped Fight Hijackers," *News & Record* (Greensboro, N.C.), September 21, 2001 (http://webcache.news-record.com/legacy/photo/tradecenter/bradshaw21.htm).

6 9/11CR 11, 29.

7 AT&T spokesperson Alexa Graf said shortly after 9/11: "On land, we have antenna sectors that point in three directions—say north, southwest, and southeast. Those signals are radiating across the land." Insofar as "those signals do go up," that is "due to leakage" (quoted in Betsy Harter, "Final Contact," *Telephony's Wireless Review,* November 1, 2001 [http://wirelessreview.com/ar/wireless_final_contact]). A story in the *Travel Technologist,* published one week after 9/11, said: "[W]ireless communications networks weren't designed for ground-to-air communication. Cellular experts privately admit that they're surprised the calls were able to be placed from the hijacked planes. . . . They speculate that the only reason that the calls went through in the first place is that the aircraft were flying so close to the ground" ("Will They Allow Cell Phones on Planes?" *Travel Technologist,* September 19, 2001 [www.elliott.org/technology/2001/cellpermit.htm]). But, of course, the planes were *not* flying close to the ground when most of the cell phone calls were reportedly made.

8 A.K. Dewdney, "Project Achilles Report: Parts One, Two and Three," Physics 911, April 19, 2003 (www.physics911.net/projectachilles). In his essay, Dewdney applied this language to the likelihood that 13 calls would have been completed. But in an e-mail letter of November 21, 2006, he agreed that it equally applied to the likelihood that 9 calls would have succeeded.

9 Rowland Morgan, *Flight 93 Revealed: What Really Happened on the 9/11 'Let's Roll' Flight?* (New York: Carroll & Graf, 2006), 49–51.

10 The results of Dewdney's twin-engine experiments are reported in Barrie

Zwicker, *Towers of Deception: The Media Cover-Up of 9/11* (Gabriola Island, BC: New Society Publishers, 2006), 375.

11 E-mail from Dewdney, November 21, 2006.

12 A. K. Dewdney, "The Cellphone and Airfone Calls from Flight UA93," Physics 911, June 9, 2003 (http://physics911.net/cellphoneflight93.htm).

13 Dewdney quoted several such statements in his article. More recently, a Delta flight attendant has written on the Pilots for 9/11 Truth website: "I have never seen a cell phone work in flight, although I have seen countless passengers try to find a signal in flight, to no avail. I even tried one myself. . . . No luck. This was one of the things that seemed very suspicious to me. . . . [C]ell phones just don't work in flight, no matter the altitude. . . . [T]he speed at which we travel makes it too difficult for the phones to find a tower to route the call through" (http://z9.invisionfree.com/Pilots_For_Truth/index.php?showtopic=12&st=15).

14 QUALCOMM Press Release, "American Airlines and QUALCOMM Complete Test Flight to Evaluate In-Cabin Mobile Phone Use," July 15, 2004 (www.qualcomm.com/press/releases/2004/040715_aa_testflight.html).

15 Stephen Castle, "Era of In-Flight Mobile Phone Use Begins in Europe," *International Herald Tribune*, April 18, 2008 (www.iht.com/articles/2008/04/18/business/cell.php). Castle wrote: "[L]ast month, Emirates became the first airline to enable in-flight mobile voice services, on an Airbus A340 from Dubai to Casablanca. On April 2, Air France began offering voice calls on one of its jets on a trial basis." Addressing the question of 9/11, Castle said: "[It] is technically possible [for mobile phones to connect to a base station] when a plane is flying below 10,000 feet. That proximity is, for example, what enabled passengers on United Airlines Flight 93, one of four planes hijacked as part of the attacks on the United States on Sept. 11, 2001, to contact emergency officials and family members before it went down in Pennsylvania." However, although this statement implies that several cell phone calls were made from Flight 93, the FBI in 2006 declared, as discussed later in the chapter, that there were only two such calls, which were made after the plane had descended to 5,000 feet. All the other calls from this flight were said to have been made from seat-back phones. Clearly, therefore, Castle—whether deliberately or not—obscured the threat posed by his story to the original official account of 9/11.

16 William M. Arkin, "When Seeing and Hearing Isn't Believing," *Washington Post*, February 1, 1999 (www.washingtonpost.com/wp-srv/national/dotmil/arkin020199.htm).

17 D9D 87–91, 292–97.

18 "[A] member of an FBI Joint Terrorism Task Force testified" that "13 of the terrified passengers and crew members made 35 air phone calls and two cell phone calls" (Greg Gordon, "Prosecutors Play Flight 93 Cockpit Recording," McClatchy Newspapers, KnoxNews.com, April 12, 2006 [www.knoxsingles.com/shns/story.cfm?pk=MOUSSAOUI-04-12-

06&cat=WW]). The person giving this testimony was Detective Sergeant Ray Guidetti of the New Jersey State Police, who had been "assigned to an FBI anti-terrorism task force in Newark" (Richard A. Serrano, "Heroism, Fatalism Aboard Flight 93," *Los Angeles Times*, April 12, 2006 [http://rednecktexan.blogspot.com/2006/04/heroism-fatalism-aboard-flight-93.html]). This story reported, based on Guidetti's testimony: "37 phone calls were made by 13 passengers and flight attendants, most of them using air phones. Two of the calls were from cellphones." (It agreed with Gordon's story, therefore, that Guidetti reported that there were 35 calls from passenger-seat phones and only two from cell phones.) Although the New Jersey State Police website pointed out that "Guidetti was the only non FBI agent selected" to head up the FBI's investigation into the four flights, it did not explain why he, as a police officer, was chosen. It merely said: "Four case agents were selected to lead the investigation. . . , one from each of the cities where a flight that was hijacked originated. DSFC Raymond Guidetti who was assigned to the FBI's Joint Terrorism Task Force (JTTF) was selected as the case agent for flight 93 which originated in Newark" ("Trooper of the Year," New Jersey State Police [www.njsp.org/info/toy00.html]).

19 See United States v. Zacarias Moussaoui, Exhibit Number P200054 (www.vaed.uscourts.gov/notablecases/moussaoui/exhibits/prosecution/flights/P200054.html). This graphics presentation can be more easily viewed in "Detailed Account of Phone Calls from September 11th Flights" at 9-11 Research (http://911research.wtc7.net/planes/evidence/calldetail.html). Although this graphics presentation is not specifically identified as coming from the FBI, this inference is warranted by its agreement with the FBI's oral testimony at the trial, combined with the fact that its information about phone calls from American Airlines is partly identical with an FBI report entitled "American Airlines Airphone Usage," dated September 20, 2001, which was cited by the 9/11 Commission (see note 21).

20 By comparing this graphics presentation with the FBI's oral testimony at the trial (see the two preceding notes), one can see that, unless the graphics presentation specifically designates a call as a cell phone call, it is considered a call from an onboard phone. By looking at the presentation for all four flights, therefore, one can see that the two Flight 93 calls that are designated as cell phone calls—one by Edward Felt and one by CeeCee Lyles—are the only two calls from all four flights that, according to the FBI, were made on cell phones. The graphic showing this for Felt's call is especially hard to access at the government site, but Jim Hoffman has made it readily visible at his site (http://911research.wtc7.net/planes/evidence/calldetail.html).

21 The 9/11 Commission, in discussing the alleged calls from Barbara Olson, referred to an FBI report entitled "American Airlines Airphone Usage," dated September 20, 2001. With regard to Flight 77, this report, the Commission said, had indicated that there were four "connected calls to

unknown numbers." These calls "were at 9:15:34 for 1 minute, 42 seconds; 9:20:15 for 4 minutes, 34 seconds; 9:25:48 for 2 minutes, 34 seconds; and 9:30:56 for 4 minutes, 20 seconds" (9/11CR 455n57). If we then compare this summary with the FBI Report entitled "American Airlines Flight #77 Telephone Calls" that was part of the FBI's report presented at the Moussaoui trial in 2006 (United States v. Zacarias Moussaoui, Exhibit Number P200054 [www.vaed.uscourts.gov/ notablecases/moussaoui/exhibits/prosecution/flights/P200054.html]), we can see that they are identical, except for one trivial difference that was probably simply a typographical error in *The 9/11 Commission Report*. (Whereas the FBI report for the Moussaoui trial had the third call lasting 159 seconds, which would mean 2 minutes and 39 seconds, the 9/11 Commission had it lasting "2 minutes, 34 seconds.") Accordingly, the report on telephone calls submitted to the Moussaoui trial in 2006 was at least partly identical with the FBI report dated September 20, 2001.

22 "Staff Report, August 26, 2004" (www.archives.gov/legislative/research/9-11/staff-report-sept2005.pdf), 45. My thanks to Elias Davidsson of Iceland for informing me of this report.

23 *Contradictions*, 173, quoting 9/11CR 12. I had also interpreted the Commission's statement that way in D9D 88.

24 *Debunking*, 84.

25 See Greg Gordon, "Widow Tells of Poignant Last Calls," *Sacramento Bee*, September 11, 2002 (http://holtz.org/Library/ Social%20Science/History/Atomic%20Age/2000s/Sep11/Burnett%20wid ows%20story.htm), and Deena L. Burnett (with Anthony F. Giombetti), *Fighting Back: Living Beyond Ourselves* (Longwood, Florida: Advantage Inspirational Books, 2006), 61.

26 FBI, "Interview with Deena Lynne Burnett," *9/11 Commission, FBI Source Documents, Chronological, September 11, 2001*, Intelfiles.com, March 14, 2008 (http://intelfiles.egoplex.com:80/2008/03/911-commission-fbi-source-documents.html).

27 In his testimony at the Moussaoui trial, Sergeant Guidetti said: "[A]irphone records indicate that Mr. Burnett made three phone calls. . . . However, Thomas's wife, Deena, reported that there may have been additional cell phone calls made to her" (see "Transcript of Jury Trial"). But Deena Burnett did *not* report cell phone calls *additional* to other calls; she said that all of the calls came from her husband's cell phone.

28 FBI, "Interview with Deena Lynne Burnett."

29 The advertisement for a device called "FoneFaker" says: "Record any call you make, fake your Caller ID and change your voice, all with one service you can use from any phone"; see "Telephone Voice Changers," Brickhouse Security (www.brickhousesecurity.com/telephone-voice-changers.html).

30 David Segal, "A Red Carpet Tragedy: Grief and Glamour an Odd Mix at 'United 93' Debut," *Washington Post*, April 26, 2006 (www.washingtonpost.com/wp-dyn/content/article/2006/04/

26/AR2006042600061.html).

31 Matthew Brown, "Hero's Family Perseveres: As Spotlight Fades, Young Wife Looks Ahead," *Record* (Bergen County, NJ), October 5, 2001 (www.highbeam.com/doc/1P1-47456022.html); Jane Pauley, "No Greater Love: The Passengers and Crew of United Flight 93 Showed Courage and Self-Sacrifice in the Face of Almost Certain Death," *Dateline NBC*, September 11, 2001 (www.msnbc.msn.com/id/14789502/page/0).

32 Longman, *Among the Heroes*, 129–30; Phil Hirschkorn, "More 9/11 Families Testify for Moussaoui," CNN, April 21, 2006 (http://edition.cnn.com/2006/LAW/04/21/moussaoui.families/index.html.

33 *Larry King Live*, CNN, February 18, 2006 (http://transcripts.cnn.com/TRANSCRIPTS/0602/18/lkl.01.html); Longman, *Among the Heroes*, 172.

34 Longman, *Among the Heroes*, 129–30.

35 For Deena Burnett's reconstruction of the calls, see www.tomburnettfoundation.org/tomburnett_transcript.html.

36 Newseum, *Running Toward Danger* (Lanham: Rowman & Littlefield, 2002), 148.

37 Ibid., 149.

38 David McCall, *From Tragedy to Triumph* (Johnstown, Penn.: Noah's Ark, 2002), 25.

39 Dunbar and Reagan, ed., *Debunking*, 90.

40 Debra Erdley, "Crash Debris Found 8 Miles Away," *Pittsburgh Tribune-Review*, September 14, 2001 (www.pittsburghlive.com/x/pittsburghtrib/s_12967.html).

41 Jonathan Silver, "Day of Terror: Outside Tiny Shanksville, a Fourth Deadly Stroke," *Pittsburgh Post-Gazette*, September 12, 2001 (www.post-gazette.com/headlines/20010912crashnat2p2.asp).

42 Erdley, "Crash Debris Found 8 Miles Away"; Bill Heltzel and Tom Gibb, "2 Planes Had No Part in Crash of Flight 93," *Pittsburgh Post-Gazette*, September 16, 2001 (www.post-gazette.com/headlines/20010916otherjetnat5p5.asp); Richard Wallace, "What Did Happen to Flight 93?" *Daily Mirror*, September 12, 2002 (http://911research.wtc7.net/cache/planes/evidence/mirror_whatdidhappen.html).

43 On the remaining fuel, see John O'Callaghan and Daniel Bower, "Study of Autopilot, Navigation Equipment, and Fuel Consumption Activity Based on United Airlines Flight 93 and American Airlines Flight 77 Digital Flight Data Recorder Information," National Transportation Safety Board, February 13, 2002 (www.ntsb.gov/info/autopilot_AA77_UA93_study.pdf). On the lack of contamination, see "Environmental Restoration begins at Somerset Site," WTAE-TV, October 2, 2001 (http://html.thepittsburghchannel.com/pit/news/stories/news-100064120011002-151006.html), and "Latest Somerset Crash Site Findings May Yield Added IDs," *Pittsburgh Post-Gazette*, October 3, 2001

(www.postgazette.com/headlines/20011003crash1003p3.asp).

44 Rob Balsamo, *The Flight of United 93*, Pandora's Black Box, Chapter 3 (available at Pilots for 9/11 Truth).

45 "America Under Attack: FBI and State Police Cordon Off Debris Area Six to Eight Miles from Crater Where Plane Went Down," CNN, September 13, 2001 (http://transcripts.cnn.com/TRANSCRIPTS/0109/13/bn.01.html).

46 Balsamo, *The Flight of United 93*. This film documents other contradictions. One involves the altitude of the plane. Witnesses who agreed with the flight data recorder (FDR) that the plane came from the north disagreed radically about the altitude, saying that the plane was only a few hundred feet high when the FDR had it at several thousand. Also, whereas the impact site suggested that the aircraft was coming down at about 90 degrees, the FDR said that it impacted the ground at a much less steep angle.

47 "Homes, Neighbors Rattled by Crash," *Pittsburgh Tribune-Review*, September 12, 2001 (www.pittsburghlive.com/x/pittsburghtrib/s_12942.html); Robin Acton and Richard Gazarik, "Human Remains Recovered in Somerset," *Pittsburgh Tribune-Review*, September 13, 2001 (www.pittsburghlive.com/x/pittsburghtrib/s_47536.html); Richard Gazarik and Robin Acton, "Black Box Recovered at Shanksville Site," *Pittsburgh Tribune-Review*, September 14, 2001 (www.pittsburghlive.com/x/pittsburghtrib/s_12969.html).

48 Won-Young Kim and Gerald R. Baum, "Seismic Observations during September 11, 2001, Terrorist Attack," Spring 2002 (www.mgs.md.gov/esic/publications/download/911pentagon.pdf).

49 9/11CR 462n168.

50 Kim and Baum, "Seismic Observations."

51 Longman, *Among the Heroes*, 147–154. She repeated her story while being interviewed by Jane Pauley on *Dateline NBC* (see "Lyz Glick's Courage," August 20, 2002 [www.msnbc.msn.com/id/3080114]).

52 9/11CR 34.

53 9/11CR 28–30; see my discussion in 9/11CROD 227–29 or D9D 66–67.

54 9/11 Commission Hearing, May 23, 2003 (www.9-11commission.gov/archive/hearing2/9-11Commission_Hearing_2003-05-23.htm).

55 9/11CR 28–29.

56 Ibid.

57 Leslie Filson, *Air War over America: Sept. 11 Alters Face of Air Defense Mission*, Foreword by Larry K. Arnold (Public Affairs: Tyndall Air Force Base, 2003), 72.

58 "9/11: Interviews by Peter Jennings," ABC News, September 11, 2002 (s3.amazonaws.com/911timeline/2002/abcnews091102.html).

59 William B. Scott, "Pilots Considered Ramming Flight 93," *Aviation Week and Space Technology*, September 9, 2002 (www.aviationweek.com/aw/generic/story_generic.jsp?channel=awst&id=news/aw090971.xml).

60 Michael Bronner, "9/11 Live: The NORAD Tapes," *Vanity Fair*, September 2006, (www.vanityfair.com/politics/features/2006/08/norad200608), 262–85, at 285.

61 Ibid., 282.

62 Richard A. Clarke, *Against All Enemies: Inside America's War on Terror* (New York: Free Press, 2004), 7.

63 "9/11: Interviews by Peter Jennings."

64 9/11CR 40.

65 9/11CR 37, 41–42.

66 Clarke, *Against All Enemies*, 8.

67 "'The Pentagon Goes to War': National Military Command Center," *American Morning with Paula Zahn*, CNN, September 4, 2002 (http://transcripts.cnn.com/TRANSCRIPTS/0209/04/ltm.11.html).

68 "9/11: Interviews by Peter Jennings."

69 Filson, *Air War over America*, 73.

70 Dave Foster, "UST Grad Guides Bombers in War," *Aquin*, December 4, 2002 (www.stthomas.edu/aquin/archive/041202/anaconda.html). For a fuller discussion, see *Contradictions*, Ch. 5, "When Did Cheney Issue Shootdown Authorization?"

71 Wayne Madsen, "Third NSA Source Confirms: Flight 93 Shot Down By Air Force Jet," OpEdNews, April 20, 2008 (www.opednews.com/articles/opedne_wayne_ma_080419_third_nsa_sour ce_con.htm).

72 Charles E. Lewis, "What I Heard LAX Security Officials Say During the 9/11 Attacks."

CHAPTER 4: BUSH AT THE SCHOOL IN SARASOTA: COVER-UP ATTEMPTS

1 "9/11: Interviews by Peter Jennings," ABC News, September 11, 2002 (s3.amazonaws.com/911timeline/2002/abcnews091102.html).

2 Sandra Kay Daniels, "9/11: A Year After/Who We Are Now," *Los Angeles Times*, September 11, 2002 (http://pqasb.pqarchiver.com/latimes/access/171354041.html?dids=17135 4041:171354041&FMT=ABS&FMTS=ABS).

3 Malcolm Balfour, "Tragic Lesson," *New York Post*, September 12, 2002 (http://s3.amazonaws.com/911timeline/2002/nypost091202.html). For these articles by Daniels, I am indebted to Elizabeth Woodworth, "President Bush at the Florida School: New Conflicting Testimonies," 911Blogger.com, July 7, 2007 (www.911blogger.com/node/9847).

4 Jennifer Barrs, "From a Whisper to a Tear," *Tampa Tribune*, September 1, 2002 (http://s3.amazonaws.com/911timeline/2002/ tampatribune090102.html). On the importance of this article, which has become virtually unavailable on the Internet, see Woodworth, "President Bush at the Florida School."

5 Kean and Hamilton, WP, 54.

6 9/11CR 39.

7 For a more complete discussion of the White House's attempt to change this story, see *Contradictions*, Ch. 1, "How Long Did George Bush Remain in the Classroom?"

CHAPTER 5: EVIDENCE OF ADVANCE INFORMATION: THE 9/11 COMMISSION'S TREATMENT

1 Stephen Braun, Bob Drogin, Mark Fineman, Lisa Getter, Greg Krikorian, and Robert J. Lopez, "Haunted by Years of Missed Warnings," *Los Angeles Times*, October 14, 2001 (http://web.archive.org/web/20030812200356/www.latimes.com/news/nati onworld/nation/la-101401warn,0,999276.story).

2 "Report Warned of Suicide Hijackings," CBS News, May 17, 2002 (www.cbsnews.com/stories/2002/05/18/attack/main509488.shtml).

3 "Excerpts from Report on Intelligence Actions and the Sept. 11 Attacks," *New York Times*, July 25, 2003 (www.nytimes.com/2003/07/25/ national/25TTEX.html).

4 Matt Mientka, "Pentagon Medics Trained for Strike," *US Medicine*, October 2001 (www.usmedicine.com/article.cfm?articleID=272&issueID=31).

5 Steven Komarow and Tom Squitieri, "NORAD Had Drills of Jets as Weapons," *USA Today*, April 18, 2004 (www.usatoday.com/ news/washington/2004-04-18-norad_x.htm).

6 Gen. Lance Lord, "A Year Ago, A Lifetime Ago," *The Beam*, September 13, 2002 (www.dcmilitary.com/dcmilitary_archives/ stories/091302/192121.shtml).

7 "President Addresses the Nation in Prime Time Press Conference," White House, April 13, 2004 (www.whitehouse.gov/news/releases/ 2004/04/20040413-20.html).

8 "Bush, Clinton Figures Defend Terrorism Policies," CNN, March 24, 2004 (http://edition.cnn.com/2004/ALLPOLITICS/03/23/911.commission/index. html).

9 9/11 Commission Hearing, April 8, 2004 (www.9-11commission.gov/ archive/hearing9/9-11Commission_Hearing_2004-04-08.pdf).

10 9/11 Commission Hearing, June 17, 2004 (www.9-11commission.gov/ archive/hearing12/9-11Commission_Hearing_2004-06-17.htm).

11 9/11 Commission Hearing, April 13, 2004 (www.9-11commission.gov/ archive/hearing10/9-11Commission_Hearing_2004-04-13.htm).

12 9/11 Commission Hearing, May 23, 2003 (www.9-11commission.gov /archive/hearing2/9-11Commission_Hearing_2003-05-23.htm). Ben-Veniste was referring to Amalgam Virgo, which was held in June 2002 but was being planned in July 2001 (see www.historycommons.org/ context.jsp?item=abefore091101virgo2&scale=0).

13 9/11CR 345.

14 9/11CR 17.

15 9/11CR 31.

16 WP 257.

17 Tom Clancy, *Debt of Honor* (New York: Putnam, 1995).

18 See http://killtown.911review.org/lonegunmen.html.

19 Christian Berthelsen and Scott Winokur, "Suspicious Profits Sit Uncollected; Airline Investors Seem to Be Lying Low," *San Francisco Chronicle*, September 29, 2001 (www.sfgate.com/cgi-bin/article.cgi?file=/chronicle/archive/2001/09/29/MN186128.DTL).

20 Allen M. Poteshman, "Unusual Option Market Activity and the Terrorist Attacks of September 11, 2001," *Journal of Business* 79/4 (July 2006): 1703–26 (www.journals.uchicago.edu/doi/abs/10.1086/503645). Although this article was not formally published until 2006, after the 9/11 Commission had completed its report, it was already available on the Internet early in 2004 and was, in fact, quoted in the notes to NPH (249n71).

21 9/11CR 499n130.

22 See Bruce Falconer, "Blackwater and the Brothers Krongard: How Cookie Crumbled," *Mother Jones*, November 14, 2007 (www.motherjones.com/washington_dispatch/2007/11/Krongard-Blackwater-State-Department-Brother.html), or Scott Horton, "The Cookie Crumbles," *Harper's*, November 15, 2007 (www.harpers.org/archive/2007/11/hbc-90001673).

23 I discussed the Commission's treatment of the put options more extensively in 9/11CROD 52–57. A still fuller discussion has been provided in Paul Zarembka, "Initiation of the 9-11 Operation with Evidence of Insider Trading Beforehand" (47–74) and "Update" (305–14), in Paul Zarembka, ed., *The Hidden History of 9-11*, 2nd ed (New York: Seven Stories, 2008).

CHAPTER 6: CONTINUING OBSTRUCTIONS AND NEW DOUBTS ABOUT HIJACKERS

1 9/11CROD, Chapter 6, "Osama, the bin Ladens, and the Saudi Royal Family."

2 Roy Gutman and John Barry, "Beyond Baghdad: Expanding the Target List," *Newsweek*, August 11, 2002 (http://bulletin.prev01.ninemsn.com.au/article.aspx?id=131723).

3 9/11CROD, 63. This discussion refers to Craig Unger, *House of Bush, House of Saud: The Secret Relationship between the World's Two Most Powerful Dynasties* (New York & London: Scribner, 2004), 255, 264–68.

4 Gerald Posner, *Case Closed: Lee Harvey Oswald and the Assassination of JFK* (New York: Random House, 1993).

5 Gerald Posner, *Why America Slept: The Failure to Prevent 9/11* (New York: Random House, 2003), xi, xii, 35, 44–47, 59, 142, 146, 150, 155, 169, 173, 178.

6 James Risen, *State of War: The Secret History of the CIA and the Bush Administration* (New York: Free Press, 2006), 187.

7 The CIA view is presented in George Tenet, *At the Center of the Storm: My Years at the CIA* (New York: HarperCollins, 2007), 241–51; the FBI view

is presented in Ron Suskind, *The One Percent Doctrine: Deep Inside America's Pursuit of Its Enemies since 9/11* (New York: Simon & Schuster, 2006), 100–01, 111, 115–18. The two views are contrasted in Dan Eggen and Walter Pincus, "FBI, CIA Debate Significance of Terror Suspect; Agencies Also Disagree on Interrogation Methods," *Washington Post*, December 18, 2007 (www.washingtonpost.com/wp-dyn/content/article/2007/12/17/AR2007121702151.html).

8 Gerald Posner, "The CIA's Destroyed Interrogation Tapes and the Saudi–Pakistani 9/11 Connection," Huffington Post, December 7, 2007 (www.huffingtonpost.com/gerald-posner/the-cias-destroyed-inter_b_75850.html).

9 Posner, *Why America Slept*, 190.

10 9/11CR 171.

11 Josh Meyer, "2 Allies Aided Bin Laden, Say Panel Members," *Los Angeles Times*, June 20, 2004 (www.truthout.org/cgi-bin/artman/exec/view.cgi/4/4932).

12 Ibid.

13 9/11CR 272, 540nn86, 88.

14 Amanda Ripley and Maggie Sieger, "The Special Agent," *Time*, December 22, 2002 (www.time.com/time/subscriber/personoftheyear/2002/poyrowley2.html).

15 "Coleen Rowley's Memo to FBI Director Robert Mueller" (www.time.com/time/covers/1101020603/memo.html).

16 9/11CR 540n94.

17 9/11CR xvi.

18 Office of the Inspector General, US Department of Justice, "A Review of the FBI's Handling of Intelligence Information Related to the September 11 Attacks (November 2004)," June 2006 (www.usdoj.gov/oig/special/s0606/final.pdf). Maltbie is referred to as "Martin" in this document.

19 Todd Lightly, "FBI Moves to Fire Outspoken Agent," *Chicago Tribune*, April 22, 2005 (www.washingtonpost.com/wp-dyn/articles/A10381-2005Apr22.html).

20 Todd Lightly, "Beleaguered FBI Agent Gets Job Back," *Chicago Tribune*, October 19, 2005 (www.accessmylibrary.com/coms2/summary_0286-31664084_ITM).

21 9/11CROD 94-101.

22 Sibel Edmonds, "Our Broken System," July 9, 2004 (http://911citizenswatch.org/?p=325).

23 9/11CR 473n25.

24 "Sibel Edmonds Letter to Thomas Kean," Scoop, August 2, 2004 (www.scoop.co.nz/stories/HL0408/S00012.htm); also available as "An Open Letter to the 9/11 Panel," Antiwar.com, August 2, 2004 (http://antiwar.com/edmonds/?articleid=3230).

25 Ibid.

26 National Security Whistleblowers Coalition (www.nswbc.org). This site has

a link to the video of a 2007 speech given by Edmonds (www.blip.tv/file/314908).

27 David Rose, "An Inconvenient Patriot," *Vanity Fair*, September 2005 (www.informationclearinghouse.info/article9774.htm).

28 Christopher Deliso, "'The Stakes Are Too High for Us to Stop Fighting Now': An Interview with Whistleblower Sibel Edmonds," AntiWar.com, August 15, 2005 (www.antiwar.com/deliso/?articleid=6934).

29 Scott Horton, "Cracking the Case: An Interview with Sibel Edmonds," AntiWar.com, August 22, 2005 (www.antiwar.com/orig/horton.php?articleid=7032).

30 David Stout, "Court Turns Down Case of F.B.I. Translator," *New York Times*, November 28, 2005 (www.nytimes.com/2005/11/28/politics/28cnd-scotus.html).

31 Horton, "Cracking the Case."

32 Pen American Center, March 29, 2006 (www.pen.org/viewmedia.php/prmMID/633/prmID/172).

33 Brad Friedman, "Exclusive: FBI Whistleblower Sibel Edmonds Will Now Tell All—and Face Charges if Necessary—to Any Major Television Network That Will Let Her," The Brad Blog, October 29, 2007 (www.bradblog.com/?p=5197).

34 Chris Gourlay and Jonathan Calvert, "Al-Qaeda Kingpin: I Trained 9/11 Hijackers," *Sunday Times*, November 25, 2007 (www.timesonline.co.uk/tol/news/world/europe/article2936761.ece). Al-Sakka (sometimes spelled "Sakra") claimed that one of the hijackers he trained was Satam al-Suqami. This claim is supported by the FBI's "Hijackers Timeline," which was released in 2008, insofar as it reports, as a *Complete 9/11 Timeline* story points out, that al-Suqami's passport showed that he spent much of the period between late 2000 and April 2001 in Turkey (www.historycommons.org/news.jsp?oid=140393703-423). Also, *The Complete 9/11 Timeline* project has compiled evidence suggesting that al-Sakka had become a CIA asset prior to 9/11 ("Late 1999–2000: Alleged CIA Informant Said to Train Six 9/11 Hijackers in Turkey" [www.historycommons.org/searchResults.jsp?searchtext=Sakra&events=on&entities=on&articles=on&topics=on&timelines=on&projects=on&titles=on&descriptions=on&dosearch=on&search=Go]). If so, and if he did indeed train some of the alleged hijackers, then they were trained by a CIA asset.

35 Luke Ryland, "Sibel Edmonds Case: Front Page of the (UK) Papers (Finally)," Let Sibel Edmonds Speak, January 6, 2008 (http://letsibeledmondsspeak.blogspot.com/2008/01/sibel-edmonds-case-front-page-of-uk.html); Ryland's identification seems confirmed by the fact that Edmonds herself included Perle and Feith in the photographs she put up (without names) on her own website under the heading, "Sibel Edmonds' State Secrets Privilege Gallery" (www.justacitizen.com/images/Gallery%20Draft2%20for%20Web.htm).

36 Chris Gourlay, Jonathan Calvert, and Joe Lauria, "For Sale: West's Deadly

Nuclear Secrets," *Sunday Times*, January 6, 2008
(www.timesonline.co.uk/tol/news/world/middle_east/article3137695.ece).
37 Ibid.
38 Justin Raimondo, "Nukes, Spooks, and the Specter of 9/11," AntiWar.com,
January 7, 2008 (http://antiwar.com/justin/?articleid=12166); quoting
Luke Ryland, "Sibel Edmonds Case: Front Page of the (UK) Papers
(Finally)."
39 Chris Floyd, "The Bomb in the Shadows: Proliferation, Corruption and the
Way of the World," Empire Burlesque, January 8, 2008 (www.chris-
floyd.com/Articles/Articles/The_Bomb_in_the_Shadows%3A_Proliferati
on%2C_Corruption_and_the_Way_of_the_World).
40 Dave Lindorff, "Sibel Edmonds, Turkey and the Bomb: A *Real* 9/11 Cover-
Up?" Counterpunch, January 7, 2008
(www.counterpunch.org/lindorff01072008.html).
41 "Worldwide Coverage of the Sibel Edmonds Bombshell," The Brad Blog,
January 8, 2008 (www.bradblog.com/?p=5527).
42 Ibid.
43 The first story was Chris Gourlay, Jonathan Calvert, and Joe Lauria, "FBI
Denies File Exposing Nuclear Secrets Theft," *Sunday Times*, January 20,
2008 (www.timesonline.co.uk/tol/news/world/us_and_americas/
article3216737.ece); the second story was Chris Gourlay, Jonathan
Calvert, and Joe Lauria, "Tip-Off Thwarted Nuclear Spy Ring Probe,"
Sunday Times, January 27, 2008 (www.timesonline.co.uk/tol/news/
world/us_and_americas/article3257725.ece).
44 Gourlay et al., "FBI Denies File Exposing Nuclear Secrets Theft."
45 Gourlay et al., "Tip-Off Thwarted Nuclear Spy Ring Probe."
46 9/11CR 1–5, 238–39.
47 David Bamford, "Hijack 'Suspect' Alive in Morocco," BBC, September 22,
2001 (http://news.bbc.co.uk/1/hi/world/middle_east/1558669.stm).
48 9/11CR 5.
49 "Hijack 'Suspects' Alive and Well," BBC News, September 23, 2001
(http://news.bbc.co.uk/1/hi/world/middle_east/1559151.stm).
50 "Panoply of the Absurd," *Der Spiegel*, September 8, 2003
[www.spiegel.de/international/spiegel/0,1518,265160,00.html]).
51 See Jay Kolar "Update: What We Now Know about the Alleged 9-11
Hijackers," in Zarembka, ed., *The Hidden History of 9-11*, 2nd ed. (New
York: Seven Stories, 2008), 293–304. (The first edition was published by
Elsevier in 2006.)
52 Jody A. Benjamin, "Suspects' Actions Don't Add Up," *South Florida Sun–
Sentinel*, September 16, 2001 (http://web.archive.org/web/
20010916150533/www.sun-sentinel.com/ news/local/southflorida/sfl-
warriors916.story).
53 Dana Canedy with David E. Sanger, "Hijacking Trail Leads FBI to Florida
Flight School," *New York Times*, September 13, 2001
(http://query.nytimes.com/gst/fullpage.html?res=9805E6DC1038F930A25
75AC0A9679C8B63); Barry Klein, Wes Allison, Kathryn Wexler, and

Jeff Testerman, "FBI Seizes Records of Students at Flight Schools," *St. Petersburg Times*, September 13, 2001 (www.sptimes.com/News/091301/Worldandnation/FBI_seizes_records_of.shtml).

54 Joel Achenbach, "'You Never Imagine' A Hijacker Next Door," *Washington Post*, September 16, 2001 (www.washingtonpost.com/ac2/wp-dyn/A38026-2001Sep15?language=printer); Peter Finn, "A Fanatic's Quiet Path to Terror," *Washington Post*, September 22, 2001 (www.washingtonpost.com/ac2/wp-dyn?pagename=article&node=&contentId=A6745-2001Sep21).

55 Carol J. Williams, John-Thor Dahlburg, and H.G. Reza, "Mainly, They Just Waited," *Los Angeles Times*, September 27, 2001 (http://web.archive.org/web/20010927120728/www.latimes.com/news/nationworld/world/la-092701atta.story).

56 John Cloud, "Atta's Odyssey," *Time*, September 30, 2001 (www.time.com/time/printout/0,8816,176917,00.html).

57 Johanna McGeary and David Van Biema, "The New Breed of Terrorist," *Time*, September 24, 2001 (www.time.com/time/covers/1101010924/wplot.html).

58 9/11CR 160. The text says: "When Atta arrived in Germany, he appeared religious, but not fanatically so. This would change. . . ." It is justifiable, therefore, to say that the Commission claimed that Atta had become fanatically religious.

59 9/11CR 253.

60 Kevin Fagan, "Agents of Terror Leave Their Mark on Sin City," *San Francisco Chronicle*, October 4, 2001 (http://sfgate.com/cgi-bin/article.cgi?file=/chronicle/archive/2001/10/04/MN102970.DTL).

61 David Wedge, "Terrorists Partied with Hooker at Hub-Area Hotel," *Boston Herald*, October 10, 2001 (http://s3.amazonaws.com/911timeline/2001/bostonherald101001.html).

62 "Terrorist Stag Parties," *Wall Street Journal*, October 10, 2001 (www.opinionjournal.com/best/?id=95001298).

63 9/11CR 248.

64 *Contradictions*, Ch. 15, "Were Mohamed Atta and the Other Hijackers Devout Muslims?"

65 For details, see ibid.

66 Daniel Hopsicker, *Welcome to Terrorland: Mohamed Atta and the 9-11 Cover-Up in Florida* (Eugene, OR: MadCow Press, 2004), 98, 283.

67 Ibid., 68.

68 "Sander Hicks Interviews Richard Benveniste [sic] on 911," YouTube (http://youtube.com/watch?v=9D8RLot2PW4). This exchange is described, with slightly different wording, in Sander Hicks, "No Easy Answer: Heroin, Al Qaeda and the Florida Flight School," *Long Island Press*, February 26, 2004 (www.mindspace.org/liberation-news-service/archives/000599.html).

69 9/11CR 154.

70 I first became aware of this evidence in Jay Kolar, "What We Now Know

about the Alleged 9-11 Hijackers," in Paul Zarembka, ed., *The Hidden History of 9-11-2001* (Amsterdam: Elsevier, 2006), section 3.

71 9/11CR 1–2.

72 9/11CR 451n1; FBI Director Robert S. Mueller III, "Statement for the Record," Joint Intelligence Committee Inquiry, September 26, 2002 (www.fas.org/irp/congress/2002_hr/092602mueller.html).

73 9/11CR 1–2.

74 Paul Sperry, "Airline Denied Atta Paradise Wedding Suite," WorldNetDaily.com, September 11, 2002 (www.worldnetdaily.com/news/article.asp?ARTICLE_ID=28904).

75 The CNN reporter, Susan Candiotti, said "Logan Airport," but this was obviously a mistake: The US Air flight was the one from Portland to Boston, and it was the flight that the Maine state police would have been in position to confirm.

76 "America Under Attack: How Could It Happen?" CNN, September 12, 2001, 8:00PM (http://transcripts.cnn.com/ TRANSCRIPTS/0109/12/se.60.html).

77 "US Says It Has Identified Hijackers," CNN, September 12, 2001; available at Afghanistan News Center (www.afghanistannewscenter.com/ news/2001/september/sep12aa2001.html).

78 "Two Brothers among Hijackers," CNN, September 13, 2001 (http://english.peopledaily.com.cn/200109/13/eng20010913_80131.html). This story is no longer present on the CNN website.

79 "Hijack Suspect Detained, Cooperating with FBI," CNN, September 13, 2001, 9:03PM (http://transcripts.cnn.com/TRANSCRIPTS/0109/13/ltm.01.html).

80 "Feds Think They've Identified Some Hijackers," CNN, September 13, 2001 (http://edition.cnn.com/2001/US/09/12/investigation.terrorism).

81 Mike Fish, "Fla. Flight Schools May Have Trained Hijackers," CNN, September 14, 2001 (http://archives.cnn.com/2001/US/09/13/flight.schools).

82 "Portland Police Eye Local Ties," Associated Press, *Portsmouth Herald*, September 14, 2001 (http://archive.seacoastonline.com/2001news/9_14maine2.htm).

83 Achenbach, "'You Never Imagine' A Hijacker Next Door."

84 "The Night Before Terror," *Portland Press Herald*, October 5, 2001 (http://pressherald.mainetoday.com/news/attack/011005fbi.shtml).

85 The FBI's cropped photo can be seen online (www.abc.net.au/4corners/atta/resources/photos/gas.htm).

86 The uncropped photo can be seen online (www.rcfp.org/moussaoui/jpg/FO07011-1.jpg) and in Rowland Morgan, *Flight 93 Revealed: What Really Happened on the 9/11 'Let's Roll' Flight?* (New York: Carroll & Graf, 2006), 85, where this discrepancy was evidently first pointed out.

87 "Boston Division Seeks Assistance," FBI press release, October 14, 2001 (www.fbi.gov/pressrel/pressrel01/100401.htm).

88 This affidavit is available at Four Corners: Investigative TV Journalism (www.abc.net.au/4corners/atta/resources/documents/fbiaffidavit3.htm). My thanks to Rowland Morgan for this information.

89 David Hench, "Ticket Agent Haunted by Brush with 9/11 Hijackers," *Portland Press Herald*, March 6, 2005 (www.atca.org/singlenews.asp?item_ID=2493&comm=0).

90 Ibid.

91 Mel Allen, "5 Years after 9/11: Former Portland Ticket Agent Mike Tuohey is Still Haunted by His Meeting with Mohamed Atta," *Yankee*, September 26, 2006 (http://web.archive.org/web/20061126072733/www.yankeemagazine.com/thisissue/features/fiveyears911.php).

92 9/11CR 451n1 (where his name is spelled "Touhey").

93 Graeme Massie, "9/11 Four Years On: I Could Have Stopped Terror Boss Getting on That Plane," *Sunday Mirror*, November 9, 2005 (www.sundaymirror.co.uk/news/sunday/2005/09/11/9-11-four-years-on-i-could-have-stopped-terror-boss-getting-on-that-plane-98487-15955447); *Oprah Winfrey Show*, September 11, 2006 (www.oprah.com/tows/slide/200509/20050912/slide_20050912_103.jhtml).

94 See two blogs by William Beutler on blog, p.i.: "The Oprah Winfrey–9/11 Ticket Agent Suicide Myth?" September 15, 2006, updated January 2007 (www.blogpi.net/the-oprah-winfrey-911-ticket-agent-suicide-myth), and "Myth Busted: Oprah Winfrey and the 9/11 Ticket Agent 'Suicide,'" January 18, 2007 (www.blogpi.net/myth-busted-oprah-winfrey-and-the-911-ticket-agent-suicide).

95 This first FBI list of hijackers appears not to be available anywhere. From the early press reports, however, we can know that it consisted of Mohamed Atta, Adnan Bukhari, Ameer Bukhari, Abdulrahman al-Omari, and Amer Kamfar on Flight 11, the present list of five men on Flight 175, the present list of four men on United 93, and, on Flight 77, someone whose name was transcribed as "Mosear Caned," who was later replaced by Hani Hanjour, plus three of the four other men on the present list (the FBI list two days after 9/11 had only four hijackers on Flight 77 and hence a total of only 18 hijackers; see "FBI: Early Probe Results Show 18 Hijackers Took Part," CNN, September 13, 2001 [http://archives.cnn.com/2001/US/09/13/investigation.terrorism]).

96 These and the other replacements are discussed in Kolar, "What We Now Know about the Alleged 9-11 Hijackers," section 3.

97 For reports that they were originally on the list, see Kevin Cullen and Anthony Shadid, "Hijackers May Have Taken Saudi Identities," *Boston Globe*, September 15, 2001 (www.boston.com/news/packages/underattack/globe_stories/0915/Hijackers_may_have_taken_Saudi_identities+.shtml), and "Saudi Suspects in US Attacks Were Not in U.S.," Islam Online, September 17, 2001 (www.911omissionreport.com/us_apology_to_saudi.html), although it spelled Kamfar's name "Kenfer."

98 "List of Names of 18 Suspected Hijackers," CNN, September 14, 2001, 10:11AM (http://transcripts.cnn.com/

TRANSCRIPTS/0109/14/bn.01.html).

99 "FBI List of Individuals Identified As Suspected Hijackers," CNN, September 14, 2001, 2:00PM (http://archives.cnn.com/2001/US/09/14/fbi.document).

100 "Four Planes, Four Coordinated Teams," *Washington Post*, September 16, 2001 (www.washingtonpost.com/wp-srv/nation/graphics/attack/hijackers.html).

101 The "Hijackers Timeline (Redacted)" has been made available by History Commons (www.historycommons.org/news.jsp?oid=140393703-423).

102 FBI, "Hijackers Timeline (Redacted)," 288 and 296.

103 On Peter Hanson's reported calls, see Karen Gullo and John Solomon, Associated Press, "Experts, US Suspect Osama bin Laden, Accused Architect of World's Worst Terrorist Attacks," September 11, 2001 (http://sfgate.com/today/suspect.shtml), and Kathryn Hanson, "From a Big Sister's Point of View" (www.petehansonandfamily.com/doc/FROM%20A%20BIG%20SISTER.doc); on Brian Sweeney, see David Maraniss, "September 11, 2001," *Washington Post*, September 16, 2001 (www.washingtonpost.com/ac2/wp-dyn/A38407-2001Sep15).

104 9/11CR 5.

105 9/11CR 6.

106 Gail Sheehy, "Stewardess ID'd Hijackers Early, Transcripts Show," *New York Observer*, February 15, 2004 (www.observer.com/node/48805).

107 "Calm Before the Crash: Flight 11 Crew Sent Key Details Before Hitting the Twin Towers," ABC News, July 18, 2002 (http://web.archive.org/web/20020803044627/http://abcnews.go.com/sections/primetime/DailyNews/primetime_flightattendants_020718.html).

108 My discussion of the reported calls by Sweeney and Ong is heavily indebted to Rowland Morgan's treatment of them in a book manuscript tentatively titled "Voices."

109 Eric Lichtblau, in recounting this story in a *Los Angeles Times* article, added: "according to an investigative document compiled by the FBI." He also reported that a spokesman for American Airlines said that they were under orders from the FBI not to discuss the call (Lichtblau, "Aboard Flight 11, a Chilling Voice," *Los Angeles Times*, September 20, 2001 [http://web.archive.org/web/20010929230742/http://latimes.com/news/nationworld/nation/la-092001hijack.story]).

110 See page 2 of "Affidavit and Application for Search Warrant," Four Corners: Investigative TV Journalism (www.abc.net.au/4corners/atta/resources/documents/fbiaffidavit7.htm).

111 Ibid. Woodward and Sweeney are not identified by name in the affidavit, which refers simply to the former as "an employee of American Airlines at Logan" and to the latter as "a flight attendant on AA11." But their names were revealed in the "investigative document compiled by the FBI" to which Eric Lichtblau referred in his *Los Angeles Times* story of September 20, 2001, "Aboard Flight 11, a Chilling Voice."

112 9/11CR 453n32.

113 Gail Sheehy, "9/11 Tapes Reveal Ground Personnel Muffled Attacks," *New York Observer*, June 24, 2004 (www.observer.com/node/49415).

114 Ibid.

115 Ibid.

116 It is also inconceivable that if Wyatt had been repeating Woodward's words into the phone, Woodward would have forgotten to tell Lechner about this.

117 Lichtblau, "Aboard Flight 11, a Chilling Voice."

118 Paul Sperry, "Flight 11 Stewardess' Kin to Sue American Airlines," WorldNetDaily.com, June 19, 2002 (www.wnd.com/news/article.asp?ARTICLE_ID=28012).

119 Ibid.

120 9/11CR 4, 6.

121 Gail Sheehy, "Stewardess ID'd Hijackers Early, Transcripts Show," *New York Observer*, February 15, 2004 (www.observer.com/node/48805).

122 9/11CR 2.

123 The reservation desk's tape recorder would record only the first four minutes of a call. These four minutes can be heard at "Betty Ong's 9/11 Call from Flight 11," YouTube (www.youtube.com/watch?v=icfkIH3j-nk). These four minutes plus only the American Airlines side of the following four minutes can be heard at "Final 8 Minutes of Phone Call from Flight 11 on 9/11," YouTube (www.youtube.com/watch?v=q-Tr0u35Tek&NR=1). A portion of this call was played at the hearing of the 9/11 Commission on January 27, 2004, and transcribed in its minutes (www.9-11commission.gov/archive/hearing7/9-11Commission_Hearing_2004-01-27.htm). This transcription can also be read at American Radio Works (http://americanradioworks.publicradio.org/features/911/ong.html).

124 Scott McCartney and Susan Carey, "American, United Watched and Worked in Horror as Sept. 11 Hijackings Unfolded," *Wall Street Journal*, October 15, 2001 (http://s3.amazonaws.com/911timeline/2001/wallstreetjournal101501.html); Glen Johnson, "Probe Reconstructs Horror, Calculated Attacks on Planes," *Boston Globe*, November 23, 2001 (www.boston.com/news/packages/underattack/news/planes_reconstruction.htm#aa11).

125 Lichtblau, "Aboard Flight 11, a Chilling Voice."

126 See note 123.

127 9/11CR 353n32.

128 This alternative version of the "Ong" transcript has been made available by Intelfiles.com (http://intelfiles.egoplex.com/911COMM-Chapter-1-We-Have-Some-Planes-04.PDF). I am indebted to Elias Davidson for calling it to my attention, and to Elizabeth Woodworth for detailing the differences between it and the other "Ong" transcript. (This transcript is also available at http://intelfiles.egoplex.com:80/2008/03/911-commission-fbi-source-documents.html, but for some reason this version is more heavily redacted.)

129 Another suspicious fact about the "Betty Ong" call, mentioned in

Rowland Morgan's "Voices," is the fact that, instead of calling the flight service department at Logan Airport, which managed her cabin crew, she called a reservations desk in North Carolina, where the employees neither knew her nor were trained to deal with in-flight emergencies.

130 "Ashcroft Says More Attacks May Be Planned," CNN, September 18, 2001 (http://edition.cnn.com/2001/US/09/17/ inv.investigation.terrorism/index.html).

131 Anne Karpf, "Uncle Sam's Lucky Finds," *Guardian*, March 19, 2002 (www.guardian.co.uk/september11/story/0,11209,669961,00.html). This article, like some others, mistakenly said that the passport had Atta's name on it.

132 Susan Ginsburg, senior counsel to the 9/11 Commission, said that "a passer-by picked it up and gave it to a NYPD detective shortly before the World Trade Center towers collapsed"; 9/11 Commission Hearing, January 26, 2004 (www.9-11commission.gov/archive/hearing7/9-11Commission_Hearing_2004-01-26.htm).

133 Sheila MacVicar and Caroline Faraj, "September 11 Hijacker Questioned in January 2001," CNN, August 1, 2002 (http://archives.cnn.com/2002/US/08/01/cia.hijacker/index.html); 9/11 Commission Hearing, January 26, 2004.

134 On the speed, see 9/11CR 14. On the plane's going into the ground, Jere Longman wrote (surely on the basis of a statement by the FBI or the Pentagon): "Traveling at five hundred seventy-five miles an hour, the 757 had inverted and hit the spongy earth at a forty-five-degree angle, tunneling toward a limestone reef at the edge of a reclaimed strip mine. . . . The fuselage accordioned on itself more than thirty feet into the porous, backfilled ground. It was as if a marble had been dropped into water" (*Among the Heroes: United 93 and the Passengers and Crew Who Fought Back* [New York: HarperCollins, 2002], 215).

135 In light of the absurdity of the claims about the passports of al-Suqami and Jarrah, we can safely assume that the ID cards of Majed Moqed, Nawaf al-Hazmi, and Salem al-Hazmi, said to have been discovered at the Pentagon crash site, were also planted. See "9/11 and Terrorist Travel," *9/11 Commission Staff Report* (www.9-11commission.gov/ staff_statements/911_TerrTrav_Monograph.pdf), 27, 42.

136 For a photograph of the bandana, see www.vaed.uscourts.gov/notablecases/moussaoui/exhibits/prosecution/PA0 0111.html, or 9-11 Research, "The Crash of Flight 93" (http://911research.wtc7.net/disinfo/deceptions/flight93.html).

137 Milt Bearden, quoted in Ross Coulthart, "Terrorists Target America," Ninemsn, September 2001 (http://sunday.ninemsn.com.au/sunday/cover_stories/transcript_923.asp). I learned of Bearden's statement in Ian Henshall, *9/11 Revealed: The New Evidence* (New York: Carroll & Graf, 2007), 106.

138 Rowland Morgan and Ian Henshall, *9/11 Revealed: The Unanswered Questions* (New York: Carroll & Graf, 2005), 181.

139 This photo can be seen in Morgan, *Flight 93 Revealed*, 85, and online (www.historycommons.org/context.jsp?item=a553portlandfilmed&scale=0).

140 Associated Press, July 22, 2004 (http://foi.missouri.edu/terrorintelligence/survvideo.html). The photo can be seen in Rowland and Henshall, *9/11 Revealed*, 117–18, along with a typical security video, which has identification data.

141 9/11CR 452n11.

142 Rowland and Henshall, *9/11 Revealed*, 118.

143 9/11CR 2.

144 Quoted in 9/11CR 19.

145 "Summary of Air Traffic Hijack Events: September 11, 2001," FAA, September 17, 2001 (www.gwu.edu/~nsarchiv/NSAEBB/NSAEBB165/faa7.pdf).

146 Frank J. Murray, "Americans Feel Touch of Evil; Fury Spurs Unity," *Washington Times*, September 11, 2002 (http://web.archive.org/web/20020916222620/www.washtimes.com/septe mber11/americans.htm).

147 Clarke, *Against All Enemies*, 13; Tenet, 167–69.

148 "Statement of Robert C. Bonner to the National Commission on Terrorist Attacks upon the United States," January 26, 2004 (www.9-11commission.gov/hearings/hearing7/witness_bonner.htm).

149 9/11 Commission Hearing, January 26, 2004 (http://govinfo.library.unt.edu/911/archive/hearing7/9-11Commission_Hearing_2004-01-26.htm).

150 The flight manifest for AA 11 can be seen at www.cnn.com/SPECIALS/2001/trade.center/victims/AA11.victims.html. The manifests for the other flights can be located by simply changing the relevant part of the URL. The manifest for UA 93, for example, is at www.cnn.com/SPECIALS/2001/trade.center/victims/ua93.victims.html. Attempts to get flight manifests directly from the airlines were futile. For example, when one researcher requested the final flight manifest for Flight 11, American Airlines replied: "At the time of the incidents we released the actual passenger manifests to the appropriate government agencies who in turn released certain information to the media. These lists were published in many major periodicals and are now considered public record. At this time we are not in a position to release further information" (e-mail from Elias Davidsson, September 9, 2004).

151 Terry McDermott, *Perfect Soldiers: The 9/11 Hijackers: Who They Were, Why They Did It* (New York: HarperCollins, 2005), photo section after page 140.

152 This is stated at "Passengers," 911myths.com (http://911myths.com/html/the_passengers.html).

153 The sheer amount of material and the way it is organized make it difficult to determine what all is contained in this evidence. But although discussions on the Internet have often claimed that these manifests were included in the FBI's evidence for the Moussaoui trial, several researchers

looking for them have failed to find them. See Jim Hoffman's discussion at http://911research.wtc7.net/planes/evidence/passengers.html.

154 To view them, see "Passenger Lists," 9-11 Research (http://911research.wtc7.net/planes/evidence/passengers.html#ref9). To download them and/or read cleaned-up versions, see "The Passengers," 911myths.com (http://911myths.com/html/the_passengers.html).

155 "Hijackers Linked to USS Cole Attack? Investigators Have Identified All the Hijackers; Photos to Be Released," CBS News, September 14, 2001 (www.cbsnews.com/stories/2001/09/12/national/main310963.shtml); Elizabeth Neuffer, "Hijack Suspect Lived a Life, or a Lie," *Boston Globe*, September 25, 2001 (http://web.archive.org/web/ 20010925123748/ boston.com/dailyglobe2/268/nation/Hijack_suspect_lived_a_life_or_a_lie+.s html).

156 "Four Planes, Four Coordinated Teams."

157 According to a commercial aviation glossary (www.airodyssey.net/reference/glossary.html), "to squawk" means "to transmit an assigned code via a transponder."

158 Peter Grier, "The Nation Reels," *Christian Science Monitor*, September 12, 2001 (www.csmonitor.com/2001/0912/p1s1-usju.html).

159 "America Under Attack: How Could It Happen?" CNN Live Event, September 12, 2001 (http://transcripts.cnn.com/TRANSCRIPTS/ 0109/12/se.60.html).

160 Ibid.

161 9/11CR 5.

162 Grier, "The Nation Reels."

163 9/11CR 18.

164 Richard A. Serrano, "Heroism, Fatalism Aboard Flight 93," *Los Angeles Times*, April 12, 2006 (http://rednecktexan.blogspot.com/ 2006/04/heroism-fatalism-aboard-flight-93.html).

165 "Silver Blaze" (the entire story), Wikisource (http://en.wikisource.org/wiki/Silver_Blaze).

166 In 2004, A. K. Dewdney wrote: "[T]he basic technology for the remote guidance of aircraft has been on hand for many years" ("Operation Pearl," Physics 9/11 [http://www.physics911.net/pearl]). On October 9, 2001, in fact, an application was filed for a patent on an "anti-hijacking system" that is "responsive to . . . [a] remote override signal to deactivate the pilot's normal flight controls and program the autopilot system to fly the aircraft." Besides allowing "remote personnel [to] assume control of the aircraft," this system has an optional feature that "disables the aircraft's communications equipment, eliminating any chance for [people in the plane to communicate with] people on the ground" (http://patft.uspto.gov/netacgi/nph-Parser?Sect2=PTO1&Sect2= HITOFF&p=1&u=%2Fnetahtml%2FPTO%2Fsearch-bool.html&r=1&f =G&l=50&d=PALL&RefSrch=yes&Query=PN%2F6641087). My thanks to Aidan Monaghan for this second reference.

167 "Lt. Col. Shaffer's Written Testimony," Armed Services Committee, US

House of Representatives, February 15, 2006 (www.abledangerblog.com/2006/02/lt-col-shaffers-written-testimony.html).

168 Ibid.

169 Ibid.

170 "Kean–Hamilton Statement on ABLE DANGER," August 12, 2005 (www.9-11pdp.org/press/2005-08-12_pr.pdf); testimony of Stephen Cambone, undersecretary of defense for intelligence, "Joint Hearing on the Able Danger Program," Subcommittees on Strategic Forces and on Terrorism, Unconventional Threats, and Capabilities, House Armed Services Committee, February 15, 2006 (www.abledangerblog.com/hearing.pdf).

171 Ibid.

172 Representative Curt Weldon (R-Penn.), US House of Representatives, June 27, 2005 (www.fas.org/irp/congress/2005_cr/s062705.html).

173 Douglas Jehl, Philip Shenon, and Eric Schmitt, "4 in 9/11 Plot are Called Tied to Qaeda in '00," *New York Times*, August 9, 2005 (http://query.nytimes.com/gst/fullpage.html?res=9400E0D9173EF93AA3575BC0A9639C8B63&sec=&spon=&pagewanted=all).

174 Mark Zaid, speaking as the attorney for Shaffer (who had been barred from testifying by the Pentagon), said: "It is Lt Col Shaffer's specific recollection that he informed those in attendance, which included several Defense Department personnel, that Able Danger had identified two of the three successful 9/11 cells to include Atta. See "Prepared Statement of Mark S. Zaid". (This statement should not be confused with "Statement of Mark S. Zaid, Partner, Krieger & Zaid" [www.fas.org/irp/congress/2005_hr/shrg109-311.html], which comes from the same hearing, the same day.) See also "Lt. Col. Shaffer's Written Testimony," House Armed Service Committee, February 15, 2006 (www.abledangerblog.com/2006/02/lt-col-shaffers-written-testimony.html).

175 "Lt. Col. Shaffer's Written Testimony."

176 Kimberly Hefling, "'Able Danger' Officer's Clearance Revoked," Associated Press, September 30, 2005 (http://tvnewslies.org/phpbb/viewtopic.php?t=2283&view=next&sid=a8f3f80f9f7a568e3eb86f08575fff10); "Prepared Statement of Mark S. Zaid"; "Lt. Col. Shaffer's Written Testimony."

177 *New York Times* reporter Philip Shenon, who had been assigned to cover the 9/11 Commission, co-authored an article the following year that said: "In a final report released last summer called the authoritative history of the attacks, the commission. . . made no mention of the secret program or the possibility that a government agency had detected Mr. Atta's terrorist activities before Sept. 11" (Philip Shenon and Douglas Jehl, "9/11 Panel Seeks Inquiry on New Atta Report," *New York Times*, August 10, 2005 [www.nytimes.com/2005/08/10/politics/10intel.html?_r=1&th=&emc=th&pagewanted=print&oref=slogin]).

178 "Lt. Col. Shaffer's Written Testimony."

179 Keith Phucas, "Missed Chance on Way to 9/11," *Times Herald*

(Norristown, PA), June 19, 2005 (www.topdog08.com/2005/08/
index.html [scroll down]).

180 Curt Weldon, Address to the House, June 27, 2005
(www.fas.org/irp/congress/2005_cr/s062705.html).

181 "Weldon Letter on 'Able Danger,'" *Fox News*, August 11, 2005
(www.foxnews.com/story/0,2933,165408,00.html).

182 Douglas Jehl, Philip Shenon, and Eric Schmitt, "4 in 9/11 Plot Are Called
Tied to Qaeda in '00," *New York Times*, August 9, 2005
(http://query.nytimes.com/gst/fullpage.html?res=9400E0D9173EF93AA35
75BC0A9639C8B63&sec=&spon=&pagewanted=all); Philip Shenon
and Douglas Jehl, "9/11 Panel Seeks Inquiry on New Atta Report," *New
York Times*, August 10, 2005 (www.nytimes.com/2005/08/10/politics/
10intel.html?_r=1&th=&emc=th&pagewanted=print&oref=slogin);
Douglas Jehl and Philip Shenon, "9/11 Commission's Staff Rejected
Report on Early Identification of Chief Hijacker," *New York Times*, August
11, 2005 (www.nytimes.com/2005/08/11/politics/
11intel.html?ex=1281412800&en=3c4c0f2346a58391&ei=5090&partner
=rssuserland&emc=rss).

183 "Kean–Hamilton Statement on ABLE DANGER," August 12, 2005
(www.9-11pdp.org/press/2005-08-12_pr.pdf); Douglas Jehl, "9/11 Panel
Explains Move on Intelligence Unit," *New York Times*, August 13, 2005
(www.nytimes.com/2005/08/13/politics/13intel.html?ex=1281585600&en
=8aebe6bed227e33f&ei=5090&partner=rssuserland&emc=rss).

184 Philip Shenon, "Officer Says Pentagon Barred Sharing Pre-9/11 Qaeda
Data with F.B.I.," *New York Times*, August 16, 2005
(www.nytimes.com/2005/08/16/politics/16cnd-intel.html?_
r=1&hp&ex=1124251200&en=0a9cf97378831bba&ei=5094&partner=h
omepage&oref=slogin); Keith Phucas, "'Able Danger' Source Goes
Public," *Norristown Times Herald*, August 17, 2005
(www.topdog08.com/2005/08/index.html); Fox News, "Agent Defends
Military Unit's Data on 9/11 Hijackers," August 17, 2005
(www.foxnews.com/story/0,2933,165948,00.html).

185 A fourth reason given by Kean and Hamilton for ignoring the Able
Danger operation is that it "did not turn out to be historically significant"
("Kean–Hamilton Statement on ABLE DANGER"). Although this was a
less important claim, it evoked much comment. For example, former FBI
Director Louis Freeh, saying that "[t]he Able Danger intelligence, if
confirmed, is undoubtedly the most relevant fact of the entire post-9/11
inquiry," called the Commission's claim "astounding" ("An Incomplete
Investigation: Why Did the 9/11 Commission Ignore 'Able Danger'?" *Wall
Street Journal*, November 17, 2005
[www.opinionjournal.com/extra/?id=110007559]). Col. Shaffer said:
"[T]hey [the Commissioners] never did an adequate investigation of the
issue. . . . Therefore, they can't make that judgment" ("Joint Hearing on
the Able Danger Program," Subcommittees on Strategic Forces and on
Terrorism, Unconventional Threats, and Capabilities, House Armed

Services Committee, February 15, 2006
[www.abledangerblog.com/hearing.pdf]).

186 "Kean–Hamilton Statement on ABLE DANGER," August 12, 2005 (www.9-11pdp.org/press/2005-08-12_pr.pdf).

187 Phucas, "'Able Danger' Source Goes Public." I would add that it seems very unlikely that, during the 75 minutes that this meeting had lasted, Shaffer would not have mentioned this all-important fact.

188 Fox News, "Agent Defends Military Unit's Data on 9/11 Hijackers."

189 "Kean–Hamilton Statement on ABLE DANGER."

190 Jehl and Shenon, "9/11 Commission's Staff Rejected Report on Early Identification of Chief Hijacker."

191 I used the term "suggested" because Shaffer's attorney, Mark Zaid, said: "At no time did Able Danger identify Mohammed Atta as being physically present in the United States," adding that it claimed only that he had been identified as having "associational links" with the Brooklyn al-Qaeda cell ("Prepared Statement of Mark S. Zaid"). Zaid, however, might not have made that defensive remark if he had been aware of the evidence that Atta had indeed been physically present.

192 "The Night before Terror," *Portland Press Herald Report*, October 5, 2001 (http://web.archive.org/web/20040404001010/www.portland.com/news/att ack/011005fbi.shtml).

193 Barbara Walsh, "Residents Sure They Had Seen Hijackers," *Maine Sunday Telegram*, September 30, 2001.

194 Pat Milton, "Investigator: Atta Visited New York," Associated Press, December 8, 2001 (http://multimedia.belointeractive.com/ attack/investigation/1208atta.html).

195 Brian Ross, "Face to Face with a Terrorist: Government Worker Recalls Mohamed Atta Seeking Funds Before Sept. 11," ABC News, June 6, 2002 (http://web.archive.org/web/20020725114958/http://abcnews.go.com/secti ons/wnt/DailyNews/ross_bryant020606.html).

196 FBI Director Robert S. Mueller III, "Statement for the Record," Joint Intelligence Committee Inquiry, September 26, 2002 (www.fas.org/irp/congress/2002_hr/092602mueller.html).

197 Philip Shenon, "Naval Officer Says Atta's Identity Known Pre-9/11: Captain is Second Military Man to Say Terrorist Was Named," *New York Times*, August 23, 2005 (www.nytimes.com/2005/08/22/politics/23cnd-intel.html?_r=1&ex=1125374400&en=a7d75762bbb6ead1&ei=5070&e mc=eta1&oref=slogin).

198 Ibid.

199 Ibid.

200 See Erik Kleinsmith's testimony before the Senate Judiciary Committee, September 21, 2005 (http://patriotsquestion911.com/#Kleinsmith). In 1998, Christopher Westphal, the CEO of Visual Analytics, co-authored *Data Mining Solutions* (www.wiley.com/WileyCDA/WileyTitle/productCd-0471253847.html).

201 Associated Press, "More Recall Atta ID'd before 9/11," September 1, 2005

(www.msnbc.msn.com/id/9163145); Thom Shanker, "Terrorist Known Before 9/11, More Say," *New York Times*, September 2, 2005 (www.nytimes.com/2005/09/02/politics/02intel.html).

202 Devlin Barrett, "Panel Rejects Assertion US Knew of Atta before Sept. 11," Associated Press, September 15, 2005 (www.boston.com/news/nation/washington/articles/2005/09/15/panel_rejects_assertion_us_knew_of_atta_before_sept_11).

203 In his testimony to the Senate Judiciary Hearing on Able Danger, former Army Major Erik Kleinsmith, who had been chief of intelligence for LIWA, testified that in the spring of 2000, he was "forced to destroy all the data, charts, and other analytical products that we had not already passed on to SOCOM related to Able Danger" (http://judiciary.senate.gov/testimony.cfm?id=1606&wit_id=4669). Also, Anthony Shaffer said he was told that all of his documents were destroyed in 2004 ("Lt. Col. Shaffer's Written Testimony").

204 CBS News, "Military Bars 9/11 Intel Testimony," September 21, 2005 (www.cbsnews.com/stories/2005/09/21/terror/main871800.shtml).

205 "Able Danger and Intelligence Information Sharing," Hearing before the Committee on the Judiciary, United States Senate, September 21, 2005 (www.fas.org/irp/congress/2005_hr/shrg109-311.html). Kleinsmith's testimony is also at Patriots Question 9/11 (http://patriotsquestion911.com/#Kleinsmith).

206 Douglas Jehl, "Senators Accuse Pentagon of Obstructing Inquiry on Sept. 11 Plot," *New York Times*, September 22, 2005 (www.nytimes.com/2005/09/22/politics/22intel.html?ex=1285041600&en=be75f65b369fa799&ei=5090&partner=rssuserland&emc=rss).

207 "Weldon Secures House Majority Signing Letter to Rumsfeld Calling for Lift of Gag on Able Danger," November 18, 2005 (http://911citizenswatch.org/?p=725).

208 James Rosen, "Able Danger Hearing Sets Intelligence Officers at Odds," *News & Observer*, February 16, 2006 (www.newsobserver.com/114/story/400682.html).

209 Rosen, "Able Danger Hearing." Another story reported that, just before the hearing, Weldon had reported "13 hits on Mohamed Atta" (Sherrie Gossett, "'Able Danger' Identified 9/11 Hijacker 13 Times," CNSNews.com, February 15, 2006 [www.cnsnews.com/news/viewstory.asp?Page=%5CNation%5Carchive%5C200602%5CNAT20060215d.html]). This, however, was a misunderstanding. Weldon had reported 5 hits on Mohammed Atef (see Weldon's statement after Stephen Cambone's testimony in "Joint Hearing on the Able Danger Program").

210 Ibid.

211 See note 214.

212 "Joint Hearing on the Able Danger Program," Subcommittees on Strategic Forces and on Terrorism, Unconventional Threats, and Capabilities, House Armed Services Committee, February 15, 2006 (www.abledangerblog.com/hearing.pdf).

213 Ibid.

214 Thomas F. Gimble, Acting Inspector General, "Alleged Misconduct by Senior DOD Officials Concerning the Able Danger Program and Lieutenant Colonel Anthony A. Shaffer, US Army Reserve," September 18, 2006 (www.dodig.mil/fo/foia/ERR/r_H05L97905217-PWH.pdf). I cite the pagination of this version of this document, because it is the original and best-known version. Unfortunately, however, it can neither be printed nor searched. A searchable and printable version does exist (www.dodig.mil/fo/foia/ERR/r_H05L97905217-PWH.pdf), but it has different pagination. A third version is valuable in having clearer graphics, although it is devoid of page numbers (http://cryptome.org/able-danger-ig.htm).

215 The spelling used by Atta himself was "Mohamed." The *New York Times*, to its credit, issued a correction, which was appended to Philip Shenon and Douglas Jehl's article of August 10, 2005. The correction said "An article on Saturday . . . misspelled [Atta's] given name. (The error was repeated in articles last Tuesday, Wednesday and Thursday.) He is Mohamed Atta, not Mohammed."

216 As the two instances of "sic" indicate, this is a carelessly written document. Its foreword, for example, is called its "forward."

217 Weldon, "Able Danger Failure," Address to the House, October 19, 2005 (www.fas.org/irp/congress/2005_cr/weldon101905.html).

218 "Weldon Rejects DOD Report on Able Danger & Harassment of Military Officer" (www.fas.org/irp/news/2006/09/weldon092106.html).

219 See, for example, Josh White, "Hijackers Were Not Identified before 9/11, Investigation Says," *Washington Post*, September 22, 2006 (www.washingtonpost.com/wp-dyn/content/article/2006/09/21/AR2006092101831.html).

220 See "Principle Deputy Inspector General, Department of Defense: Thomas F. Gimble" (www.dodig.osd.mil/BIOs/gimble_bio.html).

221 "'Able Danger' Could Rewrite History," Fox News, August 12, 2005 (www.foxnews.com/story/0,2933,165414,00.html).

222 Jehl and Shenon, "9/11 Commission's Staff Rejected Report on Early Identification of Chief Hijacker."

223 In the report as published, the names of Phillpott and the other Able Danger team members except Anthony Shaffer are blocked out. I have restored them for easier reading.

224 "Alleged Misconduct," 17.

225 Ibid., 3.

226 Ibid., 3. I wish to express my indebtedness at this point to Alex Constantine, whose critique of Gimble's report emphasized the importance of his focus on Figure 1 ("The Able Danger 'Investigation' Was a Simple but Slick Piece of Prestidigitation, A Psyop," 911review.org [http://911review.org/Alex/Able_Danger_9-11.html]).

227 "Alleged Misconduct," 22. Gimble's tendency to discredit every claim that contradicts the official story is illustrated here by his insertion of the word

"allegedly" in a sentence that was supposed to be paraphrasing Preisser's statement. She certainly would not have said, "One of the charts allegedly contained a photograph of Atta."

228 Ibid., 17.

229 Ibid., 18.

230 Ibid., 18.

231 Ibid., 18.

232 Ibid., 26n19.

233 Ibid., 35.

234 Ibid., 30.

235 Ibid., 23.

236 Ibid., 37.

237 Ibid., 55.

238 Attorney Stanley G. Hilton, Senator Bob Dole's former chief of staff, claimed in 2004 to have documents to support this suspicion, saying: "My office was broken into about six months ago. The file cabinets—it was obvious they had been rifled through. Files were stolen—files dealing with this particular case and particularly with the documents I had regarding the fact that . . . some of these hijackers, at least some of them, were on the payroll of the US government as undercover FBI, CIA, double agents. They are spying on Arab groups in the US. . . [A]ll this led up to the effect that . . . the entity . . . called al-Qaeda is directly linked to George Bush. And all this stuff was stolen. Fortunately, I had copies." I have quoted this, while improving the punctuation, from a radio interview transcription contained in Thomas Buyea, "Government Insider Says Bush Authorized 911 Attacks," Rense.com, September 17, 2004 (www.rense.com/general57/aale.htm).

Chapter 7: Motives of US Officials: The Silence of the 9/11 Commission

1 9/11CR 203.

2 9/11CR 11, 203, 337.

3 Zbigniew Brzezinski, *The Grand Chessboard: American Primacy and Its Geostrategic Imperatives* (New York: Basic Books, 1997).

4 See Ahmed Rashid, *Taliban: Militant Islam, Oil and Fundamentalism in Central Asia* (New Haven: Yale University Press, 2001), 145. Rashid first used this name in "The New Great Game: The Battle for Central Asia's Oil," *Far Eastern Economic Review*, April 10, 1997. He also used it for Part 3 of *Taliban*. Chalmers Johnson, in *The Sorrows of Empire: Militarism, Secrecy, and the End of the Republic* (New York: Metropolitan Books, 2004), refers to Rashid as "the preeminent authority on the politics of Central Asia" (179).

5 Rashid, *Taliban*, Chs. 12 (1994–96) and 13 (1997–99).

6 9/11CR 111.

7 George Arney, "US 'Planned Attack on Taleban,'" BBC News, September

18, 2001 (http://news.bbc.co.uk/2/hi/south_asia/1550366.stm).

8 9/11CR 206.

9 Johnson, *The Sorrows of Empire*, 178–79.

10 *The Frontier Post*, October 10, 2001, cited in Nafeez Mosaddeq Ahmed, *The War on Freedom: How and Why America was Attacked September 11, 2001* (Joshua Tree, Calif.: Tree of Life, 2002), 227.

11 Johnson, *The Sorrows of Empire*, 182–83.

12 9/11CR 334–36.

13 9/11CR 66.

14 "Panel Finds No Qaeda-Iraq Tie," *New York Times*, June 17, 2004 (http://query.nytimes.com/gst/fullpage.html?res=9C05E1DE1639F934A25 755C0A9629C8B63). Cheney's comment was quoted in David E. Sanger and Robin Toner, "Bush and Cheney Talk Strongly of Qaeda Links with Hussein," *New York Times*, June 18, 2004 (www.nytimes.com/2004/06/18/politics/18DEBA.html?ex=1199077200& en=74f601fe50125c89&ei=5070).

15 William Safire, "The Zelikow Report," *New York Times*, June 21, 2004 (http://query.nytimes.com/gst/fullpage.html?res=9E05EFDA1239F932A15 755C0A9629C8B63); Joe Conason, "9/11 Panel Becomes Cheney's Nightmare," *New York Observer*, June 27, 2004 (www.observer.com/node/49431).

16 9/11CR 335.

17 "Bush Sought 'Way' To Invade Iraq? O'Neill Tells 60 Minutes Iraq Was 'Topic A' 8 Months Before 9-11," *60 Minutes*, CBS News, January 9, 2004 (www.cbsnews.com/stories/2004/01/09/60minutes/main592330.shtml).

18 Richard Clarke, *Against All Enemies: Inside America's War on Terror* (New York: Free Press, 2004), 264.

19 Ron Suskind, *The Price of Loyalty: George W. Bush, the White House, and the Education of Paul O'Neill* (New York: Simon & Schuster, 2004), 96. For the document and the map, see "Cheney Energy Task Force Documents Feature Map of Iraqi Oilfields," Judicial Watch, July 17, 2003 (www.judicialwatch.org/iraqi-oilfield-pr.shtml).

20 Paul D. Wolfowitz and Zalmay M. Khalilzad, "Saddam Must Go," *Weekly Standard*, December 1997.

21 This letter, dated January 26, 1998, is available at the Project for the New American Century (www.newamericancentury.org/iraqclintonletter.htm).

22 *Rebuilding America's Defenses*, Project for the New American Century, September, 2000 (www.newamericancentury.org/RebuildingAmericasDefenses.pdf), 14.

23 Christine Spolar, "14 'Enduring Bases' Set in Iraq; Long-Term Military Presence Planned," *Chicago Tribune*, March 23, 2004 (www.globalsecurity.org/org/news/2004/040323-enduring-bases.htm). For more recent developments, which include the construction of four or more enormous (15–20 square-mile) bases, each of which is costing many billions of dollars, see Tom Engelhardt, "Can You Say 'Permanent Bases'?"

TomDispatch.com, February 14, 2006 (www.tomdispatch.com/ index.mhtml?pid=59774). For all bases, see "Iraq Facilities," GlobalSecurity.org (www.globalsecurity.org/military/facility/iraq.htm).

24 David Manning, "The Secret Downing Street Memo: Secret and Strictly Personal—UK Eyes Only," *Sunday Times*, May 1, 2005 (www.timesonline.co.uk/article/0,,2087-1593607,00.html). For discussion, see Ray McGovern, "Proof the Fix Was In," Antiwar.com, May 5, 2005 (www.antiwar.com/mcgovern/index.php?articleid=5844), or Greg Palast, "Impeachment Time: 'Facts Were Fixed,'" May 5, 2005 (www.gregpalast.com/impeachment-time-facts-were-fixed).

25 See, for example, John W. Dean, "Missing Weapons of Mass Destruction: Is Lying about the Reason for War an Impeachable Offense?" FindLaw.com, June 6, 2003 (http://writ.news.findlaw.com/dean/20030606.html); "Lies: Weapons of Mass Deception," Not in Our Name, June 9, 2003 (www.notinourname.net/war/wmd_text.htm); and "Buying the War," *Bill Moyers Journal*, PBS, April 25, 2007 (www.pbs.org/moyers/journal/btw/transcript1.html), which focuses on three Knight Ridder reporters who tried to alert the world.

26 9/11CR 47.

27 Bob Woodward, *Bush at War* (New York: Simon & Schuster, 2002), 32; "Secretary Rumsfeld Interview with the New York Times," *New York Times*, October 12, 2001 (www.defenselink.mil/transcripts/transcript.aspx?transcriptid=2097). Two days after 9/11, Bush said: "[T]hrough the tears of sadness I see an opportunity" ("September 11, 2001: Attack on America: Remarks by the President in Telephone Conversation with New York Mayor Giuliani and New York Governor Pataki 11:00AM EDT; September 13, 2001" [www.yale.edu/lawweb/avalon/sept_11/president_009.html]). Condoleezza Rice reportedly told senior members of the National Security Council: "[T]hink about 'how do you capitalize on these opportunities' to fundamentally change American doctrine, and the shape of the world, in the wake of September 11th" (Nicholas Lemann, "The Next World Order: The Bush Administration May Have a Brand-New Doctrine of Power," *New Yorker*, April 1, 2002 [www.newyorker.com/fact/content/articles/020401fa_FACT1]).

28 Roy Gutman and John Barry, "Beyond Baghdad: Expanding the Target List," *Newsweek*, August 14, 2002 (http://bulletin.prev01.ninemsn.com.au/article.aspx?id=131723).

29 Wesley Clark reported this conversation in *Winning Modern Wars: Iraq, Terrorism, and the American Empire* (New York: Public Affairs, 2003), 120, 130. He then repeated it in his later book, *A Time to Lead: For Duty, Honor and Country* (New York: Palgrave Macmillan, 2007), 231. Although in this later book, he mentioned only Iraq, Syria, and Iran, he referred to the other countries during several interviews, including one on *Democracy Now!* March 2, 2007, "Gen. Wesley Clark Weighs Presidential Bid: 'I Think about It Everyday'" (www.democracynow.org/

article.pl?sid=07/03/02/1440234). For more details, see Joe Conason, "Seven Countries in Five Years," Salon.com, October 12, 2007 (www.salon.com/opinion/conason/2007/10/12/wesley_clark).

30 See Gareth Porter, "Yes, the Pentagon Did Want to Hit Iran," *Asia Times*, May 7, 2008 (www.atimes.com/atimes/Middle_East/JE07Ak01.html). As Porter reports, Rumsfeld's letter is discussed in Douglas J. Feith, *War and Decision: Inside the Pentagon at the Dawn of the War on Terrorism* (New York: HarperCollins, 2008). Although this book blocked out the names of all the countries on this list except Iraq, Feith said, in response to Porter's question as to which of the other names on Clark's list were included in Rumsfeld's paper, "All of them."

31 Thomas E. Hicks, "Briefing Depicted Saudis as Enemies," *Washington Post*, August 6, 2002 (www.washingtonpost.com/ac2/wp-dyn?pagename =article&node=&contentId=A47913-2002Aug5&notFound=true); Jack Shafer, "The PowerPoint That Rocked the Pentagon: The Larouchie Defector Who's Advising the Defense Establishment on Saudi Arabia," Slate.com, August 7, 2002 (http://slate.msn.com/?id=2069119).

32 Michael A. Ledeen, *The War Against the Terror Masters: Why It Happened. Where We Are Now. How We'll Win* (New York: St. Martin's Griffin, 2003), 159.

33 See "If 9/11 Was An Inside Job, the Hijackers Would Have been IRAQI," George Washington's Blog, May 30, 2008 (http://georgewashington2. blogspot.com/2008/05/if-911-was-inside-job-hijackers-would.html).

34 9/11CROD 121.

35 An examination of *The 9/11 Commission Report* shows that Rumsfeld is mentioned in 53 paragraphs, Myers in 18, and Eberhart in 8. Many of these places cite interviews with them as sources of information. None of them reflect questions implying that any of their statements might have been less than fully truthful.

36 "9/11 and Prior False-Flag Operations," Ch. 1 of *Christian Faith and the Truth behind 9/11: A Call to Reflection and Action* (Louisville: Westminster John Knox, 2006); "False-Flag Operations, 9/11, and the New Rome: A Christian Perspective," in Kevin Barrett, John B. Cobb Jr., and Sandra Lubarsky, eds., *9/11 and American Empire: Christians, Jews, and Muslims Speak Out* (Northampton: Olive Branch, 2007).

Chapter 8: 9/11 Commission Falsehoods about Bin Laden, al-Qaeda, Pakistanis, and Saudis

1 Gary Berntsen with Ralph Pezzullo, *Jawbreaker: The Attack on Bin Laden and Al-Qaeda* (New York: Three Rivers, 2005), 277, 290.

2 Ibid., 290, 299, 305, 307, 314.

3 Ibid., 275, 280, 290.

4 Ibid., 291.

5 Ibid., 297.

6 Ibid., 276–77, 315.

7 "Most Wanted Terrorists: Usama bin Laden," Federal Bureau of Investigation (www.fbi.gov/wanted/terrorists/terbinladen.htm). It says: "Usama Bin Laden is wanted in connection with the August 7, 1998, bombings of the United States Embassies in Dar es Salaam, Tanzania, and Nairobi, Kenya. These attacks killed over 200 people. In addition, Bin Laden is a suspect in other terrorist attacks throughout the world." The same statement is on the Usama bin Laden page of the FBI's "Ten Most Wanted Fugitives" website (www.fbi.gov/wanted/topten/fugitives/laden.htm).

8 Ed Haas, "FBI Says, 'No Hard Evidence Connecting Bin Laden to 9/11'" Muckraker Report, June 6, 2006 (www.teamliberty.net/id267.html).

9 Ed Haas, "Fact: Osama bin Laden Has *Not* Been Indicted for His Involvement in 9/11," Muckraker Report, August 20, 2006 (www.teamliberty.net/id290.html).

10 *Meet the Press*, NBC, September 23, 2001 (www.washingtonpost.com/wp-srv/nation/specials/attacked/transcripts/nbctext092301.html).

11 "Remarks by the President, Secretary of the Treasury O'Neill and Secretary of State Powell on Executive Order," White House, September 24, 2001 (www.whitehouse.gov/news/releases/2001/09/20010924-4.html).

12 Seymour M. Hersh, "What Went Wrong: The C.I.A. and the Failure of American Intelligence," *New Yorker*, October 1, 2001 (http://cicentre.com/Documents/DOC_Hersch_OCT_01.htm).

13 Office of the Prime Minister, "Responsibility for the Terrorist Atrocities in the United States," BBC News, October 4, 2001 (http://news.bbc.co.uk/2/hi/uk_news/politics/1579043.stm).

14 "White House Warns Taliban: 'We Will Defeat You,'" CNN, September 21, 2001 (http://archives.cnn.com/2001/WORLD/asiapcf/central/09/21/ret.afghan.taliban).

15 Ibid.

16 Kathy Gannon, "Taliban Willing to Talk, But Wants US Respect," Associated Press, November 1, 2001 (http://nucnews.net/nucnews/2001nn/0111nn/011101nn.htm#300). Also available, under the title "Taliban Willing to Negotiate—Official" (http://english.peopledaily.com.cn/english/200111/01/eng20011101_83655.html).

17 "Top 25 Censored Stories of 2008: #16 No Hard Evidence Connecting Bin Laden to 9/11," Project Censored (www.projectcensored.org/censored_2008).

18 Dan Eggen, "Bin Laden, Most Wanted for Embassy Bombings?" *Washington Post*, August 28, 2006 (www.washingtonpost.com/wp-dyn/content/article/2006/08/27/AR2006082700687.html). The omission was also pointed out by Jeff Ferrell of KSLA 12 in Shreveport, Louisiana, in a report that is available on YouTube as "Bin Laden's FBI Poster Omits Any 9/11 Connection" (www.youtube.com/watch?v=fnUQczDktgI&eurl=http%3A%2F%2Fwww%2Ebrasschecktv%2Ecom%2Fpage%2F150%2Ehtml).

19 See Kevin Johnson, "FBI Retools Most Wanted List," *USA Today*, January

17, 2008 (www.usatoday.com/news/nation/2008-01-16-Top10_N.htm).

20 "Tape 'Proves Bin Laden's Guilt,'" *BBC News*, December 14, 2001 (http://news.bbc.co.uk/2/hi/south_asia/1708091.stm).

21 Ibid.

22 "Bush: Tape a 'Devastating Declaration of Guilt,'" CNN, December 14, 2001 (http://edition.cnn.com/2001/US/12/ 14/ret.bin.laden.video/index.html?related).

23 See "The Fake 2001 bin Laden Video Tape" (www.whatreallyhappened.com/osamatape.html).

24 Kevin Barrett, "Bin Laden Tapes Are as Phony as Sept. 11's Connection to Islam," *Capital Times* (Madison, Wisconsin), February 14, 2006 (www.unknownnews.org/060214a-Barrett.html).

25 Steve Morris, "US Urged to Detail Origin of Tape," *Guardian*, December 15, 2001 (www.guardian.co.uk/world/2001/dec/15/ september11.afghanistan).

26 "Transcript of Usama bin Laden Video Tape," Department of Defense, December 13, 2001 (www.defenselink.mil/news/Dec2001/d20011213ubl.pdf).

27 For the government documentation of these ticket purchases, see History Commons's *Complete 9/11 Timeline*, "August 25–September 5, 2001: Hijackers Spend Over $30,000 on 9/11 Tickets" (www.historycommons.org/timeline.jsp?timeline=complete_911_timeline &startpos=2000#a082401buyingtickets).

28 According to FBI testimony to the House Permanent Select Committee on Intelligence and the Senate Permanent Select Committee on Intelligence, the so-called muscle hijackers who arrived at the airports in Miami and Orlando settled in Fort Lauderdale, along with pilots Mohamed Atta, Marwan al-Shehhi, and Ziad Jarrah, whereas those who arrived in New York and Virginia settled in Paterson, New Jersey, with pilot Hani Hanjour (testimonies of Cofer Black, Dale Watson, and Robert Mueller, September 26, 2002). See *Complete 9/11 Timeline*, April 23–June 29, 2001: 9/11 'Muscle' Hijackers Arrive in US at This Time or Earlier" (www.historycommons.org/timeline.jsp?timeline= complete_911_timeline&startpos=1600#a042301muscle).

29 "Transcript of Usama bin Laden Video Tape."

30 Bruce Lawrence's statement is quoted in Kevin Barrett, "Top US Bin Laden Expert: Confession Video 'Bogus,'" Mujca.com, February 27, 2006 (http://mujca.com/hoax.htm). Lawrence is the editor of *Messages to the World: The Statements of Osama Bin Laden* (London and New York: Verso, 2005).

31 "Tape 'Proves Bin Laden's Guilt.'"

32 See note 70 of Chapter 10.

33 "Bin Laden Says He Wasn't Behind Attacks," CNN, September 17, 2001 (http://archives.cnn.com/2001/US/09/16/inv.binladen.denial).

34 "Interview with Usama bin Laden," *Ummat* (Karachi), September 28, 2001 (www.robert-fisk.com/usama_interview_ummat.htm).

35 "Bush: Tape a 'Devastating Declaration of Guilt.'"

36 With regard to who might have orchestrated the attacks, bin Laden said: "In the US itself, there are dozens of well-organized and well-equipped groups, which are capable of causing a large-scale destruction. . . . Then there are intelligence agencies in the US, which require billions of dollars worth of funds from the Congress and the government every year. This [funding issue] was not a big problem till the [extinction] of the former Soviet Union but after that the budget of these agencies has been in danger. They needed an enemy. So, they first started propaganda against Usama and Taleban and then this incident happened" ("Interview with Usama bin Laden").

37 9/11CR 148, 149, 153, 154, 155, 166.

38 See 9/11CR Ch. 5, notes 1, 10, 11, 16, 32, 40, and 41.

39 WP 118.

40 Ibid., 118-19.

41 Ibid., 122-23.

42 Ibid., 122, 119, 124.

43 Ibid., 124.

44 Ibid., 119.

45 Robert Windrem and Victor Limjoco, "The 9/11 Commission Controversy," Deep Background: NBC News Investigations, January 30, 2008 (http://deepbackground.msnbc.msn.com/archive/2008/01/30/624314.aspx).

46 Greg Miller, "Three Were Waterboarded, CIA Chief Confirms," *Los Angeles Times*, February 6, 2008 (www.latimes.com/news/la-na-terror6feb06,0,6365979.story?track=ntothtml). The third person to which the title of this article referred was Abd al-Rahim al-Nashiri, a Saudi suspected of involvement in the 2000 bombing of the US Navy destroyer Cole.

47 Windrem and Limjoco, "The 9/11 Commission Controversy."

48 Ibid.

49 Michael Melia and Andrew O. Selsky, "Executions May Be Carried Out at Guantánamo," Associated Press, February 13, 2008 (www.truthout.org/docs_2006/021308N.shtml).

50 "Substitution for the Testimony of Khalid Sheikh Mohammed" (http://rcfp.org/moussaoui/pdf/DX-0941.pdf).

51 See Paul Joseph Watson, "KSM 'Confessed' to Targeting Bank Founded *after* His Arrest," Prison Planet, March 16, 2007 (www.prisonplanet.com/articles/march2007/160307afterarrest.htm). Although Watson incorrectly said *four* years, he correctly pointed out that KSM had been arrested in March 2003.

52 "Statement of Lieutenant Commander Charles D. Swift, JACG, USN before the Senate Committee on Judiciary on Supreme Court Decision on Detainees: 'Hamden v. Rumsfeld,'" July 11, 2006 (www.fas.org/irp/congress/2006_hr/071106swift.html).

53 Ibid. See also Leigh Sales, "Guantánamo Trials Rigged," ABC News Online (www.abc.net.au/news/newsitems/200508/s1426797.htm).

54 Leigh Sales, "Third Prosecutor Critical of Guantánamo Trials," ABC News Online, August 3, 2005 (www.abc.net.au/news/newsitems/200508/s1428749.htm).

55 Ross Tuttle, "Rigged Trials at Guantánamo," *Nation*, February 20, 2008 (www.thenation.com/doc/20080303/tuttle).

56 Ibid.

57 Scott Horton, "The Great Guantánamo Puppet Theater," February 21, 2008 (www.harpers.org/archive/2008/02/hbc-90002460); William Glaberson, "Judge Drops General from Trial of Detainee," *New York Times*, May 10, 2008 (www.nytimes.com/2008/05/10/us/10gitmo.html?_r=2&hp&oref=slogin&oref=slogin); Michael Melia, "Disqualified General Won't Quit Tribunals," Associated Press, May 14, 2008 (www.miamiherald.com/guantanamo/story/533688.html).

58 Ibid.

59 Tuttle, "Rigged Trials at Guantánamo"; William Glaberson, "Gitmo 'Attack Dog' Turns on His Pentagon Masters," *Toronto Star*, March 4, 2008 (www.thestar.com/News/World/article/309047).

60 Ben Fox, "Ex-Prosecutor at Guantánamo to Aid Defense," Associated Press, February 21, 2008 (www.truthout.org/docs_2006/022208B.shtml); William Glaberson, "Former Prosecutor to Testify for Guantánamo Detainee," *New York Times*, February 28, 2008 (www.nytimes.com/2008/02/28/us/28gitmo.html?ref=us).

61 Quoted in Carol Rosenberg, "Lawyer: Gitmo Trials Pegged to '08 Campaign," *Miami Herald*, March 28, 2008. Although this story quickly disappeared from the *Miami Herald* website, it can be found at Truthout (www.truthout.org/docs_2006/032908Z.shtml) and the Huffington Post (www.huffingtonpost.com/2008/03/28/lawyer-gitmo-trials-pegg_n_93990.html).

62 Josh White, "Colonel Says Speaking Out Cost a Medal," *Washington Post*, May 29, 2008 (www.washingtonpost.com/wp-dyn/content/article/2008/05/28/AR2008052802966.html).

63 "Attorneys: Terrorism Trials Rushed to Influence Election," CNN, May 29, 2008 (http://edition.cnn.com/2008/US/05/29/guantanamo.commission/index.html).

64 Glaberson, "Judge Drops General from Trial of Detainee."

65 Melia, "Disqualified General Won't Quit Tribunals."

66 "Unnecessary Harm," editorial, *New York Times*, February 13, 2008 (www.nytimes.com/2008/02/13/opinion/13wed1.html?ex=1360645200&en=c99a6cfbf6b671cc&ei=5090&partner=rssuserland&emc=rss&pagewanted=all).

67 All the quotations in this paragraph come from the section entitled "Senior Military, Intelligence, Law Enforcement, and Government Officials" at the Patriots Question 9/11 website (www.patriotsquestion911.com).

68 "9/12/2001: CIA Veteran Doubts Bin Laden Capable of 9/11 Attacks, Suspects Larger Plot," Aidan Monaghan's Blog, March 11, 2008 (www.911blogger.com/blog/2074).

69 9/11CR 369.

70 DOD letter to the Bloomington 9/11 Working Group, May 20, 2008; on the significance of the assassination of Masood (spelled "Massoud" by the Commission), see 9/11CROD 110–12.

71 Amir Mateen, "ISI Chief's Parleys Continue in Washington," *News* (Islamabad), September 10, 2001; 9/11CR 331.

72 9/11CR 172.

73 Josh Meyer, "2 Allies Aided Bin Laden, Say Panel Members," *Los Angeles Times*, June 20, 2004 (http://scoop.agonist.org/story/2004/6/20/132815/063).

74 On the relation between Ahmad and Musharraf, see 9/11CROD 108.

75 According to the Pentagon, CNN reported, KSM had confessed to having beheaded Daniel Pearl, although his confession had been removed from the transcript. See "Khalid Sheikh Mohammed: I Beheaded American Reporter," CNN, March 15, 2007 (www.cnn.com/2007/US/03/15/ guantanamo.mohammed/index.html). KSM confessed to so many things, however, that it is difficult to take seriously this alleged confession (which, like other claims attributed to KSM, need to be discounted because they were likely elicited by torture). The beheading of Pearl had previously been attributed to Omar Saeed Sheikh, the ISI member who reportedly wired $100,000 to Mohamed Atta. In an interview with David Frost shortly before her assassination, incidentally, Benazir Bhutto spoke in passing of Omar Saeed Sheikh as "the man who murdered Osama bin Laden" (*Frost Over the World*, November 2, 2007 [http://investigate911.se/ benazir_bhutto_about_bin_laden.html]). Although this evoked much discussion on the Internet, she probably meant to say: "the man who murdered Daniel Pearl."

76 9/11CR 369.

77 Nathaniel Heller, Sarah Fort, and Marina Walker Guevara, "Pakistan's $4.7 Billion 'Blank Check' for US Military Aid," Center for Public Integrity, March 27, 2007, with financial figures updated in November 2007 (www.publicintegrity.org/militaryaid/report.aspx?aid=831).

78 Craig Cohen and Derek Chollet, "When $10 Billion is Not Enough: Rethinking US Strategy toward Pakistan," *Washington Quarterly* 30/2 (Spring 2007), 7–19 (www.publicintegrity.org/docs/CSIS_CSF_paper.pdf).

79 Ibid.

80 David Rohde, Carlotta Gall, Eric Schmitt, and David E. Sanger, "US Officials See Waste in Billions Sent to Pakistan," *New York Times*, December 24, 2007 (www.nytimes.com/2007/12/24/world/asia/ 24military.html?ex=1356152400&en=19a8b442b685f3fa&ei=5090&part ner=rssuserland&emc=rss&pagewanted=all).

81 Benazir Bhutto, lecture at Middle East Institute, London, September 25, 2007, re-broadcast by C-SPAN, December 27, 2007 (available at www.youtube.com/watch?v=XgRhRWsgUv0).

82 *9/11 Report: Joint Congressional Inquiry*, July 24, 2003 (http://news.findlaw.com/ hdocs/docs/911rpt).

83 Bob Graham, *Intelligence Matters: The CIA, the FBI, Saudi Arabia, and the*

Failure of America's War on Terror (New York: Random House, 2004), 215.

84 Quoted in "2/14/2008: Newly Released FBI Timeline Reveals New Information about 9/11 Hijackers that Was Ignored by 9/11 Commission: Latest Findings Raise New Questions about Hijackers and Suggest Incomplete Investigation," History Commons (www.historycommons.org/news.jsp?oid=140393703-423).

85 Graham, *Intelligence Matters*, 12–13, 224.

86 Ibid., 24, 167.

87 Ibid., 168, 223, 225.

88 Ibid., 169 (citing Dana Priest, "White House, CIA Kept Key Portions of Report Classified," *Washington Post*, July 25, 2003).

89 Ibid., 224 (quoting an Associated Press story of March 24, 2004, "FBI Concludes 2 Saudis Not Intel Agents").

90 Ibid., 226–29.

91 Ibid., 166, 216, xiv.

92 Unger, *House of Bush*, 179–80; Graham, *Intelligence Matters*, 168. Unger spells the name Basnan, Graham spells it Bassnan.

93 Craig Unger, *House of Bush*, 179–80.

94 For support, it merely says [498n122]: "See Adam Drucker interview [May 19, 2004]," without telling us how we might "see" it.

95 Michael Isikoff and Evan Thomas, "The Saudi Money Trail," *Newsweek*, December 2002 (www.newsweek.com/id/66665).

96 Philip Shenon, *The Commission: The Uncensored History of the 9/11 Investigation* (New York: Twelve, 2008), 110.

97 Ibid., 308–11, 398–98.

98 9/11CR 215.

99 FBI, "Hijackers Timeline (Redacted)" (www.historycommons.org/news.jsp?oid=140393703-423), 52.

100 Jerry Markon, "Moussaoui Pleads Guilty in Terror Plot," *Washington Post*, April 23, 2005 (www.washingtonpost.com/wp-dyn/articles/A9271-2005Apr22.html).

101 "Moussaoui Says He Was to Hijack 5th Plane," Associated Press, March 27, 2006 (www.cbsnews.com/stories/2006/03/27/ap/national/mainD8GK7DEG0.shtml).

102 "Moussaoui Withdraws Guilty Plea," Associated Press, May 8, 2006 (www.11alive.com/news/news_article.aspx?storyid=79575).

103 Michael J. Sniffen, "FBI Agent Slams Bosses at Moussaoui Trial," Associated Press, March 20, 2006 (www.cbsnews.com/stories/2006/03/21/ap/national/mainD8GFLTIGA.shtml).

CHAPTER 9: COMPLICITY BY US OFFICIALS: A SUMMARY OF THE EVIDENCE

1 WP 270.

2 9/11CR 47, 48.

3 WP 278.

4 9/11 Commission Hearing, March 23, 2004 (http://govinfo.library.unt.edu/
   911/archive/hearing8/9-11Commission_Hearing_2004-03-23.htm).
5 Kenneth Adelman, "Cakewalk in Iraq," *Washington Post*, February 13, 2002
   (www.washingtonpost.com/ac2/wp-dyn/A1996-2002Feb12).
6 Quoted in Elizabeth Drew, "The Neocons in Power," *New York Review of
   Books*, June 12, 2003 (www.nybooks.com/articles/article-
   preview?article_id=16378).
7 *Rebuilding America's Defenses*, Project for the New American Century,
   September, 2000 (www.newamericancentury.org/
   RebuildingAmericasDefenses.pdf), 4.
8 9/11CR 361. After the Commission published that statement in 2004,
   military spending continued to rise, so that by the end of 2007, it had
   increased 86 percent since 2001. See "How High is Up? The Defense
   Budget Gets Even Crazier," Democracy Arsenal, December 18, 2007
   (www.democracyarsenal.org/2007/12/how-high-is-up.html).
9 Joseph Stiglitz and Linda Bilmes, *The Three Trillion Dollar War* (New York:
   W. W. Norton, 2008).
10 D9D 18–20.

CHAPTER 10: THE STRENGTHENED CASE FOR A NEW INVESTIGATION

1 9/11CR xv, xvi.
2 WP 269–70.
3 National Commission on Terrorist Attacks Upon the United States, Public
   Law 107-306 (www.9-11commission.gov/about/107-306.title6.htm). This
   statement does also say that they were to "build upon the investigations of
   other entities." But these "other entities" are limited to the Joint Inquiry
   of the Senate and House Intelligence Committees and "other executive,
   congressional, or independent commission investigations." Although the
   reference to "independent commission investigations" might seem to have
   allowed input from nongovernmental citizen groups, it clearly was not so
   interpreted. Indeed, it probably referred to the investigations by NIST
   into the World Trade Center, and NIST, as we saw in Chapter 11, was no
   more independent than the 9/11 Commission itself.
4 WP 38.
5 Ibid., 116.
6 Ibid., 269–70.
7 Ibid., 270.
8 Philip Shenon, *The Commission: The Uncensored History of the 9/11
   Investigation* (New York: Twelve, 2008), 388–89.
9 Ibid., 389.
10 Ibid.
11 Quoted in Peter Lance, *Cover Up: What the Government is Still Hiding about
   the War on Terror* (New York: Harper-Collins/ReganBooks, 2004), 139–40.
12 Shenon, *The Commission*, 69–70, 86.

13 Ibid., 167.

14 Ibid., 69, 83.

15 Ibid., 83.

16 Ibid., 84–85.

17 Ibid., 317.

18 Ibid., 277; emphasis added.

19 Ibid., 171.

20 Ibid., 390.

21 Ernest May, "When Government Writes History: A Memoir of the 9/11 Commission," *New Republic*, May 23, 2005; cited in Bryan Sacks, "Making History: The Compromised 9-11 Commission," in Zarembka, ed., *The Hidden History of 9-11*, 2nd ed., 215–52, at 249n10.

22 Shenon, *The Commission*, 321.

23 D9D 108.

24 *The National Security Strategy of the United States of America*, September 2002 (www.whitehouse.gov/nsc/nss.html); henceforth NSS 2002.

25 James Mann, *Rise of the Vulcans: The History of Bush's War Cabinet* (New York: Viking, 2004), 316.

26 David Ray Griffin, "Neocon Imperialism, 9/11, and the Attacks on Afghanistan and Iraq," Information Clearing House, February 27, 2007 (www.informationclearinghouse.info/article17194.htm).

27 "President Bush Delivers Graduation Speech at West Point," June 1, 2002 (www.whitehouse.gov/news/releases/2002/06/20020601-3.html).

28 NSS 2002: 6, 15.

29 Emphasizing the newness of this doctrine, Stefan Halper and Jonathan Clarke wrote: "Never before had any president set out a formal national strategy *doctrine* that included preemption" (*America Alone: The Neo-Conservatives and the Global Order* [Cambridge: Cambridge University Press, 2004], 142).

30 Max Boot, "Think Again: Neocons," *Foreign Policy*, January/February 2004 (www.cfr.org/publication/7592/think_again.html), 18.

31 Stephen J. Sniegoski, "Neoconservatives, Israel, and 9/11: The Origins of the US War on Iraq," in D. L. O'Huallachain and J. Forrest Sharpe, eds., *Neoconned Again: Hypocrisy, Lawlessness, and the Rape of Iraq* (Vienna, Va.: IHS Press, 2005), 81–109, at 81–82.

32 Andrew J. Bacevich, *The New American Militarism: How Americans Are Seduced by War* (Oxford: Oxford University Press, 2005), 91.

33 Ashton Carter, John Deutch, and Philip Zelikow, "Catastrophic Terrorism: Tackling the New Danger," *Foreign Affairs*, November/December 1998: 80–94 (http://cryptome.quintessenz.at/mirror/ct-tnd.htm).

34 WP 28. Shenon adds that, although Kean and Hamilton "review[ed] the résumés of about twenty candidates, including those proposed by the White House," they decided that "there wasn't anybody even close to Zelikow" (*The Commission*, 60).

35 In NPH, I incorrectly stated that Bush himself chose Zelikow to be executive director (152). In D9D, I corrected this error, reporting Kean

and Hamilton's account of their selection of Zelikow (103, 106). Of course, given Bush's insistence that he appoint the chairman of the Commission, he indirectly selected the executive director.

36 Shenon, *The Commission*, 59.

37 Ibid., 170.

38 Ibid.

39 Ibid., 181, 104.

40 Ibid., 130.

41 Ibid., 130, 131, 133.

42 Ibid., 321.

43 Ibid., 59–60.

44 Ibid., 63–65.

45 Ibid., 62, 147, 170.

46 Ibid., 319.

47 Ibid., 87, 145.

48 Ibid., 374–78.

49 Ibid., 146, 197, 394–96. Zelikow's antipathy to Clarke and his perspective probably helps explain a curious fact—that Clarke's *Against All Enemies* is never cited in *The 9/11 Commission Report*, even though many of its points were highly germane to topics discussed in that report.

50 Ibid., 396–98. Shenon pointed out that, although this comparison was completely removed from the text, one of the team members, correctly assuming that Zelikow would pay less attention to the notes, used them to sneak in some comparisons between Clinton and Bush (Shenon refers to 9/11CR Ch. 6, notes 2 and 6).

51 Ibid., 62.

52 Ibid.

53 Ibid., 169.

54 Ibid., 169–71.

55 Statement of the Family Steering Committee for the 9/11 Independent Commission, March 20, 2004 (www.911independentcommission.org/mar202004.html).

56 WP 28–29.

57 Shenon, *The Commission*, 106–07.

58 Ibid., 107.

59 Ibid., 106–07.

60 Ibid., 171.

61 Ibid., 173–74.

62 Ibid., 173.

63 Ibid., 29. This information was reportedly given to senate majority leader Tom Daschle by Trent Lott, the leader of the Senate Republicans.

64 Ibid., 15.

65 Ibid., 19.

66 Ibid., 175–76.

67 Ibid., 174.

68 Ibid., 169–71.

69 Ibid., 205.

70 Although Shenon's book is exemplary in revealing some dynamics of the 9/11 Commission, especially with regard to Zelikow, it is not at all exemplary in its treatment of 9/11 itself—except in the sense that it exemplifies the approach generally taken by mainstream journalists: simply endorsing the official conspiracy theory and dismissing the alternative theory without revealing any sign of having studied the relevant evidence so as to be able to make a responsible evaluation of the merits of the two theories.

Shenon says, for example, that when the Commission was formed in 2003, "many of the most outrageous . . . of the [conspiracy] theories—that the attacks were an inside job by the Bush administration, that the Twin Towers were brought down by preplaced explosives, that the Pentagon was hit by a missile and not a plane—had been well debunked" (*The Commission*, 264). In making this statement, Shenon gives no indication of what for him makes a theory "outrageous." Many people call a theory "outrageous" if it seems intuitively implausible. But if that is Shenon's meaning, then the term surely applies to the official theory, according to which—in Shenon's own words—"nineteen young Arab men with little more than pocket knives, a few cans of mace, and a misunderstanding of the tenets of Islam [brought] the United States to its knees" (406).

Within the philosophy of science, an outrageous theory is one that violently contradicts the relevant facts. But if Shenon were using the term in that sense, then he would see—if he would bother to study those facts—that, again, the term would apply to the official conspiracy theory. It appears, however, that for Shenon the alternative theory is outrageous simply because it blames the attacks on people within our own government rather than Muslim terrorists. (If so, he is simply expressing what I have elsewhere called "nationalist faith" [see my DVD, "9/11 and Nationalist Faith," available at 911TV.org or Amazon.com.])

With regard to the alleged debunking of the theory that "the Twin Towers were brought down by preplaced explosives," he gives no indication of just who it was in 2003—two years before the NIST Report appeared—that had carried out this debunking. Does he mean the report put out in 2002 by FEMA? If so, is he unaware that NIST later rejected its ("pancake") theory?

With regard to the Pentagon, Shenon writes as if the only issue were whether the Pentagon was hit by a missile or "a plane," ignoring the fact that most of the debate has centered around evidence that, whatever caused the damage, it could not have been the *kind* of plane alleged by the official narrative, a Boeing 757, and, in particular, American Flight 77 under the control of Hani Hanjour.

In a paragraph evidently intended to refute the "outrageous" notion that 9/11 was an inside job, he says: "The evidence was incontrovertible that al-Qaeda was behind the September 11 attacks." In illustrating this "incontrovertible" evidence, Shenon first says: "Osama bin Laden had been videotaped bragging to his colleagues about his role in the preparations" (118). Perhaps considering it unthinkable that our government might have fabricated this video, Shenon evidently did not explore this issue sufficiently to learn that, as we saw in Chapter 8, this video's authenticity is doubted by one of America's bin Laden experts and even, it would appear, by the FBI.

Shenon next says: "There was clear-cut documentation to show that bin Laden had dispatched nineteen young Arab men to the United States to carry out the hijackings—he had chosen them personally for the mission" (118). What is this "clear-cut documentation"? As we saw at the outset of Chapter 8, the information that bin Laden had chosen Mohamed Atta and the other hijackers came to the 9/11 Commission from statements reportedly extracted from KSM by CIA interrogators. This was "information" that, Kean and Hamilton themselves have admitted, they had no way of evaluating. Shenon himself—referring to Dietrich Snell, the leader of the "plot" team—writes: "Snell knew that testimony from key witnesses like the al-Qaeda detainees would have value only if they were questioned in person" (182). Shenon also points out that many people on the Commission staff knew that any testimony extracted by torture was dubious (391). But he, nevertheless, treats statements reportedly made by KSM as if they were indubitable. Indeed, he confidently calls KSM "the mastermind of 9/11," adding: "Apart from Osama bin Laden himself, it was unlikely that anyone knew more than KSM and bin al-Shibh about the logistics of the 9/11 plot" (242, 181). With regard to "Osama bin Laden himself," we must ask: Was Shenon— the reporter assigned by the *New York Times* to deal with 9/11—unaware that the FBI has not indicted bin Laden for 9/11 because, a spokesman has said, it had "no hard evidence" of his involvement? Where is the "clear-cut documentation" to which Shenon refers?

Shenon also holds that such documentation exists for the claim that those "nineteen young Arab men. . . were aboard the four planes" (118). As we have seen in Chapters 3 and 6, however, none of that reputed evidence stands up to scrutiny. Also, Shenon's own *New York Times* provided some of the evidence against the official portrayal of these young Arab men. By reporting that Atta and others were drinking heavily at Shuckums bar in Florida a few nights before 9/11, a *Times* article, as we saw in Chapter 6, provided evidence against the image of them as devout Muslims, ready to meet their maker. Also, the claim that Flight 77 was flown into the Pentagon by Hani Hanjour was undermined by a *Times* story, as we saw in Chapter 2, that quoted one of Hanjour's flight instructors as saying that he "could not fly at all." Should Shenon not have mentioned the fact that the Zelikow-led Commission ignored these reports?

If Shenon shows no sign of having studied the evidence presented by those who consider 9/11 an inside job, how can he be so confident that it was not? He appears to trust his own intuitions. When asked by Amy

Goodman how he dealt with "those in this country who believe 9/11 was an inside job," he replied: "I have trouble believing that myself, I have great difficulty believing in vast conspiracies." But he does accept the official theory about 9/11, according to which it was a vast conspiracy between Osama bin Laden and other members of al-Qaeda. What he seemed to be saying, therefore, was simply that he could not believe in vast conspiracies carried out by people inside our own government. He then added: "I just think a conspiracy of that nature would require competence on the part of people in the federal government that I just don't believe exists in the federal government" (*Democracy Now!* February 5, 2008 [www.democracynow.org/2008/2/5/new_book_alleges_9_11_ commissioner]). So, although various political and military leaders from other countries, as we saw in Chapter 8, have stated that al-Qaeda would not have had the competence to pull off such an operation, Shenon has no doubts about al-Qaeda's ability to plan and carry out such a vast conspiracy. For him, it is the US government, which spends about a trillion dollars annually on its military and various intelligence organizations, that would have been unable to pull off such a big operation.

Shenon began his answer to Goodman's question about 9/11 as an inside job by saying: "It is a tough issue. I just haven't seen the evidence." But did he mean that, although he had studied several books, essays, and films purporting to provide such evidence, he did not find any of it convincing? Or did he merely mean that, being *a priori* certain that none of this purported evidence would be worth examining, he did not study it? This second meaning is suggested by his bibliography. To mention only the most obvious omission: Although his book is about the 9/11 Commission, he does not list my book on the subject, *The 9/11 Commission Report: Omissions and Distortions.* Was he unaware of this book? Or did he, while being aware of it, choose not to tell his readers about it? Either alternative would be problematic.

This omission brings me, in any case, to the main point of this long note: Shenon's book, in spite of its many important revelations, provides a very incomplete critique of the 9/11 Commission. Although Shenon gives us very good reasons to suspect that the Commission, under Zelikow's leadership, would have covered up evidence pointing to the Bush administration's responsibility for the attacks, Shenon limits his own discussion of this issue to cover-ups of incompetence. Although my book on the Commission documented 115 lies of omission and distortion, he mentions none of these.

For example, although Shenon mentions that Secretary of Transportation Norman Mineta testified before the Commission in 2003, he does not mention the fact that the Zelikow-led Commission did everything it could to obliterate Mineta's testimony about Dick Cheney and the young man discussing the incoming aircraft.

Likewise, Shenon refers to Cheney's appearance on *Meet the Press* five days after 9/11 as "the most authoritative account [of what had happened in the executive branch on the morning of the attacks] until the 9/11 commission's report was released in 2004" (264). But Shenon fails to point out that Cheney's account, according to which he had learned about the attack on the Pentagon only after he had entered the underground bunker, was contradicted by the Zelikow-led Commission's account, according to which Cheney did not enter the bunker until 20 minutes after that attack, which he had learned about while in the corridor leading to the bunker (see Chapter 2, above).

Shenon also, while saying that the theories about preplaced explosives in the Twin Towers have been debunked, fails to point out that the Zelikow-led Commission, even though it had read the oral histories of the members of the Fire Department of New York (which had been made available by the *New York Times*), made no mention of the fact that over 100 of these firefighters and emergency medical workers spoke about explosions going off in the towers (see Chapter 1, above).

Also, Shenon must have known that two of his fellow *New York Times* writers, James Glanz and Eric Lipton, had reported in 2001, as we saw in Chapter 1, that some pieces of steel in the debris pile from the Twin Towers and WTC 7 had apparently "melted away," even though "no fire in any of the buildings was believed to be hot enough to melt steel outright." But Shenon did not point out that the Zelikow-led Commission's report did not mention this fact, which Glanz and Lipton, as we saw in Chapter 1, had called "the deepest mystery uncovered in the investigation."

Shenon also failed to discuss one of the most criticized omissions of *The 9/11 Commission Report*—that it did not even mention the collapse of WTC 7. Perhaps Shenon believes that this omission was unimportant because this building's collapse had already been explained. In a statement that surely refers to the FEMA report on the WTC, which came out in 2002, Shenon says: "[I]t was determined that a fire that. . . destroyed WTC 7 on September 11 was probably caused by the rupture of the building's special diesel fuel tanks" (347). However, FEMA said that, although this was the best theory it could come up with, this theory had "only a low probability of occurrence"—a phrase that cannot be translated "probably." Shenon also surely knew that, as he was finishing up his book, NIST had repeatedly delayed its report on WTC 7, thereby suggesting that providing a plausible and yet politically acceptable explanation of its collapse was not easy. In light of these facts, how could Shenon have thought that the 9/11 Commission's failure to mention this collapse was itself not worth mentioning?

Moreover, while pointing out that the Commission failed to ask Rudy Giuliani any tough questions (351–56), Shenon fails to mention the toughest question raised by the 9/11 truth movement: How did Giuliani and his people know that the Twin Towers were going to collapse?

Still another example: Shenon points out that President Bush told the Commission "that he had not rushed out of the Florida schoolhouse after learning of the attacks that morning because he did not want to panic the kids" (344). But Shenon does *not* point out that such a consideration would surely not have stopped the Secret Service from rushing Bush out of there if it had feared that a hijacked plane might be bearing down on the school. Nor does he mention the fact that the White House, on the first anniversary of 9/11, tried to change the story, claiming that Bush had left the room immediately.

Given Shenon's keen interest in the tension between Zelikow and Richard Clarke, we might expect that he would at least have reported on contradictions between Clarke's assertions and those of the Zelikow-led Commission. One of those, as we saw in Chapter 3, involved the time at which Clarke received shootdown authorization from Cheney: Clarke said that he received it at about 9:50, whereas the Commission's report said that he did not receive it until 10:25. Shenon, however, makes no mention of this enormous contradiction.

Finally, although Shenon had been one of the journalists who exposed the fact that the Commission's report failed to mention Able Danger, even though two of its team members had personally talked to the Commission, he treats the issue as one of no consequence, writing: "The commission. . . said it was aware of Able Danger but had uncovered nothing in its investigation to suggest that Atta and the other hijackers were known to the government before 9/11" (417). Shenon says nothing about the kind of evidence that had been presented, the credibility of the Able Danger team members, or the fact that the DOD's inspector general could dismiss their claims only by calling them liars.

Shenon does not mention these and dozens of other omissions and distortions in *The 9/11 Commission Report*, it appears, because of his prejudgment that the story told by the government and the Commission is basically correct, so that any theory that challenges it is "outrageous" and hence unworthy of examination. As a result, he does not really give us, as his subtitle claims, an *uncensored* history of the 9/11 Commission. His account may have only been *self-censored*, and this self-censoring may have resulted from a combination of prejudice and ignorance, but his account was censored nonetheless, leaving out the most important fact about the 9/11 Commission—that its report systematically excluded all evidence pointing to 9/11 as an inside job.

Coincidentally, the same day on which I wrote this note (March 9, 2008), Shenon was interviewed on BookTV's *After Words*. When asked why 9/11 had given rise to conspiracy theories portraying 9/11 as an inside job, Shenon gave a purely psychological explanation: Whenever there is a national tragedy—Shenon used the assassination of President Kennedy as an example—some people feel the need to provide an alternative explanation. He implied, therefore, that evidence plays no role in leading people to decide that 9/11 was an inside job (which, if true, would make it puzzling why most members of the 9/11 truth movement did not join until years after the event). He then suggested that his book had shown incompetence to be a more probable explanation. His book, however, did no such thing. It could have done this only by refuting the evidence supporting the inside job theory. But he did not even mention any of this evidence. Far from showing the incompetence theory to be more probable, Shenon simply assumed it.

71 Ibid., 118–19. Cf. WP: "[I]f the military had had the amount of time they said they had. . . and had scrambled their jets, it was hard to figure how they had failed to shoot down at least one of the planes. . . . In this way, the FAA's and NORAD's inaccurate reporting after 9/11 created the opportunity for people to construct a series of conspiracy theories that persist to this day" (259).

72 Shenon, *The Commission*, 208. In endorsing the 9/11 Commission's contention that NORAD's timeline of September 18, 2001, contained lies, Shenon, like the Commission, ignored the fact that it would have been irrational for the military to tell the particular lies of which it was thereby accused. Shenon, like the Commission, finds the motive for the military's (alleged) lies in the account it had given of United Flight 93: "A central element of the NORAD cover story. . . was that air force jet fighters had heroically chased United 93. Had it not crashed in Pennsylvania because of the struggle between the hijackers and passengers, the United plane would have been blown out of the sky before it reached its target in Washington, NORAD had wanted the public to believe" (208). Shenon, in other words, believes that those who wrote NORAD's timeline, along with General Arnold and the other officers who testified to the Commission, lied simply to appear to have been more ready to defend the country than they really were. By focusing only on Flight 93, Shenon ignores the fact that the Commission's charge, which he endorses, also entails that the military falsely said that the FAA had notified it about Flights 77 and 175 in time for these flights to have been intercepted—a lie that would have been totally irrational. Does Shenon really believe that the military, in order to appear potentially heroic with regard to Flight 93, would have opened itself to the charge of extreme incompetence or even treason with regard to Flights 77 and 175?

Shenon also ignores the fact that the Zelikow-led Commission, in constructing its new tapes-based timeline, omitted any mention of reports that challenged it. For example, Shenon did not mention the fact, discussed in Chapter 2, that although Richard Ben-Veniste read the FAA memo from Laura Brown into the record—the memo that said the FAA had told the military about Flight 77 even earlier than the 9:24 time given in NORAD's timeline—the Commission's report was written as if this memo had never existed. In this and the many ways mentioned in note 70, Shenon actually helped cover up the Zelikow-led Commission's cover-up.

73 Ibid., 203–06.

74 E-mails from Hordon, December 30, 2006, and January 2, 2007, previously quoted in D9D 84.

75 Shenon, *The Commission*, 208.

76 WP, 14–15. "Set Up to Fail" is the title of the first chapter.

77 Ibid., 321.

78 "A Word about Our Poll of American Thinking toward the 9/11 Terrorist Attacks," Zogby International, May 24, 2006 (www.zogby.com/features/features.dbm?ID=231).

79 WP 268.

80 Ibid., 320–21, 319.

81 "9/11: Press for Truth" (http://video.google.com/videoplay?docid=5589099104255077250).

82 The quotations from Chiesa and Cossiga come from the section entitled "International Military, Intelligence Services, and Government Officials" on the Patriots Question 9/11 website (www.patriotsquestion911.com).

83 Fujita was referring to Captain Russ Wittenberg as quoted on the Patriots Question 9/11 website.

84 This translation of Fujita's comments is a slightly revised version of a transcript provided by Benjamin Fulford (http://benjaminfulford.com/ Transcript%20of%20Japanese%20Parliamentary%20discussion%20of%20 911.html). Videos of Fujita's presentation with Fulford's transcription as subscripts are available on the Internet (www.911video.de/ex/jap111.htm).

Atef, Mohammed, 212, 318n209
Avery, Dylan, 275nn173,176, 276n181, 277n185
Ayoub, Mahmoud Mustafa, 153
Ayres, J. Marx, 57, 280n219

B

Bacevich, Andrew, 242
Bachmann, Hugo, 44
Baer, Robert, xx–xi
Bagram Air Force Base, 180
Baker, Jeremy, 48–50
Balsamo, Rob, 75, 77–78, 264n6, 285n77, 300n46
Bamford, David, 151–53
Banaciski, Richard, 270n99
Barnett, Jonathan, 273n138. *See also* WPI professors.
Barrett, Kevin, 209
Barry, Kathy, 183
Bart, Eric, 284n66
Bartmer, Craig, 278n196
Basnan, Osama, 225, 329n92
Batista, Fulgenico
Baum, Gerald R., 71, 121–22
Bauries, George, 31
al-Bayoumi, Omar, 224–27
Bazant, Zdenek, 25
BBC: on bin Laden "confession video," 209; on premature report of WTC 7's collapse, 278n204; on story about still-alive hijackers, 151–52; TV program about WTC (2001), 278n206; Guy Smith's TV program about 9/11 (2007), 278–79n207; Mike Rudin's TV program on WTC 7 (2008), 43, 47, 274n160, 276–77nn184,185
Bearden, Milt, 171, 221
Beg, General Mirza Aslam, 221
Belger, Monte, 83

Ben-Veniste, Richard, 82, 134, 155, 302n12, 338n72
Berger, Michael, 274n153
Berger, Sandy, 246
Berntsen, Gary, 205–06
Beutler, William, 309n94
Bhutto, Benazir, 223, 224, 328n75
Biederman, Ronald R., 273n138. *See also* WPI professors.
bin Laden (Ladin), Osama (Usama): and Pakistan, 148, 223; and Saudi royals, 139–43; and the Taliban, 198, 199; as not wanted for 9/11 by FBI, 206–08, 323–24n7, 334n70; as connected to Saddam Hussein, 199, 245; as responsible for 9/11, ix, xxiv, xxv, 137, 206–15, 229, 334n70; "confession video" of, 208–11, 333n70; his inability to orchestrate 9/11 attacks, 220–21, 261n21, 335n70; 9/11 Commission's treatment of, 202, 210–15, 229–31, 239–40, 258; not captured by US, 139, 205–06, 223; on true perpetrators of 9/11 attacks, 325–26n36
bin Sultan, Prince Bandar, 225
Binalshibh, Ramzi, 212
Bingham, Mark, 118–19
Black, Cofer, 325
Blair, Prime Minister Tony, 207, 208
Bloomberg, Mayor Michael, 26
Bloomington 9/11 Working Group, 327–28n70
Bohrer, David, 92, 93, 125
Bolton, John, 200
Bonner, Robert, 174
Boot, Max, 242
Boston Center (FAA), 1–4, 83, 88, 173, 252
Bowman, Marion ("Spike"), 144, 261
Bradshaw, Sandra, 112

Britton, Marion, 112
Brokaw, Tom, 8, 83
Bronner, Michael, 264n9, 265n13, 289n135, 300n60
Brown, Aaron, 53
Brown, Laura, 4, 9, 81, 83, 88, 123, 338n72
Bryant, James, 291n161
Bryant, Johnelle, 184
Brzezinski, Zbigniew, 197, 199
Building 7. *See* WTC 7.
Bukhari, Adnan, 156–58, 162, 175, 309n95
Bukhari, Ameer, 156–58, 162, 175, 309n95
Burke, Timothy, 271n104
Burlingame, Charles ("Chic"), 62
Burma, 202
Burnett, Deena, 117, 118, 119, 165, 299n35
Burnett, Tom, 111, 117, 119, 165
Burton, Dan, 180, 187, 193
Bush (–Cheney) administration, xii, 42, 143, 150, 219, 230, 333n70, 335n70; and Guantánamo trials, 215–20; and NIST, 11; and Osama bin Laden, 205–11; and Pakistan's 9/11 role, 222–24; and Saudi Arabia's 9/11 role, 224–27; as responsible for 9/11, xv–xvi, xviii, 133, 135, 333, 335; conspiracy theory of, 215; incompetence of, 235–36; its exploitation of 9/11, xii, xvi, 242; its new doctrine of preemption, 242, 331n29; its plans to attack Afghanistan and Iraq, 197–201; its plans to refashion world, 202–03; its refusal to debate, xxv; lies by, xvi–xvii, xxi, 134, 150; on 9/11 as opportunity, 202; on 9/11 as sacred story, xvii–xviii;

Zelikow's relation to, xv, 238, 245–46, 249–51, 257–58
Bush, President George H. W., xix, 247
Bush, President George W.: and choice of Zelikow, 331n35; blasphemy about, xviii; Commission as mortal threat to reelection chances of, 250; denied awareness of terrorist airplane threat, 134; Fujita on, 255; Kean contacted by political guru of, 250; linked to al-Qaeda, 320n238; new preemption doctrine of, 242–43; on bin Laden "confession video," 209, 210; on 9/11 as opportunity, 202, 203, 322n27; on Zubaydah, 142; pre-9/11 silence about terrorism of, 247; relatives of, 39; refuses to provide proof of bin Laden's responsibility, 207–08; Rumsfeld recommended new regimes in seven countries to, 202; Sandra Kay Daniels on, 129–30; Sarasota classroom behavior of, 129–31, 336–37n70; Secret Service in relation to, 130–31; to be shown Able Danger chart, 193; White House lies about, 129–30, 337n70
Bussey, John, 29
Buswell, Donald C., 66, 67, 282n35
Buyea, Thomas, 320n238

C

C ring (Pentagon), 63, 71–72, 74, 102, 109, 233, 284
Cabell, Brian, 121
Cachia, Edward, 270n100
Callaway, Dr. Terry, 139
Cambone, Stephen, 251–53,

315n170, 318n209

Canavan, General Mike, 82

Candiotti, Susan, 308n75

Caned, Mosear, 163, 175, 309n95

Card, Andrew, 129–30

Carlsen, Craig, 270n95

Carlson, Tucker, xviii

Carr, Captain John, 217

Cass, Nancy, 39

Castle, Stephen, 296n15

Castro, Fidel, 203

cell phone calls: as evidence for hijackers, 111–12; as faked, 118, 165; FBI report on, 115–18, 296–97n18, 297nn19,20, 298n27; by Any Sweeney, 115, 166–67; by Barbara Olson, 60–61, 165, 227, 233, 280n6; by Ed Felt and CeeCee Lyles, 115, 296n15, 297n20; by Renee May, 62, 164; Flight 11-based, 115, 165–70; Flight 77-based, 60–62, 164; Flight 93–based, 111–18, 163, 164–65, 167, 227, 234, 236, 296nn15,18,20; Flight 175–based, 164; from passengers, 111–17, 234; high-altitude, 112–16; in film *United 93*, 116; 9/11 Commission on, 115–16; *Popular Mechanics* on, 116; to Deena Burnett, 117–18, 165, 298n27

cell phone technology, 60, 61, 112–15, 117, 164, 295n7, 295–96n13, 296n15. *See also* Voice morphing technology.

Charles, Lenny, 267n34

Cheney, Lynne, 91, 92

Cheney, Vice President Dick, xviii; as member of PNAC, 200; and David Addington, 217; and the Buswell case, 282n35; biography of, 289n144, 290n156; his Flight 93 awareness, 125, 126; Norman Mineta's account of, 91–94, 107, 126, 335n70; on tie between Iraq and al-Qaeda, 199; on Tim Russert's *Meet the Press*, 93, 290n153, 335–36n70; prior to Pentagon attack, 91; prior to WTC attack, 290n156; Richard Clarke on, 288n121; shootdown authorization by, 94, 234, 337n70; stand-down order by, 94, 95–96, 126–27, 234; time of entrance into PEOC, 91–94, 109, 234, 288n121, 289n144

Chiesa, Giulietto, 255, 339n82

Chitwood, Mike, 157, 159

Christison, Bill, xx, xxi, 262n34

CIA, xix, xx, xxii, 84–87, 133, 137, 139–42, 150, 171, 174, 195, 201, 211–215, 221–22, 224–25, 243, 255, 303n6–8, 305n34, 320n238, 326n45, 327n68, 328n53, 329n58, 334n70

Citgo gas station, 68, 74

Citizen Investigation Team (CIT), 74, 285n75

Clancy, Tom, 135

Clark, General Wesley, 202, 322n29

Clarke, Jonathan, 331n29

Clarke, Richard A., 84–87, 92–93, 125–26, 135, 174, 200, 231, 234, 246, 247, 249, 288nn121,125, 332n49, 337n70

Cleland, Senator Max, 84, 86

Clinton, President Bill, 201, 245, 246, 247, 332n50

Cockburn, Alexander, xviii, xix, xx, xxi

Cohen, Judge David M., 160

Cohen, Judge Lawrence P., 160

coincidence theory, 236

complicity theory, 235–36

Conason, Joe, 199

Evey, Lee, 72, 233
explosions, xix, 25–34, 39, 45–48,
    51–53, 102, 231–32, 270, 336n70
explosives, xix, 11, 14, 16, 22, 24–25,
    27–28, 31–32, 34, 36–45, 49–50,
    55, 57, 102–03, 134–35, 232,
    270n93, 277n184, 333n70, 336n70

F

FAA (Federal Aviation
    Administration): Administrator
    Jane Garvey in White House
    video conference, 85, 87–88;
    Colin Scoggins of its Boston
    Center, 2, 4, 5, 6, 88–89, 264–
    65n9; falsely blamed by military,
    5, 253; headquarters, 2, 83; its
    Boston Center, 1, 2, 4, 83, 173; its
    Herndon Command Center, 7,
    83; its Indianapolis Center, 82–
    83; its New York Center, 7; memo
    sent by Laura Brown, 9–10, 81–
    82, 87, 123, 232, 338n72; military
    liaisons at, 83; Secret Service had
    open lines to, 84; standard
    procedures of, 3–4, 265n12; the
    9/11 Commission's claim that it
    failed to notify military about last
    three flights, 6–10, 81–83, 90,
    123, 234, 338nn71–72; the 9/11
    Commission's claim that it was
    slow to contact military about
    first flight, 3–4, 231, 264–65n9;
    time of its notifications according
    to "NORAD's Response Times,"
    5–6, 8, 81, 88, 252; would have
    contacted NEADS, 1
FAA memo, 9–10, 81–82, 87, 123,
    232, 338n72
Fahrenheit 9/11, 129
al-Faisal, Princess Haifa, 225
false-flag attack (operation), xxi–xiii,

67, 201, 203, 255, 262n40
Family Steering Committee (FSC),
    130, 248
Farmer, John, 124, 252
Faulkner, Bonnie, 52
FBI: agent James Lechner, 160, 166–
    68; and Able Danger, 179, 181,
    184, 316n185; and discovered
    passports, 170–72, 312n135; and
    evidence about Moussaoui, 227;
    and Flight 93 evidence, 121,
    283n49, 319n134; and flight
    manifests, 174–75, 313n153; and
    Pentagon investigation, 68,
    283n43; and Saudi officials, 225,
    226–27; as blocked in Phoenix,
    Minneapolis, and Chicago, 143–45;
    contradicted Renee May's parents,
    62; contradicted Ted Olson's claim,
    61, 227, 233; has no hard evidence
    of bin Laden's 9/11 responsibility,
    206–08, 211, 235, 323–24n7,
    334n70; its "Hijackers Timeline,"
    163, 226, 305n34; its Joint
    Terrorism Task Force, 296–97n18;
    its Moussaoui trial report on phone
    calls, 61–62, 115, 164–70, 227,
    234, 280–81n8, 297n19, 297–
    98n21; on cell phone calls, 114–
    18, 296nn15,18, 297n20, 297–
    98n21; notified of Flight 77
    hijacking, 81; on Amy Sweeney
    call, 125, 165–68, 310nn109,111;
    on Betty Ong call, 170; on calls to
    Deena Burnett, 117, 118; on flight
    data recorders, 69–70; on Hamza
    al-Ghamdi, 163; on Hani Hanjour,
    163, 309n95; on Mohamed Atta,
    155, 156–61, 184, 235; on the
    hijackers, 151–63, 170–74, 234,
    309n95; on torture and Zubaydah,
    142, 303n7; Sibel Edmonds's

Floyd, Chris, 149
FoneFaker, 298n29
Forbes, Scott, 39
Frank, Alan Dodds, 49
Freeh, Louis, 134, 316n185
Freni, Pamela, 9, 83
Friedman, Brad, 149
FSC (Family Steering Committee), 130, 248
Fuchek, Greg, 32
Fujita, Yukihisa, 255–57, 339n83
Fulford, Benjamin, 339n84

G

Gaffney, Mark, 17, 23, 268n52, 291n166, 292n168
Gage, Richard, 266n30, 269n67
Gallop, April, 65, 100–01, 103, 105, 107, 292nn173,176
Gannon, John, 133
Ganser, Daniele, 263n48, 274–75n168
Garvey, Jane, 85, 87, 88, 125
Gayle, Frank, 33
Geyh, Alison, 32
al-Ghamdi, Hamza, 163
Gibson, Charles, 93, 125, 129
Gilroy, Captain Dennis, 64
Gimble, Thomas F., 187, 189–95, 318–19n214, 319nn220,226,227
Ginsburg, Susan, 312n132
Giuliani, Rudy, 40, 45, 52, 55, 209, 232, 273n151, 278n199, 322n27, 336n70
Glanz, James, 35, 336n70
Glick, Jeremy, 112, 122, 168
Glick, Lyzbeth, 118, 122, 300n51
Goldsmith, Gilah, 102
Gonzales, Alberto, 103, 293n193
Gonzales, Paul, 107
Goodman, Amy, 334n70
Gordon, Greg, 296–97n18, 298n25
Gorton, Slade, 185, 244

Gourley, James R., 57, 269n72, 270nn86,90
Grabbe, Crockett, 267n34, 270n85
Graf, Alexa, 295n7
Graham, Senator Bob, 224
Grandcolas, Jack, 118
Grandcolas, Lauren, 118
Gray, Captain Larry, 291n161
Gregory, Stephen, 270n101
Griffin, David Ray, xxiii
Gross, John L., 34, 272–73n136
Grossman, Marc, 149–50, 222
Ground Stop (Pamela Freni), 9
Ground Zero: dust from, 38; fires at, 57; illness of workers at, xxvii, 260n10; steel at, 32, 38, 272nn124,129 (*see also* steel, melted). *See also* World Trade Center.
Guantánamo trials, 215, 217, 326n53
Guidetti, Ray, 296–97n18, 298n27
Gul, General Hamid, 210
Guzman, Genelle, 30

H

Haas, Ed, 40, 207
Haass, Richard, 241
Hadley, Stephen, 180, 187, 193, 249
Haikal, Dr. Osama, 154
Halper, Stefan, 331n29
Hamdan, Salim, 219
Hamilton, Lee, xxv, 81, 90, 130, 135, 182–84, 199, 201, 211–13, 220, 229, 237, 238–41, 244–54, 259, 274n155, 287n102, 314n170, 316n185, 331nn34–35, 332, 334
Hanjour, Hani, 78–80, 109, 163, 175, 233, 286, 309, 325, 333–34n70
Hanson, Peter, 164, 310n103
Hartmann, Thomas, 218–19
Hayden, Michael, 139, 214
Hayes, Stephen F., 289n144
Haynes, William, 217

Jones, Al, 278n194
Jones, Steven, xii, 16, 20, 24, 38, 44,
    57, 266n32, 268n53, 269nn67,72,
    270n86, 271n114
Journal of 9/11 Studies, xi
Jowenko, Danny, 44–45
Judge, John, 294n208

K

Kamfar, Amer, 162, 175, 309n95
Karpf, Anne, 312n131
Karzai, Hamid, 198
Kean, Thomas, xxv, 81, 90, 130, 135,
    146, 182–85, 199, 201, 211–13,
    220, 229, 237–41, 244–54, 259,
    287n102, 314n170, 316n185,
    331nn34–35, 334n70
Keller, Amanda, 155
Keller, Jack, 44
Kennedy, President John F., 141, 337n70
Kerrey, Senator Bob, 249
Khalilzad, Zalmay, 198, 200
Khan, A.Q., 148
Kilsheimer, Allyn, 73
Kim, Won-Young, 71, 121–22
King, John, 97–98, 291n164
Kleinsmith, Erik, 186, 317n200,
    318nn203,205
Knesl, Edward, 22
Kolar, Jay, 152, 307n70, 309n96
Kolstad, Ralph, 64, 79
Krongard, A. B. "Buzzy," 137
Krugman, Paul, xxiv
KSM (Khalid Sheikh Mohammed),
    80, 211–18, 220, 223, 326n51,
    328n75, 334n70
Kuczynski, Lt. Anthony, 125, 127
Kwiatkowski, Karen, 63–64

L

Labeviere, Richard, 139
Ladd, Brian, 64

Lagasse, William, 74
Lance, Peter, 330n11
Land Information Warfare Activity
    (LIWA), 179, 190, 318n203
Latas, Lt. Col. Jeff, 285n84
Lawrence, Bruce, 210, 325n30, 334n70
LAX Security, 95–96, 106, 127,
    290n157
Lebanon, 202
Lechner, James K., 160, 166–68, 311n116
Ledeen, Michael, 202–03
Lehman, John, 250
Lehrer, Jim, 33
Lewis, Charles E., 95–96, 106, 127,
    200, 290–91nn157,158 291n161
Libby, Lewis, 200
Libya, 202
Lichtblau, Eric, 167–69, 310nn109,111
Limjoco, Victor, 213–14, 220
Lindorff, Dave, 149
Lipton, Eric, 35, 267n37, 336n70
LIWA (Land Information Warfare
    Activity), 179, 190, 318n203
Logan Airport (Boston), 156–61,
    166, 173, 235, 308n75, 310n111,
    311n129
Loizeaux, Mark, 56
Longman, Jere, 119, 312n124
Lyles, CeeCee, 115, 297n20

M

MacQueen, Graeme, 25–26, 27
Madsen, Wayne, 127
Maltbie, Mike, 144, 304n18
Mann, James, 241
Maraniss, David, 111
Marcus, Dan, 251
Marr, Colonel Robert, 5, 125, 127,
    265n12
Masood, Ahmad Shah, 222, 327–28n70
May, Ernest, 238, 239, 258
May, Renee, 62, 164

Mayer, Dr. Thomas, 99
McConnell, John, 290n156
McDermott, Terry, 175
McGovern, Ray, xix, 261n22, 322n24
McGowan, Dave, 67, 73
McGuire Air Force Base, 3
McIlvaine, Bob, 254, 269nn67,72
McIntyre, Jamie, 64, 281–82n20
McKeown, Lt. Nancy, 101
McWethy, John, 65, 67
media (press): mainstream, vii, ix, x,
    xii, xvii–xviii, 73, 144, 149, 153–
    54, 155, 188, 200, 213, 219, 236,
    254, 258 (*see also* Shenon,
    Philip); left-leaning, xviii–xxi
Meyer, Josh, 143, 222, 226
Meyer, Michael, 71
Meyssan, Thierry, 66, 105–06, 294n207
al-Mihdhar, Khalid, 172, 180, 224–27
military exercises, 13–34, 105
military (defense) spending, 230–31,
    330n8
Mineta, Norman, 91–96, 107–09,
    126, 234, 237, 288nn121,144,
    335n70
Mitchell, Terry, 139
Mohammed, Khalid Sheikh (KSM),
    80, 211–18, 220, 223, 326n51,
    328n75, 334n70
Monaghan, Aidan, 69–70, 282nn46,48,
    290n150, 327n68, 314n166
Moore, Michael, 129
Moqed, Majed, 312n135
Morgan, Rowland, 173, 281n8,
    308n86, 303n88, 310n108,
    311n129, 312n139
Mosiello, Steve, 278n199
Moussaoui trial, 61, 115–18, 160,
    164, 167, 169, 175, 177, 216, 227,
    297n19, 297–98n21, 298n27,
    313n153
Mueller, Robert, 225, 325n28

Muga, Ted, 79
Mukden incident, xxi–xxii
Munyak, Edward, 39
Murphy, Eileen, 64
Murray, John, 270n87
Musharraf, General Pervez, 221–22,
    255, 328n73
Muslim: 9/11 conspiracists as, ix,
    153–55, 163, 179, 202, 203, 225,
    229, 234, 333n70; Shi'a and Sunni,
    171–72; countries targeted
    by Bush administration as, 203, 230
Myers, General Richard, 84–88, 104,
    109, 125, 134, 203–04, 231, 323n35
Mylroie, Laurie, 245

N

Naik, Naiz, 198
al-Nashiri, Abd al-Rahim, 326n46
National Institute of Standards and
    Technology. *See* NIST.
National Military Command Center
    (NMCC), 9–10, 82, 265n12
National Security Agency (NSA),
    11, 127, 137, 224
National Security Council (NSC),
    200, 249, 322n27
National Transportation Safety Board
    (NTSB), 69–70, 74–75, 121,
    283n47, 285n77,82
NEADS (NORAD's Northeast Air
    Defense Sector), 1–8, 63, 88,
    124–25, 127, 264–65n9, 265
Nelson, George, xix, 68, 261
New Pearl Harbor. See NPH.
New Pearl Harbor Revisited (NPHR),
    xii, xiii
New York Center (FAA), 6, 7
Newman, Michael, 38, 40
Newman, Rick, 75
Nielsen, Michael J., 101, 293n184

9/11 Commission: and NORAD tapes, 251–52; assumed truth of government's conspiracy theory, xxiii, xxv, 215, 238–40; directed by Phillip Zelikow, xv, xxiii, 238–52, 332–38n70; its concern for truth, ix, 137, 205, 249, 251; Kean and Hamilton's inside story of, xxv, 212–15, 237, 253–54; mandate of, 237–38; refuses to debate, xxv, 40, 232; Shenon on, 226, 239–41, 244–52, 331n34, 334n70

9/11 Commission Report: and alternative conspiracy theory, x; and NPH, ix–x, xiii, xv; as cover-up operation, xiii–xiv, xv, 4, 94, 98, 129, 137, 141, 143, 155, 195, 205, 225–26, 253, 254, 335n70, 338n72; charges military with lying, 89–90; concealed Pakistani and Saudi connections, 139–43, 222–27; contradicted by Richard Clarke and Robert Andrews, 84–87; falsehoods in, xii, xv, xx, 87, 91; ignores military liaisons, 83; on Rumsfeld's and Myer's whereabouts, 84–88; its new explanation of failures to intercept, xiii, 5–10, 59, 81–87, 89–90, 231, 232; its omissions and distortions covered up by Shenon, 332–38n70, 338n72; its publication as decisive event, xv–xvi; its silence about possible US motives, 197–204, 229–31; its treatment of Mineta's report about Cheney in PEOC, 91–95, 109, 234, 287n121; on Able Danger, 180–82, 185, 195; on Amy Sweeney call, 165–66, 169; on Barbara Olson calls, 297–

98n21; on bin Laden's responsibility, 211–15; on blocking of FBI, 143–45; on C-130 pilot, 59–60, 109; on cell phone calls, 115–16, 166–67; on Flight 11 radio transmission, 173–74; on Hani Hanjour's piloting skill, 79–80; on hijackers, 151–63, 171; on military's Flight 93 ignorance, 122–26, 234; on notification about Flight 11 by FAA, 4, 231, 264n9; on put options, 136–37; on Sibel Edmonds, 145–46; on squawking hijack code, 177; on time of Flight 93 crash, 122; on time of shootdown authorization, 94, 126–27, 234, 337n70; Pentagon videos not mentioned in, 68; success of, 253–55; Shenon on, 226, 241, 245, 332n50, 335–37n70, 338n72; treatment of FAA memo by, 9–10, 81–82; use of KSM's testimony in, 211–13; WTC 7 not mentioned in, 41

9/11 truth community (movement), 11, 20, 56, 79, 81, 236, 253–54, 258, 336–37n70

9/11CROD (*The 9/11 Commission Report: Omissions and Distortions*), xv, 88, 140, 145, 151, 203, 240–41, 259, 260n1, 288n132, 303n23

9/11 Contradictions: An Open Letter to Congress and the Press, xii, xvi, 116, 155, 235, 259, 260n7

NIST (National Institute of Standards and Technology): as cover-up operation, xiii–xiv, 14, 29, 38, 268n46; as political agency, 11–12, 258, 330n3; delayed WTC 7 report, x, 10–11, 41–42, 336n70; difficulties facing

its probable WTC 7 explanation,
43–48; distortion of testimony by
Hess and Jennings, 46–48, 232,
276nn181,182,183, 276–77n184;
probable WTC 7 explanation,
42–43; refuses public debate, xxv,
30; Sunder's false claim about its
WTC 7 work, 274n160;
whistleblower, 11–12, 30, 266n32
NIST's *Final Report* (NIST NCSTAR
1), 267n41; empirically
groundless claims in, 18–20, 24–
25, 38, 231; five crucial claims of,
12–25; ignored evidence, x, 25–
40, 231; ignored explosions, 25–
30; ignored residue of explosives,
36–38; ignored horizontal ejections,
30–31; ignored melted steel, 31–
36; on cutting and stripping of
columns, 14–17, 268nn50,56; on
downward momentum of top
section, 21–25; on impact of
airliners, 12–14; on weakening of
core columns, 17–21; violates laws
of physics, x, xii, 22–25, 43
NMCC (National Military Command
Center), 9–10, 82, 265n12
NORAD (North American
Aerospace Defense Command), 1,
3, 6–10, 81–82, 85, 88–91, 95,
123–25, 134–35, 231, 251–53,
259, 266n28, 338nn71–72
NORAD tapes, 7, 10, 124–25, 251–
53, 264–65n9, 289n135
NORAD Timeline, 4, 10, 81, 232,
252, 338n72
North Korea, 202, 246
North Tower, 3, 13–17, 23–26, 29–
30, 39, 42, 45–50, 171, 276n181,
277n184. *See also* Twin Towers;
World Trade Center.
NPH (*The New Pearl Harbor*), ix, xii,

xiii, xv, xvi, xvii, xx, xxi, xxii, xv,
1, 4–5, 10, 12, 14, 26, 40, 59, 60,
62–63, 65–66, 68, 71, 74, 76, 81,
88, 89, 91, 94, 105, 108–09, 112,
114, 121–22, 127–29, 133, 136–
37, 139–40, 145, 153–55, 171,
178, 197, 200, 202–04, 222, 224,
227, 229, 231, 235–38, 241, 243,
248, 266n29, 274n154, 294n213,
303n20, 331n35
NPHR (*The New Pearl Harbor
Revisited*), xii, xiii
NSA (National Security Agency),
11, 127, 137, 224
NSC (National Security Council),
200, 249, 322n27
NSS 2002 (National Security
Strategy of the United States of
America, 2002), 241–43, 244,
245, 247, 248, 249
NTSB (National Transportation
Safety Board), 69–70, 74–75, 121,
283n47, 285nn77,82

0

Obeid, Kamal, 43
O'Brien, Danielle, 107, 294n213
O'Brien, Steve, 59
OEM (Office of Emergency
Management), 40, 45, 52, 55,
232, 278n199
O'Keefe, Sean, 290n156
O'Neill, Paul, 200, 321n17
Olson, Barbara, 60–62, 109, 165, 227,
280n6, 297n21
Olson, Bradley, 286
Olson, Ted (Theodore), 59–62, 165,
227, 233, 280n6
al-Omari, Abdul Aziz, 156, 159–62,
166, 168, 172, 175
al-Omari, Abdulrahman, 162, 175,
309n95

Omholt, Ralph, 79, 286n91, 292n179
Ong, Betty, 165, 168, 170, 177,
    310n108, 311nn123,129
Operation Gladio, xxii, 204, 255
Operation Northwoods, xxii, 203–04
Oswald, Lee Harvey, 141
Otis Air National Guard Base, 3–9, 85
O'Toole, Joe, 32

P

Padilla, José, 142
Palast, Greg, 322n24
passenger (flight) manifests, 163–64,
    174–75, 313n150
Patriots Question 9/11, xi, 262n32,
    269n78, 318n205, 327n67, 339n82
Pavoggi, Stephen J., 291n161
Peacock, Bill, 174
Pearl Harbor: new, 201–02, 203, 243;
    space, 203
Pearl, Daniel, 223, 328n75
Pentagon (building): as protected by
    anti-aircraft missiles, 106–07; claim
    that it struck by al-Qaeda pilot Hani
    Hanjour, 76–80, 109, 286n100;
    claim that it was struck a missile,
    105–06; claim that it was struck by
        Boeing 757 (Flight 77): not
        proved by eyewitness
        testimony, 72–75, 109; not
        supported by C-ring hole, 71;
        not supported by damage, 63,
        109; not supported by debris,
        63–68, 109; not supported by
        FDR, 68–70; not supported by
        seismic signal, 70, 109; not
        supported by time-change
        parts, 68; not supported by
        videos, 68, 109; supported by
        Barbara Olson's calls, 59, 109;
        first floor of Wedge 1 as target,
        76–77, 103–05, 109;

photographs of, xvi, 63, 73, 101;
    reports of bombs going off, 100–
    03, 109; time of attack on, 107–08,
    293n194, 294n213
Pentagon (officials): claims ignorance
    of approaching aircraft, 91–94,
    96; claims no fighters on alert at
    Andrews, 88–90; denied military
    ownership of white plane over
    White House, 97–98, 109; did not
    have building evacuated, 91–100,
    105, 134; whereabouts of
    Rumsfeld and Myers disputed, 84–
    88, 109; previously planned false-
    flag attacks, xxii–xxiii; retaliated
    against April Gallop, 292n176
Pentagon Building Performance Report,
    67, 70, 71, 284
Pentagon 9/11 PEOC (Presidential
    Emergency Operations Center),
    91, 92, 93, 94, 107, 126, 288n21,
    289n44
Perkal, Don, 102, 105
Perle, Richard, 148, 200, 202, 305n35
Peruggia, Chief John, 278n199
Phillips, Don, 294n213
Phillpott, Captain Scott, 179–86,
    189–94, 319n223
Phucas, Keith, 181–82
Pickering, Russell, 284n73
Pillar, Paul, 133
Pilots for 9/11 Truth, xi, 75, 77, 121,
    264n6, 285nn77,82,84, 296n13,
    299
Pincus, Walter, 303n7
Plant, Chris, 99
PNAC. See *Project for the New
    American Century.*
Popular Mechanics, xi, xxiv, xxv, 56,
    63, 67, 71–74, 116, 120, 259,
    264n50, 280n217, 289n135
Porter, Gareth, 322–23n30

Porter, Richard, 53–53
Portland Jetport, 157–61
Posner, Gerald, 139–43, 223, 303nn4–5, 304n8
Poteshman, Allen, 136, 303n20
Powell, Colin, 207
Powell, Reginald, 65
Preisser, Dr. Eileen, 180–81, 185–86, 190, 191–94, 319n227
Presidential Emergency Operations Center (PEOC), 91, 92, 93, 94, 107, 126, 288n21, 289n44
Preston, Major Robert, 217
Probst, Frank, 73, 284n71
Project Censored, 208, 324n17
Project for the New American Century (PNAC), 200–01, 203, 230, 321n21
put options, 136–37, 257, 303n23

Q

al-Qaeda: absence of proof against, 206–15, 220; as connected to Saddam, 199, 244–45; as having motive for 9/11 attacks, 202, 229, 231; as having names on flight manifests, 174–75; as identified by Able Danger, 179–95; as incapable of attacks, 220–21, 335n70; as linked to George Bush, 320n238; as paid assets of US government, 195, 320n238; as proved guilty by Atta's luggage, 156; as stupidly targeting Wedge 1 of the Pentagon, 77; as unlikely to wear red headbands, 171–72; interrogations of its members, 139, 211–15, 334n70; its guilt simply assumed in official conspiracy theory, xxiv, xxv, 136, 137, 207, 219, 239–40, 255, 258, 333n70, 334–35n70; Moussaoui's

connection to, 144; supported by Pakistanis, 222–23; supported by Saudis, 140–43, 224–27; Zubaydah's reported testimony about, 139–43
Quigley, Rear Admiral Craig, 107

R

Raimondo, Justin, 149
Rains, Lon, 105
Rashid, Ahmed, 197–98, 320n4
Rather, Dan, 55, 221, 2779n209
Ratner, Michael, 214, 220
Ray, Col. Ronald D., xix, 261–62n24
Reagan, President Ronald, xix
Reichstag fire, xxii
Remote control, 136, 179, 314n166
Rice, Condoleezza, xviii, 92–93, 134, 222, 241, 249, 322n27
Rice, William, 22
Riggs, Barbara, 84, 89
Risen, James, 141–42
Robertson, Leslie, 32
Rodriguez, William, 30, 48, 50
Rogers, Kenneth, 271n103
Ross, Brian, 184
Ross, Gordon, 23
Rotanz, Richard, 278n199
Rothschadl, Judy, 65
Rothschild, Matthew, xxiii
Rove, Karl, 125–26, 129, 249–51
Rowley, Coleen, 144, 237
Rudin, Mike, 276–77n184
Rumsfeld, Donald: and Buswell case, 282n35; and false-flag attacks, 204; and stand-down order, 203; and Stephen Cambone, 282n35; as anxious to attack Iraq, 199–200; as having Flight 93 knowledge, 125; as having not anticipated attacks, 134; as ignorant of approaching aircraft,

91; as wanting weapons in space, 203; Clarke's testimony about, 84–87, 102, 125, 231, 288n125; his whereabouts that morning, 84–88, 109, 288n125; initially forbad Able Danger testimony, 186; not challenged by 9/11 Commission, 323n35; not targeted in Pentagon attack, 76; on C-ring hole, 72, 102, 233; on missing $2.3 trillion, 104; on 9/11 as creating opportunities, 202; on 9/11 as enabling attacks on Afghanistan and Iraq, 230; on regime change in seven countries, 202, 323n30

Rumsfeld Commission, 203

Russell, Jerry, 73

Russert, Tim (*Meet the Press*), 93, 290n153

Ruvolo, Captain Philip, 32, 271n124

Ryan, Kevin, xii, 17, 20, 57, 268n56, 269n67, 269n72, 270n86,

Ryland, Luke, 149, 305n35

S

Safire, William, 199

al-Sakka, Louai, 148, 286n100, 305n34

Salomon Brothers building, 53. *See also* WTC 7.

Samit, Harry, 227

Sasseville, Lt. Col. Marc, 124, 125

Saudi Arabia, 140, 141, 143, 163, 202–03, 222, 225

Saudi royal family, 140–41, 143

Schiff, Congressman Adam, 97, 291n163

Schneider, Jörg, 44, 274n168

Scholars for 9/11 Truth, xi

Scholars for 9/11 Truth and Justice, xi, 269nn67,72

Scoggins, Colin, 2, 4–6, 88–89, 264–65n9, 265nn14–15, 288n134

Scott, Peter Dale, xi, xxiv, 261n77

Scripps Howard Poll, xi

Secret Service, 9, 84, 89, 91–94, 130–31, 336n70

Shaffer, Col. Anthony, 179–86, 188–95, 315n174, 316n185, 317nn187,191, 318nn203,214, 319n223

Shalev, Eddie, 80, 286n99

Shanksville, 121, 283n49, 299n41, 300n47

Shays, Chris, 180, 193

Sheehy, Gail, 166, 310n106

al-Shehhi, Marwan, 153–54, 180, 325n28

al-Shehri, Wail, 162, 169, 175

al-Shehri, Waleed, 151–53, 162, 169, 175

Sheikh, Omar Saeed, 328n75

Shenon, Philip, 182, 226, 239–41, 244–53, 266n19, 315n177, 319n215, 331n34, 332n50, 332–337n70, 338n72

Shepperd, Major General Don, 98

Shirer, William, 263n42

shootdown authorization, 6, 94, 96, 124, 126–27, 234, 337n70

Shuckums Bar, 153–54, 334n70

"Silver Blaze," 178

Silverstein, Larry, 50, 55–56, 277, 279–80n217

Singh, Indira, 52–53

Sisson, R.D., 273n138. *See also* WPI professors.

Skilling, John, 13, 14

Sliney, Ben, 83

Smith, Guy, 277n184, 278–79n207

Smith, James D., 184–87, 194

Snell, Dietrich ("Dieter"), 181, 183, 189–90, 192, 195, 226, 334n70

Sniegoski, Stephen, 242

Sofaer, Abraham, 245

Somalia, 202

South Tower, 5–8, 13–17, 24, 26–28,

Z

Zaid, Mark S., 186, 315n174, 317n191

Zarembka, Paul, 303n23

Zarrillo, Richard, 278n199

Zelikow, Philip: as closely aligned with Bush administration, 238, 241–42, 244, 245–46, 247; as controlling 9/11 Commission, 238, 239–41; as informed about Able Danger's identification of Atta, 180–82; as largely determining Commission's report, xxv, 238–39, 241, 332n50; as NSS 2002 author, 241–42, 244, 245, 247 248, 249; as supportive of Rice, 246–47; continued contact with Rice and Rove, 249–51; duplicity of, 243–46; failure to rebut 9/11 truth community's prima facie case, xv–xvi; FSC's opposition to, 248; Kean and Hamilton's choice of, 244, 331nn34,35; Kean and Hamilton's tolerance of, 239, 247–49; on catastrophic terrorism, 242–44; prepared outline of report in advance, xxv, 238–39; presupposed and promoted government's conspiracy theory, xxiii, 238–39; question of doctored NORAD tapes, 251–53; relation to Ernest May, 238–39; relation to Cambone, 251; relation to Clarke, 246, 249, 332n49; rewrote team reports, 226, 241; Shenon's only partial exposé of, 332–37n70, 337n72

Zogby poll, x, 253

Zubaydah, Abu, 139–43, 214, 215, 223

Zwicker, Barrie, xvii, 295n10